Confrontation

Confrontation

The War with Indonesia 1962-1966

Nick van der Bijl BEM

With a foreword by The Right Honourable Lord
Denis Healey of Riddlestone CH MBE

Pen & Sword
MILITARY

First published in Great Britain in 2007 and reprinted in 2009 by
Pen & Sword Military
an imprint of
Pen & Sword Books Ltd
47 Church Street
Barnsley
South Yorkshire
S70 2AS

A CIP catalogue record for this book is
available from the British Library

Typeset in Sabon by
Lamorna Publishing Services

Printed and bound in England by CPI Antony Rowe, Chippenham, Wiltshire

For a complete list of Pen & Sword titles please contact
PEN & SWORD BOOKS LIMITED
47 Church Street, Barnsley, South Yorkshire, S70 2AS, England
E-mail: enquiries@pen-and-sword.co.uk
Website: www.pen-and-sword.co.uk

THE SUCCESSFUL PATROL

The following poem is described by the *Durham Light Infantry Journal*
(February 1976) as a soldier's version of a patrol in Borneo:

We checked our arms and grenades too,
This was it, we fully knew:
To go abroad in jungles dark,
Through slimy swamp and bamboo sharp,
The monkeys scream and parrots too,
Where the hell are we going to?
We cross a river just in time
An alligator bites through our line.
All day we march, the next day too
When will this patrol be through?
The leading scout, he's turned around
He makes a sign, he's heard a sound.
Get in the side and you, Bill
This is where we make our kill.
We wait with our bated breath,
First one came and then the rest.
Treading silently as ghosts
Not knowing we were at our posts,
Till that fateful hail of lead
Mowed them down, they fell all dead.
That's the way we had to learn,
To watch enemy bodies twist and squirm:
Then we're back on the move again,
Back the way we had come.
Through slimy swamp and jungle lanes
We had succeeded for our pains;
For our job, plain and simple,
Was to kill the dreaded Indon.
On arrival back at company base
Old Bill gasps 'God, what a pace!'
'Arms unload! Grenades unprime!'
That's it, boys, until the next time.

Contents

Maps

Tables

Foreword

The Right Honourable Lord Denis Healey of Riddlestone
CH MBE

I am delighted that a detailed account of Britain's confrontation with Indonesia has at last been published. Our campaign was a text book demonstration of how to apply economy of force, under political guidance for political ends.

We owed much to the skills in jungle warfare possessed by General Walter Walker, who wrote: 'It was indelibly inscribed on our minds that one civilian killed by us would do more harm that ten killed by the enemy.' So I refused the RAF's request to be allowed to bomb the Indonesian ports of entry in eastern Borneo. However, I did allow General Walker to send forces across the border so as to ambush the enemy soldiers before they could enter Malaysian territory. The operations, codenamed 'Claret', remained secret until long after the war was over. A key role was played by 22 SAS. Their commander, Lieutenant Colonel John Woodhouse, was the greatest guerrilla warrior yet produced by the West – a man to compare with Ho Chi Minh. The SAS in Borneo worked in sixteen patrols of four men each, each carrying medical supplies and a variety of weapons. Both their officers and NCOs could speak Malay, Thai and Arabic, had been attached to casualty wards in British hospitals to learn how to treat all types of injury, and made a point of treating the local people as well as themselves. The British Army had learned under General Templer in Malaya that winning what is called 'the hearts and minds' of the local population was the precondition of success in guerrilla warfare.

Denis Healey
House of Lords

Acknowledgements

The Armed Forces of the United Kingdom have been engaged in over seventy military operations since 1945, which have resulted in about 3,000 Service personnel killed in action. The war against Indonesian ambitions in South-East Asia between 1962 and 1966 is, perhaps, the least well known, not because it was a secret war – it was not – but because the terrain and conduct of the war were too tough for the average journalist to contemplate reporting.

This book sets out to tell a history of the campaign and also add to the story of British military history on the world scene since 1945. I am beholden to Pen & Sword Books for giving me the opportunity.

I am most grateful to The Right Honourable Lord Denis Healey of Riddlestone CH MBE for writing the Foreword. As Secretary of Defence during Confrontation, his acknowledgements to the Armed Forces are a shining example.

Quite apart from those sources listed in the Bibliography, I am indebted to several people who fought during Confrontation. Lieutenant Colonel Charles McHardy (Queens Own Highlanders) and the late Alasdair Ker-Lyndsay for their recall of the Brunei Revolt. Dr Greg Poulgrain's research into the causes of the Brunei Revolt was enlightening. To Colonel Alan Thompson (Royal Leicesters) for describing his attack on an Indonesian machine gun and to Lieutenant Colonel Jon Fleming (2 Para) for telling me about the attack on Plamam Mapu in 1965. To Major General Ronnie McAlister for his review of 1/10th Gurkha Rifles operations in 1965-6. Brigadier Bruce Jackman reviewed his attack on Long Medan, as did Brigadier Christopher Bullock for 2/2nd Gurkha Rifle operations in 1965. Thanks also to Brigadier Bullock for allowing me to use some maps from his book *Journeys Hazardous*. Major John Burlison's (2nd Gurkha Rifles) account of events at Long Jawi was invaluable. He is involved in identifying war memorials to Allied and Commonwealth Service personnel killed during the Second World War, the Brunei Revolt and Confrontation. Denis O'Leary (1/7th Gurkha Rifles) helped with his review of the attack on Lobe Island. Mr Ian Mayman (2/10th Gurkha Rifles) commented on the Battle of Track 6/6A and Operation Blunt and R.A.M. Seeger (Royal Marines) scrutinized my account on his attack on Sebatik Island. Bombardier Peter Barnes supplied me with contemporary documents on 40th Light Regiment RA. Lieutenant Commander John Rogers supplied a mass of information of Naval Party Kilo. And John Mulholland, of the Victoria Cross and George Cross Society, helped with information on Lance Corporal Rambahadur Limbu VC. There are several others who played their part in Confrontation who wish to remain anonymous – I am most grateful to them and fully respect their decision.

Peter Wood, of GWA, was a Royal Engineer who supplied mapping during Confrontation. When he created the maps for this book, his recollections proved invaluable. The Ton Class Association provided me with photographs of naval activity.

I must thank Bobby Gainher for his scrupulous editing; John Noble, ex-Royal Navy and on a Type 12 a/s Frigate during Confrontation, for the indexing; and Brigadier Henry Wilson, formerly of the Royal Green Jackets in Borneo and now Commissioning Editor, Pen & Sword Books, for his encouragement in this project. There are also a large number of unseen 'backroom people' involved in the preparation and publication of this book who must be thanked too.

My wife, Penny, has again been invaluable in proofreading and asking searching questions about the draft.

Nick van der Bijl
Somerset

GLOSSARY

Baluka	Fern, scrub (Malay)
BMA	Brigade Maintenance Area – brigade logistic area
CCO	(Sarawak) Clandestine Communist Organisation
CIGS	Chief of the Imperial General Staff
CO	Commanding Officer
COMDBRITFOR	Commander British Forces
CQMS	Company Quartermaster Sergeant – responsible for organization of logistics in an infantry company
CSM	Company Sergeant Major
DCM	Distinguished Conduct Medal
DOBOPS	Director Borneo Operations
DSM	Distinguished Service Medal
DSO	Distinguished Service Order
FIO	Field Intelligence Officer
FLB	Forward Locality Base
FOO	Forward Observation Officer
GPMG	(7.62mm) General Purpose Machine Gun
Green Archer	Mortar locating radar
Gunong	Steep-sided hill (Malay)
HF	High (radio) Frequency
HMAS	Her Majesty's Australian Ship
HMAV	Her Majesty's Army Vessel
HMS	Her Majesty's Ship
HQ	Headquarters
IBT	Indonesian Border Terrorist(s)
IRD	Information Research Department
Kampong	Village (Malay)
Konfrontasi	Confrontation (Indonesian)
LAD	Light Aid Detachment
LCA	Landing Craft Assault
LCT	Landing Craft Tank

LMG	(7.62mm) Light Machine Gun. The .303 Bren gun fitted with a 7.26mm barrel and working parts.
LP	(Helicopter) landing point, also known as a landing site (LS) and landing zone (LZ)
LST	Landing Ship Tank(s)
MC	Military Cross
MIO	Military Intelligence Officer
MM	Military Medal
MMG	Medium Machine Gun
MRS	Medical Reception Service
NCO	Non-Commissioned Officer
NP	Naval Party
OFP	Ordnance Field Park
PCLU	Pioneer Corps Labour Unit
QGO	Queen's Gurkha Officer
Recce	Reconnaisance
RMO	Regimental Medical Officer
RMR	Royal Malay Regiment
RPG	Rocket-Propelled Grenade
RPKAD	*Regimen Pasukan Komando Angatan Darat* – Army Para-Commando Regiment
RPL	Ramp Powered Lighter
SLR	(7.62mm) Self-Loading Rifle
Sungei	River (Malay)
TNI	*Tentara Nasional Indonesia* – Indonesian Armed Forces
Ulu	Jungle (Malay)
VHF	Very High (radio) Frequency

Commonwealth Army Unit Titles

AAC	Army Air Corps
Gurkha ASC	Gurkha Army Service Corps
NZSAS	New Zealand SAS
RAAF	Royal Australian Air Force
RAC	Royal Armoured Corps
RAEC	Royal Army Education Corps
RAF	Royal Air Force
RAMC	Royal Army Medical Corops
RAN	Royal Australian Navy
RAOC	Rioyal Army Ordnance Corps
RAR	Royal Australain Regiment
RASC	Royal Army Service Corps
RCT	Royal Corps of Transport

REME	Royal Electrical and Mechanical Engineers
RMP	Royal Military Police
RMR	Royal Malaysian Regiment (infantry)
RNZAF	Royal New Zealand Air Force
RNZIR	Royal New Zealand Infantry Regiment
RPC	Royal Pioneer Corps
SAS	Special Air Service
SBS	Special Boat Section

MAP 1 - SOUTH EAST ASIA

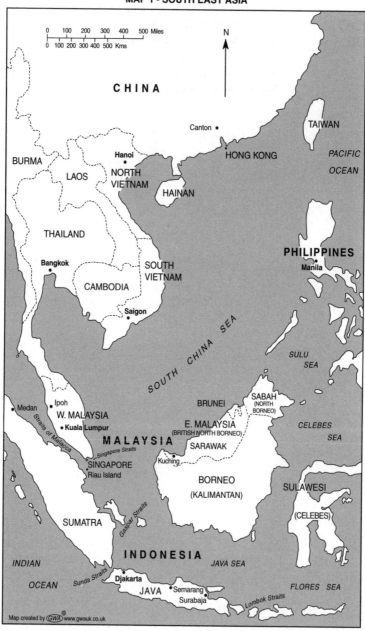

xvi

MAP 2 - MALAYSIA

Nakhon Si Thammarat

Miles 0 10 20 40 60 80 100 Miles

N

Singora
Hat Yai
Patani
LANGKAWI Kangar KEDAH THAILAND
Alor Star Kota Bahru
Sungei Patani Kroh
Baling KELANTAN
PENANG Kuala Krai
Butterworth Trengganu
Taiping TRENGGANU
Kuala Kangsar
PERAK Ipoh PAHANG
Kampah Kuala Lipis
Bidor Slim River
Telok Jerantut Kuantan
Anson
SELANGOR
Medan Selangor Bentong Pekan
Pematangsiantar Kuala Lumpur Pahang R.
Tanjunbalai Port MALAYSIA
Swettenham Endau
Seremban Gemas
Port Dickson Segamat Mersing
Bagansiapiapi Malacca JOHORE
Muar Gunang Besar
RUPAT Batu Pahat Gunang
Tanahputih Pulah Kota Tinggi
Benut Johore Bahru
Bengkalis
Pontian Kechil SINGAPORE
Kukup
Pekanbaru Batam Bintan

South China Sea
Strait of Malacca
Mud a R.
Perak R.

RIAU ARCHIPELAGO

S U M A T R A

Map created by GWA www.gwauk.co.uk

xvii

MAP 3 - KALIMANTAN

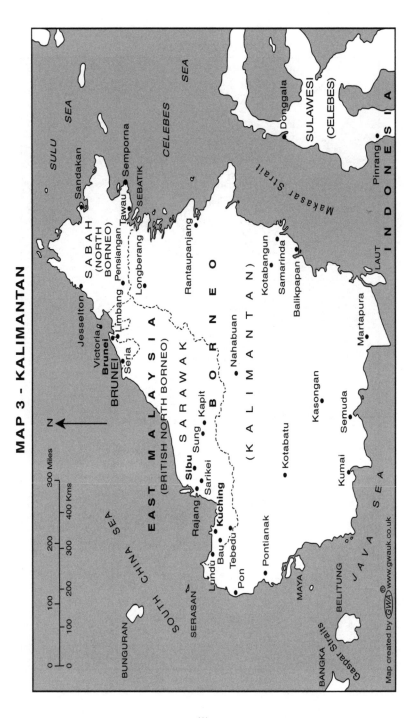

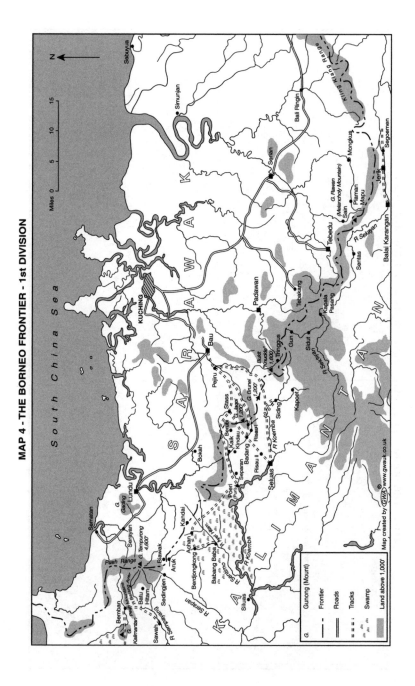

MAP 4 - THE BORNEO FRONTIER - 1st DIVISION

xix

MAP 5 - THE BORNEO FRONTIER - 2nd to 5th DIVISIONS, SABAH AND BRUNEI

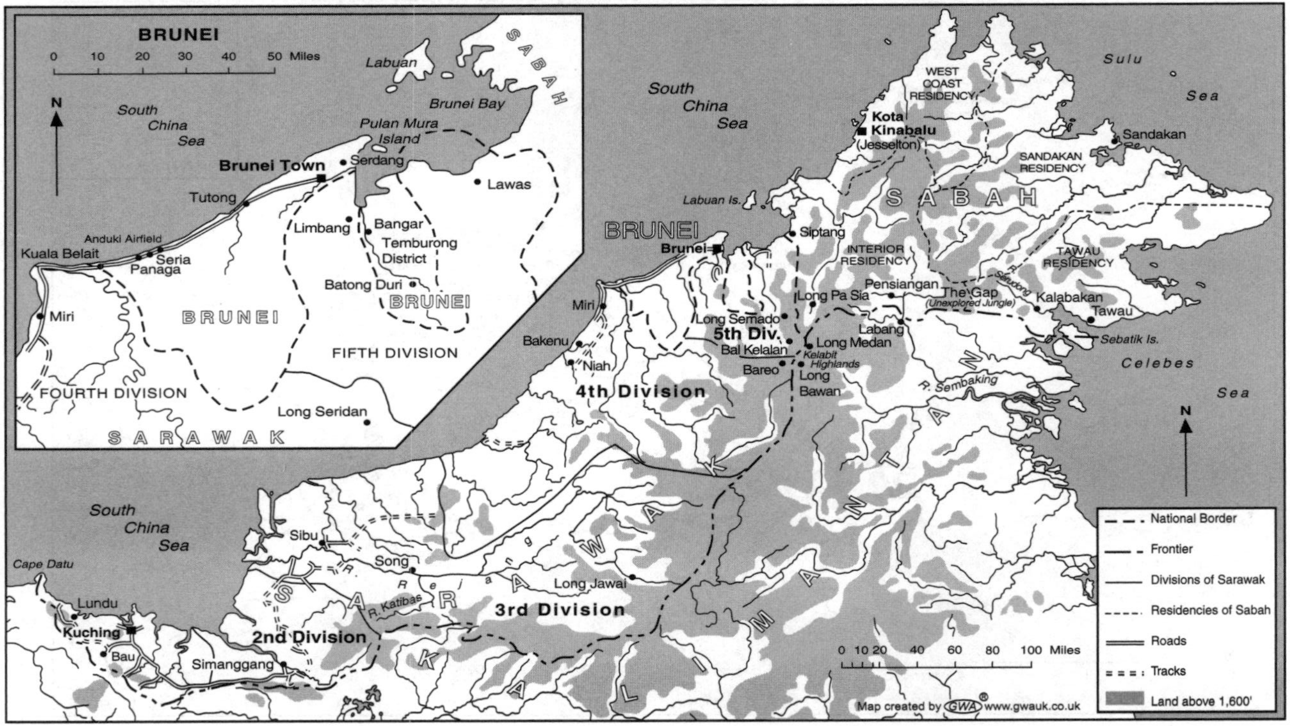

xx

MAP 6 - THE BORNEO FRONTIER - 5th DIVISION AND INTERIOR RESIDENCY, SABAH

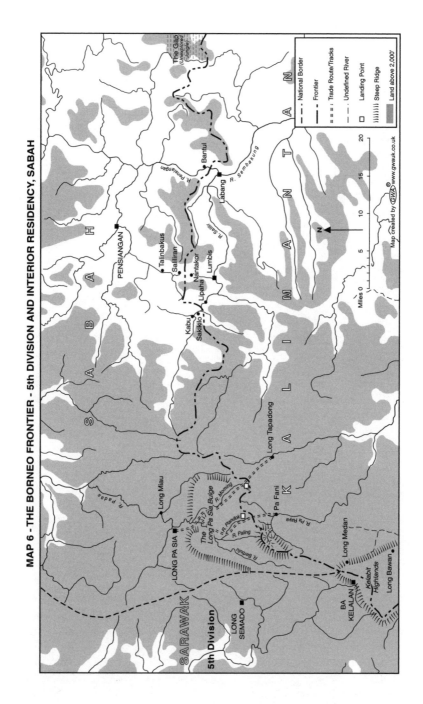

CHAPTER ONE

The Arena

The Indonesian archipelago spills across about 13,600 islands, almost half of which are inhabited and with many volcanic, stretching across some 3,200 miles of sea, covering an area of about 741,000 square miles. To the east is New Guinea and East Timor. The Equator cuts across the centre of Borneo and while it is hot day and night in the lowlands, nights are so cold in the highlands that thinly dressed men shiver.

The north-east 'dry' monsoon lasts from October to March with the heaviest rainfall between November and February. The humid 'wet' south-west monsoon runs from May to September with the daytime temperature usually climbing to 30 degrees centigrade. Humidity is high with average rainfall of about 145 inches. Extensive lowlands across Sumatra, Java and Kalimantan are rich in volcanic deposits, and ideal for small farms. Extensive forests, most concentrated in Kalimantan, Sumatra and eastern Indonesia, produce a wide variety of timber, including teak and rattan. Animal life abounds with the threatened orang-utan found only in Sumatra and Kalimantan, and the tiger in Sumatra and Java. Birds, reptiles and amphibians populate the land while the seas and rivers yield hundreds of varieties of fish. The indigenous people are mostly of mixed Malaysian origin, distinctive ethnic groups being the Javanese and the Sundanese on Java and Madura, the Balinese in Bali and the Iban and Dayak on Kalimantan. Minority groups include Chinese. More than 100 languages are spoken. Hindus and Buddhists have exerted a profound influence on the architecture of the country and Arabs have promoted Islam.

The island of Borneo, which is derived from the word 'Brunei', is the third largest island in the world, covering an area of 287,700 square miles, i.e. roughly five times greater than England and Wales. About two-thirds is bordered by mangrove swamps and covered in jungle and nipa palms. Jungle-covered hills and mountains are topped with coarse

1

grass known as *Lalang*. Sometimes known as the 'Dark Continent of South-East Asia', during the 1960s, self-sufficient communities scattered along rivers survived on subsistence farming. The shortfall in fertile soil is made up by luxuriant jungle. As the Dutch extended their influence to Java during the eighteenth century and claimed Kalimantan, they clashed with the British East India Company. From about the mid-1760s, immigrant Chinese developed gold mining in the north and then, as their communities became permanent, they developed farming and business communities. Apart from a difficult Japanese occupation from 1942 until 1945, Allied air raids against the oil refineries and the fighting conducted by the Australians between May and August, British North Borneo was a haven of colonial tranquillity, and political and economic progress.

At just 3,700 square miles, Brunei is a small country and at its widest measures 105 miles. Jungle-covered hills reach to white sandy beaches and border the Sungei Belait and Tutong. During the fifteenth and sixteenth centuries, Brunei was the dominant power in the region and generally managed to deflect the colonial ambitions of Spain and Portugal, but the arrival of James Brooke, who later became known as the White Rajah of Sarawak, spelt the beginning of the end and, in 1888, Brunei became a British protectorate. Its territory was further reduced when Limbang was ceded to Sarawak, splitting Temburong District from Brunei. Just as the country was about to be swallowed up into Sarawak in 1929, oil was found on the coast near Seria. In 1962, the population of 220,000 lived around Brunei Town (now Bandar Seri Begawan (BSB)) and in Muara. About 60 per cent of the population were of Malay origin, 5 per cent were Iban, Dayak and Kelabit and about 12 per cent Chinese. The rest were migrant oilfield workers and Europeans. Brunei is an Islamic country, which is reflected in the magnificent Omar Ali Saifudden Mosque, built in 1958. By 1962, Brunei was a wealthy country, however politics were stagnant and commerce almost entirely controlled by the minority Chinese. The sultans had little interest in democratizing Brunei and in 1953 had seen off a nationalist rebellion. However, the lessons were not learnt and little was done to address public resentment over inefficient health, education, housing and political exclusion, compared to progress in Sarawak and North Borneo.

Sarawak covers an area of 48,150 square miles and in 1962 had a population of 776,990. The hills gradually rise to 8,000 feet and the 971-mile border is ill-defined. The 450-mile coastline is a mix of idyllic beaches and mangrove. The terrain leading into Indonesia had not changed markedly except that it was less populated and there were very few metalled tracks. The rivers were the roads. Using a system developed

2

in Africa, and keen to transfer administrative authority and political power to local communities, the British had divided Sarawak into five divisions, each governed by a Colonial Service Resident reporting to the Governor. Each was broken down into districts and sub-districts administered by British and local Colonial Service officers. At the lowest level, *Penghulus* (Iban leaders) had immediate responsibility for longhouse communities, while *Tuas Kampung* (Head of a Malay/Bidayuh village) looked after the Malays, and the *Kapitan China* managed Chinese communities. By 1956, the constitution was the colonial model of an elected Council *Negri* (State) and an upper house of the Supreme Council, which was chaired by the Governor, who could override their decisions, but seldom did. By 1963, voting was universal and usually followed ethnic affiliations, which led to debates on local matters as opposed to national issues.

First Division is the most westerly and houses the capital, Kuching, which sits on the banks of the Sungei Sarawak, and is the Malay word for 'cat'. In 1962, the town was the largest population centre of 60,000 and split about two-thirds Chinese and one-third Malay. It was the commercial centre of Sarawak and provided port facilities for the Second and Fourth Divisions. Seven miles south along a narrow and winding tarmac road was Kuching Airport at 7-Mile Bazaar. The Division consisted of five districts. The Governor lived in the *Astana*, which was formerly the White Rajah's palace, across the river. When Sir Alexander Waddell lived there, he was also Commander-in-Chief, but during the war he was replaced by Sir Bernard Ferguson, whose wartime experiences included serving with the Chindits in Burma.

Lundu District was centred around a small town of the same name nestling beneath the impressive Gunong Gading (2,986 feet). The spectacular 12-mile Gunong Puteh range (4,877 feet at its highest) runs to the sea from the west of Sematan and is split by the border. The district has several beautiful beaches. To the south Gunong Raya (1,000 feet) runs east to west and is also split by the border. The terrain is mostly coastal swamp and primary jungle dispersed between shifting cultivation and consequent secondary jungle. To the north on the border are Cape Tanjong Datu and its lighthouse.

To the south, Bau District nestled among small rolling hills, with the town the administrative centre. Two comparatively low (800 feet) ridges running east to west in the middle of the District, namely the Gunong Jagoi and Gunong Brunei, divide the main plain into three subsidiary valleys, from north to south – Stass, Serikin and Gumbang. Apart from the main hills, small patches of primary jungle competed with shifting agricultural cultivation and secondary jungle. The mining around Bau and along the roads were almost entirely Chinese managed. The

3

remainder of the District is inhabited by 'Land' Dayaks. A decent 22-mile tarmac road connected Bau with Kuching. Forty-two miles south-east of Kuching is Serian, which was the main town of Upper Sadong District and the main centre for Dayaks. It is midway between Kuching and Simanggang in the Second Division. In 1962, the area had been over-cultivated, although the scenery was spectacular with jungle-covered hills. The fifth district was Lower Sadong which bordered coastal areas and swamp along the Sungei Sadong, which had a strong tidal bore. Fertile, it was the most productive rice-growing area in Sarawak. The population was mainly Malay.

Second Division was the Iban stronghold and dominated by the 280-mile long, mighty and muddy Sungei Rajang, which is the main artery into the interior. Scattered along its banks, and those of its many tributaries, were kampongs and longhouses. The Tiang Laju and Bukit Besai mountain ranges dominate the District. Trade across the border was common. A tarmac road ran from Simanggang, the small divisional capital on the banks of the Batang Lupar, east to Third Division and west to Serian in First Division. The interior is mountainous with the table-topped Bukit Lesong sitting above the Lingga, whose source is in Indonesia. The Dayaks along the Skrang were some of the most advanced in Sarawak.

Of the three districts, Lubok Antu covers the upper reaches of the Batang Lupar, with the two main centres of Engkilili and Lubok Antu, not far from the Indonesian border. Saribas District was once famous for pirates and their spirited encounters with the Royal Navy. The 'Sea' Dayaks then embraced Christianity and, by 1962, were the most advanced community in Sarawak. The saddle-backed Gunong Sadok dominates. Batong is the capital and had an ironwood fort still used for government offices. The Saribas was tidal. Kalaka District covered the area drained by the Krian and Seblakmand and, although predominantly Dayak, had a substantial Malay population. Kabong at the mouth of the Krian was one of the largest kampongs in Sarawak. Although very fertile, the District was isolated because it lacked roads and a port. In 1962, work was under way to rectify this.

Third Division was the largest in Sarawak at 25,000 square miles, much of it covered by mountainous jungle and forest, and a population of 260,000, the Foochow Chinese living downriver and Dayaks, Kayans and Kenyahs living on the banks of the Rajang and Balui. With very few roads, travellers were confined to walking, boats and aircraft. Coasters could steam as far as Kapit, 99 miles upstream from the sea. Kapit District covered a huge area of rainforest through which flowed several rivers. The Pelagus Rapids formed a major obstacle, a fact reflected in that there were no settlements south of Nanga Pila. Forty-five miles from the sea is the rough town of Sibu, which sits in the swampy ground at the junction of the Rajang and Igan. Sibu was a strategically important centre from the early days of Rajah Brooke, when he established a fort. Sibu Rural District was mainly rubber plantations cultivated by the Chinese. Binatang, on the coast, was very flat and had mangrove swamps. The thriving little port of Sarikei on the Lower Rajang, which gave its name to the District, was once an important pepper-growing centre. It had several deep-water anchorages servicing several sawmills. Mukah District was the sago-growing area of Sarawak and was inhabited by the Melanau, however the local economy was depressed. Kanowit District contained the biggest Dayak population and had resisted the ambitions of the Rajah Brooke family until the 1930s. Even after the Second World War, a rebellion broke out in the District. With its precipitous face, Bukit Sepali dominates the surrounding jungle.

Fourth Division was smaller than Third. Bintulu was an attractive little town and the commercial centre for the collection of *jelutong*, which can be made into chewing gum. With a mixed indigenous and Malay population emerging from years of isolation, it sported several jungle-covered volcanic mountains, the highest being Bukit Mersing at 3,344 feet. Miri District covered the coastal strip to Brunei. Baram District was largely uninhabited, except along the many rivers, the capital being Marudi and the limit of launch navigation at Long Lama. In 1962, the District suffered from destructive rivalry as the Roman Catholic and Evangelical missions clashed in the middle reaches of the Sungei Baram. The Evangelical were a hotchpotch of faiths drawn from the Baptists, Plymouth Brethren and other nonconformist churches, who found the isolated communities a soft touch for conversion to Christianity. Between the Sungei Tinjar and Baram, there was an uninhabited plateau at 3,000 feet where the 800-feet-high Long Julan waterfall had been discovered only a few years earlier. The upper reaches of the Sungei Baram was the centre of the isolated Punan clans. Noted for woodcarving, boatmanship and parang swords, these nomads lived in the headwaters of the Sungei Belait in Brunei and around the Baram watershed and headwaters of the Limbang; scavenging for wild sago and wild vegetables, they hunted with blowpipes and their intelligent, though scruffy, dogs. Shy, their skin colour was almost white because they disliked leaving the shade of the jungle. By no means primitive, they forsook permanent dwellings and opted for small, short-term lean-tos.

Fifth Division was the smallest administrative sector and bordered Brunei to the north and North Borneo to the east. It was ceded from Brunei piecemeal with Trusan Valley transferring in 1884, Limbang in 1890 and Lawas District in 1895. Temburong in between the Trusan and Limbang remained in Brunei. Limbang District sits astride the Limbang valley, which was one the finest in Sarawak, and had agricultural potential in palm oil. In the interior, the district is mountainous with Batu Lawas a few metres lower than Kota Kinabulu in North Borneo. Malays, Kedayans and Bisayas inhabited the lower levels, the Dayaks the middle reaches and the Kelabits on the upper slopes. Lawas District centred around the Trusan and Lawas valleys and emerged after the purchase of the latter from the British North Borneo Company in 1905. The Trusan was a long river but not navigable by any craft beyond Long Tenpoa. The Lawas was more accessible. Travel beyond the riverheads at Lawas and Long Tenpoa was only by foot, taking seven to ten days to reach the Indonesian border. At the head of the Trusan valley was Ba Kalalan, which became a major military base. Access to the Indonesian administrative centres at Tanjong via the Lawas Valley was easy. The original clans occupying the District were Murats, however they clashed with Rajah Brooke's administration and, driven into the upper reaches of the rivers, were decimated by smallpox. Resorting to the bottle, they were drinking themselves to extinction until Christian missionaries converted them in the 1930s. By the 1960s, the Trusan valley was virtually alcohol free. The Murats had a distinguished Second World War record, sheltering refugee Europeans and then hosting Australian Special Reconnaissance Department operations. Across the border in Indonesia were Murut communities with close ties with those in Sarawak. Downriver most of the population were Malays and Kedayans.

Chinese formed 31.5 per cent of the population of Sarawak and were frequently criticized in the belief that they focused on China rather than the country that had adopted them. Across the border in Kalimantan were Chinese communities, who also looked north. Business acumen and hard work allowed many to accumulate sufficient wealth to educate their children to a standard better than the indigenous peoples, however Maoist communism spreading through South-East Asia was exposing them to subversion. The largest ethnic sub-group hailed from the farming Hakkas in Kwangtung Province. In First Division, the Chinese supplied labour on the rubber estates, were heavily engaged in construction, supplied most of the fishermen and were common as barbers and coffee-shop proprietors.

Ibans formed 31.1 per cent of the population. Relatively recent arrivals in Sarawak, they lived in characteristic longhouses and tended paddy fields using an elaborate rotation of shifting cultivation. In some downriver settlements, a few took to living in houses with deplorable results. They were noted for their individualistic, enterprising and democratic society and readily accepted military discipline by supplying men

6

for the Sarawak Rangers during the Malayan Emergency.

Malays made up 17.5 per cent of the population and formed the backbone of government service. The Melanau lived as fishermen, rice farmers and sago growers in low-lying land along the coastal fringe. The Bisayas had their origins in the great clan of Dayak peoples and not only developed Sarawak, but also claimed to have founded the Brunei Sultanate generations. It was a Bisaya who, in 1858, killed Rajah Sir James Brooke's greatest enemy, Pengiran Makhota, during one of the latter's concubine-collecting expeditions along the Limbang, which encouraged Brooke to expand from Kuching towards Brunei. Largely converted to Christianity by the Borneo Evangelical Mission, the Bisayas lived in a combination of a longhouse and the ordinary separate house, which was known as a 'big-box house', usually providing accommodation for about four related families. A thin wall of bamboo down the centre separated the public place from the private quarters.

Further inland were the related Muruts and Kelabits. Murut settlements perched on jungle-clad hills between 500 and 2,000 feet and were heavily influenced by the Evangelical Mission at Lawas, or the Roman Catholic Fathers of the Mill Hill Society in Limbang. Most lived in longhouses. In early 1945, Special Reconnaissance Department teams organized the Kelabits into an effective resistance against the Japanese. Except at Long Scridan and on the Madihit, they mostly lived at 2,000 feet and above. A vigorous people and powerfully built from constant hill walking, the Kelabit longhouse was the most distinctive in Borneo of an integrated unit, with family accommodation open to all. They were noted for erecting stone memorials to their dead, which the Lawas mission actively discouraged, although this is exactly what Christians do. Both clans had a high standard of living, cultivated from rich rice irrigation, a wide variety of vegetables, fishponds and farm animals. Hospitality was a speciality of these hill people. Living in huge longhouses, with as many as fifty families in each, along the banks of the Sungei Baram and its tributaries, were the Kenyahs and Kayans, with nearly 200,000 across the border in Indonesia, which to them was a meaningless line on a map. Strong aristocratic leadership made them easy to organize.

The Kedayans occupied a large and economically powerful part of the coastal plain of British North Borneo. The legend told against them is that in the great cock fight between the Sultan of Brunei and the Sultan of Java during the sixteenth century, when royal gamblers bet fifty of their own people, the Sultan of Java's cock lost and it was from this fifty Indonesian stock that the Kedayans were alleged to have originated. Indeed, the name of the clan means 'servants or followers of the prince', and consequently they believed themselves second-class citizens. Some observers claimed they could detect a physical resemblance between the Kedayans and the Indonesians, in particular, their darker skin. Efficient farmers along the coastal strip, they excelled at working their buffaloes in the rice paddies. Subject to Islamic law, they lived their own lives without much interference from the other races. It is certainly correct that they were under-represented in Brunei public affairs and were ripe for subversion.

Finally, the Europeans at about 1,740 compromised just 0.2 per cent of the population, most Colonial administrators, police officers, teachers, businessmen, oilmen and missionaries.

North Borneo, with its capital at Jesselton (Kota Kinabalu), covered 29,388 square miles and was broken down into four residencies – West Coast, Interior, Tawau and Sandakan – and, in 1962 was governed by Sir William Goode. Interior and Tawau bordered Indonesia; a dominating feature is Mount Kota Kinabalu. Rajah Brooke had planned to secure North Borneo in order to improve the safety of ships transiting through the South China Sea, but the American adventurer, Claude Lee Moses, outwitted him by persuading the Sultan of Brunei to cede to him a large tract of North Brunei territory. In Hong Kong, Moses sold the cessation papers to four merchants who set up the American Trading Company of North Borneo, but the venture failed. One of the four, Joseph Torrey, convinced the Austrian Consul in Hong Kong, Baron von Overbeck, to speculate in North Borneo, however in 1877, a British civil servant based in Singapore, Mr W.H. Treacher, persuaded von Overbeck to cede the territory to the British. Von Overbeck then persuaded the Sultan to cede the 28,000 miles of North Borneo and by 1881 the British North Borneo Chartered Company was formed. In spite of opposition from the Brooke family, Treacher expanded the territory and after a period of instability and rashly planned projects, including the building of a railway line along the coast, by the twentieth century, profits enabled the Company to finance administrative, economic, health and education development. Timber was an important resource but frequently ran into trouble when labour was short. Indonesians made up the shortfall. In August 1945, North Borneo suffered from Allied bombing and in compensation for losses suffered during the war, the Chartered Company transferred its sovereignty to the Crown. In June 1946, British North Borneo became the British Crown Colony of North Borneo. The Kazackdusuns, 32 per cent of the population of 454,421 in August 1960, formed the largest community group. Originating from the Philippines before the last Ice Age, they were descended from notorious pirates defeated by Brookes and were converted into prosperous and stable rice farmers, fishermen and cattle ranchers. The Chinese numbered 23 per cent of the population and were engaged in a wide range of activities, including artisans, businessmen and government clerks. There were also about 25,000 Indonesians in North Borneo, mostly immigrant workers.

CHAPTER TWO

Indonesia

Two days after Japan surrendered on 14 August 1945, two Indonesian nationalists, Ahmed Sukarno and Muhammad Hatta, proclaimed the Republic of Indonesia from the Dutch East Indies colonial authorities, then in exile in Australia, and were selected as President and Vice-President respectively.

Known to Commonwealth soldiers as 'The Mad Doctor', Sukarno was born in 1901 in Surabaya, Java. Graduating from Bandung Technical College as an engineer in 1925, the next year he set out his political aspirations in *Nationalism, Islam, and Marxism*, a combination that was to direct his ambitions. Complex, flamboyant and a stirring orator, he led a scandalous private life and yet retained the goodwill of his people for twenty years while he moulded the disparate regions of Indonesia into a powerful Asian nation. Arrested again in 1933, he was exiled to Sumatra until released by the Japanese in 1942, who then encouraged him to promote Indonesian nationalism in return for mobilizing support. In March 1945, although staring at defeat, Japan supported Indonesian independence by establishing the Investigating Committee for the Preparation of Indonesia's Independence, and at a debate in July, Sukarno sided with Professor Mohammed Yamin who argued that since the Malay Peninsula was the neck of the Indonesian archipelago, the unification of Malaya and Indonesia would logically strengthen their regional influence. This formed the rationale of Sukarno's foreign policy.

While the declaration of independence surprised the Dutch and many Indonesians, the outer islanders, who traditionally distrusted the Java-dominated central government, regarded it as an attempt to impose its will on non-Javanese. However, since the government was not then controlled by one group, instability prevailed and, as law and order collapsed and extremists settled old scores, engaged in armed robberies and terrorized communities, observers believed that Indonesia would

10

not survive as sovereignty. However, three factors united the Indonesian will for self-determination: first, the Japanese had promised self-determination, which had reinforced resentment against the Dutch; secondly, the Japanese had appointed Indonesians into senior civil servant appointments vacated by the Dutch; and thirdly, there was a pressing need for an army. Until 1942, the 40,000 strong Royal Dutch East Indies Army had defended the Dutch East Indies. The Japanese then had assembled 37,000 nationalists into the auxiliary 'Defenders of the Fatherland' (*Pembela Tanah Air – PETA*), which was commanded up to battalion level by Indonesians, such as Ahmad Yani and Mohammed Suharto, all of whom played significant roles in post-1945 Indonesia. Twenty-six thousand men were assembled into home guards commanded by Japanese officers known as the *Hei-ho*, while several paramilitary guerrilla forces were collectively called the *Lascars*.

In the midst of the chaos were 129,000 interned colonialists and Allied prisoners of war, and the Allied policy was that Japanese-occupied colonies would return to their pre-war status. On 2 September, Vice Admiral Lord Louis Mountbatten, in his position as Supreme Commander, South-East Asia Command, issued orders to HQ 11th Army Group in Directive ASD 4743S:

> You are instructed to proceed with all speed to the island of Java in the East Indies to accept the surrender of Japanese Imperial Forces on that island, and to release Allied prisoners of war and civilian internees.
>
> In keeping with the provisions of the Yalta Conference you will re-establish civilian rule and return the colony to the Dutch administration, when it is in a position to maintain services.
>
> The main landing will be by the British Indian Army, 5th Division, who have shown themselves to be most reliable since the Battle of El Alamein. Intelligence reports indicate that the landing should be at Surabaya, a location that affords a deep anchorage and repair facilities.
>
> As you are no doubt aware the local natives have declared a Republic, but we are bound to maintain the status quo that existed before the Japanese invasion. I wish you God speed and a successful campaign.

The task was allocated to Lieutenant General William Slim's Fourteenth Army. On 8 September, a Force 136 team of the Special Operations Executive parachuted into Batavia (Jakarta) and reported that although Indonesian nationalists were controlling most of the administration and infrastructure, the People's Security Corps, which had been raised from

11

the Defenders of the Homeland and youth organizations, was providing a semblance of law enforcement in a country in a state of anarchy. On 29 September, the 23rd Indian Infantry Division landed at Batavia amid acceptance by the nationalists that they had arrived to evacuate the prisoners and internees, and repatriate the Japanese. The Australians landed in the eastern part of the country. However, when the Netherlands East Indies Governor, Lieutenant Governor Dr Hubertus van Mook, arrived on 7 October, he rejected political concessions to Sukarno and distanced himself from a broadcast made by Queen Wilhelmina suggesting independence. Allied hopes for a peaceful transition faded when the Indonesians promised total resistance and the British were drawn into fighting until April 1946 that cost sixty killed, five murdered, and over 2,000 wounded. Most of the casualties were Indians and Gurkhas, in a period of near total chaos and wanton destruction, implemented by the nationalists to such an extent that Japanese troops supported the British and also suffered casualties, nevertheless the internees, prisoners of war and 68,000 Japanese were evacuated. The Indonesian Prime Minister, Dr Sharir, praised the performance of the troops for 'your politeness, your kindness and your dignified self-restraint'.

The Dutch and Indonesian Republic endorsed the British-brokered Linggadjati Agreement and recognized the authority of the de facto republic covering Java, Sumatra and the Celebes, and plans for the establishment of a federal Indonesia. West Irian (Netherlands New Guinea) on Papua New Guinea remained under Dutch administration. When internecine factions in the military threatened civil war, Sukarno loyalists in the newly-formed Dutch-trained Siliwangi Division and Police Mobile Brigade restored order. In July 1947, the Dutch, claiming violations of the Agreement, launched the First Police Action to seize Indonesian-held territory until the United Nations-sponsored (UN) Committee of Good Offices, which comprised Australia (chosen by Indonesia), Belgium (chosen by the Netherlands) and the United States (chosen by both sides), sponsored, in early 1948, the Renville Agreement, which transferred the sovereignty of Java, Sumatra and the Celebes to Indonesia. However, the Dutch violated the Agreement with an economic blockade of the Indonesian Archipelago and launched the Second Police Action, although international pressure forced them into the inevitable transference of independence to the Republic of the Unitary States of Indonesia at the Hague Conference on 29 December 1949. The Dutch still retained West Irian. The Royal Dutch East Indies Army was disbanded with about half transferring to the Indonesian Armed Forces. By August 1950, the United States of Indonesia had emerged with the Legislature and House of Representatives defining the nation as a parliamentary democracy. In reality, politicians were faction torn, corrupt, and ineffective, and the predominantly Javanese government had few ties to the regions it was supposed to represent.

Among the military were several bright, ambitious and politically astute young officers, some of whom would attend Western military staff colleges during Confrontation. Abdul Nasution was aged thirty-one in 1949. Born in North Sumatra, educated at the Royal Military Academy at Bandung and then commissioned into Dutch Royal East Indies Army in 1941, during the occupation he had worked in civil administration and commanded civil defence forces in Bandung. Immediately after independence, he held a minor staff appointment until 1946 when he commanded the embryonic Siliwangi Division for the next two years. He was appointed as Chief of the Operational Staff of the Armed Forces with a remit to analyse the Dutch First Police Action and develop a military organization and countermeasures. When the Second Dutch Police Action broke out in December 1948, he was Army Commander on Java. Nasution took the Army down the 'Middle Way' of ensuring that it did not take over the government but remained active in national politics. However, he was part of an army with little command experience above battalion level, had limited strategic perception and had officers who saw no difficulty in combining military service with promoting political loyalties to protect the fledgling democracy from the excesses of a weak parliament. Nasution was implicated in a failed coup d'état in October 1952 to oppose moves by the refusal of Sukarno to modernize the Armed Forces and was barred from holding an appointment.

By 1954, Sukarno was such a dominant force that the Australian Department of External Affairs assessed:

> President Sukarno occupies a key position. As the father of the revolution, his prestige is firmly established and with the frustration and disillusionment which have resulted from the wranglings and manoeuvres of coalition governments, his importance as controller of the balance of power has increased as the reputations of others have declined. He has a remarkable understanding of the public relations technique required of a national figure and he has successfully kept Vice-President Hatta in the background.

A major factor in governing Indonesia was the deep, widely-spread, ethnic, regional, class and religious differences so that centralized decisions were communicated with difficulty. Muslim uprisings in West Java and Aceh, and Dutch-led anti-republican movements in the Celebes and the Moluccas were met with extreme counter-insurgency, which

13

hardened resistance and alerted the international community to Indonesian excesses. Into the breach blossomed the Parti Komunis Indonesia (PKI – Communist Party of Indonesia). Founded by socialist Dutch colonists and servicemen during the First World War, the PKI grew steadily and in 1945 was led by Dipa Nusantara Aidit who preached anti-colonialism and was anti-Western. In 1955, it came fourth in elections with 16 per cent of the vote from its 165,000 members. Although Sukarno did not trust the PKI, because it had had rebelled against him in 1949, he nevertheless sympathized, as we have seen, with the ideology of communism, a move barely tolerated by the Army and the majority of Muslims.

Lurking in the wings was the Central Intelligence Agency (CIA) and British Intelligence observing ideological threats to South-East Asia and looking for opportunities to undermine communist subversion.

By 1956, Sukarno had been increasingly frustrated with the restrictions placed on his power by Parliament and was developing the idea of 'Guided Democracy'. The philosophy was modelled on the government of Indonesian villages in which the elders debate a topic and the villagers then reach consensus – under the guidance of an enlightened leader. On 1 December, Vice-President Hatta resigned in protest at Sukarno's autocratic style and the government collapsed. The resignation did not improve Sukarno's popularity in Sumatra, where Hatta was well liked. Meanwhile, General Nasution, now Chairman of the Joint Chiefs of Staff, strengthened the Army's political position by replacing entrenched regional commanders with loyalists. In 1956, a coup by Colonel Zulkifli Lubis, the dismissed head of Army intelligence, led to several regional commanders, concerned by the growing influence of the PKI and encouraged by the CIA, to demand that Sukarno be appointed as president and that Hatta form a government. In February 1958, when Sukarno was out of the country, several senior Army officers in Sumatra and Celebes, prompted by the CIA, proclaimed the Pemerintah Revolusionir Republik Indonesia (PRRI – Revolutionary Government of the Republic of Indonesia) and arrested several prominent PKI. The situation was serious for without Sumatra and Celebes, there was no Indonesia. On 18 May, the shooting down of a CIA B-25 bomber on an arms supply mission over Ambon, and the capture of its pilot, Allen Pope, gave Sukarno the opportunity to accuse the US of supporting the rebels and prompted him to develop closer relations with the Soviet Union and, more especially, the People's Republic of China. By the mid-1950s, British Intelligence and the CIA had jointly developed a strategy of undermining revolutionary and nationalist groups by supposedly supporting their aspirations and then by double-crossing them, and attacking the credibility of the top echelons. In fact, the CIA were double-crossing the PRRI by passing information to Jakarta and ensured that weapon drops were seized by Sukarno's forces. When, in the middle of the year, Colonel Achmad Yani, under orders from General Nasution, suppressed the rebellion with ruthless efficiency, Lubis accused the US of treachery.

The losers of the rebellion were democracy, the people of the outer islands and the parties that had procrastinated over how to deal with the rebels. Of the winners, Sukarno reinforced his position by playing the PKI against the Army. The Army had proved its indispensability to central government and took a wider role in civil administration and politics. The replacing of outer-island officers by Javanese officers solidified Nasution's position as Army Commander; however he was not popular with some officers using their new-found powers to indulge in corruption and smuggling. The Army also developed a single command and control structure. In supporting the suppression, the PKI had declared its nationalist aspirations.

By 1957, the PKI had moved to the political centre stage by winning two elections, its success attributable to effective organization, appeal for land reform and support for 'Guided Democracy'. By 1959, membership had grown to 1.5 million. When tension between Indonesia and the Netherlands over West Irian grew in 1957, 46,000 Dutch were expelled and Nasution strengthened the military powerbase when he undermined moves by communist trade unions to nationalize Dutch-owned firms by installing officers as managers. This marked the beginning of the military involvement in economic development, and also a steep and slippery slope to progressive financial ruin.

In July 1958, Nasution suggested that Guided Democracy was achievable and, a year later, supported the dissolution of the House of Representatives and the introduction of the concept – with Sukarno as the 'enlightened leader'. Ignoring the deteriorating economic situation, Sukarno governed as President and appealed to the Indonesians to adopt nationalist ideals, however corruption was rife and although he promoted the interests of the functional groups, his aspirations were largely rejected in the outer islands. Next year, Nasution was appointed Minister of Defence.

When, in 1960, Sukarno developed the political creed of 'Nasakom' which was an acronym for *nasionalisme, agama, komunisme* (nationalism, religion, communism), the PKI saw an opportunity to gain influence as a junior partner in government. Meanwhile, the seizure of British property and attempts to seize American and other international assets failed to rescue Indonesia's economy and favoured communist ambitions. By the early 1960s, the cost-of-living index had rocketed and Sukarno took a traditional route to deflect the internal crisis by looking

15

for an external trigger to distract the rumblings from the economic debacle and, with the backing of the PKI, he began a *konfrontasi* to seize West Irian.

Konfrontasi, literally translated as confrontation, had been in wide use in Indonesia and usually referred to the diametrically opposed differences between conservative traditionalism and liberal thought and cultural expression. Sukarno believed that political success could be achieved through diplomatic lobbying accompanied by economic and military threats. The word was familiar to Indonesians but far less so to foreigners, who usually regarded confrontation as a direct intervention or open hostilities.

The only clash of note was a naval engagement. Australia objected to the seizure because she wanted Papua New Guinea as a barrier to Indonesian aspirations. The US, Great Britain and Australia had opposed the Dutch occupation of West Irian, anyway, and in 1962, the territory was placed under UN administration and then transferred to Indonesian control a year later with the proviso that a UN-sponsored plebiscite be held to determine the colony's future. The PKI, which had strongly supported Sukarno, became the centre of attention during the negotiations, a fact not ignored by the Army.

In his book *How Borneo Was Won*, Major General Walker quotes Field Marshal Slim:

> The Asian fighting man is at least equally brave, usually more careless of death, less encumbered by mental doubts and not so moved by slaughter or mutilation about him. He is better fitted to endure hardship uncomplainingly, to demand less in the way of subsistence or comfort, and to look after himself when thrown on his own resources. He has a keen practised eye for country and an ability to move across it on his own feet. He has no inherent disinclination to move through swamps and jungle nor to climb hills.

During his enforced period of reflection, in 1953 General Nasution had published the *Fundamentals of Guerrilla Warfare* (see Annex B for a summary). This is a thesis on guerrilla and anti-guerrilla warfare based on his own experiences and although one of several publications written by contemporary guerrilla leaders, such as Mao Tse Tung, Vo Nguyen Giap and Che Guevara, it is the product of independent analysis through his experiences in guerrilla warfare and in counter-insurgency. In making a clear division between the 'constructive' nature of irregular operations and the 'destructiveness' of conventional war, he analyses guerrilla warfare as:

The guerrilla movement is only the result, not the cause of the problem... A guerrilla war, sufficiently active behind the front line of the enemy, can engage an enemy ten to thirty times its number. Thus the enemy is forced to decrease the number of troops used in the actual front line. At the right time, the army can go over to the offensive in order to destroy and annihilate the enemy's army.

Nasution illustrates his theories by examining history, in particular the Spanish guerrillas in the Peninsula War, the Second Boer War, the Soviet Partisans, and significantly, Wingate's Chindit operations in Burma in 1943 and 1944, focusing not so much on disrupting enemy rear area operations, but as a means of expanding territory from sympathetic strongholds. In relation to anti-guerrilla operations, Nasution wrote that the Security Forces must:

demonstrate political, psychological, social and economic skills in order to win the hopes and faith of the people gradually...The anti-guerrilla forces movement must be able to realise what are the politico-ideological and socio-economic problems that give rise to and nourish such guerrilla resistance; in essence that good intelligence is a vital element of the security forces.. Anti-guerrilla warfare is patrol warfare.

Superiority in mobility, flexibility, aggression and skill supported by a co-ordinated and effective intelligence is critical. This he wrote before the British 'hearts and minds' activities during the Malayan Emergency became a feature of that campaign. On the terrain, Nasution wrote,

The condition of the terrain on the larger islands of Indonesia is suitable for the conduct of guerrilla warfare. There are many mountainous and jungle areas where passage is difficult and there are few roads. The country has many wet and dry rice fields which produce food and the rivers and forests yield fish and game. Being an archipelago, Indonesia is difficult for the enemy to enter from abroad since he has to cross the ocean. An enemy who can cross the ocean to attack us will also be able to control the sea communications of our archipelago. This does not mean we cannot sneak, as guerrilla fighters. From island to island, or even from aboard in spite of having to sail in small boats. In the past, we have been able to smuggle guerrilla fighters in and out of Java, Kalimantan, Celebes, Moluccas, Malaya, Philippines etc.   The people are, in general, in the best position to defend the freedom of their territory against outside aggression. However, in South East Asia it has been proved that this condition has been easily utilised by a foreign enemy to wage a guerrilla war against some of us. There is enough political, economic, social and psychological chaos in our young nation and there is enough misery and ignorance everywhere which can be used to raise guerrilla forces to fight a guerrilla war against our rear. Such troops will certainly be equipped and activated as completely as possible by the enemy. Such non-direct attacks, such as jabs from the rear, can always spread and become a civil war and in this way relieve the task of the aggressor's army. It is a common strategy in recent years to employ cold or secret war during peace-time to eat a potential enemy from the inside so that he can be invaded and sub-jugated easily and rapidly. Especially young and backward countries like ours are subject to becoming victims to such a plan.

Ten years after publishing his thesis, Indonesia was about to fight an army experienced in jungle warfare. Under the auspices of the Commander-in-Chief FARELF, *Anti-Guerrilla Operations in South East Asia* analyses potential hotspots in South-East Asia and showed that the British understood the psychology and nature of revolutionary warfare, describing the guerrilla soldier as a hardy and poorly educated peasant with low living standards – by Western standards. Able to carry heavy loads long distances, his needs are fewer than the conventional European soldier, and although adept at using ground and the natural elements, inadequate medical services ensure that casualties are a liability and abandonment is faced with stoicism. Defeating revolution-ary forces is fundamentally a joint political-military problem resolving the causes of unrest on which guerrillas base success. Since the leaders are frequently at odds with each other, the aim is to divide and conquer by exploiting the factions within the movement and then use the military in the reconstruction phase at the end of hostilities. So far as Confrontation was concerned, the British had a full dress rehearsal in Malaya against the Communist Terrorists (CTs).

Between 1962 and 1969, the Armed Forces of Indonesia (Angleatan Bersenjata Republik Indonesia) consisted of the Army, Navy, Air Force and police grouped into the National Army of Indonesia (Tentara Nasional Indonesia (TNI)), each headed by a commander responsible to Sukarno as Supreme Commander. Distance and poor communications usually meant that regional military commanders had more independ-ence than was politically healthy.

The Army (Angkatan Darat Republik) was raised from PETA in 1945 and until the PPRI rebellion was no more than an organization of loose political alliances and hidden agendas, over which Army HQ had little control. Its powerbase was limited to Java, where the best- equipped and motivated units were deployed. Encouraged by the CIA and British

Intelligence, the Army saw the PKI as the main threat to Indonesian stability; however Sukarno was canny at exploiting the traditional military conservatives against both the socialist-minded and liberal Air Force and the PKI. Army commanders doubted the wisdom of Confrontation but could not morally oppose a national campaign and undermine Sukarno without losing out to the PKI. Of the 546 Indonesians captured on Malaysian soil between 1963 and 1966, only twenty-one were Army. Officers saw no need for a professional force and most senior commanders were in the pocket of the CIA, anyway.

In 1963, from a population of about 100 million and Armed Forces of 412,000, the Army establishment stood at about 200,000 with 150,000 reservists and 130,000 para-military, home guard and police available for operations. Training focused on guerrilla ('Territorial Warfare') and anti-guerrilla operations ('Territorial Defence'), the governing principle being to raise local forces quickly to meet the threat and then disband when the crisis had passed. Operations envisaged a three-stage strategy:

- Phase One. Prevent the enemy from landing. With the weakness of the Navy and Air Force, this could not be guaranteed.

- Phase Two. Inflict maximum damage on the enemy using flexibility and mobility, and avoiding actions which could lead to serious losses. Total support of local populations were essential, however the Army track record on 'hearts and minds' was poor, even during the insurgency campaigns against the Dutch. This weakness led to a reappraisal and the Army was used to build roads, hospital and schools, and developed veteran co-operatives. This was known as Civic Action and led to political clashes with the PKI.

- Phase Three. The defeat, surrender and ejection of the enemy.

Shortly before the West Irian *konfrontasi*, the Army structure was organized into the General Staff with deputy commanders heading up Operations, Intelligence, Combat Support and Logistic Support. Three Interregional Commands covered Sumatra, Kalimantan and East Indonesia, each with three or four provincial Resort Military Commands (Komando Resort Militer – KOREM) supported by an infantry division, each with its own political affiliation. The pro-Western Siliwangi Division was based in Semarang, West Java (Siliwongi) in Military District III. Its major units usually began their titles with the figure 3. The Central Javanese (Diponegoro) Diponegoro Division was based in Bandung in Military District IV and retained Indonesian traditions. The Brawijaya Division was based in Surabaya in

19

Military District V in East Java. The importance of defending Jakarta was reflected in 1961 with the conversion of infantry battalions from the three divisions into rapid response Army Airborne Infantry, namely 328 and 330 Para-Raider Battalions, 454 Parachute Infantry Battalion and 530 Parachute Infantry Battalion. The next level down was District Military Commands (Komando Distrik Militer (KODIM) in towns and at the lowest formation level there were Resort Military Commands (Komando Rayon Militer – KORAMIL). The Army Strategic Reserve Command (Komando Serba Usha Gotong Royong – KOSTRAD) relied upon Regional Military Commands to supply troops and was thus politically influential. Alongside the conventional military units, in a structure that reflected 'Territorial Warfare', were sixteen 'territorial' regions known as Combat Commands. This network was developed to defend the country and gain political influence by integrating with the people. To simplify the organization, 'territorial units' all but paralleled civil administrations and each was supported by a brigade to fight conventional military operations alongside 'territorial' units. In Kalimantan, this was 5 Infantry Brigade with H, I and J Battalions. The Army had some Stuart tanks and Saladin armoured cars, US M2 105mm howitzers and Soviet ZSU-57-2 air-defence batteries with much based on Java defending Jakarta. Units tended to be self-sufficient in supplies.

The Air Force (Angkatan Udara Republik) was keener on Confrontation. Led by the Sukarno loyalist and left-wing Air Marshal Omar Dhani, its 1963 strength was about 20,000. Organized in a similar structure to the Army, it had a mixed air arm of about 550 aircraft of diverse origins and vintage, including US B-25 Mitchells and Soviet Tupolev-16 Badger bombers, MiG-17 Frescos, MiG-19 Farmers, MiG-21 Fishbed fighters, C-47 Dakotas and modern C-130 Hercules, however, it suffered from a chronic lack of spares. The lack of experienced pilots was filled by mercenary aircrew. Strategically and tactically, the Air Force was totally outclassed by the Commonwealth air forces.

The elite 3,500-strong Quick Mobile Force (Pasukan Gerak Tjepat (PGT)) was the oldest airborne formation in the country and had first jumped into action on 17 October 1949 when nine men dropped into Kalimantan to stir up anti-Dutch resistance. This tiny cadre was expanded into the Air Base Defence Force (Pasukan Pertahanan Pangkalan (PPP)) until, in the 1950s, it developed into the Quick Mobile Force and was used as shock troops during an Islamic rebellion in West Java, and in north Celebes in 1958. They dropped into Sumatra during the PRRI rebellion and also during the West Irian operation.

Politically the Navy (Angatan Laut Republik) played second fiddle to the Army and Air Force. In its early days, it had a mixture of old ships from the British, Dutch, American and Italian navies. In the late

1950s/early 1960s, Sukarno purchased several Soviet warships but Indonesia had neither the tradition nor expertise to man them. The pride of the fleet were a former Soviet Sverdlov class cruiser and six Soviet Whisky class diesel patrol submarines, supported by Soviet Navy personnel – otherwise the ships were a mix of destroyers, submarine hunters, mine-warfare ships, motor torpedo and patrol boats, landing craft and auxiliary oilers and transports from Italy, the United States, Yugoslavia and East Germany. During the West Irian *konfrontasi*, a two-battalion force had landed against very limited opposition and the only naval action of note was on 5 January 1962 when the East German-built 'Jaguar' torpedo boat *Madjan Tutal* was sunk by Dutch warships whilst trying to land infiltrators in Kalimantan. In 1963, the 25,000 men of the Navy were concentrated at Surabaya on the northern coast of Java, with light surface unit bases at Tanjong Priol, on Java, the Rhiau Islands and Palembang on Sumatra, Belawan and Tarakan on Borneo and Makassar on New Guinea. The fleet was exceptionally well placed to dominate the Java Sea and southern area of the South China Sea lapping the northern coasts of Borneo. Allied operations during the Second World War had shown that submarines could operate effectively in the area and it was these that posed the greatest threat to Commonwealth ships, in particular Commonwealth oilers, transports and landing craft in transit between Singapore and Borneo. The Indonesians had an estimated 10,000 former Soviet contact mines but the shallowness of the water and their indiscriminate nature made minelaying difficult.

Like the Air Force, the Navy had spent huge amounts of money buying military and naval equipment, but by 1963, it was unable to train its sailors to develop a reasonable standard of competency and capability, and maintenance and repair facilities were generally poor. These factors led the British Joint Intelligence Staff to assess the capability of the Navy to be low as a consequence of 'lack of experience, leadership and trained technicians'. The fact that the Navy, very young compared to the Royal Navy, had attempted amphibious operations was significant.

Part of the Navy, and generally loyal to Sukarno, was the 3,500-strong Marine Corps (Korps Komando Operasi (KKO)). Divided into two regiments of three battalions, each with field artillery, engineer and logistic support, it had increased to 14,000 men by 1966. During Confrontation, a brigade presented the principal threat to Sabah and Fifth Division. Like marines elsewhere in the world, they were often used for fighting in difficult terrain, however since the Navy did not have a dominant position in Indonesian politics, the marines lacked modern equipment, which undermined their fighting capabilities.

21

Although training was usually short, they were tough opponents. In 1960, several attended the British Jungle Warfare School and were followed, the next year, by a group attending US Marine Corps reconnaissance training. These two cadres amalgamated to form the Amphibious Reconnaissance Para-Commandos (Kommando Intai Para Amphibi (KIPAM)), initially numbering about 100 men. They were first committed into battle during the West Irian operation.

The fourth arm of the TNI was the police. Split by faction-fighting on a greater scale than the Armed Forces, it upheld law and order, and internal security. The para-military Police Mobile Brigade was formed in late 1946 and used extensively against the Dutch. Two cadres attended courses with the US Army Special Forces in Okinawa in 1959, and trained with US Rangers the next year. By 1964, the Brigade consisted of three battalions and had been converted into shock troops. The extent of their military use is reflected in the fact that seventy-two police officers were taken prisoner during Confrontation.

By 1962, after recovering West Irian, the PKI successfully subverted Sukarno against the Army and, in June, Nasution found himself sidelined to Armed Forces Chief of Staff. General Yani, a Nasution loyalist and the same officer who had quelled the PRRI rebellion, was promoted to Army Commander. And so, why was it that Malaya and her Commonwealth allies confronted Indonesia in the sparsely populated jungles of northern Kalimantan in a relatively unknown war from 1962 until 1966.

CHAPTER THREE

Historical Background

During the Second World War, Japanese gains in the Far East spelt the death knell of French and Dutch colonies in South Asia. With their governments in exile, only Great Britain retained influence in the region, although confidence in her had been severely shaken by the fall of Singapore. While Lieutenant General Slim's Fourteenth Army was fighting bruising battles in Burma, the controversial landings on British North Borneo by the Australian 7th and 9th Infantry Divisions under American command was the last major Allied offensive of the Second World War. Slim had no need of a Borneo base, not even as a jump-off for the invasion of Malaya, the oil was not needed and the Japanese forces were isolated. Most of the 600 Australians killed were buried in the war cemetery on Labuan and nearly 1,400 were wounded in bitter fighting.

In January 1957, following the Suez debacle the previous year, Prime Minister Harold MacMillan's Conservative Government recognized that Great Britain's retention of her Empire was no longer politically, economically or militarily viable and that the country should disengage from its colonies. This strategy fell neatly into the UN policy of decolonization and was exemplified by MacMillan's 'wind of change' speech in Cape Town in February 1960, and over the next four years, his and Sir Alec Douglas-Home's governments withdrew from those colonies that wished independence, mainly in Africa. Several territories, such as the Falklands, North Borneo, Sarawak, Brunei and Gibraltar opted to be Crown Colonies or Protectorates with associated diplomatic, economic and defence guarantees.

In April 1960, Secretary of State for War Duncan Sandys announced that National Service was to discontinue and that the Armed Forces was to restructure to meet its Priority One commitment to NATO of defending Western Europe against a perceived threat from the Warsaw Pact. Inevitably, cavalry, artillery and infantry regiments disappeared into the abyss of disbandment and amalgamation. A Strategic Reserve was created and the Territorial Army was generally confined to home defence. For the Armed Forces, the transfer from a global strategy was troubled with Great Britain becoming engaged in counter-revolutionary warfare, counter-insurgency, internal security, peacekeeping, quelling mutinies and low-intensity operations in states threatened with destabilization, seeking disciplined troops to restore order and organize national defences. In 1961, a joint Army and Royal Marines brigade deployed to Kuwait to deter Iraqi ambitions. The Army, in particular, was stretched to its limit, not for the first or last time.

President Sukarno and President Diosdado Macapagal of the Philippines both had nationalist aspirations to form a South Asia federation encompassing Malaya, British North Borneo, Indonesia and the Philippines, named *Maphilindo*. However, British North Borneo and Malaya had no such ambitions of political alliances with Indonesia and the Philippines – indeed the Philippines had strong links with the US and were strategically important to contain Japanese aspirations, admittedly unlikely.

Malaya, with its seat of government in Kuala Lumpur, achieved independence in 1957. At its head was Tunku Abdul Rahman Putra al-Haj ibni Almarhum Sultan Abdul Hamid Halim Shah, a member of one of Malaya's aristocratic families. Born in 1902, educated in Malaya and graduating from Cambridge University in law, he was dignified and quiet, but stubborn to the point of immobility. Virulently anti-communist, at a Foreign Correspondents' Association of South-East Asia lunch on 27 May 1961, he made it abundantly clear that Malaya had absolutely no wish to be involved with Indonesian and Philippine regional ambitions:

> Malaya today as a nation realises that she cannot stand alone. Sooner or later, Malaya must have an understanding with Britain and the peoples of the territories of Singapore, North Borneo, Brunei and Sarawak ... Where-by these territories can be brought closer together in political and economic co-operation.

He also mentioned the word 'Malaysia'. Generally the reaction to the Tunku's proposition was favourable, even by Lee Kuan Yew, the formidable Prime Minister of Singapore. Singapore had been granted independence in 1954. Lee Kuan 'Harry' Yew, born in 1923, had been educated in Singapore and had gained a Double First in Law at Cambridge University. Meeting in September, both men agreed that federation was inevitable and that Singapore would be accorded rights of finance, education and labour.

So far as British North Borneo was concerned, in 1892, the year after the Dutch East India Company and the British colonial authorities agreed to demarcate North Kalimantan, the British openly discussed the viability of a loose federation of the North Borneo colonies combining with Malaya and Singapore, largely because the majority of the indigenous peoples looked north towards Malaya. In 1945-6, British attempts to impose the 'Malayan Union' were rejected outright by nationalist Malays because it envisaged a system of equal rights, which would lead to a democratic self-government with the probability of a future Chinese majority and the possibility of a communist state. In July 1947, in line with its policy of economically and politically viable small colonies, the Colonial Office, through the Commissioner-General for South-East Asia, Malcolm MacDonald, revived a 1931 proposal to form a federation of Sarawak, North Borneo and Brunei within about four years, and identified Labuan as the capital. However, the concept was coolly received in Sarawak and was replaced, in 1948, by a Federation Agreement in which the Borneo colonies accepted partial loss in sovereignty, in particular the management of defence and foreign affairs, in exchange for federal government from Kuala Lumpur. Several anti-secessionist groups unleashed civil unrest and on 13 December 1949, two Malays of the small, militant, Sibu-based Malay Youth Movement (Pergerakan Pemuda Melayu) stabbed Governor Duncan Stewart of Sarawak. Official retribution was swift. The Movement was proscribed and the killers together with three of its members were hanged, while others received lengthy prison sentences. Tunku Abdul Rahman later proclaimed the killers as freedom fighters and was instrumental in raising a memorial to them in Kuching in 1990. Nevertheless, 'Borneoisation' continued with the establishment of a centralized High Court, although progress to a common administration system was protracted.

Within two months of the Foreign Correspondent's speech, the Tunku had persuaded the Malayan House of Representatives to approve negotiations with Prime Minister MacMillan, and then in November he signed the London Agreement proposing Federation. Meanwhile, Lee Kuan Yew was persuading Singaporeans of the inevitability of federation on the basis that without it, Singapore, as a shop window in South-East Asia, could not survive and that sooner or later the psychological barrier of the Johore Causeway would be swept away by commercial and economic pressures. After the Malayan Emergency, Malaya had a strong policy of anti-communism and although Lee, a Singaporean Chinese, was reliant upon the Chinese for his political success, he encouraged them to identify the advantages of self-determination. He also warned them against using Singapore to undermine

25

Malaya, and challenged them to place the development of Singapore and Malaya above their ideological whims. Indonesia, through Foreign Minister Dr Raden Subandrio, welcomed the Federation initiative by:

> disclaiming any territories outside the former Netherlands East Indies, though they are part of the same island (of Borneo), but more than that, when Malaya told us of its intentions to merge the British Crown colonies ... as one federation, we told them we had no objections and that we wished them success with the merger so that everyone might live in peace and freedom.

Comforting though the statement was, to a certain extent it was a blind because if Sukarno was to achieve his greater Indonesia, he envisaged Malaysia to be part of it. So far, he had never made any direct claims on the British colonies, only an indirect one in which he saw the whole island of Kalimantan as part of Indonesia. So far as Washington and London were concerned, the critical issue was to stem Chinese subversion in South-East Asia, which is reflected in a comment made by Prime Minister MacMillan to President J.F. Kennedy in 1962 that the situation in South-East Asia was as dangerous as anything since the Second World War.

With Chinese forming 31.5 per cent of the population, they would potentially soon be in the majority. Ready to take advantage of any issue that would give them an advantage, political intelligence sources were suggesting that the communists were seeking to establish a state in Sarawak. Communism in British North Borneo had been evident before the Second World War and was manifested by the guerrilla Anti-Japanese Sarawak Anti-Fascist League which, by 1956, had been renamed the Sarawak Advanced Youths' Association. The same year, the colonial authorities adopted the title Clandestine Communist Organisation (CCO) to cover communist organizations in British North Borneo. As with most subversive organizations, local structures were designed to resist infiltration and had small cells at branch level working upwards to district, town, area and divisional committees which reported to a central committee at the top of the triangle. Talent spotting was carried out at organized picnics and recreational cultural events, and those attracted to the ideology underwent training before being accepted as a Party member.

The communists' first foray into direct action in Sarawak happened on 5 August 1952 when three men and a woman 'liberated' Batu Kitang in First Division – to help the poor. Firing their weapons, cutting telephone lines, forcing shopkeepers to open their doors and demanding money, they claimed that there was a 1,000-strong army in Kalimantan, before heading south toward the border in a taxi. At 27th milestone, they ran into a police road block where they killed Lance Corporal Matu and wounded two constables; the police actually had no idea that Batu Kitang had been raided. The incident precipitated a state of emergency during which five Chinese were deported and several detained. Intelligence-gathering on the Chinese became a high priority.

Critically Sukarno, with his ideological commitment to communism, was seen to be part of the problem. His nationalist ambitions were essentially discounted. Sukarno's complaint with the Tunku was his willingness to remain part of the Commonwealth and its colonial connections. Nevertheless, the Tunku made every effort to maintain friendly relations with Sukarno and even allowed Indonesia to recruit Malays for the West Irian campaign. About fifty passed Indonesian screening and were despatched to Jakarta to receive training. Sukarno later formed them into a clandestine organization designed to overthrow the Malayan Government by inciting civil disturbances, particularly amongst the Chinese.

The British, while acknowledging the viability of Federation, would not agree until the people of the British North Borneo territories had been consulted; the Sultan of Brunei would be consulted separately. On 16 January 1962, Lord Cobbold headed a commission to elicit the views of Sarawak and North Borneo peoples. Their terms of reference issued by the Malaysian Commission of Enquiry were:

Having regard to the expressed agreements of the Governments of the United Kingdom and the Federation of Malaya that the inclusion of North Borneo and Sarawak (together with other territories) in the proposed Federation of Malaysia is a desirable aim in the interests of the peoples concerned:

(a) to ascertain the views of the peoples of North Borneo and Sarawak on this question; and

(b) in the light of their assessments of these views, to make recommendations.

The Commission spent two months travelling widely and then on 25 March, in a masterpiece of diplomacy, Cobbold reported:

• A third of the populations of Sarawak and North Borneo were in favour of federation.

• A third agreed prejudicial to certain guarantees.

• A third wanted independence or continued colonial government. Although Sarawak was the most politically developed, progress to a full democracy was slow.

27

- The indigenous peoples and Chinese led separate lives in peaceful harmony under a benevolent colonialism by a respected colonial government, however most wanted a local head of state.

- Political parties had developed along racial lines, for instance the left-wing Sarawak United People's Party, led by Ong Kee Hui, and was strongly Chinese.

North Borneo was less politically aware, however it had a major advantage in that it was not plagued by communism. The Chief Minister, the Eurasian Donald Stevens, believed that Federation would inevitably lead to domination by the Peninsula Malays. The Philippine claim over the colony developed in 1878 when North Borneo was transferred to British administration from the Sultanate of Sulu, which was now part of the Philippines and was complicated in that the North Borneo Company still made regular payments to Sulu. Tunku Abdul Rahman was conciliatory and regarded the claim to be diversionary internal politics, nevertheless as the concept of Federation gathered speed, he eventually made it absolutely clear that North Borneo would be included in Malaysia.

The persuasive powers of Tunku Abdul Rahman and Lee Kuan Yew persuaded Sarawak and North Borneo representatives to support Federation with several conditions:

- They would have direct authority over immigration, including Malays from other states.

- Malay would be the national language. English would remain official in the legislatures and in schools for ten years.

- Islam was the official faith and others faiths would be tolerated.

- The two states would enjoy exactly the same political, economic, financial and social privileges of Malaya and Singapore.

- A separate federal administration would be developed and expatriate officers phased out in favour of local officials.

In September, Lee Kuan Yew proposed the idea of a Malaysian Federation in a referendum, and his People's Action Party won a significant victory. Communist aspirations were rejected. Only in Brunei was there opposition, but Tunku Abdul Rahman rejected this by suggesting that it was too small to survive on its own outside the Commonwealth. This remark infuriated A.M. Azahari, an aspiring nationalist politician of Arab extraction in Brunei.

CHAPTER FOUR

The Brunei Revolt
December 1962 to May 1963

As early as 1951, British Intelligence had identified A.M. Azahari bin Sheikh Mahmud as a potential nationalist leader in Brunei. Trained in Indonesia as a veterinary surgeon during the Japanese occupation, he had fought for Indonesian independence and then, in 1952, had returned to Brunei where he had become involved in several failed business ventures before being jailed. Developing political acumen by exploiting popular dissent with the Sultan's regime and the regional drive for independence, he formed the nationalist Brunei People's Party (Partai Ra'ayat Brunei) in 1956, and attracted many of the intelligentsia and politically astute. When his proposals for a single autonomous North Kalimantan state proved to be a steady recruiting sergeant, the Sultan became concerned that Brunei would be forced to share its oil wealth with its poorer neighbours, while the British were anxious that independence would risk access to Brunei's oilfields. In 1959, the Sultan finalized negotiations with London to replace the Protectorate treaty drawn up in 1905-6 with a Constitution in which executive authority for internal affairs was vested in the Sultan, while a British High Commissioner oversaw defence and external affairs. By April 1962, Azahari, with his nationalist credentials, was an influential member of the Executive.

In 1957, a decision was made to eliminate Azahari politically, particularly as he had close connections with Indonesia and therefore, it was believed, with Indonesian communists. With Special Branch and British Malayan Petroleum as a front, British Intelligence penetrated the Brunei People's Party and hatched a scheme to induce an Indonesian response to a crisis in British North Borneo and then persuade British North Borneo of the advantages of merging with Malaya. Using the same tactic with the PRRI rebels in 1958, when a scheme failed to stir up disaffection among Sarawak Chinese, the CIA, in a joint operation organized from Singapore, supplied underground groups with weapons and encouraged subversion, before double-crossing them.

From dissidents in the Brunei People's Party spawned the communist North Kalimantan People's Party and the underground National Army of North Kalimantan (Tentera Nasional Kalimantan Utara – TNKU), largely from disaffected Kedayans and Chinese. The TNKU was commanded by Yassin Affendy. Training was rudimentary and weapons amounted to shotguns, axes, parangs and spears; it was hoped to capture police weapons. Active Indonesian complicity is unclear even today, nevertheless about sixty members of the TNKU trained in the Malinau area of Kalimantan under the auspices of the commander of the Kalimantan Combat Command, Colonel Supardjo, but complained of a frosty reception. In 1961, Azahari had proposed that the Indonesians form the Brunei Regiment and that the Malays recruited for the West Irian operation should be transferred to North Kalimantan. Assured of assistance from the Philippines and Indonesia, the dissidents believed that the Sultan should remain as head of state with Azahari as his prime minister. When the *Brunei Bulletin* reported the Indonesian connection, British units and the Sarawak Police conducted a large military 'exercise' in North Borneo, but patrols found no sign of the TNKU.

In November 1962, the Sultan assured Tunku Abdul Rahman of Brunei's support for Federation, however during Legislative Council elections, Azahari scored a massive electoral victory on the basis of a federation of Brunei, North Borneo and Sarawak and the transformation of Brunei into a republic with a socialist economy. When the result conceivably relegated the Sultan to a puppet monarchy, he neutralized Azahari's majority by nominating a majority to the Council. When he then cancelled a debate on Federation scheduled for 5 December, this seems to have been the catalyst for TNKU couriers to take despatches that the outbreak of rebellion was to coincide with the proposed visit of Tunku Abdul Rahman to Jesselton, in North Borneo, in December. A split then developed between the Brunei People's Party and the TNKU that military action should take place, with 24 December eventually being selected. Although the TNKU believed their security was tight, it was actually porous. For instance, on 23 November, the newly-arrived Fifth Division Resident Richard Morris was told that insurrection was planned for sometime after 17 December. A week later, the Sarawak Police in Lawas were asked by a grandmother to help to release her grandson from 'the army' so that he could help her till the fields. 'And which army might that be, madam?' she was asked. 'The local one,' she said, showing them a jungle-green shirt. When the police checked the markets, they discovered that there had been such a run on jungle-green cotton that extra cloth had been sent from Singapore.

When Tunku Abdul Rahman expressed his concerns about the security situation in British North Borneo to Lord Selkirk, who was the Commissioner-General of the Far East, Selkirk reviewed the situation, as did Sir Claude Fenner, the Inspector-General of the Malayan Police. When Fenner briefed Admiral Sir David Luce, Commander-in-Chief (C-in-C) Far East, that unrest was simmering in Brunei, Luce instructed his Chief of Staff, Major General Brian Wyldbore-Smith, to review Plan Ale, the military contingency plan drawn up after the 1953 rebellion to support the Brunei Police with two infantry companies and a small headquarters of Royal Engineers, Royal Signals and a Military Intelligence Officer (MIO). When Morris reported disquiet among the Kedayans to Governor Waddell, Waddell advised North Borneo Governor Goode, and Mr Outram and Mr Mathieson, Commissioners of Police for Brunei and North Borneo respectively, to put their constabularies on full alert. Wing Commander Graves, the Station Commander at RAF Labuan, sent a 209 Squadron Twin Pioneer aircraft to collect a North Borneo Police Field Force platoon as reinforcement for Outram in Brunei.

When Azahari left to visit Manila, this gave Superintendent Roy Henry, head of Special Branch in Sarawak, the opportunity to ignite rebellion by arresting ten senior TNKU officers in Lawas. After transferring them to Limbang Police Station and by leaking to a magistrate that more arrests were imminent, he convinced the TNKU to believe that the time had come to act and Affendy ordered the TNKU to deploy at 2.00 am on 8 December. The power station was captured and Police Headquarters in Brunei briefly overrun; attacks on the Sultan's summer palace and Prime Minister's residence were repulsed, as was an attempt to seize Brunei Airport. The Seria oilfields were overrun and Europeans and Malays taken hostage. In Limbang, the TNKU led by Salleh bin Sambas, a former police weapons instructor, captured Morris and his wife and overran the police station, during which four police officers were killed, five captured and one was missing. In Fourth Division, sheer ineptness prevailed and a TNKU attack on Miri withered when insufficient activists turned up. In North Borneo, John Parry, the Sipitang Assistant District Officer in the Interior Residency, and the police scattered about sixty TNKU waiting inland for a fishing boat to deliver arms and ammunition from Brunei.

Even though his political future was doomed, as 'Prime Minister of the Unitary State of North Borneo' (Utara Negara Kesatuan Kalimantan), Azahari broadcast next day that the three territories had been unified under the Sultan. In fact, the Sultan appealed to UN Secretary-General U Thant to intervene 'to prevent further bloodshed', and asked Great

31

Britain for military aid. When the Philippines distanced itself from the rebellion, claiming no official dealings with Azahari, and the expected support from African and Asian heads of state withered, Azahari flew to Jakarta where he received qualified support for the rebellion.

In Singapore, Admiral Luce, under Plan Ale Yellow, instructed HQ Far East Land Forces (FARELF) to place two infantry companies from 99 Gurkha Infantry Brigade group on forty-eight hours notice under the command of Brigadier Jack Glennie DSO, Brigadier General Staff, with orders, 'You will proceed to Brunei and take command of all land, sea and air forces for Borneo Territory and restore the situation.' The idyllic life that British servicemen and families enjoyed in Singapore was about to be shattered as the RAF found aircraft and aircrew, Ordnance depots were opened and the Royal Navy assigned ships.

As information trickled in, Plan Ale Yellow was ratcheted to Ale Red and just after 2.45 pm on 8 December, four transport aircraft left with elements of 1/2nd Gurkha Rifles for Brunei. Communications with Brunei then failed, and it was only when a message was passed by a British Overseas Airways Corporation pilot en route from Australia that a British officer and a rifleman had been killed reach Singapore, that HQ FARELF realized the seriousness of the situation. During 9 December, 1st Queen's Own Highlanders (Lieutenant Colonel Charlie McHardy) recaptured the Seria oilfields by launching two simultaneous airlanding attacks from the east and west to seize Anduki Airfield, and released the hostages from the police station. Early on 12 December, L Company, 42 Commando (Captain Jeremy Moore MC) landed at Limbang from two Z-craft commercial landing craft manned by sailors from the minesweepers HMS *Chawton* and *Fiskerton* and rescued eight hostages, including Richard Morris, but at the cost of five killed and eight wounded. Moore was awarded a bar to his Military Cross (MC) won in Malaya. The cruiser HMS *Tiger* landed 1st Green Jackets at Miri at about the same time and, after a difficult overnight approach through dense jungle, seized Bekanu and Niah from rebels next morning. Within five days, the British had smashed the insurrection at a cost of seven killed and twenty-eight wounded.

With a communist threat apparently evident and the probability of direct interference from Indonesia, HQ 3 Commando Brigade (Brigadier Billy Barton) took over operational responsibility for the defence of Sarawak. On 13 December, a State Executive Committee was formed in Brunei. Brigadier Glennie was still Commander, British Forces, Borneo, pending the arrival of the charismatic Major General Walter Walker, commander of 17th Gurkha Division, on his way from Nepal. Two days later, Indonesia dropped a heavy hint supporting the rebellion.

Born in Tiverton, Walter Walker served with 8th Gurkha Rifles in 1933 on the North-West Frontier, and then joined 4/8th Gurkha Rifles as Commanding Officer in February 1944. Training his men to 'Move quickly, fight fiercely and shoot low', the Battalion joined 7th Indian Division in Burma in the pursuit of the Japanese withdrawal from Arakan. Walker was awarded the first of three Distinguished Service Orders (DSO). On partition of India in 1947, 8th Gurkha Rifles was transferred to the Indian Army and Walker joined 6th Gurkha Rifles, one of the four Gurkha regiments that remained with the British Army. From his experiences in the Malayan Emergency, he was instrumental in setting up the Jungle Warfare School at Johore Bahru, where skills developed by Fourteenth Army were taught to National Servicemen about to fight Communist guerrillas who had been living in the jungle since 1942. Walker's training methods were unpopular but they brought success. Towards the end of the Emergency, Walker was appointed to command 99 Gurkha Infantry Brigade Group in South Johore. By now, he was probably the best British exponent of jungle warfare, but was regarded as a maverick by the military establishment. That he was a Gurkha did not help, nevertheless Walker was promoted to command 17th Gurkha Division in Singapore. Its role was to defend Commonwealth interests in the Far East and it had battalions in Singapore and Hong Kong.

At the conclusion of the Malayan Emergency, the government had proposed reducing the Gurkhas to two regiments. In early December 1962, Walker, assured by HQ FARELF that there were no military or political threats on the horizon, had departed on a three-month trip to visit Gurkha pensioners in Nepal in his capacity as Major General, Brigade of Gurkhas. At an audience with the King of Nepal, he mentioned that the disbandment proposals would affect his country's economy. The US Ambassador was unhappy about the proposals because he believed that firm British and Nepali relations helped stabilize a region under threat from the Chinese, notably in Tibet. When Walker heard about the Brunei rebellion, he was back in Singapore by 17 December, and two days later took over command of British forces in Brunei from the indefatigable Brigadier Glennie, reporting directly to the Commander-in-Chief, Far East. Walker was convinced that Indonesia was the real threat and, while flying to Brunei, scribbled his ingredients for success:

- First-class intelligence machine.

- Timely and accurate information.

33

- Speed, mobility and flexibility of Security Forces, particularly the Army.

- Security of our bases, what they may be, wherever they are; whether an airfield or patrol base or whatever.

- Domination of the jungle.

In the first meeting of the Borneo Security Council three days after he arrived, when Governor Waddell objected to concentrating the Royal Marines in Brunei and North Borneo, and replacing them in West Sarawak with a Queen's Royal Irish Hussars (QRIH) armoured car squadron, Walker had it minuted that he was the military commander, not the Governor. By the New Year, in a strategy that remained solid throughout Confrontation, Walker had created two tactical areas of operations:

- Western Sarawak. Lieutenant Colonel Pierson QRIH was Military Commander, West Sarawak (COMKUCHFOR) with his HQ at Kuching.

- North-Eastern Sarawak, Brunei and North Borneo. Commanded by Lieutenant Colonel John Heelis (1/7th Gurkha Rifles).

Insisting that there was no 'rear' area in Borneo, just areas in depth to be defended, Walker's first priority was defending the 971-mile border with Kalimantan – about the same distance by sea from England to Spain. Rejecting as 'too little, too late' a HQ FARELF suggestion to fly battalions from Singapore to meet an incursion, he intended to dominate a 100-mile-deep sanitized zone in British North Borneo so that every time there was an incursion or civil unrest, it would be dealt with quickly before it disappeared. Walker familiarized himself with Sarawak by spending time in the field and liaising with local information sources. One of these was Tom Harrison DSO OBE, the Curator of the Sarawak Museum and a wartime member of the Australian Special Reconnaissance Department. At the request of Walker, he wrote a booklet, entitled *Background to a Revolt: Brunei and the Surrounding Territory* for the benefit of all ranks of the British Armed Forces in Borneo. Not a comprehensive study, it outlined the history and anthropology of Brunei in a readable form. Walker recommended that all officers and men serving in Borneo should read it.

Two thousand Iban irregulars were assembled into Harrison Force and, by 15 December, were deployed in a wide arc south of Brunei and contributed to the capture of about 100 TNKU and CCO. From 28

December, a patrol from M Company, 42 Commando, commanded by Lieutenant Rupert van der Horst, investigated reports that a TNKU group had set up a stronghold on Bukit Pagon, a 6,070-feet-high mountain on the southern border with Sarawak. His projected seven-day patrol lasted over ten days during which the Royal Marines were compelled to hunt for food.

While the CCO were successful in subverting the Chinese education system and labour movements through trades union, and were politically disruptive, they were now faced by colonial authorities prepared to use emergency powers legislation. Over 100 suspected CCO were detained and four deported, while interrogations by Special Branch in West Sarawak led to the seizure of large quantities of arms, ammunition and training pamphlets, and indications that the CCO was in the advanced stages of planning insurgency, had rehearsed attacks on police stations, and had planned assassinations and intimidation. Over the next six months, the Security Forces, with the help of loyalist Kenyahs, Kayans and Ibans, mopped up the TKNU by sealing river headwaters, ambushing escape routes and using psychological operations to convince dissidents that further resistance was pointless. A few communities, persuaded by the TNKU not to surrender their weapons, soon changed their minds when the irregulars reminded them where their loyalties ought to lie. Some disappeared, no doubt dying of starvation and disease, and some slipped into Indonesia. A few 'on the run' in the jungle were pursued relentlessly.

A month after arriving in Brunei, Walker, drawing on his Malayan experiences, added 'winning the hearts and minds' to his list. Kuching, which was about five days' march from the border, was under particular threat, as was the airport. With the need for infantry to meet the threat, he needed timely accurate information of activity along the border. While the police could maintain internal security in urban areas and along the coastal strip, the key to guarding the border was to minimise the risk to the villagers, most of whom regularly crossed the border to trade, and were a potential source of intelligence. When Walker deployed infantry sections among the longhouses, the British soldiers revelled in their new role. Medics played a valuable role in treating illness, inoculating against diseases and in dentistry. These early 'hearts and minds' ensured that throughout Confrontation the Indonesians fell well short of a classic requirement of a successful guerrilla campaign – local support.

After its nine years in Malaya and with no foreseeable role, 22 Special Air Service (SAS) had been reduced from four squadrons to two with the disbandment of B Squadron and C (Rhodesian) Squadron, and an internal debate had emerged between those who saw the Regiment supporting NATO and those who saw it with a global role. When the Brunei Revolt broke out, the Commanding Officer, Lieutenant Colonel John Woodhouse, who supported a global role, lobbied that the SAS should be sent there and by 11 December, was in Brunei. Within three weeks, A Squadron (Major John Edwardes), in civilian clothes, arrived in Singapore from a ferocious winter in the UK and were loaded on to military transport vehicles. It is doubtful that its arrival fooled anyone – not that the reputation of the SAS in 1962 was as public as it is today. Major General Walker originally wanted to use the SAS as quick reaction and reserve force 'tree jumpers' to recapture jungle airstrips, but Woodhouse persuaded him that the Regiment be better spread along the border as information gatherers reporting direct to his HQ. 'Tree jumping' was a dangerous technique developed in Malaya when the parachutist jumps onto the jungle canopy, falls until the parachute is trapped by branches and then abseils to the ground using a 100-foot rope. Serious injuries were not unknown. Within days, four-man patrols were deployed along the border on about a 20-mile frontage. From discreet hides near kampongs and greatly helped by Tom Harrison in Sarawak and John Warne in Sabah, Edwardes personally introduced the patrols to the elders, requiring his men to develop dossiers on longhouse habits. Fortunately, many jungle communities did not need to be bribed with gifts; common courtesy, an acceptance of their lifestyle and a cast-iron stomach was all that was required. As planned, the SAS began to collect information on the Indonesians.

Early in the New Year, the worst monsoon in living memory struck Brunei, and Belvedere and Wessex helicopters hunting the TNKU resorted to rescuing frightened and soaked people from the roofs of their shaky huts and trees, while assault boats visited kampongs with food and medical supplies. This also had a major impact on 'hearts and minds'. Psychological warfare operations – using the distribution of transistor radios to village headmen, leaflet distribution, safe-conduct passes and Valetta and Twin Pioneer Voice Aircraft broadcasting – was an important facet in convincing TNKU dissidents in the jungle of the futility of continued evasion, inviting them to surrender and warning their families of the consequences of not doing so. They also advised on curfew times and generally helped restore confidence. Unkempt and starving young men drifted back to their kampongs, although this was not the case in the centre of the rebellion in Limbang and Temburong. By 19 January, 55 TNKU had been killed, 33 wounded and 3,288 captured, of whom 794 were released.

Initially, the Indonesian threat was less easy to analyse. Reports suggested that about 1,000 volunteers were preparing to infiltrate into British North Borneo, while behind them, not necessarily in support, were reported to be about 8,000 Indonesian troops en route to North Kalimantan. President Sukarno's stance finally emerged on 20 January 1963 when Foreign Minister Dr Subandrio broadcast on Radio Jakarta several inflammatory statements designed to destabilize British influence in the region and declared that Malaya represented the 'accomplices of neo-colonists and neo-imperialist forces that were hostile to Indonesia'. From henceforth, Indonesia would adopt a policy of *konfrontasi*. Radio Jakarta claimed that volunteers were ready to help liberate the three protectorates of British North Borneo from colonialism. Defence Minister General Nasution knew Azahari and supported an independent North Kalimantan.

Although Colonel Hassan Basri, a Kalimantan Inter-Regional Command intelligence officer, established links with Chinese refugees from Sarawak, most of whom had links with the Chinese in north-west Kalimantan, the Army were outsmarted when Subandrio's Central Intelligence Bureau actively supported the Brunei Revolt by supporting generally badly equipped 'volunteers'. Apart from the TNKU, this included 1,600 Chinese assembled south of the border under the control of Wong Ki Chok, an executive member of the Sarawak United People's Party. Most were members of the left-wing and anti-Federation Sarawak Guerrilla Army (Pasukan Guerrilla Rakyat Sarawak (PGRS)) and the North Kalimantan Army (Pasukan Rakyat Kalimantan Utara (PARAKU) – the majority being Chinese refugees. Wong Ki Chok formed a cadre that fought against a federated Malaysia until 1974. Most were assembled into companies of the Brunei Regiment with such stirring titles as 'The Thunderbolts', 'Night Ghosts' and 'World Sweepers', although interrogations established that it was beefed up with former Indonesian Army, TNKU with police experience, and convicted criminals and pirates cajoled into the militias. The British collectively nicknamed these insurgents as Indonesian Border Terrorists (IBT). Although a welcome resource, and even though some were loosely subverted to the PKI anti-colonialist views, Sukarno was careful not to insinuate that Malaya was under threat from communists. Most groups were concentrated in towns, villages and hamlets near tracks or rivers that headed north toward Chinese communities in First, Second, Fourth and Fifth Divisions, and North Borneo, however their presence was not always welcome, particularly when strong-arm tactics were applied. One village became so frustrated that one night in 1964, they packed their belongings and, in a planned operation, seventy-two villagers trekked across the border and were met by B Company, 1st Royal Ulster Rifles (1st RUR) and were resettled in an area they called

Kampong McGonigal, named after the Quartermaster. General Yani, the Army Commander, declared 'fullest moral support' to the TNKU and assured that his 'troops were awaiting orders'. The 'Voice of Freedom Fighters of North Kalimantan', through Radio North Kalimantan, broadcast anti-Malayan propaganda to Borneo. On 13 February, Indonesia formally declared its opposition to the Federation of Malaysia.

The warmongering by Indonesia led to Tunku Abdul Rahman fearing a resurgence of communist activity throughout the Malayan Peninsula and he insisted that Singapore round up its communist activists before Federation. Lee Kuan Yew acted quickly and in February, in Operation Coldstore, police arrested 107 prominent politicians and trade unionists under public security legislation, because they strongly supported a socialist state, as opposed to Federation.

In mid-January, Major General Walker moved his HQ into Brunei Girls' School and occupied the headmistress's office. Emphasizing that there was no room for inter-Service politics, he insisted Joint Service representation must include civil authority and police components at all levels. Typically, Walker arrived from his accommodation at Muara Lodge, which was on loan from the Sultan of Brunei, at 8.00 am for 'daily prayers', the Army adage for the intelligence, operations and logistics brief. At 5.30 pm, he usually returned to Muara Lodge.

Although determined to flush out the remaining TNKU in time for Federation in August 1963, Walker remained convinced that the Revolt was a prelude to something more sinister from Indonesia, nevertheless, in spite of the hawkish declarations from Jakarta, military activity from North Kalimantan was not evident. His assessment was intuitive and, having no alternative but to reduce his force levels, Walker recommended that for future Far East operations, HQ 17th Gurkha Division and 99 Gurkha Infantry Brigade Group should be nominated as the regional strategic reserve, as opposed to the War Office despatching the Strategic Reserve from the UK. By the end of March, Walker's men were under orders to return to their barracks in Malaya, Singapore and Hong Kong.

Meanwhile, Walker's comments about the proposed disbandment of the Gurkhas reached London. As Major General, Brigade of Gurkhas, he was entitled to resist the proposals, however three field marshals with a Gurkha background – Harding, Slim and Templer – regarded Walker as disloyal and, under the threat of enforced resignation, Walker apologized to Field Marshal Sir Richard Hull, the Chief of the Imperial General Staff. Thereafter, Walker's judgment was frequently called into question, particularly by Hull, who suspected that every request he made was designed to save the Gurkhas.

The war that became known as Confrontation broke out on Good Friday, 12 April, when thirty guerrillas attacked Tebedu Police Station, which was located about 3 miles from the border in the First Division. Under cover of darkness, they crawled along a monsoon ditch, slipped underneath a 10-foot-high chain-link fence surrounding the compound and took the Sarawak Police completely by surprise, killing a corporal in the Charge Room and wounding two constables in the barracks. The raiders then scavenged the bazaar for food and scattered pamphlets suggesting the raid had been carried out by the TNKU. However, the raid had been effectively planned and was strongly suspected to have been executed by Indonesian commandos. It took a British relief convoy over three hours to travel the 30 miles from Serian, such was the poor state of the roads. Lieutenant Colonel John Strawson, who was the local military commander and had recently taken over command of the QRIH, was so concerned about the Indonesian threat that, next day, he sent a FLASH signal to HQ FARELF:

In view of likely further incursions from Kalimantan and probability of CCO insurgency, I have recommended to HE The Governor, who agrees with me, the instant despatch of a brigade of troops from Singapore to ensure the security of Sarawak.

The urgency of military teleprinter signals is determined by the content and graded by 'Priority' to 'Immediate' to 'Flash'. 'Flash' signals are rare, however Strawson's recommendations had the desired affect and HQ FARELF contingency plans swung into action. On the same day, the Sarawak Emergency Committee sought urgent military assistance from Great Britain, in particular to enforce an amnesty to collect an estimated 8,514 shotguns held on the firearms register. HQ 3 Commando Brigade and 40 Commando were recalled from Easter leave and deployed immediately, while 2/10th Gurkha Rifles was placed on short notice to move. Major General Walker now had two brigades:

- West Brigade. HQ 3 Commando Brigade (Brigadier Barton) took over from Strawson as Commander, British Forces, West Sarawak, and defended First Division, Second and Third Division.

- East Brigade. HQ 99 Gurkha Infantry Brigade (Brigadier Pat Patterson) continued anti-TNKU operations in Brunei and guarded Fourth and Fifth Divisions.

Good military communications were a critical asset. 17 Gurkha Signal Regiment supported 17th Gurkha Infantry Division, and its four squadrons supported the four Gurkha Infantry Brigade HQ and Signal

Squadrons in the Far East. 3 Commando Brigade had its own Signal Squadron. Long-range communications were undertaken by 18 Signal Regiment, with 1 Squadron providing the communication centre and telephone exchanges, 2 Squadron running line in the HQ, and 3 Squadron providing the Signal Training Centre at Calcutta Camp, Singapore. The Regiment was distinctive in that, in 1964, it absorbed 4 Independent Company, Women's Royal Army Corps (WRAC) into its order of battle. 19 Signal Regiment (Air Support), which had a history of air support going back to 1943, provided ground-to-air communications and had detachments in Kuching, Labuan and Tawau. In 1963, when the Army established rear-link Signal troops for airportable battalions in the UK, and the two Gurkha battalions and one British battalion of 99 Gurkha Infantry Brigade Group, troops were assembled from the UK and Far East and stayed in position as units rotated through Borneo. In total, fifteen Signal troops were deployed to Borneo with 606 Signal Troop being enlarged to 266 Signal Squadron in 1964, until 25 January 1965, when it was converted to the Joint Communication Unit, Borneo and was staffed by the Royal Navy, Army and RAF.

Operation Parrot began on 19 April and not only netted 7,188 licensed firearms, but a 2/10th Gurkha Rifles patrol stumbled on twenty Chinese youths doing physical training in a jungle clearing in the middle of the night.

Ten days after the Tebedu raid, eight guerrillas attacked the Sarawak Police Field Force post at Gumbang, which was only 200 yards from the First Division border, however it had been reinforced by a section commanded by Corporal Radford of B Company, 40 Commando, and he personally accounted for two of them. His leadership gained him the MM. Documents suggested that the TNKU were again responsible and blood trails led across the border, although Indonesian military involvement was suspected once more. Imposing a 'shoot-on-sight' curfew between 8.00 pm and 4.00 am, 5 miles in depth along the border, Brigadier Barton ordered Operation Falcon Strike in which First Division Police Field Force detachments were reinforced by L Company, 42 Commando, and despatched to about fifteen defended forts near kampongs to cover likely border-crossing points. Nevertheless, on 27 April, Tebedu Police Station was again attacked by three raiders who crawled to within 20 yards of the compound, cut the alarm system, removed some punji sticks, and opened fire with a shotgun and a Bren gun. A half-section from C Company, 40 Commando, returned fire but a dog tracker team had little success when the spoor was weak.

Meanwhile, the net had closed on the surviving TNKU commanders on a small island near Kampong Serdang, which is north of the mouth of the River Brunei. Several raids resulted in captures of a number of TNKU, but at the cost of Captain Keith Burnett, a Royal Artillery officer acting as a MIO, killed on 17 April. A month later, the interrogation of a young food supplier led to the capture of the last TNKU in an attack on Serdong Island by B Company, 2/7th Gurkha Rifles. Prisoners included Yassin Affendy, the TNKU military commander and Salleh bin Sambas, a senior commander at Limbang.

The Brunei Revolt was over. Although the Indonesian dissident, Pramoedya Ananta Toer, claimed the activities of British Intelligence 'reprehensible', the fact is that Indonesia's ambitions were exposed and the people of British North Borneo spared her ruthlessness. The British also brought stability to a region in turmoil, as communists attacked South Vietnam. Opposition parties in British North Borneo, who had largely rejected Azahari's claim as an opposition mouthpiece, condemned it. The local population had generally not supported the rebellion; indeed it highlighted their vulnerability to interference from Indonesia and even the Philippines. In elections held in North Borneo that year, the Sabah Alliance, on a ticket of pro-Malaysia, scored a massive victory, although the Sultan of Brunei still elected not to join the Federation.

But lurking in Jakarta was the 'Mad Doctor', determined as ever to destabilize regional stability by challenging colonialism and the Federation. And so began a war which, to this day, is known in Great Britain as Confrontation. Many at home did not even know about this strange war – and still don't.

CHAPTER FIVE

Jungle Warfare

'The jungle is neutral.' So wrote Spencer Chapman describing, in *The Jungle is Neutral*, his three years in Malaya during the Second World War. The 'ulu' (jungle) is probably the most difficult environment in which to fight. When Lieutenant Colonel Corran Purdon MC, of 1st Royal Ulster Rifles (1st RUR), arrived in May 1964 and flew over his area of operations around Sibu in Third Division, he later wrote:

> We had crossed a coastline of mangrove swamps and nipah palms intersected with inlets, creeks and great brown, powerful-looking rivers, which, with their narrower offshoots, writhe beneath the green canopy of the jungle. Scarcely a road or logging track was visible and I already knew from my reconnaissance earlier that until the arrival of our security forces with their helicopters the main means of travel had to be by the waterways or along jungle trails. We flew over longhouses where whole villages lived under one long roof inside a building built on stilts high above the river bank to escape the flooding waters, access being by notched tree trunks leant against the building and leading up to a long, wide, communal veranda. The domestic animals lived below.

At night, unless it is raining, the jungle is silent except for the occasional rustle as insects and reptiles disturb fallen leaves. Rivers, some shallow and clear, were the easiest form of travel. Salt-water crocodiles lurked among some coastal estuaries. Snakes were not uncommon, the most aggressive being the King Cobra. Yellow and green bamboo snakes perched on branches were virtually invisible. Mosquitoes, leeches, spiders and insects of all sorts abounded, including a mammoth beetle fondly known as the 'Flying Halftrack'.

After the British had been defeated in Malaya in 1942, Brigadier Orde Wingate's Chindits in 1943 and 1944 had shown that European troops could fight and survive in the jungle, and the Japanese crumbled before the formidable British, Indian and African divisions of Lieutenant General Slim's Fourteenth Army. Wartime skills were then revised to equip Gurkhas and British National Servicemen to defeat the Communist Terrorists in Malaya, themselves thoroughly familiar with surviving and fighting in the jungle since 1942.

The four years of Confrontation proved to be a difficult period for the British Armed Forces. Although international tension was cooling down after the Cuban missile crisis in October 1962, nationalist pressures in the volatile Middle East had led to the establishment of the Aden military base the same year. Within the year, a state of emergency was declared and operations in the Radfan were followed by a vicious campaign conducted by the Egyptian-supported National Liberation Front. Cyprus was still tense after the defeat of the Greek-Cypriot nationalist EOKA campaign in 1959. In 1963, the last National Serviceman soldier was discharged and in 1964, direct government from London was imposed on Aden, Rhodesia declared Unilateral Declaration of Independence and British forces quelled a mutiny in East Africa. In South Vietnam, Australian and New Zealand contingents were dragged into the war with the US against the Viet Cong and the North Vietnamese. In the summer of 1962, 28 Commonwealth Brigade had practised counter-insurgency on Exercise Trumpeter, in case it was deployed to Vietnam, the enemy being controlled by Major Chris Batchelor of 7th Gurkha Rifles. He later commanded a wing at the Jungle Warfare School at Kota Tinggi training South Vietnamese officers and visited South Vietnam to evaluate British training methods. The combination of these deployments, plus the need to supply four armoured divisions for the British Army of the Rhine against an unlikely Soviet invasion of Western Europe, and providing overseas garrisons in such places as Hong Kong, Gibraltar and Singapore, meant that Confrontation would stretch the Army to the limit.

The infantry provided the backbone of the defence of North Borneo with thirty British, Gurkha, Australian, New Zealand, Malaysian and Brunei battalions represented, the onus falling on the eight Gurkha battalions, two Commandos and a few British battalions. There was a huge wealth of jungle experience in the Gurkhas. Not only had some senior and middle-rank British officers and Queen's Gurkha Officers (QGOs) and other ranks in the Gurkha units fought in Burma, many had participated in the Malaya Emergency. The British units, trained primarily to fight a mechanized war in West Germany and with transferable skills learnt in Libya and on operations in Korea, Kenya, Aden and Cyprus, were quick to learn. The British also had a cadre of Second World War veterans. Every British soldier trains to be an infantryman, irrespective of his cap badge, and, with very few exceptions, everyone completed a jungle warfare course so that by the time the men arrived in Borneo, they were lean, fit and competent at living and fighting in the jungle. Inevitably, some, such as those in a Field Ambulance, when it arrived in the Far East in July 1966, found the course a 'week of pure hell'. For most of the campaign, the Jungle Warfare School was at Kota Tinggi in Johore Bahru state in Malaya, which had been established by the then Lieutenant Colonel Walker during the Malayan Emergency. When Great Britain decommissioned its base in Malaysia, the Jungle Warfare School was transferred to Paradise Camp not far from Jesselton. By the 1970s it was on the banks of River Tutong in Brunei. By then, British forces were in Belize deterring Guatemalan aggression in a jungle environment different from the Far East – in particular there are no leeches!

Following the murder of Lance Corporal Matu by Communists in 1952, the Sarawak Constabulary was trained by the Singapore Police Training School who took over the Kuching training school and although efficiency had improved by 1962, accidental discharges of weapons had been averaging 154 annually since 1945 and was still problematic. The 1,400 officers were divided into the urban Sarawak Constabulary and the Sarawak Police Field Force, which patrolled long-houses and isolated communities, and included the Public Order Company. Special Branch dealt with political intelligence and subversion, and worked with military and civilian agencies. The difficulty of attracting Chinese handicapped its dealing with the CCO. Enlistment into the Auxiliary Constabulary was confined to those who had served in the Sarawak Police, the Armed Forces and the Colonial Police. By 1960, it was organized into the Field Force Reserve, the Oilfields Reserve and the Police Reserve. The shadowy Senoi Praaaq, which was formed by British Military Intelligence in 1956, was a Special Forces unit with an intelligence-gathering role not dissimilar to the SAS.

As the threat developed in 1963, platoon and company forts, known as Forward Locality Bases (FLBs), were hacked out of the jungle or near kampongs to cover probable incursion routes. The FLBs invested in local economies with locally-employed labour and thereby maintained the 'hearts and minds' campaign. The defence was arranged in three zones, the strategy being the deeper the enemy penetrated, the more forces could be assembled to their front and rear. Since British battalions were structured to meet the mechanized infantry requirements of three rifle companies and a Support Company, and the new defensive strategy called for four rifle companies, the Coldstream Guards, Irish Guards, South Wales Borderers and Royal Artillery frequently provided reinforcement platoons. Support Companies were also converted into rifle companies. By 1964, battalions were deploying two companies forward to cover their tactical area of operations (TAOR). With two of the three

44

platoons dominating sectors covering the border, a battalion frontage was about 120 men watching the front and flanks, the size of the TAOR being dependent on the threat, with the third and fourth platoons held in reserve, and a detachment of two Support Company medium mortars usually in support. For the Indonesians, the four platoons lurking near the border always threatened withdrawal routes south. Behind the platoons were the two Company HQs, sometimes hosting a 105mm Pack Howitzer 'on call'. The remaining two companies formed the third and rear line of defence, usually with a Mortar Platoon detachment and another Pack Howitzer on call. FLBs mutually supported each other. In an age when military operational security was respected by journalists, *The Times* defence correspondent wrote in August 1964:

> On a hot and tropical morning with white clouds towering in a pale blue sky over the canopy of trees, the atmosphere in a jungle fort is deceptively idyllic. Soldiers stripped to the waist potter about repairing the defences and exchanging genial insults. Little village girls, chattering like birds, hang out the washing to dry. This is what soldiers always hope will lie behind the recruiting posters – no cere- monial parades; not a sergeant-major in sight; the constant stimulus of shared danger; and the warm sense that they are physically pro- tecting the villagers among whom they live ... Living huts ingeniously contrived from split bamboo and usually decorated with spectacular double page colour photographs from Playboy magazine.
>
> Between the forts are miles of thick and mountainous jungle that have to be constantly patrolled to discourage terrorists from infil- trating to the less heavily defended villages farther from the border. Living deep in primary jungle has a powerful fascination. It is cool, dark and filled with the damp smell of leaves and flowers. The trunks of the trees sweep up to 200ft like grey cathedral pillars to a dark green canopy. By day there are strange jungle noises of birds and insects that perfect disconcerting imitations of circular saws and other unmusical instruments; and there are brilliant butterflies with huge lazy wings ...There are, of course, other ways of describing the jungle. Soldiers on patrol tend to use much shorter words, especial- ly when they are carrying a machine-gun and 90lbs of rations and ammunition up a slope of four in one.

Royal Engineers and Gurkha Engineers designed and built the FLBs. Until the Malaysian Engineers developed air-portable construction material and equipment, plant was parachuted from Beverleys or flown in pieces by helicopters or light aircraft. The TAORs were supported by over 1,000 numbered helicopter landing places (LP), winch/down rope sites and, sometimes, a drop zone (DZ) for parachuted deliveries hacked out of the jungle by Sappers or battalion assault engineers walking, or roping from helicopters or ferried by boat. Trees were felled with chain saws or, in some instances, Plastic Explosive (PE). When the LPs were booby-trapped with mines, sappers 'deloused' them. Some FLBs were supported by airstrips, such as the 1,300-foot strip at Long Semado, which had been built by the Borneo Evangelical Mission in 1961 and was suitable for Twin Pioneers and Caribous. The Royal Engineers built fourteen airstrips capable of taking aircraft. Improving Long Akah airstrip, which is on the Sungei Baram, deep inside Fourth Division and over 200 miles from Brunei, tested the ingenuity of A Troop, 67 Gurkha Independent Field Squadron. Two D4 bulldozers and a Wobbly Wheel roller were dropped by parachute while other equipment was flown in by naval helicopters. Lorries then transported 200 tons of Pierced Steel Planking (PSP) from Seria by the 85 miles road that degenerated from tarmac to a sand track at the head of the Baram. The PSP was then loaded onto a 10 Port Squadron Ramped Powered Lighter (RPL), ferried 90 miles to Long Lama where they were transferred to local longboats, each of which took up to 10 tons, for the final 200 miles.

Vegetation around the FLBs was pruned to improve fields of fire and perimeters were protected by complementing natural obstacles, such as streams, gullies and clearings, with barbed wire, fire-hardened bamboo sharpened 'punji' sticks and Claymore mines covering likely approaches and forming-up areas. The Claymore is an American mine consisting of a curved box supported on four legs, which can either be pressed into the earth or perched on undergrowth or fixed to a tree. Fired remotely or triggered by a tripwire, anyone in its 75-yard killing zone is likely to be caught by the 700 small steel balls ejected over a 60-degree arc. A drawback was that the 16 feet to the rear were also at risk. Machine-gun bunkers provided the strength of the perimeter defence, the number depending on the size of the FLB. In depth in the centre were usually 2-inch mortars, which could fire high-explosive, smoke and illuminating bombs. Although officially obsolete, it was an excellent short-range jungle warfare weapon and when ammunition stocks ran low, a Royal Army Ordnance Corps (RAOC) officer in Singapore remembered that 2-inch mortar ammunition had been sold to Australia, so an Ammunition Technical Officer (ATO) was sent to Canberra to buy back the stocks.

Initially lightly defended, in late 1964, when the threat from artillery, mortars and rocket-propelled grenades (RPG) increased, bunkers were strengthened with communication trenches connecting them to the Command Post (CP), administrative areas and accommodation. The Gunners achieved the reputation of having comfortable bunkers – deep, dry and lined with parachute silk to help to screen earthen walls. Keeping the bunkers dry in the 'wet' monsoon was a problem, as snakes often sought shelter in stores, lockers and on beds. The prefabricated timber and corrugated Bowen Bunker was adapted for a variety of uses ranging from machine-gun posts to accommodation. Erected by Royal Engineers from a production line manned by 54 Corps Field Park Squadron and a Malaysian Engineers Park Troop, foundation posts for the frame were collected from the jungle, while the corrugated-iron roof and plywood walls were delivered. It was then surrounded by sandbags and, ideally, oil drums filled with soil. Inside were hooks for mosquito nets.

Although rain and sunken wells provided water, this rarely catered for the thirty recommended gallons per man per day for drinking, showering, laundry and cooking. After a week of being soaked by rain and sweat on patrol, exposing the body to the sun helped recovery, and hot showers reduced skin infections. For large FLBs, when water collection and purification by a single Farelf Filter, supplied by the Engineer Base Workshop, Singapore, and consisting of an Alcon pump feeding water into interconnected 44-gallon storage drums perched on timber towers, proved unreliable, they were replaced by Double Farelf Filters fitted with a No. 4 Pump. This could produce 1,000 gallons per hour, however the system needed to be back-flushed about every fifteen minutes, a responsibility of the incumbent infantry unit. However, the Royal Engineers sometimes found that the maintenance schedule was insufficiently meticulous. For platoon FLBs with water supply problems, the Royal Engineers developed the Murcott Filter. This contraption consisted of a 4-foot-long, 4-inch casing containing parachute cloth wrapped around fine wire gauze on an angle frame, through which water from a river or a well was filtered.

The Borneo Latrine of a stack of three 40-gallon oil drums set in a pit avoided the use of soakaway sumps. The 1st Scots Guards built an exemplary 20-seater that was used by a Royal Army Medical Corps (RAMC) lieutenant colonel to show visiting dignitaries. To delouse the human waste, and the bugs and insects that frequent such places, a white-phosphorous hand grenade lobbed into the mess by a medic usually did the trick. When the Scots Guards handed over to a Gurkha battalion, there was clearly a misunderstanding for a Gurkha medic hurled in a high explosive (HE) grenade, which blew the magnificent 20-seater, its hessian privacy screens and several pounds of excrement across the base.

Typically, a platoon routine was eight to twelve days on patrol and four days in base. Camp duties revolved around cleaning weapons and equipment; 'dhobi-ing' from the previous patrol; preparing for the next patrol; and manning bunkers. Some of the unpopular but essential 'fatigues', such as peeling potatoes, cleaning pots and pans, and collecting/disposing of garbage was devolved to locally-employed labour in exchange for payment or supplies. Dress in camp was dependent on the unit culture, the only stipulation being that every man's personal weapon with a full magazine had to be carried at all times. Mail was eagerly awaited and boredom tackled by training, sport, books, magazines, cards, darts, indoor games and listening to the British Forces Broadcasting Service (BFBS) beaming from Singapore to transistor radios. Alcohol was generally limited to two cans of Tiger or Anchor lager per person per day, although it was not unknown for commanding officers to ban alcohol. Units adopted pets which included honey bears, snakes, rats and tortoises. The 1st RUR mascot was a bear cub named Sticky, which eventually ended up in Belfast Zoo. A proposal to give a Rhinoceros Hornbill named Fitch to Dublin Zoo ended when the bird died. Captain Barry Courtney, a Beaver pilot with 130 Flight, RASC, was en route to Labuan when he heard a Wessex pilot carrying three crew and twelve members of 42 Commando with their mascot, reply to an Air Traffic Control request for number of souls on board with 'Fifteen souls on and one bear'. Invitations to the longhouses were common.

Units usually spent their entire tours in a FLB with rest and recuperation (R&R) of about a week every six months. The Royal Artillery established an R&R centre near Kuching with beach and water activities. When 1st RUR moved to First Division in 1964, Major Mike Esteridge, the Quartermaster, found a large house with a swimming pool in Kuching, built a volleyball court and a bar, and organized a cinema showing the latest films sent from Singapore by the Services Kinema Corporation (SKC). The men could go anywhere in town that was in bounds but permitted to drink and revel as much as they liked only within R&R centres. Any soldier who broke this code usually led to his entire platoon being threatened with an immediate return to operations. The system was only occasionally breached.

The Army Catering Corps (ACC) was formed in 1941 as part of the RASC and gained independence in December 1964. Generally, a combination of unit and ACC cooks prepared meals in FLBs. A report in 1968 on Confrontation concluded that while the food had improved, JNCOs were inexperienced in supervising small kitchens and officers and SNCOs lacked management and leadership skills. On patrol, the troops were, at first, issued with tins of high-protein temperate composite ('compo') rations, however, as the troops in the tropics had found during the Second World War, the heat converted the rations into an uninviting soggy mess – hardly a morale-boosting fillip after a day's patrolling or lying in ambush. In 1965, the lightweight dehydrated jungle ration packs pioneered during the Malayan Emergency were reintroduced, the contents including a main meal of chicken, beef or pork, and sundries including Garibaldi biscuits, tea and coffee, orange or lemon powder to flavour water, boiled sweets, chewing gum, water purification tablets and a few sheets of 'Government Property' toilet paper. Since the intake was only about 1,800 calories, after about ten days, recuperative feeding was essential to rebuild muscles and fat reserves. Troops usually departed on patrol with half rations, in order to reduce the weight to be carried.

Few who have experienced jungle warfare would disagree that its skills suit any theatre of war, including nuclear warfare. In many respects, it is similar to night-fighting in which soldiers are close but cannot see each other and therefore experience the anxiety of isolation. In his book *How Borneo Was Won*, Walter Walker predicted that the more civilized we become and the more soldiers are drawn to the bright lights, the more 'frightened' they will be of the jungle and forest. Within a very few years, the US Military Intervention Command in Vietnam would experience just that. Walker never allowed his soldiers to sample shops and bars on patrol and, by confining them largely to their FDLs, ensured that they retained their jungle instincts. Fortunately, the British experienced no such concerns, although the Malaysians initially did. Jungle warfare is arduous and requires long periods of intense mental and physical concentration to deal with hostile terrain, the weather and shock action at very short range, maybe less than 20 yards.

Patrols were often fruitless but there was always the risk of the unexpected – the enemy, lightning, a charging animal, rotting branches falling from trees, or, in the case of a 2/2nd Gurkha Rifles patrol in August 1965, seventy men gingerly moving around a small Krait snake curled up among leaves. The defeat of the Communist Terrorists in Malaya by an established government supporting disciplined Commonwealth forces adept at fighting in the jungle laid the foundations of the victory in Borneo, and led to the acknowledgement that the British, Gurkhas, Australians, New Zealanders and, to a lesser extent, Malaysians, were competent jungle warfare warriors. In spite of their experiences in the Pacific, the American strategy in South-East Asia against a highly politically committed enemy was less subtle and eventually undermined military and civilian morale. While US forces usually wore steel helmets, Commonwealth soldiers wore floppy hats so that they could hear better and reduce the possibility of the helmet knocking a rifle or radio. Those who live and operate in the jungle must adopt the strategies of wild animals. The fragrance of scented soap, hair oil and

Old Spice aftershave, so important to the young men of the 1960s, had to be dispelled before going on patrol with a dip in a river or swamp. Some units insisted on shaving. Others argued that a cut could turn sceptic and an unshaven face helped camouflage. Anyone below peak fitness and those with sniffles and coughs were left behind. Walker's aim was to dominate the jungle and the frontier, week in, week out, day and night:

> There was no galloping over the jungle canopy in helicopters. We used all our cunning and guile to get within striking distance of the enemy by helicopter but without being seen or heard. Then we tracked him down, stalking and closing in on our feet for the kill. The sure way to beat a guerrilla is to operate more quietly, smoke less, and talk less to possible enemy agents before an operation. In Borneo, it was always the Indonesians who fell into booby traps and triggered the Claymore mines and trip flares set by patrols.

On patrol, the men carried as little as possible. Toothbrushes were shortened and a spoon the only cutlery. Survival kits might be sewn into uniforms or carried in the belt order. A personal medical pack was essential, as was the issue clasp knife. Dress was the ubiquitous floppy hat, olive-green shirt and trousers, and canvas jungle boots, although these would later be replaced by Australian canvas and leather jungle boots. Webbing was generally the 1944 pattern of braces supporting a belt onto which was attached two Bren magazine pouches, water bottle and a cup, a machete, bayonet and any other pouches that could be purloined. Into this order and the side pockets of the pack were crammed the soldier's requirements and rations. The 1944 pack was quite small and additional space was gained by sewing Bren gun pouches to the sides. The centre pocket was filled with stores, such as extra ammunition, radio ancillaries and air identification panels.

If the soldier took everything with him, the (19)44 Basic Individual Load weighed 24lb 6oz. Add to this rations, extra machine-gun ammunition belts, a couple of Claymores at 6lb 8oz each, SLR at 9lb 4oz and radio batteries, and the soldier could end up carrying about 80lb, although this decreased as rations were eaten and perhaps ammunition used. Strict track discipline required soldiers to take garbage back to camp for disposal with tins flattened to make room in the pack. Water was collected from a variety of sources, including rivers and rain, filtered through Millbank muslin bags in order to remove visible impurities, such as insects and soil, before being poured into water bottles and then sterilized with chlorinated tablets. Most carried at least two water bottles, with the Gurkhas renowned for carrying rum in one. Later, the

1958 pattern emerged with the same belt order supported by a harness. Heavy equipment, such as radios, was carried on a rectangular aluminum frame or an A-Frame. Some soldiers purchased civilian Bergens.

Depending on the tactical situation, patrols filed from their FLB or were flown to a LP. Single file was the patrol formation, the length of the column being dictated by not losing contact with the man in front. A platoon of thirty men could cover a considerable distance. Scouts led, sometimes carrying shotguns, the 12-Bore Browning Automatic being favoured. No grabbing trees as one slithered down slopes in case the sudden waving of leaves on a still day might be seen by an enemy, a jungle inhabitant or indeed by a monkey, which would then screech in alarm. 'Wait-a-while' thorns caught in uniforms must be disentangled.

Jungle patrolling is thirsty work and a quick swill in a stream is always welcome but has its pitfalls of bad water. When it rains, it is like standing underneath a punishing waterfall. It hurts. There is little shelter except under a tree or palm frond. Lightning is a problem with a Gurkha officer, a veteran of the Second World War and Malaya, being killed on 8 September 1963. Hacking is exhausting, noisy and very slow. Talking is done only when necessary, for instance to issue orders; otherwise everything else must be by hand signals passed down the column. Troops had to learn a whole new language: A fallen log across a track, a clearing and streams are obstacles that must be negotiated with a machine gun covering scouts checking that the enemy are not waiting in ambush on the other side. 'Forward' (Palm up and wave forward with the hand) and everyone silently moves back on the track and crosses the obstacle. Riverbank patrols are tiring because the patrol follows undulating riverbanks and the countless streams must either be waded or crossed by precariously balancing on a fallen tree. Not everyone could swim and several men were drowned. Waterborne patrols in local or military boats probed inlets and streams. Marine David Lee of 42 Commando described his experiences during the Brunei Revolt:

One such patrol took us to a charcoal kiln, with a very long jetty and this was on our list to search as an empty kiln would provide an ideal hiding place. We pulled up at the jetty and were just about to secure the boat when a huge bull terrier came bounding toward us, yellow pus oozing out of one eye and saliva dripping from its mouth. 'What to do?' The situation was saved by the kiln owner, who having seen us point a rifle at the dog, because of its aggressive manner, shouted, which calmed it down. We then explained our purpose and were allowed to search all buildings and kilns but there was no sign of the enemy so we withdrew. Our river patrols took us

51

down small tributaries, which were good places to lay up and watch for other boat movements on the main river but these would be mostly locals going about their daily business, each village being reliant upon their boats for trading and essential supplies.

Rivers can be dangerous obstacles – a wide area of open space. Crossing is slow, cumbersome and exposes the column to attack. Again machine guns cover swimmers looking for exit routes and a beachhead. Prior to crossing, a defended forming-up place is found so that loads can be wrapped in ponchos and air trapped inside to create a floatable bundle. On fast-flowing or deep rivers, perhaps in flood during or after heavy rain, then a strong swimmer, carrying a rope or vine, enters the water some distance upstream and is carried across the river to the opposite bank by the flow of the current.

When looking for a patrol base, the commander has several requirements:

- Concealment, defendable and easily vacated in a hurry or as a matter of routine.

- Good radio communications.

- Near water.

- Fairly level and dry, although in the monsoon season this is usually not possible. Several fatalities were caused by sites being near dead trees or rotting branches.

- If an airdrop is expected, a DZ must be found.

Once occupied, a clearing patrol scouts outside the perimeter and then the commander indicates arcs of fire and sectors, and vulnerable approaches to be defended by sentries. In Confrontation, at first a circle was usually the shape of the base, with a cord defining the perimeter, although a triangle was later adopted. Anyone outside after a given period is assumed to be enemy. Pairs known as 'basha buddies' work together with one on watch, while the other prepares a meal, cleans his weapon and maybe scrapes mud from uniforms before taking over on watch. Weapon pits and latrines might be dug, ammunition redistributed and medical treatment given. In rain, when shelters might be erected, the British and Gurkhas were reliant upon a groundsheet or a poncho strung between trees, until the Australian Lightweight appeared. This versatile equipment consisted of three rubber tubes fed into a hammock that doubled as a mattress, a float, a lightweight blanket and poncho. Soldiers were encouraged to sleep in dry clothes, often a light-weight siren suit made from cotton of parachute silk and nicknamed 'the zoot suit'. There is nothing more uncomfortable than buttoning a wet, cold shirt first thing next morning! Even when asleep, boots were worn, loosely laced. Everything had to be completed at least half an hour before stand-to at dusk. The base was then silent except for the occasional rustle as sentries on the machine guns changed and signallers shuffled. After stand-to next morning, Claymores and booby traps were collected and the base concealed and vacated. Breakfast would be taken later.

An anonymous author of the 1st King's Own Scottish Borderers (1st KOSB) described a patrol in Third Division in 1965:

The helicopter gradually loses height and gently drops into the cleared patch of jungle. Hovering a few inches above the cleared ground a couple of soldiers with mine detectors quickly jumped out and gave the thumbs up signal. Rising suddenly, the helicopter started to circle slowly and move to and fro above the clearing, while down below two tiny figures moved slowly up and down searching for Indonesian booby traps and mines. When the landing pad was cleared, the helicopter dropped again. The red light went on, then the green and tumbling out, the men doubled out into the sunshine and moved quickly to the edge of the jungle. Shielding themselves beside trees, they peered into the dark shadows watching and waiting. Rising once more the helicopter tilted and wung away, gradually its noise grew fainter until only the sound of the crickets and jungle birds remained. The contrast in noise and movements was uncanny, another patrol had begun.

A large vulture-like bird slowly flew across the clearing and settled in a tree looking down at the motionless figures of men. Then a whining in the air, steadily rising to a deafening roar, a whirling blast of hot air and another helicopter appeared. Before its wheels had touched the ground men were springing out clutching their weapons and dashing into the shadow at the edge of the clearing. Over a period of half an hour more helicopters disgorged bodies and sped away until the whole patrol had arrived and was ready to move. A low whistle from the platoon commander, a quick 'O' Group and silent men began to move in single file into the jungle. The burning heat of the clearing gave way to the coolness of the jungle. Giant trees stretched up letting through only vague glimpses of blue sky. Birds and insects kept up a continuous background chorus, while the noise of a stream roared away down below.

Moving carefully the men pushed aside branches of undergrowth and moved towards the stream. One man at a time waded across while those waiting on the bank fanned out fingering their rifles. Were there Indonesians there, lined out on the other bank or along that track patiently waiting for us? Waiting until we came into view, to slip the safety catch forward and take the first pressure on their triggers.

In the jungle you can never relax, never be sure that up on that ridge or round that corner in the track, the world won't suddenly split open with machine gun fire. When camp is made before dusk and your back is sore and your shoulders ache from the weight of your pack, you still cannot relax, while you silently cook and whisper to your friend or crawl into your basha at night, all the time you half wait for the sound of a twig cracking or a man crawling up the bank towards you. Naturally as the days of the patrol pass by, the senses become blunted, it also becomes easier to relax and boredom begins to set in. Men whisper 'Why are we here, there's no enemy here, where's the enemy?' But always in the back of everybody's mind is the feeling of awareness, the feeling that in the claustrophobic vastness of the jungle, one can never be sure of anything.

Two weeks later the patrol is ready to be moved out of the jungle back to the Company base. Many miles have been covered, mountain ridge after ridge have been climbed, sometimes on hands and knees, sweating with the weight of the pack and pulling oneself up a few feet at a time, desperately trying to stop sliding down the other side. Days of perpetual motion, whether it be moving to a new camp area, or a series of small patrols searching the track for infiltrators.

After several days of cutting down trees to make a clearing and a flat platform on the perilous side of a ridge so the helicopter can land, the men pack their kit, fill in the litter pit and sit down to wait. The jungle ceaselessly drips after a rain storm. The men amuse themselves by comparing their two-week old beards or sit quietly smoking looking over for the last time the trees they have cut down. The Platoon Commander listens on the set waiting to be told when the helicopters will arrive. But over the set a crackling voice informs the Platoon that our helicopters have been postponed for twenty-four hours. Cursing everybody under their breaths from Company HQ to the whole RAF, the men unpack their kit and in a short while bashas are up. Because there is no food, hunting parties move out and by mid afternoon four skinned monkeys and a squirrel are being boiled. Monkey meat is tough and has a wild taste, however when you are hungry it tastes very good. Once again the radio crackles into life and we are informed the Army Air Corps is coming to the rescue and dropping food. Far away a little black dot appears and starts to circle the distant mountain tips far away across the valley, and then it sees our flares and turns straight toward the camp. Dropping a parachute can be a tricky business, if you are lucky it lands in a clearing; if you are not lucky it lands nearby on a small tree. Our parachute landed fifty yards away up what was undoubtedly the biggest tree in Borneo. Felling the tree took two hours of solid cutting by our Iban Border Scouts.

The next morning, dirty, wet, bedraggled men jump out of the helicopter at the Company camp, carrying their packs up the hill for the last time until the next patrol. Now is the time for that cold beer, a square meal and a thoroughly relaxed sleep – good night!

As the campaign developed, Iban trackers, whose jungle lore was legendary, frequently guided patrols. Some were locally employed, while others were members of the Sarawak Rangers, which had first come to note in 1952 during the Malayan Emergency as Ferret Force. Renamed the Sarawak Rangers (Malaya Unit) until 1957 and the Sarawak Rangers (Far East Land Forces), they had a liability for service anywhere in the world. Its core recruiting area remained along the Sungei Undup in Second Division. By 1962, the Sarawak Rangers, consisting of five British and one Iban officer, and 156 other ranks divided into three platoons, an animal transport platoon using North Borneo ponies and a dog section, was deployed during the Brunei Revolt. Locally recruited Iban trackers attended courses so that they knew how the military operated on patrol and were familiar with some weapons. Their favoured weapon was generally a shotgun. During Confrontation, many Malayan Emergency veterans volunteered to act as guides now they were on their own turf.

Combat Tracking Teams usually consisted of a commander, three Ibans, a dog and handler, and three riflemen as cover. Information gleaned from tracks often includes direction, age of tracks, number in party, sex and whether loads were being carried. Deception included walking backwards, jumping to one side, moving across ground that was difficult to track, such as water rocks and stones, and covering footprints with leaves and twigs. In a cross-grain search, the tracker 'ploughs' the jungle through several 180 degrees until the search reaches a Finish Point. Patrol commanders had to remember that tracking teams were not 'killer groups' and must be supported by a military or police pursuit.

Dogs, which had proven successful in Malaya, were equally adept in Borneo. The infantry patrol dog, normally an Alsatian or Labrador, points toward the threat and was valuable in alerting troops in ambush, for camp patrols and on recce patrols, however, a dog cannot differentiate between friend and foe, and is equally likely to point at animals as human beings. Limitations included fatigue, sensory deterioration in tropical rainstorms and confusion when a large number of people gather in a small area. All dogs were trained by the Royal Army Veterinary Corps (RAVC) at the War Dog Training Wing at the FARELF Training Centre in Singapore. While the Corps helped select and train the dogs, units sent men to train as handlers and learn the basics of kennel management and basic veterinary procedures. On patrol, the handler carried 1lb tins of meat and a bag of biscuits in addition to his own individual load. Most dogs received treats from soldiers and at least one delighted in curry and rice.

Confrontation was not a conventional war of holding ground against sustained assault. Encounters were fleeting and contact with the enemy was often over in seconds, with patrol clashes on the same track usually resulting in frantic, close-range firefights. A patrol might see an enemy patrol and melt into the jungle until the enemy had passed, or open fire in a quick ambush. Tactics were no different than in other military environments except that far greater control had to be exercised by commanders. This is not always possible in the heat of the moment and regular training was required so that a reaction to a contact became second nature.

An ambush is essentially picking the ground to kill the enemy and was usually laid as a consequence of an intelligence assessment that the enemy were using a particular route. Careful planning is essential to manage long periods of waiting in the same place, and still be sufficiently alert to execute the ambush. Sites include 'linear' along roads, paths, tracks and rivers, and 'area' in which more than one approach is covered. The ambush is broken down into several elements:

- Killing zone with cut-offs and flank protection.

- Ambush base at the rear of the ambush.

- Checkpoint through which ambushers are counted in and out.

- Strongpoint, a defensive position through which the ambush party withdraws to the administrative base. Might double with ambush base.

- Administrative base. Administrative area usually about 400 yards from the ambush and sited in deep jungle to preserve the security of the operation; used to rest ambush occupiers and collect casualties.

Considerable self-discipline is required to lie silently on the jungle floor, perhaps pestered by ants and insects, with the prospect of a snake slithering across the legs, either in intense humidity and heat, or soaked and cold from rain. Troops communicate with tugs on vines or a cord, giving simple messages. When the enemy appears, the instinct is to wriggle into better cover, but this must be avoided in case a twig snaps or a bird takes fright. Failures were attributable to weapons being cocked and fire being opened prematurely. The ambush is sprung with the signal to 'Open fire' and then the aim is to kill as many of the enemy as possible with maximum firepower. After the cease fire is ordered, if there is time a small party checks the killing zone to search for items of intelligence interest, such as documents, maps and equipment, however the priority is to leave the area quickly.

Being ambushed requires courage and leadership with the survivors in the killing zone giving covering fire as the rest of the column counter-attacks the ambush flank with a right-angled attack.

If there is an environment entirely unsuited for the Royal Armoured Corps, it is the jungle, nevertheless, a 42 Commando officer wrote of the QRIH: 'They drive, march, boat and helicopter and there's nothing they won't try.' The Saladin armoured cars and Ferret scout cars of the Armoured Reconnaissance Regiment were deployed throughout Sarawak and dominated areas accessible by road. Each sabre squadron had an Assault Troop carried in a Saracen Armoured Personnel Carrier (APC), trained as infantry and assault engineers. Armoured crews needed to be multi-skilled and when the infantry required support, some crews were sent as Browning machine gunners to FLBs, while others supported short-handed Royal Artillery gun crews. Most found these deployments a welcome opportunity to experience front-line activity and an opportunity to add 'tone to a vulgar brawl'. After the 4th Royal Tank Regiment (4 RTR), which tended to recruit from Scotland, had served in Borneo in 1964, its second-in-command, Major Richard Vickers, commented:

> In three years of active operations in Borneo ... not one single shell or machine-gun belt of the many thousands fired was aimed at an enemy target. It is a doubtful if a single casualty was caused. There was not one ambush, encounter or incident ... A number of arrests, much useful information and an incalculable amount of 'hearts and minds' support was achieved but only 95% of this work was dismounted. To be brutally honest, the armoured reconnaissance squadrons were odd-job men carrying out rear area tasks to relieve infantry manpower for its main task of dominating the border.

The poor roads took a heavy toll on the armoured cars with servicing reduced from 1,000 miles to 250 miles.

While the RAF could generally predict their engineering needs, the Army were less able to so and were reliant upon the size and duration of the deployment. All units brought their own Royal Electrical and Mechanical Engineers (REME) Light Aid Detachments (LAD) for the first-line repair of vehicles, weapons and equipment. The REME had a policy of sending soldiers to Borneo not likely to be promoted within the year and therefore not needing educational, trade or military qualifications. The perpetual humidity and rain frequently affected the equipment designed for Europe – for instance, FARELF had no Base Workshops to repair the Green Archer mortar-locating radar. Initially, second-line faults were fixed by two Workshops, with major repairs sent to Singapore, Malaya and Hong Kong, which meant that equipment could be missing for up to eight weeks. When Lieutenant Colonel B.G. Heelis arrived as Commander REME in 1964, he created a conventional field repair system with 9 and 10 Infantry Workshops attached to Central and West Brigades, and the Gurkha Workshops on Labuan. 78 Aircraft Workshop in West Brigade and 21 Air Maintenance Support Platoon in Central Brigade supported the Army Air Corps. As the build-up of forces developed in late 1964, Heelis insisted that first-line repairs be completed within fourteen days and organized mobile workshops, ranging in size from a platoon of twenty-five men to an individual, to carry out repairs at the scene, but since the infantry had the first call on helicopters, it was not unknown for detachments to become isolated. Two technicians sent to mend a generator, which usually took two days, returned to their parent unit a fortnight later. Another found himself defending a base under attack. To meet the fortnight deadline, the problem of spares taking a month to arrive from Singapore was resolved when RAOC Stores Sections attached to the Workshops over-scaled stocks and organized a counter service. The deployment of landing craft and small boats led to the creation of maritime repair sections in the Workshops.

FLBs often needed specialist equipment such as water pumps, power saws and refrigerators, all of which needed to be maintained and repaired. REME tradesmen designed 'off-the-shelf' equipment such as a beer can crusher, field mountings for 0.50-inch Brownings, tree-climbing equipment and mine-exploder boxes, all of which required considerable ingenuity to develop.

CHAPTER SIX

Skirmishing
May to 16 September 1963

The first phase of Confrontation is characterized by Indonesian interference to Malaya's march toward Federation by political pressure,
international conferences and military action, all of which fell into line
with *Konfrontasi*. Although throughout Confrontation, the Indonesian
strategy centred on creating Wingate-style strongholds in 'liberated'
zones from which to launch attacks, Sukarno had four critical weaknesses:

- The Indonesian Armed Forces were unprepared for anything more
  than low-intensity operations.

- Command, control and communication difficulties.

- Lack of amphibious capability.

- Taking on the Commonwealth, the British had been fighting in the
  jungle since 1942, and in Malaya, between 1947 and 1957, had
  learnt how to deal with revolutionary warfare.

Commanding No. 4 Combat Command along the border with British
North Borneo in Kalimantan Inter-Regional Command was the left-
wing Brigadier General M.S. Supardjo. Aged thirty-nine and formerly an
Assistant Military Attaché in Washington and Military Attaché in Kuala
Lumpur, he had recently attended the Pakistan Army Staff College at
Quetta. With the Army lukewarm toward the campaign, he soon found
that Army commanders had permitted local commanders to retain
control of their units despite orders that they be transferred to his
command.

At HQ Far East, new arrivals heralded hardening intent. Admiral Luce
was replaced by Admiral Sir Varyl Begg as Commander-in-Chief. A

modest man, he was surprised to be promoted to the senior ranks of the Royal Navy, nevertheless his performance was impressive. A strong advocate of unified command, he recognized Major General Walker to be the best field commander that Great Britain had in the Far East. Lieutenant General Poett had not appreciated the regional strategic importance of 17th Gurkha Division and had been criticized for not sending HQ 99 Gurkha Infantry Brigade Group to Brunei. Walker was not sorry to see him depart into eventual retirement, however his relations with Poett's successor, the gunner, Lieutenant General Sir Reginald Hewetson, who had just handed over as Commander, British Forces Hong Kong, were no better, largely because Hewetson, as Commander-in-Chief, FARELF and with some justification, wanted Walker to report direct to him, as opposed to Begg. When Walker wanted to raise morale in Borneo by introducing a command shoulder flash depicting a Brunei eagle in flight superimposed on a dark blue, red and light blue, representing the three Services, set against the green of the jungle, Hewetson refused on the grounds that the famous 'Black Cat' insignia of the Gurkha Division was sufficient for Army units in the Far East. He was overruled by Begg.

Walker recognized that helicopter flexibility and mobility would be battle-winning, however, unlike the 3,100 helicopters available to US forces in Vietnam, the maximum available in Borneo was about eighty, which, according to Walker in his book, *How Borneo was Won*, was forty short of the minimum needed. Several factors hindered flying. Thick early morning mists rose from the jungle until it was burnt off by the sun by about 10.00 am. On good days, this allowed about five hours of clear skies before afternoon cloud accumulation led to turbulence and invisible sudden downdraughts. In the 'wet' monsoon, cloud cover was low. Low-level night flying was almost impossible. Initially, maps covering British North Borneo were almost non-existent, which meant that aircrew were compelled to know the lie of the land until better maps appeared.

Walker convinced Royal Navy commanders that helicopters were no different to lorries and armoured personnel carriers, except that pilots were better paid. He also emphasized that troop delivery from a landing craft or helicopter was not a mystic available only to the Royal Marines, and that the Army could do them both equally well. Unlike the 1st (US) Cavalry Division developing massed helicopter assault in Vietnam, Walker was determined that helicopters must be used in direct support of ground operations, and aircrews trained accordingly. In the jungle, a minute in a helicopter equals a day's march of about 3,000 yards by a company, and 5,000 yards by a platoon; one hour airborne equals five days on the ground; and a battalion using six troop helicopters equals a brigade with none. Fortunately, converting the Fleet Air Arm (FAA) was easy because 845 and 846 Naval Air Squadrons (NAS) lived cheek by jowl with the Royal Marines on the two commando carriers, HMS *Albion* and *Bulwark*. 45 Commando had carried out the first major heliborne assault at Suez in 1956. Admiral Sir Desmond Dreyer, the new Commander-in-Chief, Far East Fleet, agreed with Walker that carrier-based helicopter operations were impractical in terms of distance and a quick reaction, and they must be landed. Both squadrons proved so expert at jungle operations that they became adept at moving troops, supply runs and evacuating casualties and prisoners, and achieved a fine reputation by winning the Boyd Trophy in recognition of hours flown over the hostile jungle in 1963 and 1964. It was a remarkable achievement considering that both had only recently converted from naval operations. As Confrontation developed, Dreyer commanded all naval forces in the region, which eventually included a third of the Royal Navy's surface fleet. Fortunately, he had an excellent relationship with Admiral Begg, developed over weekly meetings at the Royal Singapore Golf Club.

The main base of 845 NAS was at Sibu airport in a collection of attap huts known as Royal Navy Air Station Sibu, or HMS *Hornbill*, the hornbill being the national bird of Sarawak. In 1964, the Commanding Officer was the legendary Lieutenant Commander 'Tank' Sherman. Described as 'pirates' by one admiral, forward operating bases were established at Belaga and Nanga Gaat. Nanga Gaat was 150 miles inland and only 30 miles from the border; it usually held half a squadron and also a Hiller liaison and recce helicopter trainer. Opening up this base allowed all Third Division to be within the 100 miles of the Wessex radius of action. All ranks lived in attap huts and during the evenings piled into the legendary Anchor Inn, where hospitality was second to none. Illuminated by a fluorescent light powered by an ancient generator, the duty barman dispensed iced drinks from the only paraffin-powered fridge for miles around. Naval ground crew soon learnt Iban and some nights were spent in the local longhouse, watching ceremonial dancing and sampling the lethal local rice brew – *tuak*. Although the base was defended by an infantry company, it was supported by an Iban home guard known as the Junglewood Squad. Some tribesmen sported helicopter tattoos and at least one baby was apparently named 'Helicopter'. Dress was informal, usually a colourful sarong and beaded Iban necklace. The Sick Bay soon became the surgery for the Ibans too. When a cholera epidemic hit the Nanga Gaat area in 1964, 845 NAS worked with 1st RUR to fly the victims to hospital, often with food, pots and pans – another fine example of keeping the local people friendly.

61

845 NAS was equipped initially with twelve Wessex HU1 anti-submarine warfare helicopters, which had entered British service in 1961. In April 1962, it converted to assault helicopters by replacing the anti-submarine equipment with facilities for either up to sixteen fully-equipped soldiers, seven stretcher casualties or a 4,000lb inboard or an underslung load. It could be armed with four air-to-surface, wire-guided, anti-tank missiles (SS-11), or 2-inch, free-flight rockets mounted in pods. However, it had a high attrition rate of mechanical failure, but it was not until February 1964 that the Wessex HU5 tactical transport entered service with better durability in the tropics and a higher ceiling. The Whirlwind had first seen service as an assault helicopter in 1961 when 42 Commando landed in Kuwait. It filled the gap between the Belvedere and Wessex.

In dealing with the RAF, Walker was faced by the Second World War dogma that anything that flew must contribute to air power. This meant that close air support favoured the RAF as opposed to the troops, and thus, at first, Nanga Gaat was considered to be too dangerous and too difficult to defend. In predicting that Great Britain's future campaigns would be internal security, counter-insurgency and low-intensity campaigns, a *Times* correspondent wrote in August 1964: 'It is time, as one of its officers has said, [for the RAF] to come down from 50,000 feet, to bury the dying cult of the bomber and organise the air arm as a tactical air force, equipped with aircraft designed to transport and give close air support to ground forces.'

When the socialist-minded, former fighter pilot Air Vice-Marshal Sir Peter Wykeham took over as Air Officer Commanding in Chief, Far East, he insisted that air operations must reach such efficiency that 'no one else can claim they could do the job better.' Eventually, RAF aircrew threw away most of the rule book and showed the same flair as the naval pilots.

66 Squadron, which had recently converted from Hawker Hunter fighter ground attack to Belvedere heavy-lift helicopters, arrived in the Far East in May 1962 and was deployed to the Naval Air Station, HMS *Simbang*, in Singapore, where it was initially accommodated in tents, much to the shock of the aircrew. The Belvedere was the first twin-rotor, twin-engine helicopter to enter operational service and, the forerunner of the CH-47 Chinook, could carry eighteen fully-equipped men, or 2.5 tons internally and 2.25 tons with an underslung load. However, it had a 48-foot wingspan, which meant that preparing a jungle LP was laborious and tiring, nevertheless a pair could move a 105mm Pack Howitzer, its first-line ammunition and crews, and all their equipment in one sortie. The Belvedere was first deployed during the Brunei Revolt when three aircraft flew the 750 miles to Labuan in a single day and set

a helicopter distance record. Shortage of spares and agreement about the role of the helicopter resulted in delays, but once this was resolved it became an important asset in achieving heavy and mass-lift tasks. British domination of helicopters was undermined when a Belvedere flown to Malta from Great Britain by the one-eyed former Spitfire pilot, Wing Commander 'Cyclops' Brown, awakened United States interest.

The Army Air Corps (AAC) was initially regarded as a minnow by the RAF. Its pilots included SNCOs posted from other Arms and Services while naval and RAF pilots were all officers. It flew two helicopter types. The Westland Scout appeared in 1958 and deployed to Borneo in 1963. Fitted for casualty evacuation with external stretcher panniers, it was also a gunship with two forward-firing 7.62mm GPMGs. Sighting was rudimentary with the aiming cross chinagraphed on the windscreen! The Augusta Sioux, with its distinctive cockpit glass bubble, appeared two years later. Both aircraft had observation, recce, airborne 'taxi' and airborne command post roles. The distinctive Taylorcraft Auster was a gallant little aircraft that had seen service in every Second World War theatre on air observation, artillery spotting and communications tasks. It was joined by the Air Observation Post-9 Auster; both aircraft were also used as airborne command posts. Midway through the campaign, units were given their own Flights, usually of two Sioux, which gave commanding officers greater flexibility.

30 Flight RASC, formed in April 1964 from two flights of 656 Squadron, AAC, flew fixed-wing De Havilland of Canada Beaver Mark 1s. Designed for rugged bush flying with minimum engineering support, it had a short take-off facility of 250 yards and was ideal for jungle flying. Walker described it as 'a wonderful aircraft and certainly one of the best buys the Army ever made'. With a capability to fly five fully equipped soldiers, the seats could be removed to accommodate stretchers. Technically in direct support to HQ FARELF, its six aircraft were based at Brunei and Tawau, and were involved in close air support operations and naval gunfire support. The demand for light aircraft became so urgent that the Flight was reinforced from the War Maintenance Reserve and the 3rd Armoured Division Flight, which was with the UN Forces in Cyprus. In July 1965, 30 Flight was renamed 130 Flight, Royal Corps of Transport (RCT) and remained in Borneo until the end of Confrontation.

On 8 September 1954, Australia, France, New Zealand, Pakistan, the Philippines, Thailand, the United Kingdom and the United States signed the South-East Asia Collective Defence Treaty, which is also known as the Manila Pact, in Bangkok, to preserve self-determination, equal rights, independence and freedom from the scourge of communism, which was then rampant in some parts of South-East Asia. From the pact emerged the South East Asia Treaty Organisation (SEATO) with a military philosophy very similar to NATO. With its headquarters in Bangkok and although primarily a defensive shield, it had agencies to which underdeveloped and developing countries could refer on economic, agricultural, industrial and cultural matters. A Council controlled the organization, with ambassadors working with the Permanent Working Group before issues were debated at Council level. The Military Affairs Group directed military activities with the commander of the Military Planning Office reporting directly to the Secretary-General. A Military Advisers Group studied specialized military affairs such as intelligence, topography, mapping and communications.

Exercises are an important element of testing command, control and communications, quite apart from demonstrating muscle. Between 22 April and 9 May 1963, forty-five SEATO ships took part in the three-phase Exercise Sea Serpent in the South China Sea, with friendly 'Blue Forces' defending a convoy en route from Singapore to Manila against 'Red Forces' simulating attacks by Soviet submarines, Krupny-class guided-missile destroyers and aircraft. The British 6th Minesweeping Squadron was meant to take part in this phase but was committed to operations off British North Borneo. Even though Exercise Sea Serpent was a regional test, Indonesia cannot fail to have noticed that windows of opportunity to compete with the Royal Navy were slim. It was a significant show of strength.

From 7 to 11 June, the Malayan, Indonesian and the Philippine foreign ministers met in Manila to discuss regional security – the Manila Conference. Indonesian Foreign Minister Subandrio's commitment to peace must be set against his interception, in 1962, of official correspondence from the constitutional monarch of Malaya inviting Sukarno to a meeting to discuss Federation. The letter was passed through the Foreign and Commonwealth Office but never reached Sukarno, and was found a year later in Indonesian Embassy files. By the time Sukarno was made aware of the letter, relations between Kuala Lumpur and Indonesia were such that a visit was impossible. Malaya was determined to proceed with Federation while President Macapagal of the Philippines remained hooked on the loose amalgamation of the three nations into *Maphilindo*, primarily because he was keen to promote closer ties with Asia and the Malay brotherhood, as opposed to Chinese Malays and their associations with communism. Indonesia, focusing on anti-colonialism and her strategic need for national identity, made unhelpful comments on Malaya's reliance upon Great Britain and on the Philippines' close connection with the US, nevertheless, the Manila

Accord was drawn up and embodied the following:

- The three countries would share responsibility for the maintenance of the security of the region of South-East Asia from subversion.

- General support for the confederation of *Maphilindo*.

- Admission by Malaya that the Philippine claim to North Borneo would not prejudice the latter's incorporation in the proposed federation of Malaysia.

- The principle of self-determination by their respective peoples, as promoted by the UN. For the British protectorates, the UN Secretary-General must appoint independent observers to ascertain the wishes of the people.

The conference closed to enable the three foreign ministers to ratify the Accord, however when Dr Subandrio returned to Jakarta, he faced opposition from the PKI, who declared that the people of British North Borneo had already made their choice by rebelling in Brunei. The communists conveniently forgot that only a fraction had supported the outbreak and that it was not an entirely pro-Indonesian rebellion.

Malaya then upset the applecart when Tunku Abdul Rahman and Lee Kwan Yue signed the London Agreement on 9 July, extending existing defence ties with Great Britain. When the signatories agreed that the Federation would be formed on 31 August, this did not allow much time for the electoral survey proposed by the UN, nevertheless when Foreign Minister Razak of Malaya agreed to allow limited confirmation of the people's wishes, Sukarno angrily accused the Tunku of an inability to keep his promises. On 16 July, as Indonesia announced that her fleet had been mobilized, the proposed summit at prime ministerial level to ratify the Manila Accord seemed unlikely. Ten days later, Indonesia announced joint naval-air exercises in the South China Sea and Malacca Straits, and '*Ganjung* Malaysia!' ('Crush Malaysia') became the Indonesian battle cry. On 27 July, Sukarno's warmongering continued when he declared that 'to crush Malaysia, we must launch a confrontation in all fields. We cannot talk sweetly to the imperialists.'

As diplomatic moves stumbled towards the Manila Summit, throughout the summer, British North Borneo was tense as CCO subversion and IBT insurgents pecked at stability, and intimidation generated civil insecurity, particularly in Sibu. Diplomatic relations in North Borneo were damaged when two Indonesian diplomats were expelled from Jesselton in May, as we shall see.

65

Since the Sarawak Rangers had proved a success during the Malayan Emergency, in May, Major General Walker reasoned that an indigenous force would be equally valuable in their own country and instructed Lieutenant Colonel John Cross, a 7th Gurkha Rifles veteran of the Emergency, to raise and train 1,000 Border Scouts as a tripwire along the border. 40 Commando had already proved the value of local guides by recruiting a diminutive Iban they christened 'Tom Thumb' and equipping him with a uniform, shotgun ammunition and rations in return for guiding patrols and information-gathering. Unfortunately, most recruitment took place along the coastal strip, as opposed to inland, followed by a three- week basic training course run by the SAS and Gurkha Independent Parachute Company, and managed by the Gurkha battalions, before Cross was appointed. Formed in January 1963 from the Brigade of Gurkhas, the role of the Gurkha Independent Parachute Company was to overcome the airlanding problems faced by the 1st Queen's Own Highlanders when it seized Anduki airfield during the Brunei Revolt.

In spite of Scouts demotivated by the prospects of soldiering in the shadows of the jungle, Cross organized them into sections commanded by Gurkha corporals, with a lance corporal or experienced rifleman as second-in-command. However, this proved cumbersome because some young Gurkhas, isolated from their sergeants and officers, were uncomfortable with their independence and did not always trust the loyalty of the Scouts. Nevertheless, Cross worked hard to develop the Scouts into a useful home guard organization, and eventually a network of guides, discreet observation posts and intelligence sources emerged. In 1963 in Second Division, 1/10th Gurkha Rifles had thirteen sections working with A Company in the Engkilili, ten with B Company in the Lubok Antu area and seven in the Sungei Tenggang area with D Company.

An attack on three traders at Nangga San, in the Second Division, on 17 May by thirteen IBTs indicated that Indonesia would support a rebellion, however, apart from a few dissident Chinese and Malays offering shelter, food and guides, the response was limited and consequently the raiders resorted to stealing from shops and longhouses. An attack on Gumbang kampong during the early hours of 13 August was beaten off by a section from L Company, 42 Commando and a Border Scouts section commanded by Sergeant Alastair Mackie. Several more attacks were launched over the next week, the last, on the 23rd, by about sixty men, being thrown off balance when the IBTs were ambushed near the border. It was the first time that a large force had been used. Some British patrols were of an exploratory nature. In June, Captain Andrew Dennison and Sergeant Edward Lillico, of the SAS, led a patrol of three local Murats and five Sarawak Police Field Force to recce the Pensiangan Gap, an area of unexplored, pristine jungle in North Borneo and thought to be a probable infiltration route.

In spite of the rising political and military tension, the Manila Summit opened on 30 July 1963, four weeks before the proposed Federation. On the same day, in Kuching, Governor Waddell unveiled the memorial to the police officers and Royal Marines killed at Limbang, and announced gallantry awards to several Limbang police officers and civil awards for outstanding service by civilians during the Brunei Revolt.

Inevitably the Soviet Union, China and regional communist parties objected to a politically powerful and culturally influential Malaysia, while capitalist states welcomed the concept as a buffer against the growing influence of communism. Malaya's Minister without Portfolio, Khaw Kai Boh, a lawyer with an intelligence and security background gained during the Emergency, and Indonesia's Dr Sudjarwo Tjondronegoro, also a lawyer and a formidable debater, were the main players. Colonel Koesta, the intelligence chief at the Indonesian Embassy in Kuala Lumpur, encouraged anti-federalists to attend a conference in Sumatra with a view to inciting civil unrest and insurrection in order to overthrow Tunku Abdul Rahman, by sending telegrams to Manila that Federation should not be agreed without a referendum in British North Borneo. Indonesia voiced her objections to the London Agreement and demanded that British forces must withdraw from Singapore. Koesta also insisted that if bases in Singapore and Borneo were needed in the event of hostilities, then Great Britain must seek permission from the proposed confederation of *Maphilindo*. Relations between Tunku Abdul Rahman and Sukarno were initially strained until the latter, in uniform, met the Tunku in his suite and then negotiations became sufficiently cordial for the Manila Accord to be ratified. The UN Secretary-General U Thant was asked to determine the wishes of the people of British North Borneo and even though disagreements on the organization of the UN team surfaced, the Summit broke up on 7 August. The Joint Statement contained an interesting paragraph:

> in which foreign bases – temporary in nature – were not to be used directly or indirectly to subvert the national independence of any of the three countries. In accordance with the principles enunciated in the Bandung Declaration, the three countries will abstain from the use of arrangements of collective defence to serve the particular interests of any of the big powers.

Although political distrust deepened when a British diplomat thoughtlessly confirmed 31 August as Malaysia Day, the Big Powers, namely the

US and Great Britain, reassured Indonesia that her sovereignty would not be invaded from either the Philippines or the proposed Malaysia. In England, Dr Stephen Ward died of an overdose in a London hospital after having been convicted of living off the immoral earnings of Christine Keeler, who had been a central figure in the Profumo affair and the Conservative Government wobbled. When the UN accepted, under pressure, that a full plebiscite in the three protectorates was not possible by 31 August, Malaya agreed to a brief delay in declaring Federation in exchange for Indonesia abandoning her demand for a full plebiscite.

Throughout the Manila Summit, internal security in British North Borneo was tense.

Table 1. Borneo Incursions 12 April to 16 September 1963				
Location	Division	Date	Intruders	Incident
Tebedu	First	12 April	75	Police station overrun; two SF killed and one wounded
Gumbang	First	23 April	10	2 TNI killed and 3 wounded
Pang Ampat	First	4 June		Flare ignited
Ensawang	Second	6 June	8	One Iban and one SF wounded
Wong Panjoi	First	17 June	30	Deflected by Voice Aircraft
Kampong Enteboh	First	20 June		Grenade thrown and three shots fired
Kandai/ Panchau	First	3 July	4	One Indonesian killed in ambush
Sungei Taping	Second	4 July	25	Longhouse raided
Sungei Putting Lulu	Second	6 July	20	One Indonesian and one civilian killed
Kampong Silik	Second	8 July	2	One Indonesian killed and one wounded
Gua	Second	4 August	10	SF ambush
Tinting Lalang	Second	8 August	15	TNKU contact
Song	Third	8 August	70	SF officer, 15 IBT killed and 3 captured
Tinting Lalan	Second	9 August	6	TNI wounded
Kapit	Third	9 August	9	TNI wounded in SF ambush
Lubok Antu	Second	10 August		SF ambush
Tebakang	First	10 August	3	Exchange of fire
Gumbang	First	13 August	35	Exchange of fire
Stass	First	15 August	1	Interference to SF booby-trap
Long Lopeng	Fifth	19 August	26	One SF killed and one wounded. 6 TNKU captured
Long Akah	Fourth	20 August	1	1 TNI captured
Gumbang	First	21 August	8	Exchange of fire
Gumbang	First	22/23 August	30 to 40	SF wounded and 5 TNI killed.
Gumbang	First	23 August	2	Exchange of fire
Pang Tebang	First	23/24 August		Exchange of fire
Long Lopeng	Fifth	25 August	3	3 IBT from Long Bawan captured
Long Merarap	Fifth	26 August	2 to 3	Exchange of fire
Stass area	First	30 August	3	2 IBT killed and 1 wounded in curfew
Sungei Angkuah	Third	2 September	6	6 IBT killed and one SF wounded.
Sungei Angkuah	Third	3 September	3	3 IBT killed and one captured
Sungei Angkuah	Third	4 September	1	One TNI captured
Kiek	First	7 September		Indonesian body found with TNKU leaflets
Kuching	First	14 September	1	Grenade thrown at SF patrol in Market

Source: *Indonesian Involvement East Malaysia, Kuala Lumpur; Public Printers 1965, Appendix 11, Part One, pp. 47-51.*

On its first tour in Third Division, 2/10th Gurkha Rifles had helped in Operation Parrot and was particularly effective in disrupting CCO activities. Moved to Simanggang for the rest of its tour, it patrolled Second Division intercepting incursions and pioneered the numbering of every helicopter LP in its sector, thus simplifying the passage of information. The Border Scouts were blooded in June when information from police informers led the Battalion to intercepting fifteen uniformed IBT at Mawang en route to attack a Border Scouts outpost. Although allocated a single 846 NAS Whirlwind, with imaginative tactics complementing physical fitness and operating from its base at Sarikie, a small trading post on the Sungei Rajang, C Company and the Border Scouts killed three guerrillas and wounded two. One of the dead was a local headmaster who had joined the TNKU and among the weapons recovered was a .303 rifle taken from Tebedu Police Station. Of concern was that the IBTs had covered 40 miles before being reported and when they were, it took the Gurkhas hours of marching through the jungle before they reached the scene. Major General Walker then instructed that battalions must always have a section-sized heli-borne quick reaction force at instant readiness to move.

1/10th Gurkha Rifles (Lieutenant Colonel 'Bunny' Burnett) arrived from Singapore and took over from its sister Battalion. Over the border, 602 and 608 Airborne Infantry Battalions and an Army Commando Regiment company had been identified, but being Army, were considered less of a threat than the Brunei Regiment and other 'volunteers', quite apart from the about 20,000 CCO in Sarawak. Burnett was determined to dominate Second Division and when an Auster pilot saw camp fires across the border, plans were developed to shell them using the Saladins of B Squadron, QRIH. Their first contact came on 9 August when a patrol investigating reports of Indonesians visiting a longhouse clashed with fifteen IBTs. Deploying men by helicopter, Burnett, for a short time, was so short of Gurkhas that he took charge of a 3-inch mortar crew consisting of himself, two riflemen and a police superintendent and constable, with corrections given by an officer in an Auster. In the follow-up, several large camps inside Sarawak were found.

Meanwhile, Brigadier Supardjo was concentrating on Third Division and assessed that Song, a small town at the junction of the Rajang and Katibas rivers, was ripe for Wingate-style occupation as a demonstration of Indonesian solidarity to the UN policy of decolonization. Crossing the Third Division border using the Sungei Ayer, IBTs supported by the Indonesian Army forced four Ibans from Man longhouse to be guides. On 11 August, when several Ibans informed Song Police Station of the incursion, a D Squadron SAS patrol training Border Scouts in the town warned 2/6th Gurkha Rifles (Lieutenant

Colonel 'Slim' Horsfield MBE MC), which had arrived in late June from Hong Kong. The Military Commander for the Division, under command of HQ 3 Commando Brigade, was Major Geoff Walsh, the Battalion second in command, with B Company at Sarikie and C Company at Sibu.

A patrol sent by Major Walsh to investigate reported boatloads of refugees hurrying downstream along the Katibas and Bangkit rivers. Meanwhile, Major Tom Leask, who commanded D Squadron, had suggested to Captain Peter Walter (Parachute Regiment and former SAS), who was on local leave in Sarawak, that he visit the Song Border Scouts. It was while he was at their HQ that a villager from Masam longhouse reported that one of the four captured Ibans had escaped. Walsh then agreed that Walters could accompany a Gurkha patrol tasked to debrief the guide and insisted that it be joined by the SAS, three Border Scouts, two Sarawak Police Field Force officers and the Kapit District Officer. On 14 August, the twenty-one strong patrol arrived by boat in Masam and, after interviewing the Ibans, continued upriver. They then met two more Ibans who had escaped from the IBTs, who reported that the incursion numbered about fifty uniformed and well-equipped CCO led by Indonesian regular officers and NCOs, who were an advance guard of 300 due to cross the border within the week, to be followed by 600 a fortnight later. With the first major incursion threatening Sarawak, Walsh sent Walter's patrol to Blayong to cover likely approaches from the border along the Ayer, and next day reinforced it with fifteen Gurkhas commanded by Lieutenant Hugh Wallace, who had arrived by Belvedere. Wallace had cut short his long leave and had taken over command of C Company the previous day. Communications were made difficult not only by storms but Walter had just two radios.

On 16 August, when he encircled Blayong with ambushes, Walter believed the IBTs to be sufficiently well trained not to enter the kampong without a recce and advised Wallace to observe from the jungle. When Walsh then instructed Walter to send two patrols to search for the enemy, Walsh established his patrol base at Blayong with a radio and then set off with the second radio to search the Ayer, while Lieutenant (QGO) Matbarsing Gurung, without one, patrolled on foot to Man.

At about 1.00 pm, when Wallace saw about ten IBTs on the riverbank, the patrol landed, however, as it was moving into positions to engage them, an Iban hunting party, who happened to be on high ground above the river, fired a shotgun. The police corporal's invitation to surrender was met with a volley of automatic and rifle fire. Covered by Walter firing the Bren, Wallace and a few men were manoeuvring to outflank the enemy when Wallace had his knee shattered by a bullet and the attack faltered. Walter, unsure what was happening, then faced a further difficulty when the Iban boatmen scurried downstream taking the patrol's kit. Clashes continued throughout the afternoon and then the IBTs withdrew, leaving the jungle to return to near silence. Believing he was facing a strong force, Major Walter assembled his patrol, and, after a five-hour march, reached Blayong where Walsh told him to wait for reinforcements. Walter sent the SAS to cut a LP at Man.

Meanwhile, Matbarsing's patrol reached Man late on the 16th only to

MAP 7 - THE BLAYONG OPERATION, 11 August to 18 September 1963

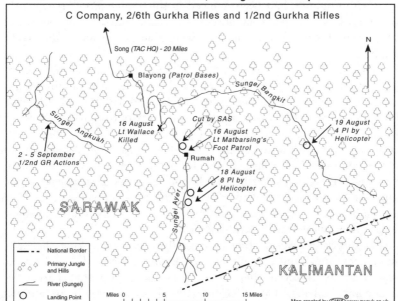

find found the longhouse deserted except for three men and an elderly woman. The Gurkhas covered the approaches all night and were about to withdraw at 6.45 am, when several IBTs, guided by a Kayan in civilian clothes, appeared. After wounding one of them and capturing the guide, they then became involved in a firefight that lasted all day, with IBTs in the jungle across the river keeping the Gurkhas pinned down. At 5.00 pm, Matbarsing withdrew to high ground behind the longhouse and, after making several unsuccessful attempts to arrange a helicopter extraction, was compelled to walk out, reaching Bayong on 19 August.

Early on the 17th, Major Walter returned to the scene of his battle and confirmed the presence of TNI from discarded uniforms, American-made boots and field dressings. Lieutenant Wallace was found not far from where his orderly had left him the previous afternoon. It seems that he had stood up and loosed off all his ammunition before being fatally wounded. At mid-morning, when another storm interfered with communications, Major Walsh deployed with his Tactical HQ to Song. Next day at 4.30 pm, 8 Platoon landed at two LPs downstream of the action and shot up a small boat containing several IBTs, killing one and capturing five, including two wounded. 4 Platoon then landed on a LP south-east of Blayong on Bangkit and effectively prevented the enemy from using the rivers. By the beginning of September, the incursion, after a fortnight of operating 15 miles inside Sarawak, without local support, hungry and hunted, had been reduced to thirty-nine. Some reached the top of a hill not far from the border and encountered 8 Platoon, which was waiting for reinforcements, and were able to slip across the border at night.

From interrogations, it emerged that the incursion had been hopelessly ill-prepared, the force had crossed the border without maps and compasses and were intending to live off the land with the help of locals. The operation marked a turning point in Confrontation. Whereas Indonesia had not admitted that TNI were crossing the border into Sarawak, the British now had proof and had learnt from the encounters in the summer that although the Indonesian Army was aggressive, planning was weak. Nevertheless, the incident was of sufficient importance for Major General Walker to send the two companies from 2/6th Gurkha Rifles to rejoin their battalion in Fifth Division and Sabah, and replace them with 1/2nd Gurkha Rifles.

After directing several other exhausted insurgents seeking shelter to the Sungei Angkuah, a longhouse headman informed Tactical HQ at Song that he believed they were from the group that had killed Lieutenant Wallace. Two C Company platoons already in ambush positions upriver pursued them for two days until, on 2 September, they were engaged at a range of over 400 yards while wading up a river bed. The Gurkhas deployed, killed one IBT and recovered documents that proved the group had indeed been part of the force that had killed Wallace. Next day, Lieutenant (QGO) Lalitbahadur cornered another group on a steep jungle-covered slope and when his invitation to surrender drew heavy automatic fire, the Gurkhas charged and killed five insurgents. On the 4th, D Company killed the incursion leader and next day another was accounted for by Ibans armed with a shotgun and a parang. On 18 September, the last man, exhausted and lost, was captured.

On 8 August, meanwhile, the UN Ascertainment Mission started its self-determination survey of British North Borneo. Inevitably, there were delays as the Philippines and Indonesia squabbled over the number of observers and consequently the survey did not commence until 16

August, the same day that Lieutenant Wallace was killed. Not everyone in Sarawak was pro-Malaysia and when the nine-man UN delegation arrived in Kuching, they were met by anti-Federation demonstrations at the airport. Hearings held in Kuching, Bau and Serian were hostile, while those at Kanowit and Bintulu were non-committal. Meetings at Sibu and Miri dissolved into riots. On 1 September, after there had been disagreements over the issue of visas, eight Indonesian and seven Philippine observers joined the UN team, and then a fortnight later, Secretary-General U Thant delivered his conclusions:

> The majority of the peoples of Sabah (North Borneo) and Sarawak have given serious thought and thoughtful consideration to their future and to the implications of them participating in a Federation of Malaysia. I believe that the majority of them have concluded that they wish to bring their dependent status to an end. There is no doubt that the wishes of a sizeable majority of the peoples of these territories want to join the Federation of Malaysia.

The Malayans were delighted and the Indonesians incensed, with the PKI pressurizing Sukarno to reject the findings and reduce ties with the West. When the Federation of Malaysia was declared next day, on what became known as Malaysia Day, and Tunku Abdul Rahman was elected as its first leader, Indonesia refused to recognize Malaysia. While Sarawak and Sabah (formerly North Borneo) settled in relatively quickly, the Sultan of Brunei, keen on protecting his country's wealth and with no great desire to share the revenue and profits, did not join. As an existing head of state, he also had no wish to rotate with the Malaysian sultans to be the federal president. The arrogance of Malayan officials helping to write the constitution two years earlier had not been forgotten and neither had the comment made by the Tunku that Brunei was too small to join the Commonwealth. Economic and commercial tensions, and jockeying for power between the Tunku and Lee Kuan Yew simmered over the next three years, although both agreed the priority was to deal with Indonesian aspirations. Since Malaysia was a member of SEATO, the Tunku now called upon member countries to help defend her against the aggression of Indonesia. The colonial campaign waged by Malaya and Great Britain changed overnight into a war fought by the Commonwealth, supporting one of its members defending its sovereign territories. Even when faced with internal instability – a financial liquidity crisis fuelling spiralling inflation, expenditure limits overreached and economic intervention being threatened by the International Monetary Fund – Sukarno was determined to eject the British from the region and again promised a 'terrible confrontation'.

CHAPTER SEVEN

The Defence of Borneo
September to December 1963

The day after Malaysia Day, anti-British anger spilled into violence when 10,000 demonstrators converged on the British Embassy opposite Hotel Indonesia at the end of Jakarta's most fashionable street. The Defence Attaché, Colonel Beck, allowed six delegates to present their concerns to the Ambassador, Sir Andrew Gilchrist. Gilchrist had previously completed a tour in Iceland during the Cod Wars and was familiar with hostility to Great Britain. However, through the front doors stepped Major Muir Walker of the SAS, the Military Attaché. Provocatively, he placed that most colonial of British musical instruments, his Highland bagpipes, under his arm and blew. The enraged mob tore down the Union flag, only for the Assistant Military Attaché, Sergeant Marshall, of the QRIH, to nail it back into place. A second surge succeeded in ripping the flag from the pole and then the crowd burst through the perimeter fence and rampaged around the compound until Gilchrist agreed to meet the mob leaders. The Singaporean Embassy was also attacked, as was the Indonesian Embassy in Kuala Lumpur.

Initially, this serious breach of diplomatic protocol did not affect links between Indonesia and Malaysia, however when British commercial interests were taken over, Malaysia severed diplomatic relations with Indonesia and the Philippines on 19 September. This sparked the second attack on the Embassy, a puzzling affair since it was Malaysia, not Great Britain, which had severed relations. Orchestrated by the Indonesian National Party, youths set fire to the shattered Embassy, and then a crowd trapped Gilchrist and several British diplomats against a wall, subjecting them to a hail of stones and bottles. For the first time, the police took action and only a police car driven straight through the mob saved them from serious injury. Throughout that afternoon, British houses, businesses and cars were attacked. A few businesses linked with the Indonesian Army, such as those owned by John McLeod, were left untouched. Australian and American properties in the same neighbourhoods were ignored. Indonesian Security Forces were noted by their absence. The unrest necessitated the evacuation of about 400 British passport holders in two 48 Squadron Argosy transports and a Hastings flying from RAF Changi. From henceforth, flying over Indonesian airspace by British aircraft was restricted. This had a major impact on Transport Command, which rerouted its flights to and from Australia via Singapore, increasing flight times, fuel consumption and inconvenience.

On 21 September, Indonesia formally severed commercial ties with Malaysia, which led to the US announcing that it was no longer financing Sukarno's attempts to stabilize his country and suspending his US$50 million credit. Proposals by Japan and Thailand for Malaysia, Indonesia and the Philippines to negotiate their way out of the crisis made a little headway, although it did seem that Foreign Minister Dr Subandrio was more receptive than Tunku Abdul Rahman.

Federation led to changes in command structures. Operations in Borneo were subordinated to the newly formed Malaysian National Defence Council, which was chaired by Tunku Abdul Rahman and linked to London through the British High Commission. As it was customary for London to assist newly independent states with security expertise, the MI5 officer, David Stewart, arrived to supervise British regional security liaison officers and, as a member of the Joint Intelligence Committee (Far East), he helped co-ordinate, collate and distribute political, military and economic intelligence. Strategic decisions were relayed to a subordinate committee, whose members included the Commander-in-Chief of the Malaysian Armed Forces, the British Commander-in-Chief Far East and the Inspector-General of the Malaysian Police, Sir Claude Fenner. Major General Walker, as Commander, British Forces, Borneo (COMDBRITFOR) and Director of Borneo Operations (DOBOPS) took his orders from HQ Far East and FARELF. The one area that risked being cumbersome was the interface with the police, particularly as the constabularies in Borneo each had their own command structures subordinated to Fenner in Kuala Lumpur. Fortunately, Walker and Fenner had served together during the Malayan Emergency and agreed that while the police led internal security operations, the Armed Forces would defend Borneo from external aggression. Sabah and Sarawak both had Security Advisory Committees, while Brunei had the State Advisory Council, which was chaired by the Sultan. Walker's HQ remained in Brunei.

The next military stage of Confrontation sees communist irregulars trained by the Indonesian Central Intelligence Bureau and stiffened by the RPKAD mounting attacks. On paper, the Indonesian Army consisted of about 100 conventional infantry battalions, most of which were under strength to the extent that only about twenty-five were assessed to have reasonable combat efficiency. Most of these were deployed on internal security in Java. The few available to Kalimantan Combat Command lacked command commitment and were hampered by long lines of communication. In September, General Nasution admitted for the first time that 'volunteers' had been crossing into Borneo for several months. The Indonesian UN representative, Dr Tjondronegro, qualified the admittance:

> Volunteers in Indonesia come from all quarters of the population and not only from Indonesia but also from the territory now called Malaysia. It is a people's fight from freedom against colonialism and neo-colonialism, against Malaysia as a political nation. For the volunteers, national boundaries do not exist. Their boundaries are political.

Walker's principal task remained to prevent IBTs establishing Wingate-style strongholds in CCO-sympathetic areas. FDLs covered virtually every major border track and waterway, however, distinguishing between legitimate traders, locals visiting relatives and IBTs proved problematic. The second task was internal security and keeping the people north of the border onside. Although the Sarawak CCO had about 2,000 hardcore activists, most were known to the Security Forces. There was also potential support from 3,000 Indonesian migrants and loggers, and in Sabah, at least 24,000. Since the British could not cross the border, the Indonesians held the initiative. Walker still had two brigade headquarters:

- *West Brigade*. HQ 3 Commando Brigade with responsibility for 623 miles of the border covering First to Third Divisions.

- *East Brigade*. 99 Gurkha Infantry Brigade Group had returned to Singapore leaving an 'ad hoc' headquarters commanded by Brigadier Glennie. The length of border was 378 miles of land and over 500 miles of coast of Fourth and Fifth Division and Sabah.

On internal security were 1st Queens Own Highlanders, 1st King's Own Yorkshire Light Infantry and 1st Green Jackets. 28 Commonwealth Brigade continued to rotate British units to Borneo.

While it is sometimes said that Confrontation was an infantry company commander's war, for the Royal Engineers, it was a corporal's war. By December 1964, British, Gurkha, Malaysian and Australian Field Squadrons, supported by stores detachments at Brunei and Kuching and 522 Specialist Team, Royal Engineers were rotating through Borneo with a Field Troop supporting the brigades. Typically, Field Squadrons were organized into an HQ, Motor Transport, Park and three Field Troops. Workshop Troops were usually spread among the Troops with the Stores Section centralized with the Resource Detachments at Brunei and Kuching. In January 1966, 67 Gurkha Independent Field Squadron took over from 69 Gurkha Independent Field Squadron in Central Brigade and, for the next eleven months, was based at Seria in Brunei. A Troop took eight months to build a stone airstrip at Long Pasia after the grass strip had collapsed. B Troop deployed detachments throughout the Brigade area maintaining FLBs and their equipment, repairing water points and 'delousing' LPs and laying mines. C Troop was at Bareo for nine months and built a camp of sixty-nine buildings. Although road building was not a high priority, 21 and 22 (Australian) Construction Squadrons built a road linking Keningau in Fifth Division to Sepulot in Sabah. Even with local labour, building and repairing roads took a disproportionate number of men, calculated to be one squadron per mile per month. The Postal and Courier Communications established field post offices to process mail and classified packaged information and materials.

During the war, the Allies had mapped most of Borneo with a scale of 1 inch to 4 miles, however it was unreliable. In 1946, when only three of eighteen proposed maps of 1 inch to 2 miles had been produced, to meet the need for large-scale maps, RAF Mosquitoes from Singapore surveyed the three territories so that by 1953 about 75 per cent had been plotted. By 1961, 145 maps of the planned 206 had been produced although only eight were fully contoured. Thus, in the early days of Confrontation, maps were black and white and contained such phrases as 'Reliability Uncertain' and 'These maps must not be used on authority of the delineation of international boundaries'. Although rivers and inhabited areas were marked, ground contours were approximate, which made jungle navigation difficult. Army cartographers added grid overlays on maps originally compiled by the Directorate of Colonial Survey in the 1950s, from information supplied by the Land and Survey Department, Sarawak. By 1962, 84 Survey Squadron in Dover Street, Singapore, reinforced by A Troop, 42 Survey Engineer Regiment flown from UK, was in the forefront of producing accurate maps. Consisting of three Topographical Troops, a three-phase operation was developed to collate all existing mapping into a 1:150,000 scale, but such was the lack of historical survey that most sheets were near blank. Phase Two was to compile all survey data and air photographs into 1:250,000 maps and the final phase was to produce standard contoured 1:50,000 and 1:250,000 mapping. This was the critical phase for it was these maps that were most commonly used by the battalions and units.

Attached to the Sarawak-based 1 Topographical Troop at Sibu and Nanga Gaat, was the Air Survey Liaison Staff/Joint Air Reconnaissance Intelligence Cell (ASLS/JARIC), tasking 81 Squadron photo-recce Canberras flying from RAF Tengah. 2 Troop deployed to Sabah. Iban and Murut tribesmen helped survey parties. The actual making of maps was complex. At the ASLS, Sapper 'Mac' Hawkins did two tours in Borneo:

Our job was to plot those areas designated for map making. We used an overmap to see what areas had been covered and whether the mission was deemed a success: correct overlaps and not too much cloud cover. If this wasn't the case, the block would have to be overflown again. It was a very time-consuming and a gradual process to build up a complete coverage of a designated area or region – in this case practically a whole country. From Labuan, the photos were flown daily in an RAF Hastings to Singapore. Once the selected photos were handed over to 84 Survey Sqn, they used infor-mation gained separately from trigonometrical surveys carried out on the ground, which determined fixed and triangulated positions that could also be defined on the aerial photos. In addition, at least four identifiable points (could be individual trees or river junctions) had to be visible on adjoining or pairs of photos. Once these points had been selected, tough celluloid sheets were overlaid on each of the photos and a pin prick marked each identifiable point. Then slotted templates were fabricated from these sheets, with each 'slot' radiating towards a centre point. Pegs then were inserted into each of these elongated slots and the adjoining or corresponding photo templates were thus linked (both lat and long) and could then be expanded or contracted in concertina fashion, so different scales could be accommodated. Once the required map scale was deter-mined, the known, fixed or triangulated positions were then pegged onto a huge board that represented the area to be mapped. The slotted templates were then incorporated onto this. Once this had been achieved, it was then necessary to draw on this template, using chinagraph pencils, the mapping information (like rivers, villages or other landmarks) extracted from the photos. This information then

78

had to be transferred with a pencil on to an overlay of tracing paper. Eventually, the resulting map, now drawn with an ink pen, was then used as the basis for the printed product. 84 Survey Sqn had their own litho department and printing presses in Dover Road.

By the end of Confrontation, 566 Field Survey Depot in Singapore had issued over 500,000 map sheets, many of them contoured in colour. Much of the financial effort was picked up by the Government of Malaysia.

In an important decision, the SAS realized that while they could tickle the Indonesians, the infantry were the hammers and consequently a SAS liaison officer was attached to the battalions guarding the border. The relationship did not last after Confrontation, largely because some senior SAS officers believed that the Regiment should be independent. The Regiment was based in a large villa loaned by the Sultan not far from Brunei town, known as 'The Haunted House', because it was reputed to house the spirit of a girl who had died at the hands of the Japanese Kempei Tei. That the locals believed the building to be haunted ensured that the SAS had the independence, privacy and security that they demanded.

Of the commanders who have fought battles without intelligence, few have succeeded. One of Major General Walker's key principles was the timely acquisition of information and intelligence, a lesson that he learnt under Lieutenant General Sir Gerald Templer during the Malayan Emergency. The HQ of the Intelligence Corps in Ashford, Kent was named Templer Barracks and the Corps motto aptly describes its role – 'Knowledge Gives Strength to the Arm'.

The British had a formidable array of strategic intelligence resources ranging from long-range Canberra PR7 air photo recce to the Government Communications Headquarters listening posts at Phoenix Park in Singapore, Shau Ke Wan in Hong Kong and electronic warfare units in Borneo. Indonesian ciphers were broken early in the campaign and their diplomatic telegrams lost their integrity; British Intelligence and the CIA, operating deep inside Indonesian government circles ensured that some Army officers grew rich.

Interrogation was a valuable resource. Early during the Brunei Revolt, 19, 21 and 22 Intelligence Platoons, reinforced from Malaya and Hong Kong, supported Brunei police interrogation centres. When Confrontation developed, a composite platoon was formed to support 3 Commando Brigade. In early 1964, Captain Nigel Flower and Staff Sergeant John Tucker developed the idea of deploying interrogation teams to units holding prisoners. By the end of Confrontation, over 200 prisoners had undergone detailed interrogation, including a signaller who had served at Army HQ, a Marine Corps battalion commander, and three officers and a warrant officer rescued by 42 Commando in February 1965 when their boat capsized near Sebatik Island.

The Corps developed a network of about twenty Warrant Officers and NCOs operating as Field Intelligence Officers (FIO) spread initially in West Sarawak and then throughout Sarawak and Sabah. Working closely with Special Branch and local MIOs, who were non-Intelligence Corps, they ran networks of sources and informers and provided crucial intelligence continuity for the rotating infantry battalions. Traders proved to be valuable. One FIO established himself as an immigration officer and gave his sources cameras to photograph Indonesian bases. FIOs were expected to integrate in local communities, which meant sampling local food and the local brew, which was usually pretty powerful, and were encouraged to wear civilian clothes. One is reputed to have worn flip-flops, a sarong and an Army shirt on which was perched a bird. Most welcomed the challenge, in spite of the threat of being turned over by subversives to the Indonesians. The strategy was later used with considerable success in Belize against the Guatemalan threat, in Hong Kong and in Northern Ireland.

From the mass of information, Intelligence Platoons collated and analysed information, and then graded its value, all in time to be of use to commanders. Intelligence assessments became so efficient that while predicting where enemy patrols might cross the border was not easy, once they were across, they could hardly move without someone reporting it, so that senior Indonesian officers believed the Commonwealth forces had special radar equipment tracking their patrols. The Intelligence Corps also security surveyed military and associated establishments ranging from large facilities, such as Ordnance depots, to units occupying single offices auditing classified information, and conducted counter-intelligence operations to control subversion, espionage and sabotage from seeping into loyal units and individuals.

As we have seen, Sukarno reacted with venom after Malaysia Day and promised the Federation a 'terrible confrontation'. The British expected some sort of military action and alert states in First and Second Divisions were raised. Across the border, Brigadier General Supjardo was still focusing on Third Division with its fast-flowing rivers bisecting jungle-clad mountains and selected Long Jawi, a large kampong on the upper reaches of the Rajang in an unmapped area about 30 miles west of the border, for a Wingate-style raid with a secondary aim of undermining Border Scout commitment. South of the border was Long Nawang, with whom the Kayan inhabitants at Long Jawi traded. Since the kampong was on a river used by Indonesians working in Third Division sawmills, he had good intelligence on the area. The kampong consisted of a longhouse, a school, several outhouses and a rough airstrip, and was defended by a Border Scout post of four soldiers from 1/2nd Gurkha Rifles, twenty-one Border Scouts and two Police Field Force radio operators. It was about 50 miles south of the administrative centre at Belaga, which was also the location of a Border Scout HQ. About 10 miles upstream from Belaga was Long Linau, with a small outpost. Both kampongs were connected to Belaga by radio, however voice communications were so bad that Morse code was frequently used. At stand-to in the morning and evening, posts confirmed their status with a radio check – if they could get through.

When an SAS A Squadron patrol led by Corporal George Stainforth on 'hearts and minds' in the area intercepted two strangers in early March and they turned out to be senior members of an Indonesian political cadre, it was suspected that Long Jawi was of interest to the Indonesians. When A Squadron was replaced by D Squadron, Stainforth remained until August, however, none of these events was made known to 1/2nd Gurkha Rifles.

On 16 September 1963, about 100 IBTs, supported by about 200 porters, commanded by Major Surjowardojo Muljono, with a small RPKAD cadre, left Long Nawang and reached Long Jawi undetected. Muljono was an experienced officer with left-wing views, who had fought with the Japanese against the Dutch and had attended the British Jungle Warfare School. He had served with the Diponegoro Division and had spent some time in Sarawak in July 1948. He was now the Military District No. 9 Intelligence Officer in North-West Kalimantan.

Captain John Burlison, who had recently taken command of the area with the Battalion Bugle Platoon, left Belaga by boat to visit the bases, taking with him an Administrative Officer, Corporal Tejbahadur Gurung, who was to relieve the corporal at Long Jawi, and a Bren gun team to reinforce the post. Arriving at Long Jawi during the afternoon of 25 September, Burlison instructed that the post HQ be moved from the school to a small hill to the east and selected flat ground across a shallow stream running alongside the kampong as the LP. At a village meeting, he then persuaded the villagers to help dig five trenches and bunkers on the hill and instructed the Border Scouts not to stay overnight in the longhouse, but to join the Gurkhas. Next day, the trenches were dug, however the radio antennae had yet to be resited and so the signallers stayed at the school. Burlison then described to the villagers how Long Jawi should be defended, but was unaware that in a storeroom was a small IBT recce patrol, who left and warned Muljono that the Gurkhas was being reinforced with an 'extra' machine gun and

81

advised him to wait until Burlison had left. Next day, 27 September, Burlison's party departed leaving Corporal Tejbahadur as Military Commander, Long Jawi. He refused permission for a Border Scout to see his pregnant wife.

MAP 8 - DEFENCE OF LONG JAWI, 28 September 1963

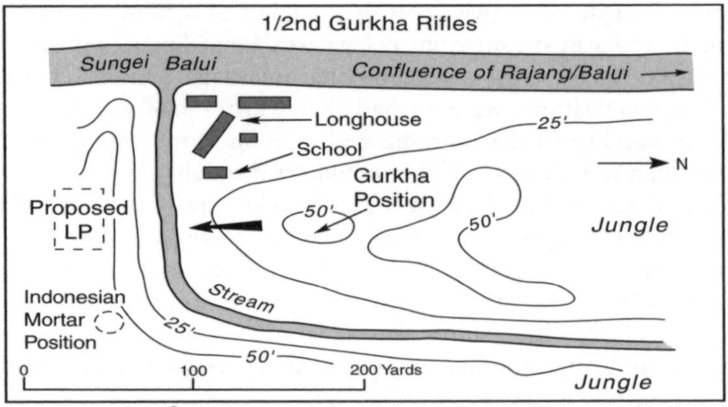

Map created by GWA® www.gwauk.co.uk

During the night, Muljono's men silently entered Long Jawi, but were spotted at about 5.30 am by the Scout visiting his pregnant wife after being on guard. Running up the hill and alerting the Gurkhas, Tejbahadur ordered stand-to and then ran to the school where he instructed the signallers to advise Belaga of the Indonesian presence. Grabbing a box of grenades, he was returning up the hill when he came under automatic and light mortar fire from the proposed LP and lost the grenades when he was bowled over by an explosion. The Indonesians killed two of the signallers and then set fire to the school. Impeded by a shattered knee, the surviving policeman staggered up the hill. The first attack was broken up, but some Border Scouts, unnerved by the fighting, slipped across the stream into the jungle near the LP where all but one were captured. The survivor, seeing the sorry plight of his captured colleagues, returned to the hill. During the second attack, Rifleman Kharkabahadur Gurung was wounded in the thigh when he was scrambling into an adjoining trench after abandoning his position when it was laced by a machine gun. Rifleman Amarbahadur Thapa was coolly picking off IBTs with his Bren. Rifleman Dhanbahadur and a Border Scout were killed and two Border Scouts were wounded when a mortar bomb exploded in the trees above them. By 8.45 am, unsure whether the signallers had radioed Belaga, with ammunition running low and unfamiliar with the topography, the tiny force of three fit Gurkhas, two badly wounded men and a frightened Border Scout were

82

in an unviable position, Tejbahadur decided to abandon his position. Ignoring Kharkabahadur's demands to be left behind, over the next two hours, the group slowly dragged the two wounded across the stream into deep virgin jungle on another hill. An hour later, the IBTs attacked the hill and when they found it deserted, they speculatively machine-gunned and mortared the area for the rest of the day. After plundering Long Jawi in the evening, they then returned upstream with several Border Scout prisoners. One named Bit Epa, although bound hand and foot, dived over the side of a longboat. Others had escaped during the day. At Belaga, the failure of Long Jawi to radio in during the morning stand-to was attributed to poor communications.

Corporal Tejbahadur's group remained undetected. Low on food and medical supplies, in heavy rain, they had a miserable time. Anxious to report the situation and knowing that Battalion HQ would not yet be worried by the lack of communications, Tejbahadur hid the two wounded in deep jungle and then he and the remainder set off for Long Linau. Two days later, they reached the longhouse at Labuai and, although fed by the Iban headman, stayed in the jungle overnight. Next day, they paddled downstream in a borrowed longboat. By now, one of the escaped Border Scouts had reached Long Linau with a confused account of the fighting. Four days after the battle, when Tejbahadur's tattered and exhausted group also reached Long Linau, they hired a boatman to ferry them to Belaga where the cleanliness of their weapons impressed the Border Scout HQ.

The 1/2nd Gurkha Rifles Commanding Officer, Lieutenant Colonel John Clements MC* a tough veteran of the Burma and Malayan Emergency campaigns, believed that Muljono had established a staging post at the junction of the Jalangai, Rajang and Balui rivers, 5 miles downstream of Long Jawi; however the pursuit would be hindered by the mass of ridges, dense jungle and rivers pounded by monsoon rain. Attached to the Battalion were four 845 NAS Wessex helicopters and a naval ground crew, equally split between Song and Sibu. Keen not to compromise information gathered so far, Clements instructed the naval pilots to avoid flying over the area where the Indonesians were thought to be.

When Major Mole and a platoon from C Company landed at Long Jawi, they found the hamlet ransacked and deserted. Rifleman Kharkabahadur and the wounded policeman were crawling from their hiding place when they were shot at until they were recognized. Mole established Company HQ in the kampong and then set off to find Muljono's camp, however the going was atrocious – up and down jungle-clad ridges in torrential rain and always the threat of ambush.

Guided by Bit Epa, Mole arrived at the Bahau, another tributary, to find a torrent of muddy water hurtling toward the Rajang. Two helicopters were sent to ferry the Gurkhas across the river to a shingle bank. At this stage, Major Mole returned to resume command of C Company and Captain Digby Willoughby, the Battalion Adjutant, assumed command of the search.

Meanwhile on 1 October, 11 Platoon (Lieutenant (QGO) Pasbahadur Gurung) roped down to a prepared LP upriver from Long Jawi near Batang Balui, with instructions to block a likely escape route. The LP had been sabotaged with stakes but was not defended. Soon after they had landed, the sound of chugging outboards was heard and, springing a quick ambush, Pasbahadur, at point-blank range, shot up two longboats packed with twenty-six uniformed IBTs. One sank midstream and the other beached on rocks across the river, where it was abandoned, however none of his Gurkhas were good enough swimmers to search it. Next day, Willoughby, who had been sent by Clements to debrief Pasbahadur and gather items of intelligence value, swam to the longboat on an improvised line, and found a dead Indonesian, the 60mm mortar used at Long Jawi and the police radios taken from the school.

On 10 October, after two IBTs, thought to be survivors of Pasbadabur's ambush, were intercepted on the Sungei Aput and one killed, 845 NAS Squadron dropped a platoon to cover the boat stations at the junction of the Balui and Aput. A boat station marks the watershed and final navigable reaches where users left their boat, crossed the border and collected another boat. Another patrol was using a power saw that had been lowered 100-feet from a Wessex through the canopy so that the Gurkhas could widen a LP, when there was near disaster as parts of a tree they were cutting clipped the helicopter under-carriage. Three IBTs opened fire with a 0.30-inch machine gun but then walked into an ambush laid by the platoon landed half an hour earlier, one man was killed and the Browning captured.

On 12 October, Willoughby's platoon found the Indonesian camp through the dripping trees across the swollen Jalangai and when he and Bit Epa, on tethered lines, swam across the river, they found it was big enough to accommodate 150 men, and was now empty except for five new graves, seven mutilated Border Scouts and three longboats. These were used to ferry the platoon across the river, however one capsized in the swirling water and a Gurkha was drowned. Bit Epa made several tethered dives to find him without success, although he recovered weapons and equipment. Clements correctly believed that the camp was a staging post. Of five powered longboats known to be have been collected by the IBTs, two had been sunk by 11 Platoon and another had been abandoned after being surprised by an Auster near the Balui-Aput river junction. The remaining two were thought to have taken some of Muljono's men back across the border. The surviving IBTs faced a difficult trek to safety. Clements set more ambushes, however by the end of October there were no more signs of Muljono's men and it was assumed that those who had not crossed the border had died in the jungle.

The Indonesians thereafter infrequently penetrated Third Division. When A Squadron SAS moved into the Division, 3 Troop located Major Muljono's camp just inside Kalimantan, however retaliatory action was not permitted. It is not known why he executed the Border Scouts. It may have been because prisoners are an impediment to guerrilla forces – more likely, it was a warning of their fate if captured. In any event, the killings and the reaction by the two Gurkha battalions rebounded on the Indonesians and the locals began to trust the British. Long Jawi doomed the Scouts as uniformed auxiliaries and Lieutenant Colonel Cross was instructed by Major General Walker to convert them into maintaining the loyalty of the border communities and as an intelligence-gathering agency. Muljono was executed in 1967 after being found guilty of deposing the military commander of Yogyyakarta and declaring himself chair of the Revolutionary Council during the attempted coup by the PKI in October 1965. Long Jawi again reinforced the value of helicopters and proved that if pilots flew tactically using the contours of hills and valleys to screen engine noise, troops could be landed close to the enemy. Tactical flying could persuade enemy forces they were being pursued by a large force.

On 12 October, B Company, 1/10th Gurkha Rifles scored its first kill but also lost a man when a four-man enemy patrol attacked an ambush in the Nanga Biru area. From information collected at the scene, the indications were that the patrol was Indonesian Army. Twelve days later, a Border Scout rest and recreation camp at Selepong was attacked and the IBTs lost a man wounded and captured by the Scouts. When D Company, 1/2nd Gurkha Rifles despatched a clearing patrol and came under fire from a nearby ridge, the Gurkhas dislodged the enemy from a depression and killed a sentry and two others. C and D Companies then pursued the enemy to the border and captured several IBTs unable to keep up with the main body. A Chinese activist turned in by locals and two IBTs captured by Ibans lived to tell the tale. Another was shot dead by a Border Scout. Interrogation of the first prisoner suggested that three groups of fifty had crossed the border to attack border villages. With more incursions evident, the SAS asked for the Gurkha Independent Parachute Company to help strengthen the tripwire along the border.

85

In October, Dr Subandrio, who was becoming more influential in Confrontation, was appointed to command the new Crush Malaysia Command (Komando Ganyang Malaysia – KOGAM). He also controlled Section V of the Supreme Operations Command (Komando Operasi Tertinggi – KOTI) and had developed the Central Intelligence Bureau into a powerful rival to the Army's intelligence machine. Operations against East Malaysia came under Army command, while those against mainland Malaysia were devolved to the Navy.

On 13 November, a lull in activity was interrupted when an Indonesian Air Force B-25 Mitchell and two Mustang P-51 fighters flew over Kuching and buzzed several First Division positions, including Tebedu. When an Intelligence assessment suggested that Kuching Airport was at risk from an airborne assault, reinforced by two infantry battalions crossing the border, 2/10th Gurkha Rifles (Lieutenant Colonel Jack Fillingham), having spent just three weeks in Singapore after its first tour, were rushed back to Sarawak and deployed to Third Division. HQ 99 Gurkha Infantry Brigade had just taken over as HQ West Brigade and Fillingham complained to Brigadier Patterson that his deployment was ridiculous because his Battalion knew Second Division well. Major General Walker agreed and the Gurkhas moved to the west. HQ 3 Commando Brigade replaced Glennie's 'ad hoc' HQ as HQ East Brigade in North Borneo. Anti-aircraft guns and DShK 12.7mm machine guns in Kalimantan frequently fired on Commonwealth aircraft flying close to the border. And on 18 December, a Bofors shot down an Auster in Lundu District killing an RAF Chaplain, Wing Commander A.M. Ross, and wounding Sergeant Thackeray, the pilot.

In First Division, 40 Commando were bemused on 28 November when Indonesia radio announced that its forces had captured three of its bases. On New Year's Day, a four-man patrol led by Corporal Michael Marriot surprised a large group of IBTs resting in the jungle near Bau, despatching two but losing Marriot, killed. During the follow-up which lasted until 6 January, two rocket-propelled grenade launchers (RPGs) and an AR-15 Armalite rifle were recovered. The Armalite was not even on general issue to the US Armed Forces and Major General Walker had asked for some. It had probably been supplied by the CIA as part of its operations to undermine Sukarno.

Early in the New Year, 1/7th Gurkha Rifles (Lieutenant Colonel John Heelis), which had arrived in November 1963, were dealing with a seaborne incursion in Third Division by a sergeant commanding ten TNI and thirteen IBT. They had landed in September from a fishing boat near the estuary of the Sungei Rajang to arm, equip and train the CCO in preparation for the proposed uprising, to be stimulated by the attack on

86

Long Jawi, and were sheltered by Malays and Chinese in Paloh and Binatang, which were both at the mouth of the river. When news of the incursion reached Special Branch and HQ West Brigade, Brigadier Patterson instructed Heelis to deal with the problem. Heelis, who was directing operations against the CCO being supported by Indonesian gun-runners, tasked A Company (Major Denis O'Leary MBE MC), at Sarekei, to intercept the group. During the afternoon of 7 January, O'Leary embarked with Company HQ in the launch the *Jolly Bachelor* while 2 and 3 Platoons filed onto another launch, the *Layang-Layang*. Both towed two motorized longboats, each with a Jungle Police Squad section. About half an hour after the force had departed, a launch carrying a Special Branch officer from Sarikei intercepted the convoy and told O'Leary that it was imperative he assess very recently received information. Returning to the Police Station he learnt that an informer had ferried eight IBTs to Pulau Lobe Balei island, about 20 miles from the mouth of the Rajang. O'Leary feared that the Indonesians might be

MAP 9 - BATTLE OF LOBE BALIE ISLAND, 7 January 1964

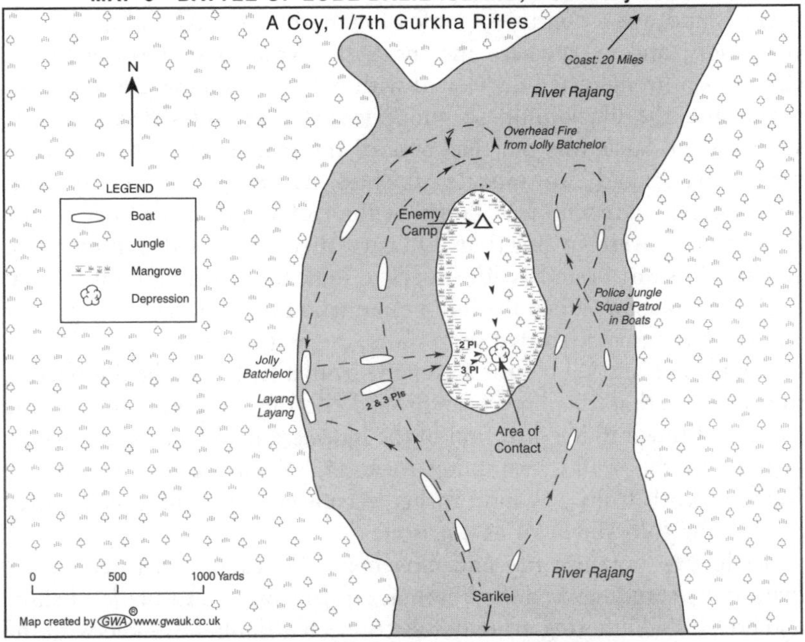

setting a trap, an experience he had encountered when pursuing the Red Flag Burmese insurgents in 1946, and was concerned about the reliability of the information, however he had precious little concrete knowledge of the intentions and strength of the group. Returning to the convoy chugging downstream, he planned that the *Jolly Batchelor* would hover at the northern end of the island, while 2 and 3 Platoons advanced from the south end.

The *Layang-Layang* was to lurk to the west while the Jungle Squad completed the encirclement to the east of the island.

At about 4.35 pm, the two platoons clambered into the two longboats off the south-west coast of Lobe Island. With radio silence in force, O'Leary, circling at the northern tip of the island, guessed that the platoons had landed and instructed his Company Sergeant Major (CSM) to fire a long speculative burst over the island, the idea being to stampede the IBTs from their, as yet, unidentified camp toward the cut-off group. Silence. Three more bursts. Still silence. Shortly after the *Jolly Bachelor* had joined the *Layang-Layang* near the western riverbank, there was the thump of grenades and crackle of rifle fire. When Sergeant Shamsherbahadur Rai, who was commanding 3 Platoon, radioed that he was in contact and had a man wounded in the face, O'Leary landed on the island with his runner and found the wounded Gurkha, a LMG gunner, angry at being hit but wanting to rejoin his platoon. O'Leary sent him back to the *Jolly Bachelor*.

The island was a confused tangle of mangrove and coastal trees, with vegetation, and everywhere the insatiable whining of mosquitoes. A close-range firefight had developed with bullets smacking into the vegetation and the black mud so slippery that both sides had difficulty standing up. Such was the thickness of the mangrove that shots were being exchanged at muzzle flashes. O'Leary found Sergeant Shamsherbahadur who told him that the LMG had opened fire before the platoons were in position. O'Leary then instructed 3 Platoon to advance in short bounds with orders to look for anything unusual that might be a person. When the Indonesian who had shot the LMG gunner was seen, O'Leary fired two snap shots, the first missing and the second taking his hat off. Asking for a grenade from a Rifleman, he discovered, to his horror, that it had not been primed. Slotting the detonator into the base, he threw it in the direction of the Indonesian and watched it feebly explode in the mud. Scrambling forward, O'Leary found his quarry feigning death from a wound to his shaven head and he was bundled back to the *Jolly Bachelor* as a prisoner.

Needing to organize fire and movement, O'Leary tried to contact 2 Platoon by standing up and shouting, but this drew a fusillade of shots and grenades. Slithering around 3 Platoon's left flank, he linked with the right-hand section of 2 Platoon, which was commanded by Rifleman Sherbahadur Limbu, but it was pinned down 30 yards from the enemy. While giving them orders, he then learnt that Sergeant Shamsherbahadur had been wounded and was lying in great pain about 15 yards in front of 3 Platoon. O'Leary tried to crawl to the Sergeant but after he was beaten back, he directed two men to protect him. He then he led both platoons in a systematic search for the Indonesian position and found it nestling in a shallow waterlogged depression protected by a few shady palm trees. Changing the direction of attack so that the Gurkhas advanced from the north, in the gathering gloom of a tropical evening, O'Leary, in Malay, invited the Indonesians to surrender. Someone replied, 'We can't. We are all dead,' but as the Gurkhas rose to advance, a big man dressed in muddy green fatigues charged but was cut down by rifle fire. In the depression, the Gurkhas found four badly wounded defenders. With one man already captured, two others wounded and one killed, the final two could not immediately be found. One was later captured by 2 Platoon as they swept through the island toward the Indonesian base at the northern end. Back at 3 Platoon, Rifleman Sherbahadur had crawled to Sergeant Shamsherbahadur and found that a bullet had grazed his spine. Two Royal Navy helicopters winched up the wounded Gurkhas and Indonesians, and took them to hospital in Sibu.

The eighth man, after swimming across the Rajang, gave himself up three days later to a Dayak longhouse. These Indonesians had proved determined. Meanwhile the hunt for the remaining insurgents continued. Eight days later, a Department of Marine Customs inspector noticed a fishing boat, previously reported as stolen, chugging downstream. A boarding party from A Company and several Sarawak Police Field Force was assembled, the boat was rammed when it failed to stop and the remaining Indonesians were captured. Rifleman Sherbahadur was awarded the MM for his leadership and courage and Major O'Leary received a bar to the MC that he had been awarded during the Second World War. In October 1966, he was appointed to command 1/7th Gurkhas Rifles after serving almost continuously through the Malayan Emergency and Confrontation.

CHAPTER EIGHT

The Defence of Fifth Division and Sabah

In October, Secretary of State for Defence, Peter Thorneycroft, wrote to Prime Minister Alec Douglas-Home outlining events in Borneo, and suggested that with increased Indonesian military involvement, there was a minimum requirement for eight infantry battalions. Five were already in Borneo, two were expected from the Malaysians and the eighth would have to come from either 28 Commonwealth Brigade or elsewhere in the Far East or UK, unless Australia and New Zealand could be persuaded to commit troops from the Brigade. There was also a need for additional field artillery. In any event, a third brigade HQ would have to be found from the UK and the shortage of troop-carrying helicopters resolved by converting RAF squadrons to fly Whirlwinds. Concerned that if Confrontation developed into a long commitment, Thorneycroft pondered if Great Britain could:

- Commit to NATO.

- Commit to SEATO.

- Maintain forces for intervention in Kuwait against Iraq.

- Provide its commitment to 28 Commonwealth Brigade and its role as the Commonwealth Strategic Reserve in South-East Asia.

- Respond to unforeseen circumstances.

In short, the Army was overstretched and in danger of losing its flexibility. On the plus side, the defence of Malaysia was essential to the stability of SEATO and the British contribution significant, nevertheless the financial implications were serious. The memorandum reminded the

Conservative Government that events in Malaysia needed to be taken seriously. When a report from Admiral Begg to the Chief of the Imperial General Staff resulted in confirmation of the British commitment in Borneo, by December, Major General Walker had created a third brigade in the knowledge that he would be reinforced:

- *West Brigade* (HQ 99 Gurkha Infantry Brigade) – First, Second and Third Divisions.

- *Central Brigade* (HQ 3 Commando Brigade) – Fourth and Fifth Divisions.

- *East Brigade* (an embryonic brigade HQ commanded by Brigadier Glennie) – Brunei and Sabah. Glennie was still Deputy Director of Operations.

By this time, the Army had raised a commando-trained Ordnance Field Park for the Royal Marines, but they spent so much time earning their Green Berets and on jungle training that they spent barely ten months in Sarawak, before being withdrawn with the Brigade to Singapore in February 1965.

Meanwhile, 4 Troop, A Squadron SAS was on a six-week patrol of the Pensiangan Gap watching for incursions through the seemingly difficult jungle. The only notable event was Sergeant Maurice Tudor being chased by a huge python that reared up to 4 feet. In November, Indonesian interest in Pensiangan was confirmed by a malaria control operator who reported that about thirty Indonesians had visited Bantul, Sabah on the 20th and, after throwing his kerosene into the river and stealing food and clothes, said that they would soon seize the town. Since the terrain was almost trackless with the only approaches into North Borneo from Labang and Lumbis, the Border Scouts information tripwire, some acting as fishermen on the rivers, spread out.

When Intelligence suggested an increase of Indonesian military activity, 1st Royal Leicesters (Lieutenant Colonel Peter Badger) replaced 2/6th Gurkha Rifles in East Brigade, they covered an area the size of Wales consisting of Fifth Division, Brunei and the Interior Residence of Sabah, except that it was not grassy mountain slopes but cultivated areas dispersed with jungle ridges. Earmarked as reinforcement during the Brunei Revolt, the Battalion was returning to the UK after an unaccompanied tour in Hong Kong and would complete five and half months in Borneo, the longest to be served by a British unit so far. The Battalion was reinforced by a composite 100-strong Troop (Lieutenant P. Barker) from 4th Field Regiment, Royal Artillery as 11 Platoon. Battalion HQ was in a partially built school in Brunei town and A

Company was based 250 miles away in Tawau, involved in operations against the Indonesian Marine Corps based on Sebatik Island. B Company was 20 miles away at Bangar in Fifth Division and C Company was 85 miles away at Lawas, patrolling the steep jungle-covered ridges, rugged tracks, rivers and streams flowing south across the border.

On 6 December, a villager reported that the previous day two Border Scouts had been captured by three IBTs north-west of the Pensiangan Gap and had been questioned on military activity around the town. When one of the Scouts escaped and was debriefed by C Company (Captain Colin Marshall) next day, it was obvious that a Wingate-style incursion commanded by a RPKAD major was aimed at Pensiangan. With the Indonesians north of the border and their target known, Lieutenant Colonel Badger conceived Operation Inglenook. It would be the first time a British battalion would be pitched against the Indonesians. Badger planned to lure the enemy 'sufficiently far into our territory so that he could be struck when he had no easy access over the border'. The lure was Pensiangan. Reinforced by a 1st Green Jackets platoon, 1st Leicesters surprised the incursion with ambushes and forced the IBTs to abandon some equipment. On one occasion, the Green Jackets spent several hours wading in a fast-flowing river, sometimes shoulder-deep, looking for an exit point. In spite of radio communication failures, it was clear by the 15th that the threat against Pensiangan had been defeated, nevertheless the Battalion was disappointed because of the lack of contacts. An interesting comment in *The Green Tiger*, the Battalion periodical, was 'There can never be too many or even enough helicopters.'

5 Platoon, B Company (Second Lieutenant Alan Thompson) at Ba Kelalan had developed an Intelligence network that included corresponding with a TNI Intelligence sergeant. The IBTs attacked the FDL several times and then, in mid-December, when Thompson heard that the Indonesians intended to install a DShK anti-aircraft machine gun on the border, on 29 December, he led patrol and found an Indonesian OP, which they booby-trapped. Returning on New Year's Day, Thompson, Lance Corporal Danny Dance (ex-Glosters in Korea, Israeli Army deserter and French Foreign Legion), three riflemen and a tracker found the loaded DShK on a tripod underneath a tarpaulin in a clearing about one hundred yards south of the border. In a nearby 'basha' were four TNI in blue shorts, white singlets and peaked soft caps. With the riflemen covering them, Thompson then invited the Indonesians to surrender. In the ensuing scuffle, one TNI was shot dead, two dived through the back of the 'basha' and the fourth was killed when the British tried to take him prisoner. While Thompson was photographing

the machine gun, he came under fire and so Dance quickly spiked the weapon before the patrol left the area. Since he had crossed the border, Thompson spent several anxious days worrying about it and was told not to discuss the action with Defence Secretary Thorneycroft when he visited the Battalion. He need not have worried and was later awarded the MC.

During this operation, Secretary of State for Defence Thorneycroft and Secretary of State for War James Ramsden visited Borneo, however neither impressed Major General Walker because they failed to ask him inquisitorial, searching questions. Instead, they seemed satisfied with briefings that they had received in London and Singapore, nevertheless Walker gave a justifiable tribute to Thorneycroft on the SAS: 'I regard 70 troopers of the SAS as being as valuable to me as 700 infantry in the hearts and minds, border surveillance, early warning, stay behind and eyes and ears with a sting.'

Unfortunately the quotation has been frequently misquoted by journalists and authors as 'I regard 70 troopers [a squadron] of the SAS as being as valuable to me as 700 infantry [a battalion].' This may well be the first occasion in which the SAS were inferred to be better trained than the rest of the Army, nevertheless Walker's statement should not be seen as doubting the quality of the Infantry. The small SAS patrols were part of an information-gathering process and were able to get close to the enemy. As we have seen and shall see, infantryman can also do that. But even for this to happen, the mundane business of information collation and analysis had to be carried out by Brigade, Divisional and Theatre Intelligence Sections. The role of the Infantry was to guard the border, react to incursions and maintain internal security, something that the SAS could not do. Later, infantry companies would slip into North Kalimantan and ambush communication and logistic routes. The Opposition Defence spokesman, Denis Healey, then arrived and impressed Walker with blunt comments and a firm grasp of the situation. It has often been said that the best allies of the Armed Forces is a Labour Government because few members have been officers. Healey, a former Royal Engineers officer, would prove a valuable ally.

The US was wary of Confrontation because she saw Indonesia as a strategically important regional chess piece in South-East Asia. President John F. Kennedy believed the PKI to be nationalist in outlook and therefore a valuable buffer against international communism. But London regarded negotiation as appeasement with an unpredictable head of state. Although US Assistant Secretary of State for the Far East, Averill Harriman, had been shown a highly classified document suggesting that Indonesia had little intention of negotiating a settlement with Great Britain and Malaysia, US Attorney-General Robert Kennedy surprised London by brokering a conference in Bangkok in February 1964 to establish a political platform from which to develop a solution. While UN Secretary-General U Thant appealed for a resolution to Confrontation, Indonesia needed a bargaining counter and selected Kalabakan, Tawau and Sandakan for a 'Wingate-style' incursion.

Sukarno believed that crippling the Malaysian economy would help his cause. Nestling around Tawau was a thriving maze of logging camps, most owned by the Bombay-Burma Company and worked by about 7,000 Indonesian migratory workers. Kalabakan was a town of 5,000 inhabitants, most employed by the Wallace Bay Ltd logging company, surrounded by tea estates, rubber plantations and cocoa and oil palm farms. From May 1963, until they were expelled in July, Major Moenardjo and Mr Bambang Sumali, both officials at the Indonesian Consulate at Jesselton, had been talent-spotting individuals for guerrilla training, and had weaned Indonesian and Chinese cultural, sport and social associations into subversive fronts. When the Indonesian Consulate in Sabah was closed after Malaysia Day, the pair targeted Indonesian workers with offers of land, better working conditions and pay.

Training camps had been established in October by the Indonesian Army and Marine Corps in North-East Kalimantan, and a massive publicity campaign of speeches, posters and cinema advertisements incited the rejection of Malaysia. Special Branch tackled these efforts and although there was some haemorrhaging to Indonesia, generally the local response was muted. The Indonesians then resorted to less subtle methods of forcing arrested cross-border traders, convicted criminals with knowledge of Sabah and former workers in Tawau district to enlist into 'volunteer' (pramuka) units. Eventually, thirty-five Indonesian Marine Corps and 128 volunteers, some of whom had had just two days instruction, were assembled for the operation. The leader was a pirate named 'Hendrix', who was well known to 1/10th Gurkha Rifles as a hardened criminal they had pursued in 1959 while on exercise in North Borneo. The force was divided into four detachments:

- N1 – eight marines and twenty-eight guerrillas commanded by Marine Sergeant Benni.

- N2 – fifteen marines and twenty-one guerrillas commanded by Sergeant Wayang.

- W1 – thirty-four men commanded by Sergeant Lasani.

- W2 – twenty-two men commanded by Marine Sergeant Lasani.

The plan was:

- Seize Kalabakan.

- Replenish with supplies.

- As Indonesian immigrants and sympathizers flocked to their colours, attack Tawau to the east.

An assumption was made that the Indonesian workers on the Borneo Abaca Estate and others sympathetic to Sukarno would provide safe areas, food and rest. Brigadier Glennie assessed that since the guardship deterred approaches from the sea, an attack on Tawau was more likely through the swampy jungle to the south. Raising the alert states and ordering aggressive patrolling, the SAS were instructed to cover the Pensiangan Gap. By 21 December, the Indonesians had reached Serudong and warned of their presence by raiding a shop for food. They lurked in a jungle camp near Kalabakan over Christmas week and then during the night of 29 December, approached Tawau to attack two Security Force bases.

C Company, 3rd Royal Malay Regiment (RMR), occupied the military post of two huts and several trenches. Battalion HQ was across Cowie Harbour at Wallace Bay. N Group approached the post from hills to the south, stealing food and weapons as it did and then, shortly before 11.00 pm, attacked by throwing grenades into the two huts, following up with machine-gun and rifle fire. The inexperienced Malaysians were totally unprepared and eight soldiers, including the company commander, Major Zainal Abidin Yaacob, were killed and sixteen wounded. They hardly returned fire. It was the greatest number of casualties suffered in a single attack on Commonwealth Forces during Confrontation.

Four hundred yards downstream was a fortified Sabah Police Mobile Force post, manned by fifteen officers, overlooking the estuary into Cowie Harbour at Kalabakan. When the Army post was attacked, the corporal in charge alerted his men and several local Home Guard and, in a two-hour battle, prevented the enemy from scaling the compound wire fence, forcing them to withdraw after losing one killed and four wounded. When the Indonesians rampaged through the village, the timber company manager ran to the Army post and encouraged the Malaysians to counter-attack, however, the shattered survivors had been shocked into inaction. Stealing a large quantity of rice, the raiders commandeered a Land Rover bringing loggers from work, killing one and wounding another. Three wounded IBTs were instructed to change into civilian clothes and make their way to Kalabakan, while three loggers were conscripted to guide the party to Brantian to the north, where the raiders lingered, waiting for the uprising – a fatal decision.

When Major General Walker learnt of the attack early on 30 December, he visited Tawau next morning and then asked Admiral Begg that 1/10th Gurkha Rifles (Lieutenant Colonel Burnett) be sent from Malacca. The Battalion had returned from Borneo three weeks earlier, nevertheless on 2 January 1964, Burnett was instructed to deploy to Sabah for a two-week emergency deployment. It would be reinforced by a 1st KOYLI company, two Ferret Scout Car Troops of the 1st (Malaysian) Federal Recce Regiment and helicopters initially provided by 103 Squadron RAF, and then by 846 NAS. A small RASC HQ (Lieutenant Frank Falle) and 31 Company, Gurkha Army Service Corps, distributed supplies shipped from 50 Supply Depot on Labuan and from local resources. Also available was the Tawau Assault Group which patrolled the inlets, creeks and swamps of Sabah. Formed by Brigadier Glennie, who was a keen yachtsman, it consisted of a disparate group of Royal Malaysian Navy patrol craft and several military and local motor vessels manned by the Royal Navy and Army, including a raft, named *Monitor*, which mounted a 3-inch mortar, and the Governor of Sabah's private launch named *Petrel*. A patrol base was on Simandalan Island and a patrol craft covered the channel between Sebatik Island and Sabah. On occasions, this vessel was subjected to harassing fire from Nunukan Island.

Major General Walker briefed Tunku Abdul Rahman, who had flown from Kuala Lumpur to visit the Malaysians, as diplomatically as he could, that they had been overwhelmed in a skilful attack, without mentioning that they had been unprepared. By late afternoon on 3 January, in a move not dissimilar to that of 1/2nd Gurkha Rifles responding to the Brunei Revolt, Burnett, his Tactical HQ and B Company (Major Richard Haddow) were at HQ East Brigade at Tawau. The rest of the Battalion arrived over the next two days, although 11 Platoon had fourteen men hospitalized in Singapore when a 3-ton truck tumbled down an embankment.

There was precious little intelligence, however the area where the Indonesians were believed to be was full of logging camps and thick secondary jungle littering the numerous rivers, lakes and swamps. To the east was the sea and Sebatik Island, half of which was occupied by the Indonesian Marine Corps. To the west was primary jungle leading to the rugged Brassey mountain range. There was still plenty of evidence of the Japanese occupation, including a destroyed railway bridge reminiscent of the film *Bridge over the River Kwai* and a complete narrow-gauge railway siding. Patrols had found wrecked Allied and Japanese aircraft in the jungle. B and C Companies, 1/10th Gurkha Rifles had several contacts and a 1st KOYLI patrol found a recently occupied camp for at least twenty-five men moving north. A useful piece of information gained by the Gurkhas was that some Indonesians had raided a shop in Brantian and that the remains of a chicken had been found on a jungle path a short distance upstream from Kalabakan. Based on this single report, Burnett assumed that food was the IBTs' first priority and therefore he decided to keep them hungry. Calculating that Brantian was the next target, he replaced the shattered Malaysians with an A Company platoon. When reports circulated that the Indonesians were begging, borrowing or stealing food, Burnett temporarily cleared several villages and kampongs and, sending a 1st KOYLI platoon to Kalabakan, corralled them into a killing triangle bordered by Kalabakan, Mawang and Brantian, and by ambushing the road from Wellawatta to Mawang. On 7 January, 5 Platoon (Lieutenant (QGO) Indrajit Limbu) was patrolling along a ridge 12 miles north of Kalabakan in going so bad that most of the platoon were 'portering' the packs of the leading section. At about 11.00 am, when the section ran into a frontal ambush, without hesitation they charged the Indonesian position, killing nine Indonesians, but losing a Corporal and a Rifleman. In this action, Lieutenant Indrajit was awarded the MC and Lance Corporal Nanabahadur the MM.

Both N Groups were trapped in the triangle and, over a period of ten days from 10 January, were decimated as they tried to breach the cordon of ambushes laid by A and C Companies, losing fifteen killed and six wounded. Two more Gurkhas were killed, one by a falling tree. Harried by A Company, which refused to allow them to break contact, the IBT survivors headed west toward the Sungei Serudong. While Gurkha OPs watched several villages, Wellawatta and the hamlet at the 16th Milestone were razed to prevent the enemy gathering food. Group W1 crossed the Serudong downstream and reached a logging camp at Umas Umas where A Company killed four more. By 30 January, twenty raiders had been killed, thirteen wounded and thirteen captured. C Company emerged after a month of operations in rags, wearing worn-out jungle boots and their hair uncustomarily long.

At the end of January 1964, HQ 5 Malaysian Brigade (Brigadier Dato Ismail) took over East Brigade from Glennie and, over the next month, maintained the immense pressure on the IBTs trapped in the web. Group W1 tried to break out by attacking HQ A Company at the Umas Umas logging camp but were interrupted by the guardship, the frigate HMS *Loch Killisport*, firing starshells at intermittent intervals throughout the night. The reinforcement of a platoon arrived during the night in a launch bravely skippered by a Chinese, who had been ambushed the previous day. W2 struggled through the mangrove hoping to be evacuated by the Marine Corps on Sebatik Island but after running into the Tawau Assault Group then had to contend with prowling helicopters during the day, with Shackletons dropping illumination flares and the frigate firing starshells at night. The IBTs did not stand a chance and by the end of March, 96 of the original 128 had been killed or captured, including 21 marines and Sergeants Lasani and Wayang. The survivors struggled across the border.

The Kalabakan raid was a major defeat from which the Indonesian Marines Corps never recovered and was a little-publicized victory for the Commonwealth Forces. When it again established, beyond doubt, Indonesian military involvement in cross-border operations, Sukarno's response was that such was the commitment of some military personnel to Confrontation that they were prepared to discard their unit loyalties to fight as volunteers. It was nonsense and everyone knew it. The discredited leader of the Brunei Revolt, A.M. Azahari, made an appearance at a press conference in Pontianak with Dr Subandrio and denied that the TNI was engaged in a border war. The attack was a deep embarrassment to Malaysia because its government had insisted its soldiers be placed in the same danger as the British, and although Malaysians deployed to East Malaysia did so with pride, many tailored their uniforms and were obsessively clean, used hair oil and talcum powder, and found it difficult to live like animals in the jungle. Interestingly, and in direct contrast to awards made in Northern Ireland, Burnett was the only battalion commander throughout Confrontation to receive the DSO, for his leadership in this operation – such are the eccentricities of those who scrutinize citations. Some officers suggested that the lean issue of awards was because Major General Walker was unpopular among the political and military establishment in London. In the confused chaos of Aden, gallantry medals were in equally short supply.

When a UN ceasefire was suggested for 25 January 1964 in preparation for the Bangkok Talks, Sukarno agreed because his battered forces in North Borneo needed time to recover and be seen as liberators. Major General Walker was unconvinced of Indonesian sincerity and issued orders that patrols were to engage only in self-defence, however the Malaysian National Operations Council instructed him to reduce internal security operations. This gave the CCO time and space to provoke internal unrest, reduce confidence in the Security Forces and heighten the political aspirations of Indonesia's disagreement with Malaysia by targeting the Sarawak Youth Front and the Borneo

Communist Party. The talks commenced on 5 February, however agreeing the terms of the ceasefire provided the first stumbling block. Whereas Malaysia regarded it as a signal for Indonesian forces and their surrogates to withdraw from East Malaysia, Sukarno took the conventional route as 'Weapons tight and stand fast until further orders.' This induced angry exchanges, which were heightened when the Malaysians infuriated the Indonesians by dropping surrender leaflets into areas known to contain IBTs. The Indonesians then issued a 'Stand firm and retaliate' followed by Indonesian aircraft flying 30 miles into Sabah airspace and dropping leaflets to reinforce the 'Stand firm' order to the Kalabakan raiders. These actions proved, beyond reasonable doubt, the presence of TNI units inside East Malaysia. As Malaysian Deputy Prime Minister Razak commented:

> As there are members of the Indonesian Armed Forces, Regulars as well as Irregulars, on the Malaysian side of the border, their presence will provoke incidents. The Malaysian Government therefore considers that the ceasefire would not be fully effective unless the Governments concerned agree to limit their activities and movements of their Armed Forces, Regulars as well as Irregulars, within their respective territories.

Dr Subandrio undertook to pave the way for the withdrawal of the 'volunteers' from East Malaysia, but this never materialized. The Indonesian delegation was disinclined to debate details to such an extent that the Malaysians accused them of inventing problems after solutions had been agreed. When the role of the British was discussed, the Indonesian argument seemed so imprecise and ill-informed that one frustrated Malaysian delegate asked, 'What do you want us to do about the British? Please be more precise.' Their answer was for Britain to withdraw from the region and Malaysia to work toward an Asian Malaysia as opposed to a member of the Commonwealth. Tunku Abdul Rahman emphasized that Malaysia was the aggrieved party and therefore unable to concede anything in the face of the aggression of Confrontation. It was up to Indonesia and the Philippines to offer alternatives, however Sukarno was under heavy pressure from the PKI and a further wave of violence and requisitioning of British companies reminded him against weakening. Eight days later, when Indonesia advised Thailand, who was supervising the ceasefire, that she wished to drop supplies to her 'volunteer' forces in East Malaysia, the Tunku was incensed, because it implied that they had good reason to be there, and announced that Malaysia would not attend any negotiations until Indonesian forces had withdrawn from Malaysian territory, and that captured enemy personnel would be treated as criminals, not as prisoners of war. Relations between the two protagonists worsened when Indonesia accused Malaysia of publicly compromising an opportunity for the Indonesian forces to withdraw without losing face. Dr Subandrio threatened that if Malaysia continued military operations, Indonesia would drop supplies to its forces. Malaysia closed her airspace and warned Indonesia not to do so. The talks finished on 10 February without agreement.

On 22 January 1964, three days before the Bangkok Talks ceasefire, Sergeant Bob Creighton's A Squadron SAS patrol covering the Long Pa Sia Bulge reported to HQ Central Brigade military boot prints of a large force using a track heading north from Long Tapadong into the Interior Residency. When his scouts then found a large abandoned enemy camp to the west of the Sungei Moming, Second Lieutenant Michael Peele and ten men from 6 Platoon, B Company, 1st Leicesters at Long Semado were ordered to destroy the enemy incursion in Operation Arrant. Flown to the Long Pa Sia border post perched 3,000 feet on a mountain top next day, Peele, unaware of the ceasefire, collected a section from 9 Platoon and two Border Scout guides. Next morning, the patrol found boot prints heading east, not north as expected, west of the Sungei Moming. Dumping their packs in a hide, Peele followed the spoor and found a large empty camp about a mile north of the border. When three distant shots were heard, the Scouts refused to carry on. At about 1.00 pm, the Leicesters came upon a second camp astride a stream and Peele despatched a fire support group of seven men under Corporal Walton to find a cut-off site to the south while he led the eleven-strong assault group toward the camp. Although the constraints of the jungle forced them into a narrow frontage, for twenty minutes, the eleven edged forward on their stomachs to within 40 yards of the camp until an Indonesian answering the call of nature literally stumbled onto them. Surprise lost, Peele shot him and then led a charge into the camp. A .30-inch Browning machine gun spat bullets across the clearing from behind a tree until its gunner was silenced by Private Tinsley, who fired a shot through the 18-inch tree trunk. Four other Indonesians were killed. Peele's men reorganized and beat off a courageous counter-attack by two men, killing one. None of the enemy who ran into Corporal Wallace's fire support group survived.

Peele estimated that the camp had accommodated at least sixty enemy, among the abandoned equipment being an incongruous black bus conductor's hat. Next day, he used plastic explosive to create a LP and relays of helicopters collected half a ton of captured equipment, arms and ammunition, including a Browning automatic rifle, a Sten gun, two

2-inch mortars and thousands of rounds of ammunition. Documents referred to 'Platoon S, Brunei Regiment, Kalimantan Utara' and named three TNKU thought to be in Temburong district. Another urged 'Down with Malaysia. Down with white neo-colonialism. Support AM Azahari', signed by a TNKU colonel '55001'. Sergeant Creighton arrived next day and captured two IBTs, who were more than happy to carry his Bergen. Under interrogation, they later revealed that the aim of the incursion was to carry out several raids with the help of TNKU activists in Brunei. Peele's action was a major coup and disrupted Indonesian aspirations in Temburong. It was the second action in which the Leicesters had clashed with the Indonesians. No longer would British battalions be relegated to internal security.

In the second week of March, Sergeant 'Smokey' Richardson was searching for evidence of Indonesian activity south of the Long Pa Sia Gap in a SAS patrol that is sometimes known as the Three Rivers Patrol. The 2/7th Gurkha Rifles platoon FLB at Long Pa Sia had regularly been mortared, an attack on Ba Kelalan was thought to be imminent and the presence of the RPKAD at Long Bawan was making the area tense. The area was mountainous and navigation sometimes so difficult that Richardson occasionally did not know where the border was. Two days after receiving a helicopter supply drop on 10 March, the patrol reached the Sungei Plandok and, while heading north intending to meet Sergeant Creighton at the Sungei Plandok, they found boot prints on a sandbank. An hour later, when a fisherman they hailed in Malay fled along a track, the SAS followed and discovered a TNI camp and then two large TNKU camps, both south of the Sungei Paling. From the information supplied by Richardson, HQ Central Brigade put out an alert.

When it turned out that the fisherman was one of a trio of sentries protecting the TNI camp, Major Roger Woodiwiss instructed Richardson to investigate the tracks heading north, however, when the depth of the jungle forced Richardson to use the track, Woodiwass, concerned that the patrol might be ambushed, instructed it to turn about. But Richardson, unsure of his location and believing that his patrol had been compromised, was concerned that returning to the two TNKU camps would take him deeper into Kalimantan. Nevertheless, he had reached them by the late afternoon, turned east and while looking for a place to lie up for the night, clashed at dusk with four RPKAD. In a frantic firefight, the SAS shot two Indonesians and then scattered to the emergency rendezvous, but by dawn, the signaller, Trooper James 'Paddy' Condon, had not arrived. Richardson and his scout, Corporal Tony Allen, found his Bergen but of Condon there was no sign. Woodiwiss became concerned when the patrol missed its scheduled radio transmission; a helicopter failed to find them. In fact, Richardson and his men were prowling around the three camps looking for Condon until, on 18 March, Woodiwass collected the three survivors. It later transpired that Condon had been captured after being badly wounded in the thigh. Thereafter, his fate remains a mystery in that he was either taken back to Jakarta, died in captivity or he was shot because he could not walk and was a hindrance to his captors. In any event, the body of this Irish member of the Parachute Regiment was not returned. He was the first British soldier to be killed operating inside Kalimantan and the circumstances of his death did not endear the SAS to the Indonesians.

On 1 June, Major Woodiwiss was leading a strong D Squadron patrol recceing the camps near the Plandok when they came under fire and withdrew a short distance. They then followed a frequently used track heading north of the river to Long Pa Sia where another set of tracks was found north of the border. On 6 June, the patrol was joined by the reinforced 14 Platoon, D Company, 2/7th Gurkha Rifles, but it was ambushed next day and Sergeant 'Buddha' Bexton, a SAS scout, was killed. Sensibly, the Indonesians gave the force no time to counter-attack and withdrew. Woodiwass found a camp for ninety men and, in a 'hot pursuit' operation, a Gurkha ambush was compromised by a dog.

Bigger commitments in the Radfan in South Yemen and the increase in infiltrations opposite Fifth Division and Sabah meant that the combination of border watching and 'hearts and minds' activities by the two SAS Squadrons was beyond their operational capability. To offset the shortages, HQ SAS reformed B Squadron and when the tough No. 1 (Guards) Independent Parachute Company (Major John Head, Irish Guards), which was on internal security duties with 16 Parachute Brigade in Cyprus, was earmarked for deployment to Borneo, they dismounted from their Ferret Scout Cars and Land Rover-mounted 120mm Wombat anti-tank guns. Re-organizing into four troops each of four patrols of four men, they began training with the SAS at Hereford. SAS proposals to raise additional squadrons, two from the Gurkhas and three from 16 Parachute Brigade and a second (Guards) Independent Parachute Company were rejected, however the Parachute Regiment agreed to form independent patrol companies. By August 1964, the SAS had raised an indigenous force of forty Ibans, known as the Cross-Border Scouts, to find forward Indonesian operating bases, watch SAS targets, scout for evidence of infiltration and provide guides. They were initially commanded by Major Muir Walker, the same officer who had infuriated the mob in Jakarta with his bagpipes. SAS 'hearts and minds' activities remained vital to maintaining an effective intelligence 'tripwire' so that when incursions occurred, the Security Forces could be warned. In Sabah, Sergeant 'Gypsy' Smith built a hydro-electric generator from a paddle and a bicycle in a stream near Talibakus, which, when connected to the house of the headman, provided the only lighting for 450 miles. He also distilled 'jungle juice' through the hollow frame of his Bergen. A concept pioneered by Woodiwiss was the 'Step Up' aimed at convincing Iban communities living near the border that if the Indonesians appeared at a longhouse, or were seen, then troops could be summoned very quickly by 'sending a message into the sky' (i.e. by radio).

CHAPTER NINE

Indonesian Escalation
January to May 1964

The collapse of the Bangkok Talks and the air incursions led to the Malaysian National Operations Council, on 24 February, ordering the Far East Air Force to impose an Air Defence Identification Zone (ADIZ) around East Malaysia to 3 miles offshore, the Rules of Engagement permitting attacking Indonesian aircraft. To police the airspace, pairs of 60 Squadron, and later 64 Squadron, Javelin Mark 9 all-weather interceptors, equipped with Firesteak air-to-air missiles, were deployed to Labuan and Kuching. 20 Squadron despatched eight Hawker Hunters with four each at Labuan and Kuching. Complementing the defence were 205 Squadron Shackletons patrolling the coast and liaising with Royal Navy and Malaysian Navy ships. Indonesian violations were not uncommon, however there is only one recorded interception when a Javelin met an Indonesian C-130 head on in a valley near the border. By the time the Javelin pilot had hauled his aircraft out of the valley and set off in pursuit, the C-130 had banked away into Kalimantan. Fighter ground attack was rare.

In early December 1964, the Infantry Trials and Development Unit from Warminster trialled the 'electronic ambush' in which a Tobias Intrusion Detector would detect the enemy and Claymore mines would be triggered remotely. On 30 December, C Company, 1/2nd Gurkha Rifles (Captain Bruce Jackman), after ten days in an electronic ambush on the border south of Ba Kelalan, reported that 11 Platoon (Lieutenant (QGO) Sukdeo Pun) was cut off by Indonesian marines after the technology had failed. The marines had stumbled across the ambush base while returning to Long Medan after getting lost on their way to attack the 6th Gurkha Rifles at Bario. Both sides were cut off. Without artillery support, outside the C Company mortar umbrella, with helicopters arranged but not immediately unavailable for at least four hours,

Hunter ground attack out of range and knowing it would take at least five hours on foot, Jackman despatched 9 Platoon and told Sukdeo to hang on. After about two and half hours, when Jackman was told that air support was arriving, to his surprise, a Javelin appeared. Directed from the ground to attack everything to the left of a large tree, the pilot, Flight Lieutenant Bob Langford, came in twice at low level and, as his jet reached the ridge, it reared up followed by two huge explosions as it soared into the clouds. Expecting to find the jungle flattened and burning, follow-up patrols by Jackman and 9 Platoon found only blood trails and abandoned weapons. In an aircraft not designed for ground attack, Langford had 'bombed' the marines by triggering his afterburners as he climbed, which caused huge bangs. It transpired that the Javelin had been scrambled to an Indonesian air incursion and had been diverted to support C Company.

While RAF Changi at Singapore was the main rear base, with its good, all-weather runway, Labuan became fully independent and developed into an important staging post supporting the forward bases throughout North Borneo. Initially a station of seventy-eight men, this rose to 500 in May 1964 and doubled the following year, most of whom lived in prefabricated huts. An initial problem with Labuan was that most RAF detachments left their Squadron HQs in Singapore and thus air traffic control was sometimes difficult. When the twelve Whirlwind 10s of 230 Squadron arrived with its air traffic control in March 1965 as the permanent helicopter force, there was relief.

Since there was no accommodation to house a battalion of 600 men at Labuan, troop rotations developed into a slick 24-hour operation, provided that the weather held and there were no mechanical breakdowns. During the early morning darkness, the incoming battalion arrived in Transport Command aircraft from Singapore, and, after transferring immediately to Belvedere and Whirlwind helicopters, were flown to their FLBs. Outgoing troops returned to Labuan in the helicopters where, still wearing their sweaty jungle uniforms and with their personal equipment, they were transferred to the transports for the evening flight to Singapore. Unit Emplaning Officers and RAF and RASC movement staff were kept busy checking destinations against manifestos to ensure that the correct troops embarked in the right aircraft at the right time. To give an idea of the air support given to the ground forces, between November 1964 and October 1965, the monthly average of consignments was 19,000 troops airlifted, 1,900,000 lb of supplies landed and 2,000,000 lb dropped by parachute or freefall from low level.

Generally two 34 Squadron Beverleys and two 215 Squadron Argosys were in Borneo supplying the military bases with heavy lift parachute drops. The robust Twin Pioneers of 209 Squadron, often operating to rough strips close to FLBs, provided close support by flying in men and supplies, and flying out casualties and small loads. They were also particularly valuable during troop rotations. The three-day cycle developed during the Malayan Emergency to air deliver supplies was activated:

- Day One. Brigade HQs collate and prioritize unit requisitions.

- Day Two. RAOC depots deliver consignments to Air Supply platoons who prepare them for loading.

- Early on Day Three. Stores assembled and packed into aircraft, which then depart at about midday.

Heavy drop systems included the Boscombe Down Stressed Supply Platform delivering 11,000 lb and the Medium Stressed Platform, which was eminently suitable for deliveries up to 18,000 lb. However, the platform wastage rate was high and delays could develop in recovering them, so the One-Ton Container was used extensively. Consisting of a plywood base board, a harness, canvas and parachute fixing points, and designed for loads up to 2,300 lb, Army air despatch could drop sixteen manually from a Beverley. The 3,000-lb net designed for helicopters could carry seventy-two jerrycans, seventy-two 10-man ration boxes or a mix of other supplies. The Belvedere could lift two nets. Parachutes recovered in East Malaysia, and not 'liberated' by the Army, were sent back to Singapore for drying, cleaning and repackaging, because no such facility existed in Borneo.

When 45th Light Regiment, RA (Lieutenant Colonel Lydekker), arrived in the Far East from Dortmund in October 1963, it supported 28 Commonwealth Brigade counter-revolutionary operations in north-east Thailand. Sent to Sarawak, it took over from 29 Commando Regiment after converting to Pack Howitzer from 25-pounders, and brought with it 2 Locating Radar Troop, 3rd Royal Horse Artillery (RHA) and its Green Archer mortar locating radar. 70 and 176 (Abu Klea) Light Batteries were reinforced by 103 Battery, Royal Australian Artillery, to bring the Regiment up to strength. The gun used was the Italian Oto Melara 105mm M56 Pack Howitzer. Designed to be broken down into portable components, it had a maximum range of about 11,000 yards, which was nearly 1,000 yards shorter than the 25-pounder, but it fired a more powerful shell. Its six gunners could fire an average of six rounds per minute. The Regiment also had 170 (Imjin) Medium Battery under command. Equipped with those reliable veterans of the Second World

106

War, the handsome 5.5-inch wheeled howitzers could throw an 82-lb shell up to 18,100 yards. Initially, there was disbelief when Lydekker was told that the Battery was to replace 145 (Maiwand) Commando Battery as the West Brigade reserve infantry company, however when a threat developed in Second Division in December, the Battery reverted to its gunner role under the command of 2/10th Gurkha Rifles. In the event that gun positions were overrun, the Director of Ordnance intended to replace lost artillery by shipping several 25-pounders, scheduled to be tipped into the South China Sea, from Singapore to some rear bases in Sarawak.

By 1964, the artillery was beginning to play an important role in providing close support, indirect fire missions to neighbouring FDLs and the registration and harassing of likely incursion routes. The problem of unreliable maps to register tracks was resolved by placing coloured parachutes on trees above the targets from which adjustments could then be made. The main enemy of inactivity in the FLBs was reduced by rotating gun crews through front and reserve gun detachments, and internal security patrols as 'infantilleria'. Maintaining gun positions revetted with corrugated iron and sandbags was a never-ending task, particularly during torrential downpours when positions were drained to ensure they were in a fit state for the guns to be brought into action with the minimum of delay on 'Take Post!' Doctoring revetments with cement and growing pineapples proved only partially successful. Ammunition Technical Officers (ATOs) inspected the quality of ammunition and destroyed, on site, deteriorating stocks exposed to hot, wet and humid conditions. 105mm ammunition was prone to damage when airdropped. It took one ATO forty days to inspect West Brigade. They also investigated accidents and defused terrorist devices and Second World War ordnance.

Gunner Paul Treen served with 16th Light Air Defence Regiment and completed two tours in Borneo. Posted from the All Arms Junior Leaders Regiment in 1964, weighed down with temperate and Far East uniforms in his issue suitcase, and with personal equipment and a greatcoat crammed into a kitbag, he reckoned the most difficult part of the journey to the Far East was the Underground from Woolwich to the Air Trooping Centre near the Houses of Parliament. Flown to Kuching from Singapore, Treen joined 30 (Roger's Company) Battery protecting the airfield. The Battery was divided into two 40/70mm Bofors Troops, each of four-gun subsections:

The daily routine was varied – gun drills, radar operating, manning the command post on the Battery radio net listening watch, equipment maintenance and site maintenance, much of it filling

107

sandbags, and aircraft recognition. Personal weapons were carried everywhere – towel, flip flops and SLR for a trip to the shower was a bit strange, at first. Whilst on the gun sites, each subsection had a ration allowance to purchase fresh food from a local contractor. The downside to this was one of the Gunners had to cook it. Troops would either be on Alert 2 readiness (two minutes warning), which entailed stand-tos at dusk and dawn or Alert 10 (ten minutes warning). If Alert 0 (imminent threat/or an unidentified aircraft warning), all Battery gun detachments would take post. Battery HQ staff manned observation posts several miles away from the airfield and would report all aircraft sightings on the Battery radio net.

On several occasions, the Gunners were flown to the border areas where the Battery also manned a 4.2-inch mortar. In spite of the effectiveness of artillery in the Burma campaign, some infantry were initially suspicious of guns. To them, the Royal Artillery motto 'Ubique' meant 'All over the place' as opposed to 'Everywhere'. The Gunners, ever the optimists, knew the jungle was not a hindrance and became indispensable.

Each battalion had a Forward Observation Officer (FOO), plus three signallers to provide artillery support. Part infantryman, part gunner, the teams had to be suitably matched with fit tough 'nuts' able to carry heavy loads up steep muddy slopes as important as the signaller with technical ability. The team carried an A41 VHF radio on the same frequency as the infantry command net and an A42 VHF radio to communicate with the guns, and also provide a back-up radio net for the infantry. The biggest problem was to site the antenna effectively. In contact with the enemy, FOOs usually moved forward to give corrections to the guns. Sometimes the closeness of the jungle meant that the fall of shot could not be seen, in which case a grid reference was given for a ranging shell, bold corrections given and then fire for effect.

The arrival of HQ 51 Infantry Brigade (Brigadier Harry Tuzo), from the Strategic Reserve, enabled Walker to reorganize for the second time in the year:

- *West Brigade* (HQ 99 Gurkha Infantry Brigade) – First, Second and Third Divisions. The border frontage of 623 miles was generally held by four battalions, including a Malaysian one. Kuching was defended by a battalion of the Singapore Regiment.

- *Central Brigade* (HQ 51 Infantry Brigade) – Fourth and Fifth Divisions and Brunei. Its border frontage was about 267 miles and defended by two battalions in Sarawak with a Singapore-based

British battalion on rotation in Brunei.

- *East Brigade* (HQ 5 Malaysian Infantry Brigade) – Sabah with a Royal Marines Commando and an infantry battalion but no helicopters. Offshore was the guardship and boats patrolling the creeks and waterways. The brigade patrolled 81 miles of land and 500 miles of coastal border.

With three Brigades in East Malaysia, HQ 17th Gurkha Infantry Division (Major General Peter Hunt, Cameronians) was established on Labuan. Major General Walker remained as Commander British Forces, Borneo, and Director of Borneo Operations, with his HQ still in Brunei town. The total number of troops under his command was about 10,000 men, far less than would be deployed in Northern Ireland throughout most of the Troubles.

51 Infantry Brigade was originally 63 Gurkha Infantry Brigade, which had arrived in Tidworth from Malaya in April 1962 with a small battle group built around 1/6th Gurkha Rifles. It was the first time that Gurkhas, some of whom were accompanied by their families, were stationed in the UK. The Brigade trained in West Germany and Norway, the intention being to rotate the eight Gurkha battalions with the Reserve. Their return to the Far East was greeted with sadness by many Britons impressed by the quiet dignity of the Gurkha soldier, about whom they had heard so much. The Battalion arrived in Borneo in February for its first tour and was initially posted to the western half of Third Division, except for B Company which was the West Brigade reserve. In March, the Battalion less C Company was deployed to First Division.

Throughout the Bangkok Talks, First Division was troubled by enemy activity. Two IBT platoons, assisted by the Sarawak United People's Party, penetrated Lundu District intent on a Wingate-style raid in the vicinity of Gunong Gading, a towering mountain that overlooked forest and cultivated farmland. 42 Commando, in its fourth tour since December 1962, had arrived in Lundu in late January. Joined by B Company, 1/6th Gurkha Rifles, which was the Brigade Reserve, the Commando was instructed by HQ West Brigade to deny the insurgents food in Operation Dragon's Teeth. Initially, things did not go well for the Royal Marines.

On 20 February, 5 Troop, L Company (Second Lieutenant Christie-Miller), which had suffered so grievously at Limbang, were searching communities north of Sekabal, about 3 miles north of Lundu, when Corporal Chapple's section came across an anxious Chinese farmer keen to dissuade them from searching his hut on the edge of the jungle. When it was, Marine Jim Gooding found three large sacks of rice and two outboard engines, which immediately aroused suspicion. Leaving Chapple and a half-section at the hut, Christie-Miller returned to his patrol base, unaware that the search had been watched by twenty IBTs commanded by Kasson bin Somento. Somento had not attacked because the Royal Marines had a Bren gun. At about 10.30 pm, the silence of the night was briefly undermined by automatic gunfire and explosions from the area of the hut, and then Marine 'Oggie' Howes staggered into the base with the news that Chapple had been killed and the remainder of the patrol wounded in a short battle. In pitch darkness, Flying Officers Warren and Danger, of 225 Squadron, left Lundu in two Whirlwinds loaded with troops. Howes insisted on guiding the Royal Marines through the darkness to the hut, each man linked with a toggle rope, which they reached at about 1.30 am. It was still being defended, but it was a wreck and there were two badly wounded Royal Marines. At least the Chinese was a prisoner and while he was being interrogated by a Sarawak Police Field Force policeman, a detailed search of his land unearthed incriminating evidence of his collusion with the IBTs; he admitted to harbouring Samento's group. The second helicopter landed an 'infantilleria' patrol from 170 (Imjin) Medium Battery commanded by Second Lieutenant Carter. His Iban scouts quickly found tracks and over the next thirty hours, the Gunners harried Somento and his men, forcing them to discard weapons and equipment as they hurried for the frontier, which they crossed just twenty minutes ahead of Carter.

Next night, the Sarawak Police Field Force post at Tringgus was attacked by about fifty IBT and although they lost two officers killed and six wounded, the police fought back with vigour. For the next two months, the Security Forces struggled to contain this incursion. During the last three days of February, the Gurkhas killed three enemy in three days and the Police killed four IBT in an ambush. The interrogation of two shocked IBTs who surrendered to K Company, 42 Commando, suggested that, contrary to the suspicions that the IBTs had crossed back into Indonesia, some had actually filtered into the area around Pang Tebang. Four more incursions infiltrated into Lundu District in March.

When locals reported lights in the area of Sempadi Forest Reserve, Lieutenant Paddy Ashdown, the future Liberal Democrat politician, led a combined Royal Marines/Gurkha force in pursuit, which then developed into a paperchase as the IBTs discarded equipment, rations and documents. Surprise was lost whilst attacking a camp on 6 March when a patrol was seen by an Indonesian filling his water bottle, nevertheless, in a brisk battle, the Indonesians split into small parties, leaving behind a mass of equipment. Dayaks later reported finding bodies in or near the river, suggesting that some survivors had returned across the border. On 21 March, a dog team commanded by Sergeant Howe, of 42 Commando, following tracks near Biawak, practically walked into a jungle camp when the dog failed to point in heavy rain. A K Company cordon and search of Musi on 30 March trapped eleven Sarawak United People's Party suspected of supplying the Indonesians with food, supplies and information. A week later, after villagers had reported that several IBT had stolen food from a shop near Serbabak, 3 Troop ambushed an IBT patrol and killed three, but were themselves ambushed on 13 April, losing Corporal Hinds, Marine McCrea and two Border Scouts. By the end of Operation Dragon's Teeth, five Indonesians had been killed and four captured including a platoon commander, who turned out to be a regular NCO.

The second round of the Bangkok Talks opened on 4 March with Malaysia again insisting on a complete withdrawal of Indonesian forces from East Malaysia and reminding Dr Subandrio that he had undertaken to seek authority, at the first conference, to do so. Subandrio denied making any such suggestion but claimed Indonesia was prepared to accept a staggered withdrawal – dependent on political progress toward an Asian Malaysia. When Malaysian Foreign Minister Razak declared this unacceptable, his remarks were constrained by elections in April. With the ceasefire now virtually in tatters, Malaysia, fully expecting Indonesia to invade Borneo and widen its regional operations, announced the conscription of 100,000 men from the 21 to 29 age group. This was not a symbolic gesture but a clear signal to Indonesia that Malaysia was determined to resist interference. Orders were sent by the Malaysian National Operations Council to Major General Walker to resume operations and using 'all possible means ... by eliminating all Indonesian border terrorists in Malaysian territory'. Tunku Abdul Rahman's overwhelming victory in the elections then wrecked any notion of negotiations so long as Indonesian forces were on Malaysian territory. Attempts by the Philippines and Thailand to break the deadlock foundered, nevertheless the door was left ajar for Indonesia to withdraw without losing face with agreement for talks to be held in Tokyo in the middle of the year. Meanwhile, the fighting continued.

As we have seen, the north-east coast of Borneo was defended by a guardship, usually a destroyer supported by a minesweeper support ship and vessels from the British 6th Minesweeper Squadron and, from 1964, the 16th (Australian) Minesweeper Squadron. The ships quietly exerted such pressure that only on a very few occasions did the Indonesians infiltrate men and material into Sabah by sea. The Ton-class minesweepers, which could carry up to 200 troops, were sometimes used to transport troops down rivers, such as the Rajang, although this did lead one Royal Navy officer to complain that 'We sometimes think the Army imagines that we exist to transport them. I suppose from a soldier's outlook this is understandable and they are quite right in thinking we are the only safe, effective and fast means of moving sizeable bodies of troops operationally in Borneo.'

How often through the centuries have Royal Navy officers expressed the same sentiments, even if few complained when Royal Marines used ships as a method of transport! Confrontation turned out to be suitable for waterborne operations and, like the raiding forces of the Western Desert in the Second World War, several units emerged.

In October 1964, 2 Special Boat Section (2 SBS) joined the Tawau Assault Group as a specialist raiding force to disrupt Indonesian ambitions to target the timber trade in Sabah. From its Wallace Bay headquarters, it patrolled the coast in Gemini inflatable boats and a launch monitoring coasters, junks and local boats, and manned an OP from a dead tree near the border on the Sabah side of Sebatik Island with a view to Indonesian bases on Nanukan Island. The Indonesian Marines kept a similar watch from the south-east coast of the island.

Naval Party Kilo (NP) was evolved after two officers and several ratings from the escort maintenance ship, HMS *Hartland Point*, which was on refit in Singapore, were drafted to Sarawak to patrol the coast and rivers from Kuching in armed native boats called 'kotaks'. Replaced by several Boom Defence Technicians from HMS *Safeguard*, whose trade required them to be expert small-boat handlers, NP Kilo was strengthened by two vessels skippered by NCOs from the RASC maritime branch. Former Second World War Landing Craft Assault (LCA), pleasure cruisers, naval stores tenders and pinnaces joined the flotilla, and since the work demanded junior leadership, vessels were commanded by a Leading Seaman (or a Corporal), with a ship's company of an Able Seaman (or Lance Corporal), a radio operator, a mechanic and a Malaysian Marine Police officer as an interpreter. The boats were armed with a LMG. In *The Times* Letters to the Editor in January 2003, a correspondent suggested that NP Kilo achieved the distinction of using cutlasses for the last time in action. Each vessel usually had bunk accommodation supported by scrounged tables and chairs, and flew their respective naval White and Army Blue ensigns. Drinking water was carried in jerrycans. The rig of the men was usually black issue swimming trunks, or shorts, and a sheath knife, although when searching, a shirt was usually worn – to add formality and not to offend locals. On official visits to communities, the rig was jungle greens and a sailor's cap for the Royal Navy and beret for the Army. On occasion, while working inshore, assistance was sought from minesweepers to stop seagoing vessels. Such opportunities were taken to shower and have a square meal. The flotilla had its own broadsheet, *The Kilo Herald*, with a regular readership of fifty. Every week, Senior Naval Officer, Kuching, such as Lieutenant Commander John Rogers, visited the detachments to hand out pay and deal with operational and administrative issues. Rogers, a naval pilot who once managed to ditch a Gannet, named one boat *Fishhead*.

A prime role of NP Kilo was to patrol the 60 miles of coves and inlets from Kuching and to the border at Cape Datu. The Tanjong Dato lighthouse was a valuable OP for watching for smuggling and incursions from the sea. A forward base was established at Sematan. Patrolling rivers, searching native craft, 'hearts and minds' visits, ferrying patrols and gathering intelligence on subversive and coastal activity was standard. When demanding to search, the little ships raised the internationally blue and yellow K flag – 'Stop Instantly' – although it is doubtful if the average Sarawak boatman knew it. More influential was the LMG. The RASC Vessel *Forsa*, a cabin cruiser which was reputed to have been used previously as a senior officer's *banyan* (picnic) boat, intercepted a group of CCO in August 1964. Not everyone wanted to be stopped. After the landing craft HMS *Skull* had been rammed by a passenger craft, its commander reinforced the sides with robust wood so that when the two next met, the riverboat came off worst. Some vessels were enticed onto rocks and shoals by 'wreckers' shining lights.

When the SBS maritime patrols were withdrawn, Lieutenant Colonel Lydekker was asked to produce a force from 45th Light Regiment. Among his officers was Second Lieutenant Tony Hunter-Choat, of 176 (Abu Klea) Battery, who had been decorated while serving with the French Foreign Legion 1er Regiment Etranger de Parachutiste as a NCO in Algeria. When the Royal Marines objected to '176 SBS', it was renamed 176 Observation Post and Small Boat Party. Allocated Sergeant Buxton, from 102 Field Battery, RAA, five bombardiers and lance bombardiers, and ten gunners, most of whom were not wanted by their parent batteries, they rose to the challenge. Introduced to watermanship by the Royal Marines, the principal craft was the Gemini inflatable powered by the Johnson 40 outboard, an engine not renowned for its reliability. Two members of the Party and a Royal Marines sergeant spent seven hours drifting out to sea in a 15-foot swell, when their engine and radio failed, until they were rescued by the Royal Navy. On 1 September 1964, 176 Observation Post and Boat Party was declared operational but such was the poor state of the Geminis that a bid was sent to 3 Commando Brigade in Singapore for replacements; the silence was deafening. Based at Sematan, the Party took over several OPs, some as close as 100 yards to Indonesian positions. Patrols usually left after dark and, for the next twenty-four hours, loitered in the operational sectors. Changeovers at shore OPs sometimes meant surfing ashore in a heavy swell. When, in October, it became too dangerous for close inshore work, the patrols and OPs were withdrawn and 176 Observation Post and Small Boat Party was disbanded to a well-deserved accolade from Brigadier Patterson.

At dusk on 6 March, Ibans living in a longhouse near the 2,000-foot Kling Klang range, in Second Division, reported to A Company, 2/10th Gurkha Rifles (Major Ian Mayman) that they had seen smoke rising from the border area near Track 6. Tracks 6 and 6A were about 400-yards apart and separated by a steep escarpment until they gradually converged to meet in Sarawak and led down to the road linking Kuching, Serian and Simanggang. It was always of some surprise that the Indonesians rarely attacked this artery.

On receiving this report, Mayman ordered 2 Platoon (Lieutenant (QGO) Karamdhoj Sunwar) to ambush both tracks during the night and if nothing happened, to move up the two tracks towards the border simultaneously at first light. When, during the morning of 7 March, Karamdhoj reported to Mayman that military radio and music was blaring from a transistor radio at the top of the ridge, Mayman joined Karamdhoj and summoned 1 Platoon (Lieutenant (QGO) Purandhoj Rai). Two recce patrols then reported uniformed Indonesians occupying positions among rocky outcrops on the ridge straddling the border. It was almost an impregnable position. Lieutenant Colonel Fillingham, CO of 2/10th Gurkha Rifles, had arrived at the bottom of Track 6 and, after receiving a report from Mayman, he ordered A Company to attack the Indonesians without delay. After a quick recce, Mayman ordered 1 Platoon to carry out a deep encircling movement to trap the Indonesians north of the border and prevent their return to Kalimantan. 2 Platoon was to keep the enemy occupied with a feint assault up Track 6 until 1 Platoon was ready to attack.

Hardly had Mayman given his orders when firing broke at the top of Track 6A. It emerged that a 2 Platoon section commander, Corporal Birbahadur Rai, had moved forward from his ambush position with two Gurkhas to observe the enemy and, in the thickness of the jungle, had been killed in a close-range clash with an Indonesian outpost. When the Indonesians tried to seize his body, Birbahadur's two colleagues resisted until the rest of the Section arrived. From the controlled fire developing from the main Indonesian position, it was obvious that the enemy were well trained and, fearing that they might withdraw, Mayman ordered an immediate frontal attack having instructed 1 Platoon to find a way around to their rear.

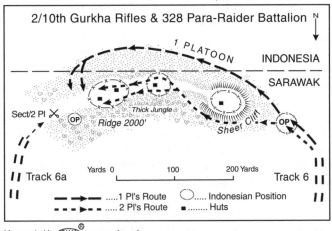

MAP 10 - BATTLE OF TRACK 6, 7 March 1964

2/10th Gurkha Rifles & 328 Para-Raider Battalion

1 PLATOON

INDONESIA

SARAWAK

Sect/2 Pl

OP

Thick Jungle

Ridge 2000'

Sheer Cliff

OP

Track 6a

Yards 0   100   200 Yards

Track 6

— ➤ — .....1 Pl's Route   ◠..... Indonesian Position
- - ➤ - .....2 Pl's Route   ■ .... Huts

Map created by GWA® www.gwauk.co.uk

As 2 Platoon began their feint attack, it came under fire from the outcrops and lost a Rifleman killed. Two sections attacked the Indonesians' left flank and forced them to abandon a forward OP, however as they emerged from the jungle, the Gurkhas found themselves on a narrow ledge at the foot of a steep hill under heavy fire with bullets pinging off the rock faces. To their left was an escarpment. The Gurkhas could only move in single file and were trapped. Mayman instructed them to take cover as best they could and went to contact 1 Platoon.

Learning from Purandhoj that 1 Platoon was scaling the steep hill to the enemy position, Mayman told him that he must take the pressure off 2 Platoon and quickly. Returning to 2 Platoon, Mayman found that there were two casualties, ammunition was running short and morale was wobbling. Believing that the best alternative was a charge, he posted Lance Corporal Keshbahadur's section on the left and Lance Corporal Damberbahadur to the right, and then charged through a smoke screen into unexpectedly open country interspersed by tall trees. Heavy fire was coming from an Indonesian position covering the exit from the ledge and unless this was silenced, the two sections would be pinned down. Mayman and a Bren gunner reached a small hump, however the gunner was fatally wounded and Mayman manned the gun while Damberbahadur's section overran the position. When the Indonesian commander realized that he was in danger of being outflanked and withdrew to a third position to the east, covered by his machine guns, 2 Platoon gave him little opportunity to settle down. Although the Indonesians resisted fiercely, the Gurkhas, some with drawn kukris, drove them from the outcrop into the path of 1 Platoon who had cut the

115

track south by crossing the border. By 4.15 pm, after a three-hour battle, the Indonesians had withdrawn at the cost of five killed and eight wounded. In an intercepted radio transmission to their HQ the following day, when they stated that they had wounded and were in considerable difficulties, they were told to get on with the operation because there were plenty of replacements. They withdrew, leaving a mixed force of eighty TNIs and Chinese IBTs on a large hill near Kluah commanding an excellent view of British activity to the north.

Among the material captured was the nominal role of 328 Para-Raider Battalion, which was part of the Kujang Regiment of the elite Siliwangi Division, and again conclusively proved TNI collusion in East Malaysia. The battle was the first in Confrontation to develop from a platoon commander's engagement into a company commander's action – from it Major Mayman identified some serious deficiencies, in particular that after years of training and using Malayan Emergency tactics, his Gurkhas had forgotten basic fire and movement tactics and must relearn from *The Infantry Platoon in Battle* pamphlet. The passage of information over the radio had failed because signallers did not find positions for successful communications. Following the Malayan Emergency experience, troops carried sufficient ammunition for a short engagement. This battle had lasted over three hours of near continuous firing and 2 Platoon had used nearly all their ammunition. Proper fire control was essential, as was a heavier ammunition load. More importantly, some section commanders had failed to lead.

Continued incursions in the same area became evident when, on 24 March, a captured Border Scout was taken to the Kling Klang range and shown three separate camps, each for about 100 men, inside Sarawak and was told by his Indonesian captors that they could, and would, cross the border at will. Lieutenant Colonel Fillingham assumed them to be elements of 328 Para-Raider Battalion connected with the Track 6 group and drew up Operation Blunt. In one of the few all-arms actions of Confrontation, he was reinforced by two Saladins from B Squadron, QRIH, a section of three Pack Howitzers from B Troop, 70 Light Battery (Major J.B. Keenan) and Wessex helicopters of 845 NAS equipped with SS-11 missiles, which could only be fired with the direct permission of the Chief of the Defence Staff, Lord Louis Mountbatten – in London.

Fillingham was keen to resolve this incursion because Intelligence reported that a 240-strong enemy force had been reported by Ibans making their way up the Sungei Ai in the Jambu area. Needing to fight one battle at a time and since the Indonesian camps were in its area, Fillingham instructed A Company to attack them, however the Scout's description of their position was vague. Spending two days with him in a helicopter and on foot searching the Kling Klang crest line, Mayman identified three probable positions, right on the border, each consisting of three huge 350-foot slabs of rock poking through the jungle canopy. In the final helicopter recce, Mayman and the Border Scout were accompanied by Major General Walker. Fillingham decided to winkle the enemy from their positions using artillery and would control operations himself from an Auster.

Two anxious days were spent waiting for Mountbatten's authority to use the SS-11s and when it arrived on 31 March, H-Hour was slipped until the sun had burnt off the mist protecting the Indonesian positions. At 9.29 am on 31 March, the Wessexes fired five missiles and then the Saladins and B Troop opened fire. A Company was advancing up the feature when a fusillade broke out above them as the Indonesians opened fire on Fillingham's Auster. The Gurkhas pressed on and, by about 10.30 am, had reached the first camp to find it abandoned and badly damaged by the shelling. The leading platoon then broke into the second camp, killing one enemy and finding it also damaged. The third, larger camp was a further 200 yards on top of the hill, also evacuated, however machine gunners were covering the Indonesian withdrawal south. Operation Blunt was achieved without a single casualty. As important was the fact that Indonesians never returned to the area for the rest of Confrontation.

While A Company was dealing with 328 Para-Raider Battalion, B Company (Major Tony Benn) searched for the 240 Indonesians reported in the Jambu area. Locals suggested that about ninety TNI had returned across the border with IBTs and porters, but another incursion was expected. When Fillingham returned to Battalion HQ after the Battle of Track 6, C Company reported that the expected incursion had occurred in the Jambu area in deep jungle about 30 miles north-east of Simanggang and consisted of thirty-six men from the Black Cobra Battalion plus several IBTs commanded by Major Audy Patawari. The country favoured them and it was not until 5 April that Intelligence confirmed the Black Cobras were inside Sarawak when they opened fire at an Iban hunting party. Fillingham assigned the rest of his tactical area to Major Mayman and concentrated his Battalion to deal with the incursion. By 10 March, B Company was covering likely incursions 20 miles from the border and was supported by D Company, the Gurkha Independent Parachute Company, 845 NAS, which included a Wessex fitted as a gunship, and a Sarawak Police Field Force company. In Operation Sabre Tooth, Fillingham planned to invite the Indonesians into a net and then bounce them through real and supposed ambushes, and reduce their effectiveness by keeping them on the move, undecided what to do next.

C Company, which was the Battalion reserve at Jambu and in position to cut the Indonesian escape route, followed the spoor of the Black Cobras, and, in teeming rain, harried them along tracks skirting the razor-backed hills, across rivers and through occasional cultivated patches near isolated longhouses. Leaving B Company in a blocking position near Jambu, Fillingham covered border crossing points with the rest of the Battalion and the Gurkha Independent Parachute Company, and then, using the 'deception and guile' demanded by Major General Walker, had Wessexes pretend to drop troops into the jungle while the 'gunship' patrolled the Rajang, firing occasional machine-gun bursts to persuade the Indonesians to turn toward C Company. 2/10th Gurkha Rifles later claimed that one IBT had been killed by the 'gunship'. Platoons forced-marched through the night to be in ambush positions by dawn and survived on one meal a day to avoid supplies being dropped. Unnerved by the activity and bounced around in the 2/10th Gurkha Rifles' net, which prevented them from collecting food from longhouses or even finding something to eat in the jungle, Major Patawari withdrew south. On 7 April, his column was attacked by B Company while resting. Grabbing personal weapons, the Black Cobras abandoned packs, weapons and supplies and some left the IBTs to their fate by making for the border. Gurkhas dropped by helicopter closed gaps in the cordon and over the next three days in three contacts, seven more Black Cobras were killed.

Six, scavenging for food, were captured by a Sarawak Police Field Force Sergeant Major on leave in his longhouse and were then decapitated by Iban headhunters. Meanwhile, Lieutenant Brian O'Flaherty, who was detached to the Border Scouts from 2/10th Gurkha Rifles, was being poled along the Rajang to visit his men. Invited to stay at the longhouse, when supper turned out to be rice topped by six heads, he arranged for them to be sent in biscuit tins by helicopter to Kuching for identification, however when this was completed, the heads became muddled with fresh rations and were dropped to B Company. On 12 April, B Company Lance Corporal Mandhoj Rai and another Gurkha were moving between two positions when they were ambushed by four enemy. Diving for cover as a grenade was thrown at them, Mandhoj calmly stepped back onto the track and picked off three Indonesians while his companion shot the fourth. By the time Operation Sabre Tooth was terminated in mid-April, 2/10th Gurkha Rifles had accounted for seventeen Black Cobras killed, including three who died of their wounds, and captured seven from the thirty-six who had crossed the border. B Company had been in ambush positions for five weeks. The sheer physical fitness of the Gurkhas and their shooting were skills that the Indonesians simply could not match.

Meanwhile, 70 Battery had initially been deployed as infantry role in First Division. When, on 22 March, Intelligence confirmed increased cross-border Wingate-style raids by the Indonesian Army, two Troops reverted to their artillery role, leaving A Troop (Captain Don Quinn) based at the Batu Kitang waterworks, not far from Kuching. Quinn was on loan from 103 Battery, Royal Australian Artillery, as was his Battery Sergeant Major, Warrant Officer II Almond. B Troop (Captain Flowers) supported 2/10th Gurkha Rifles from Batu Lintang in Second Division, which had been the site of a civilian internment camp during the Second World War. On 26 April, after six of the Troop were wounded when the longhouse was mortared and machine-gunned, Lieutenant Colonel Lydekker dispersed the Pack Howitzers in single detachments in FLBs. Each detachment consisted of the gun crew, a signaller, a surveyor and either a fitter, cook or member of a FOO party – the idea being that if a detachment was overrun, the risk to other trade groups was minimized.

CHAPTER TEN

Special Operations and Hot Pursuit

For nearly a year, the Indonesians had been sending surrogate forces into East Malaysia without much interference until they crossed the border. The pattern of Indonesian operations generally remained deep Wingate-type incursions to seize 'liberated areas', and shallow penetration to inhibit and destabilize the local communities along rivers close to the border. The first three months of 1964 had seen increased evidence of the Indonesian Army and, as a consequence, the fighting had become harder. Unless they cannot sally forth, military commanders do not like defending because a fundamental military principle is that attack is the best form of defence for it can destabilize enemy intentions.

In a highly classified assessment dated 25 March, Brigadier Patterson wrote to Major General Walker his assessment that West Brigade was facing 328 Para-Raider Battalion of the Siliwangi Division, and that it was reinforced by three companies of 428 Para-Raider Battalion from the Diponegoro Division, totalling eight Para-Raider companies. There were also about six Brunei Regiment battalions in First and Second Divisions, each about 200 all ranks, with a seventh one facing Third Division, giving an estimated combat strength of about 2,500 men. It was known that in 1963 at least 1,000 CCO had crossed into Kalimantan as refugees and were now infiltrating back in dribs and drabs. They would be supported by nearly 24,000 sympathizers throughout Sarawak, supplying moral backing, shelter, food, medical supplies and guides. Patterson believed that while the Indonesian strategy was for the IBTs and TNI to cross the border, establish Wingate-style strongholds and then generate civil unrest with the CCO, he believed there might be a conflict of interest. Assessing that the long-term aim of the Chinese was to take over Sarawak as part of the spread of regional communism, if they conformed to Mao's theories of guerrilla warfare, they would wait for a suitable opportunity to rebel openly; in the meantime, the population would be subverted. Patterson believed that the Indonesian strategy was short term and portrayed as the people of East Malaysia fighting a war of liberation from their colonial oppressors. While assessing that the strategy would not prevail, he acknowledged that the Indonesian campaign was being led by an experienced soldier – Brigadier General Supardjo – who had injected imaginative planning and had stretched the defending forces with simultaneous incursions into rural areas worked by Chinese, backed up by feints on a wide front. Patterson acknowledged that some infiltrations were bound to breach the defences, and unless there was some way to deter and defeat incursions, the solution was to beat the enemy at his own game. No longer should British Forces, Borneo wait to be attacked

Two days later, Walker wrote to Admiral Begg outlining Patterson's views and suggested that the Indonesians would take advantage of the Bangkok Talks to step up infiltration at a time when British military offensive operations were constrained by political indecision. Unless it was halted, British Forces, Borneo would face a steady increase of Indonesian and their surrogates' activity and, within four months, could be fighting a guerrilla war. In highlighting the Indonesian need for safe bases, Walker used as examples the Viet Minh in Indo-China sheltering in China, and Algerian rebels operating from Tunisia. The answer was to ensure that Indonesian bases south of the frontier were unsafe. While appreciating the political implication of the strategy, Walker suggested this needed to be weighed against the threat of a full-scale guerrilla war, which would take years to defeat, against defeating incursions within months. He recommended retaliatory operations against bases in North Kalimantan because the Indonesians had undoubtedly dropped their guard. Since the border was so ill-defined, patrols south of it were deniable. In suggesting that small enemy posts 2,000 yards south of the border be attacked, Walker cited Second Lieutenant Thompson's attack on 1 January as a good example of what could be achieved. A series of 'Maquis' raids designed to knock out logistic and communications centres, and aircraft on the ground, would pay dividends, however they needed determined leadership.

Walker mentioned that since the imposition of the ADIZ, there had been no Indonesian air incursions, nevertheless, if his strategy was accepted, he suggested that warships join the air defence of Kuching, Labuan and Tawau and that when weapons were fired from Indonesia, naval bombardment should retaliate, particularly opposite Sabah. The artillery should carry out target registration. In Walker's opinion there were two options – large-scale reinforcements to deal with a guerrilla war, or retaliation. Walker concluded that if the prospect of a long-drawn-out guerrilla campaign was accepted, then there was no problem. Using Patterson's terminology, he continued: 'The alternative is to cut the bonds which bind our hands behind our backs. Militarily it is to Sukarno's advantage to spin out the present negotiations as long as possible.' An early decision was sought.

After the Joint Intelligence Committee in London had assessed the comments, Confrontation entered a top secret phase when Walker received authority from Admiral Begg for 'hot pursuit' up to 3,000 yards south of the border. These became known as 'special operations'. The decision was taken after considerable high-level political, diplomatic and military discussion because if patrols were detected, the Indonesians would have a valuable propaganda tool and therefore operations had to be deniable. The strategy took a turn in April when Prime Minister Douglas-Home, in discussing the Borneo situation with Australian Prime Minister Sir Robert Menzies, sent a diplomatic telegram that 'British and Malaysian security forces in Borneo are to be permitted to cross the Indonesian border in hot pursuit for a distance of up to 3,000 yards.'

Secrecy surrounded 'special operations' with only commanding officers and one company per battalion aware of planning and execution. Major General McAlister, in his book *Bugle & Kukri*, describes that in May 1964, 1/10th Gurkha Rifles were reforming in Singapore, following their second tour in Borneo, when the order came to form reduced companies of picked men for special duties operations across the border in Sarawak. The order was cancelled within the week because the Battalion considered everyone suitable.

For the SAS, the decision proved to the 'European' doubters that the Regiment had a global role to do what it does best, and always has done – deep penetration, information-gathering patrols. In 1963, Lieutenant Colonel Woodhouse had introduced a policy of avoiding contact – 'shoot and scoot' – which was met with resistance by some SAS, who, it seems, did not appreciate the political implications of military forces crossing international borders. Special operations formalized SAS operating south of the border. Sometimes known as the 'Tiptoe Boys', patrols literally crept through the jungle, mostly off track and deep in the shadows, maybe taking an hour to cover 100 yards and ensuring that not a twig broke, objectives being to close recce military kampongs and plot layouts and purpose. Rucksack weights were reduced from 50lb to 30lb because 'You cannot go head down, arse up when you are near the enemy.' Nothing was to indicate British origins and so foreign boots were encouraged or sacking wrapped around the soles to disguise prints. All the time there was the threat of dogs. The patrolling was so physically and mentally demanding that most SAS managed three patrols before being sent to England to rest and recuperate.

When A Squadron (Major Peter de la Billiere) arrived in Borneo in April for its second tour, de la Billiere found D Squadron mentally and physically drained from long-range patrolling, and angered by the death of Trooper Condon, as indeed was A Squadron. Condon, an Irishman from a republican family, was formerly A Squadron and had volunteered to join D Squadron when they sent an urgent appeal for a radio operator. In de la Billiere's opinion, which is usually forthright, he believed that the Brigade HQs were not familiar with using Special Forces, and that SAS operations must be directed from the highest command level in theatre.

On 8 May, No. 1 (Guards) Independent Company, the Parachute Regiment, arrived in Borneo for a six-month tour and was deployed to Sibu in Third Division. Covering 300 miles of high mountain ridges broken up by rivers, within the week eleven patrols were monitoring likely incursion crossing points while four remained in Sarawak on intelligence gathering, mapping and 'hearts and minds' visits, including medical assistance to isolated longhouses. While Captain Tom Brooke (Irish Guards) monitored the likely trouble spot of the Ulu Aput boat station, Captain Algy Cluff (Coldstream Guards), an unorthodox soldier, and his patrol joined the British monarchist Punan, and roamed both sides of the border with the nomads, who proved a valuable source of intelligence. When the second-in-command, Captain The Lord Patrick Beresford (Royal Horse Guards (The Blues)), met Cluff for a patrol in North Kalimantan with Punan guides, he was presented with a rattan mat to be delivered to Queen Elizabeth II. In return, he arranged for a photograph of him shaking hands with the Queen at a polo match to be flown out to him. Suitably impressed, the Punan on both sides of the border hosted the patrol and in a five-day Operation Annabel, which was named after the London nightclub frequented by Guards officers, the Indonesian base at Long Kihan, which was thought to house a battalion of about 600 men, was recced.

By May, President Sukarno was losing patience with *Konfrontasi* and the first indications that he intended to escalate hostilities emerged on 3 May when he formed the People's Double Command (Dwi Komando Rakyat – DWIKORA) of 'Indonesian volunteers' to 'dissolve the puppet state of Malaysia'. Six days later, he told his Chiefs of Staff that unless advantageous negotiations with Malaysia developed, he would escalate the campaign with air strikes on the Brunei oil installations. Fortunately, Sukarno never committed his Air Force and, after Walker's request to Begg, his aircraft would most certainly have been intercepted. To rub salt into Army discomfort over its lacklustre commitment, on 16 May, Sukarno appointed the left-wing Air Marshal Dhani to command

Vigilance (or Alert) Command (Komando Siaga-KOGA) to control military operations in Sumatra, Kalimantan and Java.

By creating Vigilance Command, Sukarno wanted to apply the co-ordinated operational model developed during the West Irian campaign of diplomacy coupled with low-intensity operations. But, while West Irian was about 'liberation', the objective of Confrontation now involved 'crushing Malaysia' and, to that extent, low-intensity operations were not the answer. From its inception, the Command was plagued with political, organizational and logistic problems, and was seen by Army commanders as a move to restrain their influence, particularly because of the empathy between the Air Force and the PKI. To soothe Army suspicions, Brigadier General Achmad Wirantakusumah, was appointed as Deputy Commander to Dhani. During his speech on National Resurrection Day on 20 May, boasting that Malaysia would be crushed by dawn on 1 January 1965, Sukarno appealed for more volunteers to assist in the struggle against colonialism, as he saw it, and to protect the Guided Democracy. Dhani assumed that Vigilance Command would control offensive operations in East Malaysia, however, Lieutenant General Yani, the Army Commander, persuaded Sukarno that Dhani's authority, in relation to East Malaysia, was limited to retaliation. The retention of Brigadier General Supardjo commanding No. 4 Combat Command in North Kalimantan was a concession to Dhani by Army commanders. They reckoned that they could limit operations against North Borneo by starving him of troops and confining him to low level-incursions by Air Force, Marine Corps and police units. This led Dhani, in October 1964, to complain that not all the troops he had requested for Vigilance Command had arrived and that 5 Brigade was not fit to fight in the jungle.

In May, when 1st Green Jackets (Lieutenant Colonel David House MC), took over the defence of the west of First Division from 42 Commando, House received a personal directive from Brigadier Patterson outlining the threat to the First, Second and Third Divisions. He still believed that it could take any form ranging from regular forces infiltration to guerrilla attacks, with the total number of enemy troops available estimated to be approximately 2,740 men, a few of whom had infiltrated into the West Brigade tactical area of operations. In relation to the CCO threat, this remained strongest among the Chinese communities in First and Third Divisions, with the banned Sarawak Farmers Association and the Sarawak United People's Party thoroughly subverted – in spite of the appalling treatment of the Chinese in Java. The Borneo Communist Party in Third Division was less professional than the CCO, but more aggressive. Patterson referred to pro-

Indonesian Muslims organizing incursions and arms smuggling from the Tanjong Datu peninsula. In his operational instructions, House was ordered to detect and destroy all hostile incursions into Kuching District, disrupt subversive activity, prevent smuggling and 'prosecute the battle for the hearts and minds of the people'. In support he was given a Troop from A Squadron, QRIH, 70 Light Battery and ten sections of Border Scouts.

2/2nd Gurkha Rifles (Lieutenant Colonel Nick Neill) also arrived from Singapore on its first tour and moved into Second Division. Neill was a tough individual who had fought in Burma and in the Malayan Emergency, and would prove a formidable opponent to the Indonesians. Transported in Gurkha ASC trucks along the 120-mile road from Kuching to Simanggang, A Company deployed to the once-thriving kampong at Lubok Antu, a rather unhealthy cluster of buildings on the sluggish Sungei Lupar, while B Company went to Jambu. D Company was in a pleasant hilltop camp in virgin jungle between Jambu and the border. The Assault Pioneers, Recce Platoon and the Bugles were assembled into E Company (Major Johnny Lawes) and prevented the Indonesians on Kling Klang Ridge interfering with the road to Kuching by hot pursuit 'special operations', driving them onto the defensive 1,000 yards south of the border by retaliating to every Indonesian threat.

The next round of peace talks, with particular emphasis of the withdrawal of Indonesian forces from Malaysia, began, as agreed, in Tokyo on 8 June. Both sides agreed to a Thai-monitored checkpoint at Tebedu. When thirty-two Indonesians, alleged to have been in Sarawak for several days but wearing new uniforms, appeared from the jungle and formally returned to North Kalimantan, the Tunku accused Sukarno of deception. It was a charade. By 18 June, all was ready for the Foreign Ministers' meeting, which, it was hoped, would produce tangible agreements for a ceasefire, however, disagreements still centred on the interpretations of the Manila Agreement and demands by Deputy Prime Minister Razak that all Indonesian forces must withdraw from East Malaysia within four weeks. Dr Subandrio insisted that these demands were unacceptable and implied that although the Federation of Malaysia was a fait accompli, Indonesian 'volunteers' were now fighting British colonialism. The conference descended into a series of accusations in which politicians bickered while soldiers died. In any case, Malaysia could do little until Sukarno called off his Confrontation.

While the conference was underway, the clashes continued in East Malaysia. 2/2nd Gurkha Rifles were a little surprised not to be tested

125

until 10 June, six weeks after arriving, when about twenty IBTs visited the longhouse at Batu Lintang and restricted their activities to slashing the canopy of a civilian Land Rover. Captain Quinn of 70 Light Battery then learnt that a cockfight was to take place at Empedi longhouse, which was about 3 miles from Batu Lintang. Suspecting that the Indonesians had already cached weapons and would use the event as a cover to return to Sarawak using Track 34, which led to a fortified Indonesian longhouse at Langgau, Quinn informed 2/2nd Gurkha Rifles. Lieutenant Colonel Neill instructed the Assault Pioneer Platoon (Lieutenant (QGO) Nandaraj Gurung) to ambush the Indonesians.

Nandaraj and Quinn agreed that 70 Battery would shell Track 34 and convince the Indonesians to use another one which meandered through several longhouse communities and offered better opportunities for ambushes. Nandaraj then told Quinn, to his discomfort, that if he needed artillery support, he would use the target/map/grid procedure, in which corrections are given using grid references, and is reliant upon the observer's ability to read a map. Early on 13 June, while the Tokyo Talks were still underway, the Assault Pioneers filed through rubber plantations and secondary jungle, and reached the ambush site at the junction of several tracks in jungle noisy with heavy rain. Nandaraj showed every man his place and told them to expect a group of Indonesian civilians. At about 6.00 pm, when the cut-off group reported a column of TNI approaching from the border, Nandaraj sprang the ambush and pinned the lead section in the killing zone. The Indonesians reacted quickly and when a frantic close-range firefight developed in the evening gloom, Rifleman Resembahadur Thapa doubled forward with his Bren and killed two troublesome TNIs trapped in the killing zone by firing from his hip. 51mm mortar bombs then exploded on the Gurkhas' left flank, as a classic right-angled counter-attack developed. In danger of being rolled up, Nandaraj moved men to the left flank and cut the attack to pieces with controlled volleys, and then called for artillery fire from Quinn with two white phosphorous to every three high-explosive shells exploding in the soaking jungle. After forty minutes, the Indonesians withdrew across the border in disarray, harassed all the way by A Troop. As a precaution against counter-bombardment, Nandaraj withdrew to another ambush site for the night. Next morning, a patrol found thirteen dead Indonesians, all shot through the forehead. At 8.15 am, E Company took over the pursuit and the Assault Pioneers returned to camp to enjoy their first hot meal in forty-eight hours. Most of the Gurkhas had been in the Army barely seven months and this was their first action. Lieutenant Nandaraj was awarded the MC for an ambush that was described by the School of Jungle Warfare as classically executed.

Late in the afternoon of the day after the end of the Tokyo Talks, two Platoons made up from the 1/6th Gurkha Rifles Pipes and Drums were resting during a ten-day patrol at the disused platoon base at Rasau, not far from the border in First Division, when they were attacked by a TNI company. Over the next five hours, the Indonesians launched five attacks, killing five Gurkhas and wounding several more before withdrawing. It had been a costly mistake to occupy a well-known position devoid of any cover. Once again, the Indonesian attack was executed by aggressive troops who knew exactly what they were doing.

In July, Indonesian incursions threatened Kuching on thirty-four occasions, most by experienced TNI. The aggressive 328 Para-Raider Battalion had been replaced by the cautious 305 Infantry Battalion. On 1 July, Captain Quinn was asked to fly a Pack Howitzer to the fortified border police post at Lubok Antu to shell a particularly aggressive TNI unit at Badau that was pestering Support Company, 2/2nd Gurkha Rifles (Captain Christopher Bullock). Lieutenant Andrew Pinnion, the B Troop Gun Position Officer (GPO), led the detachment, however poor weather and operational commitments prevented them arriving for ten days. Eager to help Bullock, Pinnion and his nine-man detachment calculated the likely position of an offending mortar, without the benefit of an air observation post or sound-ranging, and fired ten rounds. The Troop Sergeant, Sergeant Metcalfe, a former Irish Guardsman, contested the methodology. When a patrol slipped across the border and found that six shells had landed within 200 yards of the mortar and that the Indonesians had hurriedly evacuated the area, leaving equipment and ammunition behind, Metcalfe admitted to being deaf in one ear. Since retaliation was expected, when Lieutenant Colonel Neill ordered Pinnion to move the Pack Howitzer into the FLB and stay a few days, as the gun was being re-assembled after being squeezed through the gun pit entrance, an important component broke. An immediate request for a replacement arrived from Singapore within eighteen hours, such was the efficiency of the logistic chain.

4 RMR (Lieutenant Colonel Noordin) arrived on the left flank of West Brigade in a cultivated sector split by the road from Kuching to Simanggang and dotted with hillocks, thick undergrowth and small streams with a maze of paths connecting the kampongs, some extending to the border. When Brigadier Patterson asked 70 Light Battery (Major Ferry) to support the Malaysians, Noordin and Ferry devised Operation Burong (Malay for 'bird') – four days of consecutively moving a Pack Howitzer by helicopter to register targets of likely border crossing points by day, and then harass them at night. Operation Mallard involved flying two 70 Light Battery guns to the platoon FLBs at Stass and Serikin to register border-crossing points. Generally, moving a Pack Howitzer,

its detachment, ammunition and other essential equipment by Belvedere required three lifts.

Meanwhile on 18 July, Lieutenant Miers, who commanded the Bukit Knuckle FDL occupied by 5 Platoon, B Company, 1st Green Jackets, was told by a fisherman that he had seen 100 TNI. The base was in the centre of the First Division midway between Serikin and Padawan. That night, the moon was obscured by low cloud and mist swirled in ghostly folds on the ground. When a sangar reported movement 200 yards to the south-east, it seemed that the Indonesians were moving around the left flank to high ground. Then, from a position across a stream about 200 yards to the south, another sangar came under fire, damaging a radio and LMG. 5 Platoon returned fire and thereafter there were sporadic exchanges until midnight when the Indonesians withdrew. The following day, a tracker dog team found evidence of at least three wounded being taken across the border. Both artillery operations were interrupted when the Indonesians retaliated by again attacking Bukit Knuckle at midnight on 20 July. Operation Mallard was brought forward twenty-four hours and adjusted so that Sergeant Steele's howitzer could be flown to Serikin from where it shelled tracks and watercourses along the border. No further attacks developed. Operation Burong was equally successful. Guided by an Auster Air OP, Sergeant Arrowsmith's gun at Tebedu registered targets along 30 miles of mountain crests on four consecutive afternoons and carried out harassing fire at night.

Any notion that the SAS would not underestimate the Indonesians was reinforced on 6 August when Sergeant Tudor's 4 Troop, A Squadron patrol, led by Lance Corporal Roger Blackman, was investigating shooting heard by 1/2nd Gurkha Rifles at Long Pa Sia the previous day. Tudor was en route to Singapore to attend a language course. The patrol was following a trade route from Long Tapadong and was about 2 miles south of where the Leicesters had attacked in January, when Blackman's scout, Trooper Billy White, shot an Indonesian preparing a meal near a tree. The jungle erupted into a fierce firefight as Indonesians on a ridge turned on the SAS. Discarding their Bergens, which unfortunately included the radio, Blackman and Trooper Jimmy Green 'shot and scooted'. Lieutenant Geoff Skardon, who was attached from the 1st (Australian) SAS Company, Royal Australian Regiment, saw White fall wounded and, returning to help him, saw that he was bleeding profusely from a thigh wound. Forced to abandon him under pressure from five charging Indonesians, he became entangled in 'wait-a-while' thorns and abandoned his webbing containing his personal and survival equipment. Next morning, Blackman and Green reached a LP not far from the border where they met Corporal Wally Poxon's patrol, who had

128

reported the shooting to the Haunted House and had then been ordered to secure the LP for reinforcements. Skardon turned up two hours later and the three were extracted back to Brunei. It was thought that the TNI were probably from 518 Infantry Battalion.

Meanwhile, Tudor had returned to Squadron HQ and was instructed to intercept the Indonesians with a 1/2nd Gurkha Rifles platoon but failed by a hair's breadth. On the 8th, White's body and items of intelligence interest found on several dead Indonesians were recovered. When White's death, the third by the SAS in 1964, was analysed, it became clear that Skardon's gallantry was natural instinct but it could have resulted in two deaths. It led to a reassessment of 'shoot and scoot' with most SAS believing it was the right tactic. The Indonesians evidently knew their opposition was SAS because three days later Poxon's patrol found inscribed on a tree near the border 'Go no further, winged soldiers of England.' Once SAS candidates pass selection, they are awarded a set of blue wings to wear on their uniform sleeve.

On 10 August, 70 Light Battery was relieved in West Brigade by 176 (Abu Klea) Light Battery (Major G.D.S. Truell). Truell, a Korean War veteran, took 70 Light Battery's single gun concept a stage further by deploying its six guns to six FLBs to cover the border in First and Second Divisions and immediately registered an average of twenty-six targets per gun, most selected by platoon commanders. Some target indication was achieved by infantry patrols firing a Very flare to indicate their position and were then given twenty minutes to get clear of the impact area – a short distance in the jungle. The 5.5-inch howitzers of 170 (Imjin) Medium Battery were flown from Sabah to Kuching, one being towed to Pejuri and the other to Tebedu.

Toward the end of August, Major B. Koe, commanding B Company, 1st Green Jackets at Bukit Knuckle, received good intelligence that 7 Platoon (Second Lieutenant P.G. Chamberlain) at Stass was to be attacked. Chamberlain was supported by a Support Company 3-inch mortar and Sergeant McDonald's Pack Howitzer. McDonald was also a Korean veteran. During the night of 30/31 August, Koe sent 11 Platoon (Second Lieutenant Roberts) from D Company, 1,000 yards to the south as a cut-off. At about 2.30 am, just after a sentry had reported a light to the west of the kampong schoolhouse, a LMG opened fire and three 2-inch mortar bombs sailed over the base, and exploded in the jungle. The Green Jacket retaliation was immediate. Guided by 2-inch mortar illumination rounds drifting over the jungle, the mortar crew plastered the gully in which the enemy were thought to be assembling and Chamberlain's FOO guided two 105mm shells to within 150 yards of the perimeter. At about 3.00 am, the Indonesians withdrew under fire from Sergeant Cole's gun at Serikin and the 3-inch mortar. Adrenalin running high, talking excitedly and badly spaced, they walked straight into Roberts's ambush and, illuminated by two large flares, the killer group decimated the column. A string of grenade necklaces attached to a tree caused further damage. Roberts then withdrew to high ground and had the ambush site shelled. Next day, a patrol found eleven bodies and evidence of two men impaled on punji sticks. It was later reported that of the casualties, six – a lieutenant, a sergeant and four privates – were from 305 Infantry Battalion.

It was not all one-sided. On 29 August, C Company, 2/2nd Gurkha Rifles (Major John Aslett) was emerging from a patch of secondary jungle onto a track heading north from the border, after an unsuccessful ambush, when it was ambushed and the leading LMG gunner from 10 Platoon was killed and three Gurkhas wounded. It is at times like this, when everything seems to have gone 'pear shaped', that someone restores the situation. Under heavy fire, Lance Corporal Amarjit Pun, who was armed with a Sterling, ran forward but, as he picked up the Bren, a bullet damaged it. Grabbing his Sterling and yelling, he stood on the edge of the track in the centre of the killing zone and sprayed the ambushers with automatic fire. Aslett, who was pinned down with 10 Platoon, instructed its platoon commander to form a fire base for the rearguard platoon to counter-attack and drive the Indonesians south across the border, leaving three killed and two wounded. The Gurkhas lost two killed and three seriously wounded. The Regimental Medical Officer, Major R.S. Blewett, came forward in a helicopter to administer life-saving battlefield surgery to the seriously wounded.

In 1964, as part of the strategy to undermine Sukarno, X-rays taken of his body and handed to British Intelligence by Washington showed that he had a gallstone and his consultant was suggesting that unless he underwent surgery, he could die. This information was of considerable value because if he died, then Confrontation would probably wither. What the British did not know was that Sukarno suffered from persistent bouts of gallstones and kidney problems, and would do so until his death in 1970. It was also suspected that he had a form of blood poisoning known as uraemia, which London was warned could produce mania and rash decisions. Sukarno was unpredictable, impulsive and his next act certainly caught London and Kuala Lumpur unawares.

CHAPTER ELEVEN

The Defence of Malaysia
August 1964 to August 1966

As soon as President Sukarno set up Crush Malaysia Border Area Command in October 1963 and handed over military operations against Malaysia outside Borneo to his naval commanders, it was inevitable that he might well consider using it. Even though there were doubts that the Indonesian Navy had the strategic ability to undertake naval operations from Sumatra, the British had recognized that Confrontation would probably spill to the Malaysian mainland, nevertheless Britain agreed with Malaysia that while Indonesian incursions onto the mainland would be resisted, retaliation to destabilize Indonesian operations would not be permitted. The same concept was in use in North Borneo and Sarawak. By the New Year, analysis of Indonesian activity indicated that covert and subversive operations were being planned from Sumatra against South Johore and Singapore, where the Chinese communities tended to be concentrated.

By the end of 1963, Brigadier General Magenda, who was Dr Subandrio's deputy at Supreme Operations Command, believed that he had sufficient intelligence, from Chinese fishermen and smugglers plying the Straits of Malacca, that some communist groups were ready to re-ignite the Malayan Emergency and would welcome Indonesian support. Magenda accepted that landings would be risky but if they were small enough, then a major British response was unlikely. In May, Air Marshal Dhani, as commander Vigilance Command, welcomed the proposals as an initiative in which the Air Force could play a big role and despatched the Air Base Defence Force and Quick Mobile Force to Sumatra to train for operations. In late June 1964, raiding parties from the naval, military and home defence forces of Crush Malaysia Border Area Command in Sumatra landed on the southern mainland coast of West Malaysia, which was not difficult because the defending naval and

131

maritime police forces were badly organized. Typically, a raid consisted of about twelve uniformed and armed men ferried to an isolated beach on the Straits of Malacca in a seagoing Chinese-manned trading sampan or a fishing boat captured a few days earlier. They would strike inland quickly and set up a base camp, their targets being to blow up Merdeka Bridge in Singapore; puncture the water pipeline between Johore and Singapore; and derail the Singapore to Kuala Lumpur express, which had been a favourite target of the Malayan Communists during the Emergency. None were successful but acts of sabotage continued on the Malaysian peninsula throughout the remainder of Confrontation and although very little damage was caused, the disruption affected local morale badly.

In July, serious race riots broke out in Singapore, which left four Chinese dead and 178 injured, and resulted in an eleven-day curfew. This led the Joint Intelligence Committee (Far East) to assess Indonesian intelligence operations, and found that its propaganda station, Radio Kemam in Sumatra, had been conducting psychological operations with the spreading of rumour, slogans on walls and 'black' news-sheets. An example given was that four days before the riots, the station had claimed that a Chinese had killed a Malay with a pork knife and others had forced Malays to eat pork.

Dr Sukarno, seeing an opportunity to broaden hostilities by opening a second front in Malaysia on Independence Day, told his people that in Confrontation, it was time to live dangerously, 'Vivero pericoloso!' On 17 August, Indonesian Naval Headquarters on Riau Island landed a force of 21 marines, 53 Quick Mobile Force, 21 Malayan Communists and 2 volunteers on three beaches near Pontian in south-west Johore with orders to rendezvous on Gunung Pulai, a jungle-covered mountain north-west of Singapore, establish training camps for Javanese immigrants and Chinese sympathizers near Labis and stir up the embers of the failed Communist insurrection between 1957 and 1960. A patrol was to make for 4,000-foot Gunung Besar and link up with airborne reinforcements dropped two weeks hence in the former Communist stronghold of Labis. The saboteurs were then to disrupt the main railway line running north-south through central Malaysia by blowing up bridges, derailing trains and heightening sufficient economic, social and political pressure to hasten the collapse of the government. Both forces were then to find a western beachhead for exfiltration to Sumatra. It was estimated the entire operation would take two months.

However, within hours 4 Federal Infantry Brigade, which had just quelled the rioting in Singapore, was alerted to the landings by locals and, moving into the area, captured the group which had landed on the southerly beach at Kukup within two days. Four marines managed to return to Sumatra. The centre group at Pontian Kechil beach was scattered by the Malaysian police, who captured substantial quantities of equipment and all but four within two weeks. Interrogations divulged the Indonesian strategy. The northerly group landed at Benut; however it lost four men when it ran into 4 RMR. The survivors reached swampy jungle to the east and contacted dissident workers on a pineapple plantation, however, on 6 October, Security Forces surrounded their camp and practically wiped out the group, although a few hardy souls evaded capture until the middle of 1965. Ten days after the landings, while attacking the maritime fuelling station on Esso Island, Indonesian fast patrol boats clashed with a Malaysian patrol craft.

Defence Minister Nasution, unimpressed with the operation, denied Indonesian Armed Forces had been involved but admitted the infiltrators might be 'volunteers'. When he suggested to Supreme Operations Command that Indonesia should consider buying Soviet medium-range missiles that could threaten Malaysia and Singapore from Sumatra, this startled Sukarno because it meant escalation. General Yani was unaware of the landings and raised the possibility that army commanders were not only being cut out of planning but were unwittingly being drawn into a campaign far wider than they had originally perceived. Their influence on Confrontation was less than the PKI, who now had greater influence on Sukarno than had been possible during the West Irian campaign, and were keen to see the campaign slide into regional instability. The Army was in an invidious position because it could not be seen to be undermining national aspirations.

Although Malaysia considered the landings to be sufficiently insignificant not to declare a state of emergency, concern was raised at the possibility of Indonesia intercepting Commonwealth-flagged warships and merchantmen passing through the Java Sea. Under the 1960 Internal Security Act, ships acting as internal security forces were permitted to detain and, if necessary, open fire on vessels acting suspiciously in international waters. Indonesia's 1958 claim of a 12-mile coastal limit was disputed by other nations, particularly the Straits of Malacca between West Malaysia and Sumatra; it also effectively turned the Flores and Java Seas into an inland lake. None of the Commonwealth countries wanted to be provocative and so Great Britain, Australia and New Zealand undertook to inform Indonesia when their warships intended to enter the disputed zones, and merchantmen were advised to stay outside the 12-mile limit. When Jakarta then announced the Sunda Straits were being closed to warships for a month for exercises, London objected on the grounds that this interfered with rights of passage in international waterways. Orders were sent to a powerful task force built around the aircraft carrier HMS *Victorious*, en route from Australia to Singapore, to pass through the Sunda Straits into the Java Sea and sail through Gaspar Straits, thereby breaching the 12-mile territorial limit. The course took her Gannet anti-submarine torpedo-bombers within range of Jakarta. Admiral Begg was not convinced that the proposal was strategically sound because he did not believe that Indonesia wanted to escalate Confrontation into a regional war. When he sought more naval escorts he found Canberra unenthusiastic about providing its Daring Class destroyers, and Auckland was concerned about provoking Indonesia, if HMS *Victorious* was attacked, he must be in a position to enact Plan Althorpe, which was one of several contingency strategies drawn up to dominate the 12-mile limit:

- Addington. Strong retaliation against Indonesian military bases in response to overt attacks.

- Althorpe (former Cougar). Limited attacks using the Vulcan bombers of 57 Squadron and the Royal Australian Air Force (RAAF) and Fleet Air Arm.

- Hedgehog. Widening retaliation by attacking selected targets in Sumatra.

- Hemley (revised to Plan Dagger). The destruction of Indonesian offensive capabilities to ensure that the sea lines of communication between West and East Malaysia were protected. Indonesian vessels entering the Malaysian 3-mile territorial limit were to be destroyed. Patrol groups were to be formed at Kuching and Tawau to deter and prevent landings, provide naval gunfire, general escort, search-and-rescue and anti-pirate operations.

- Fabian. Conventional response to widespread Indonesian attacks against western Malaysia, in particular amphibious operations mounted from Sumatra.

- Shalstone (revised to Plan Mason). Bombing, bombardment and coast artillery shelling of Indonesian bases in the Rhiau Islands in the event of low-level enemy operations.

- Spilliken. Defensive operations against Indonesian incursions into East Malaysia.

In addition to the Vulcans, a second Super Sabre squadron joined 3 Squadron at RAAF Butterworth. The RAF Regiment was reinforced with 1, 26 and 63 Light Anti-Aircraft Squadrons to protect the airfields in Singapore and Penang and the RAAF Regiment protected Butterworth. All were equipped with 20mm Bofors. 65 Squadron, which was carrying out six-month tropical trials with Bloodhound Mark II surface-to-air missiles at RAF Seletar, placed one Section on immediate readiness to defend Singapore. On 28 October, a full air defence exercise helped boost civilian morale.

The appearance of the task force and her ability to deploy counter-measures worried Jakarta sufficiently that she dispersed her ships and, on 11 September, informed London that the Straits were not going to be closed, however the naval exercises were going ahead. When the task force was invited to use Lombok Straits, London sent only the escorts. There was no reaction from the Indonesians, which was contrary to events in the Gulf of Tonkin in August when US warships were fired on by the North Vietnamese and drew the USA into war. When Sukarno instructed his embassies to establish the extent of British intentions, intercepts enabled the Joint Intelligence Committee to report that the deployment had caused a considerable impact: 'Our recent actions impressed them far more than any word could have done.' The Commonwealth naval forces were careful not to provoke Indonesia over the Sunda and Lombok Straits until October 1966 when the communist coup in Jakarta and the change in relations with Indonesia gave London another opportunity to test right of passage from the Java Sea to the Indian Ocean.

Race riots again broke out in Singapore on 3 September, resulting in 13 deaths, 106 injured and 480 arrests. Malaysia and Singapore, both of whom had been surprised by the level of inter-racial tension, attributed the unrest to Indonesian fifth columnists working with Chinese sympathizers to coincide with the next incursion. During the night of 1 September, four C-130 Hercules aircraft left the Indonesian Air Force base at Jakarta with 151 Quick Mobile Force and forty-one parachute-trained communist Malay-Chinese. Their mission was to link up with the force that had landed on 17 August and establish a guerrilla base. The drop was planned to be astride the arterial railway line. Engine trouble grounded one aircaft, leaving three heading north into the night. One aircaft disappeared, never to be seen again, presumably ditching into the sea. The remaining two aircaft reached Labis at 1.45 am just as a fierce storm broke out. Although visibility was poor, one stick of forty-eight parachutists dropped onto the correct DZ but were spread over 8,000 yards. The second aircaft had difficulty finding the DZ and spread its stick over 10,000 yards. Most groups failed to link up with each other and their containers of weapons, supplies and explosives. Communications also failed. Worst of all, the men were divided into penny packets, the largest group being eighteen.

The local Federation Land Development Area manager reported to Labis Police Station that coast watchers had seen parachutists dropping from an aircraft over Kampong Tenang. When a patrol despatched to the area found a military parachute, 7 Platoon, 6th Malayan Police Field Force moved into the area and early next day killed a parachutist and captured another. 6 RMR was alerted and, during the morning, captured two parachutists. 7 Platoon then killed a Malay-Chinese and captured another. Over the next three days, the Security Forces killed several more parachutists and captured four.

The fact that Indonesian aircraft had penetrated Malaysian airspace was of immediate concern to the Far East Air Force and HQ 224 Group placed all available aircraft on high alert. This applied to all operational Commonwealth squadrons in Malaysia and Singapore and the Meteor Mark 8s of 1574 Target-Towing Flight at RAF Changi. In spite of several alerts, only the 20 Squadron Hawker Hunters were summoned to support the ground forces when they attacked an Indonesian force corralled into 1,000 square yards of jungle, their presence signalled by white parachutes scattered on the tops of trees and lying in clearings. Armed with sixteen 3-inch rockets tipped with 60-lb armour-piercing rounds and a full load of 30mm Aden cannon, the Hunters carried out fourteen sorties that blasted the jungle and kept the Indonesians on the move.

On 4 September, HQ 1 Malaysian Federal Brigade (Brigadier Abbas) took over the hunt for the Indonesians in Operation Lilac. When Abbas was instructed to send 6 RMR to Singapore on internal security duties, it was replaced by 1/10th Gurkha Rifles two days later. The Battalion had returned to Malacca three weeks earlier from the Kalabakan operation in January. Although most of the radios were in workshops, the Regimental Signals Officer, Captain (QGO) Birbahadur Gurung, made up the deficiencies by begging and borrowing. Before Lieutenant Colonel Burnett had driven the 100 miles to Labis, the Malaysians had moved out so there was no handover. The Gurkhas were reinforced by C Battery, Royal Malaysian Artillery, two troops of the Federation Recce Squadron and B Company, Royal New Zealand Infantry Regiment (RNZIR), from 28 Commonwealth Brigade, and were driven south by 31 Company, Gurkha Army Service Corps. The force was joined by 845 NAS Whirlwinds, which were later replaced by those of 815 NAS from HMS *Victorious*. Although the position was still confused, the ineffective handover had given the Indonesians, thought to number about forty, a day's breathing space.

As he had done in Kalabakan, Burnett encircled the Indonesians. Success came quickly on 7 September when A Company chased three Chinese into a swamp near the original DZ, killed one and captured the other two. Two days later, C Company, which was in the jungle-clad hills dominated by Gunung Besar, killed three more in two separate actions. From an analysis of the actions and the interrogations of prisoners, it then became clear that there had been two drops, one at Kampong Tenang and the other 15 miles to the north, and it was this group that was moving south to link up with their colleagues. The examination of captured equipment established that the Indonesians had set their compasses on a common setting; none had been scrambled in the event of capture. In spite of at least one naive attempt to get a prisoner drunk to make him talk, the Intelligence Officer, Captain Kay of the Royal Army Education Corps (RAEC), produced a complete order of battle and list of personalities who had landed. On 11 September, B Company (Major Haddow) patrolling the area east of Kampong Tenang, persuaded a prisoner to guide a patrol to his colleagues. The Company had already lost a man in a clash and when Lieutenant Bill Dawson arrived at their camp, the Indonesians had departed, abandoning equipment and weapons. Tracks were followed until late in the afternoon on the 13th when three raiders were killed. Two days later, a C Company patrol fought a fierce battle with eighteen Indonesians, killing eight and capturing two, but at the cost of Lance Corporal Tejbahadur Rai killed by the only Indonesian to escape. Tejbahadur was the Battalion champion shot and had distinguished himself on 9 September when he killed a concealed Indonesian with a single shot. On 21 September, the Indonesian commander of the operation, Lieutenant Sutikno was captured and, under interrogation, admitted he had no idea why he had been selected to command, particularly as he was due to retire in 1965.

On 9 September, at an urgent meeting at the UN Security Council, demanded by Malaysia, to review Indonesia's 'blatant and inexcusable aggression', her delegate, Minister of Home Affairs Dato Ismail caused a storm by producing a 51mm light mortar, an AK-47 rifle, a parachute, a camouflaged uniform and other military material from a sack, all captured in Malaysia. In spite of the President, the Soviet Mr Morozov, telling him to remove the evidence as no precedent had been set for such an act, Dato Ismail accused Indonesia of blatant aggression. While deploring the Labis drop and calling upon both parties to respect each other's territorial integrity, nine members voted for the Resolution. The Soviet Union used its veto.

On 22 September, 1/10th Gurkha Rifles were tasked to search a mine about 20 miles north of Segamat by HQ 1 Malaysian Federal Brigade. Collecting clerks, cooks, orderlies and the Intelligence Section, the Adjutant, Captain Ian Corden-Lloyd, left a Malaysian Police Field Force platoon as a stop and, after following tracks in fading light and killing one in the jungle, the Indonesians replied with heavy fire and withdrew deep into a swamp. Corden-Lloyd withdrew to open ground. Next morning, B Company tracked the enemy for six hours with a tracker dog and when it pointed, the Company advanced to contact. The Indonesians reacted quickly and a skirmish developed around a huge tree, behind which they had taken cover. When the Gurkhas had fought to a standstill, Major Haddow threw a grenade at the Indonesian position and when he stood up to analyse the effect, he was shot by an Indonesian Army Airborne sergeant major with his pistol. Captain (QGO) Aitbahadur Limbu took command and, in a fierce battle, B Company killed six Indonesians. The loss of Haddow was a blow to 1/10th Gurkha Rifles and a sad end to an operation that had seen the Battalion kill 24 and capture 27 Indonesians at a cost of 2 of its men. On 6 October, 1/10th Gurkha Rifles returned to Malacca on a journey that was akin to a liberation drive as relieved villagers showered the trucks with flowers, beer and fruit. By the time Operation Lilac was complete, 90 of the 96 parachutists had been accounted for with 31 killed and 59 taken prisoner. C Battery had killed one Indonesian and taken two prisoners while the New Zealanders captured two. The Gurkha Independent Parachute Company had also helped in the pursuit.

After Long Jawi, the Gurkha Independent Company supported 3 Commando Brigade in Lundu District before returning to Malaysia. When Lieutenant Colonel Woodhouse had sought reinforcements for the SAS and had requested the Company, it was reorganized into sixteen five-man patrols of a commander, medical orderly, two assault pioneers and a radio operator, plus a Company HQ and logistic support. The rationale behind the five-man patrols, as opposed to the standard four-man patrols of British Special Forces, was that there were only enough radios in the Company to equip sixteen patrols. The second-in-command was Captain David Morgan, who, in 1982, commanded 1/7th Gurkha Rifles during the Falklands campaign.

A captured Indonesian Air Force corporal was tried, convicted and sentenced to death on 17 October after the judge ruled that he should not be regarded as a prisoner of war. The sentence was commuted; nevertheless the status of captured Indonesians remained obscure until April 1965. Second Lieutenant Sutikno, who had already expressed disillusionment over the operation, was induced to pen a message instructing

1. 10 December 1962. The 1st Queen's Own Highlanders unload stores from a 34 Squadron Beverley at Brunei Airport. *(Will Fowler)*

2. In Seria, Major General Walter Walker talks to Lieutenant Colonel Charlie McHardy (CO 1st Queen's Own Highlanders) and Major Ian Cameron (A Coy). *(Will Fowler)*

3. 12 December 1962. Z-Craft return to Brunei Town after L Coy, 42 Commando had released hostages from the TNKU from Limbang. *(Author's Collection)*

4. Lieutenant Alan Thompson MC (1st Leicesters). It was his attack on an Indonesian machine gun on 1 January 1964 that was used as an example by General Walker to promote Operation Claret. *(Colonel Alan Thompson)*

5. 7 March 1964. Photo of 328 Para-Raider Battalion soldiers captured by 2/10th Gurkha Rifles after the Battle of Track 6. The soldier on the left carries a M1 Carbine. His colleague carries a M3 sub-machine gun and wears a hat covered in foliage. *(Author's Collection)*

6. June 1964. An 81 Squadron PR7 Canberra lands at Labuan after a recce sortie over Sarawak. *(Mac Hawkins)*

7. June 1964. An air photograph taken of longhouse by an 81 Squadron Canberra. *(Mac Hawkins)*

8. July 1964. HMAV 4073 *Ardennes* RASC Landing Craft Tank moored alongside a Victoria Harbour jetty, Labuan. *(Mac Hawkins)*

9. The Ton-class minesweeper HMS *Picton*. Not only important to off-shore patrols, these ships were able to motor up the Sungei Rajang as far as Kapit. *(Ton Class Association)*

10. On board a minesweeper, British sailors clean their small arms. While the soldiers were equipped with SLRs the Royal Navy had .303 rifles. *(Ton Class Association)*

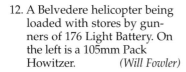

11. Royal Marines on board a launch flying the White Ensign. In the background a typical 'kampong ayer'. *(Will Fowler)*

12. A Belvedere helicopter being loaded with stores by gunners of 176 Light Battery. On the left is a 105mm Pack Howitzer. *(Will Fowler)*

13. July 1964. A QRIH Troop of two Saladin armoured cars in between two Ferret Mark II scout cars. *(Author's Collection)*

14. Described in a Jak cartoon (*London Evening Standard* – 11 August 1964) as 'We're the most savage, bloodthirsty, treacherous tribe in Borneo – We're 845 Squadron RN', Wessex helicopters at Nanga Gaat. *(FAA Museum)*

15. August 1964. A 1st Royal Ulster Rifles river patrol with a local boatman at the helm. Note the machine gunner has a newly-issued GPMG. *(Author's collection)*

16. September 1964. Two QRIH Ferret scout car crews watch a Whirlwind landing. *(Will Fowler)*

17. 1964. RAF Tengah, Singapore. On the dispersal areas are naval Sea Vixens, 20 Squadron Hunters and a Wessex helicopter. *(Patrick Walsh)*

18. 1964. F Troop, 176 Light Battery in action. Part of 45 Light Regiment RA, the Battery was in Borneo from August 1963 to January 1966. *(Will Fowler)*

19. September 1964. Viewing down the Long Bawan Valley, one of the first photos taken of Long Medan military kampong, which was attacked by C Coy, 1/2 Gurkhas in January 1965. The river is to the right of the kampong and Sarawak is 2 miles to the left (north). Pa Bawan airfield is on the other side of the far ridge. Taken from Fire Support Base hill. *(Brigadier Bruce Jackman)*

20. 1964. A typical Forward Locality Base on the border. The steps have been reinforced with ammo boxes and sandbags reinforce bunkers and huts against rocket and mortar attacks. *(Will Fowler)*

21. December 1964. General Hunt meets 6 Troop, B Company, 40 Commando after their attack on Sebatik Island. With the bandaged arm is Lieutenant Seeger. *(R.A.M. Seeger)*

22. February 1965. Mortar Platoon, 1st Scots Guards in action in Sabah. *(Will Fowler)*

23. June/July 1965. Military Survey was a critical need. Royal Engineer Sergeant Pete Mansell and a group of Iban on Bukit Tasu (4,109 ft) in Third Division. *(Brian Holdershaw)*

24. A Border Scout platoon being given orders by a European officer from the Sarawak Constabulary. *(Will Fowler)*

25. Flight Lieutenants 'Sherry' Davies (navigator) and Bob Langford (pilot) alongside a Javelin. They carried out the only fighter ground attack during Confrontation in support of a 1/2nd Gurkha Rifles patrol on 30 January 1964. *(Brigadier Bruce Jackman)*

26. Brigadier Pat Patterson whose 99 Gurkha Infantry Brigade played a significant role during the Brunei Revolt and throughout Confrontation.

27. 1966. A dog handler and his Labrador tracker lead a 2nd Royal Green Jackets patrol.

(Will Fowler)

28. A 5.5 inch medium howitzer of 170 (Imjin) Medium Battery at Pejuri. This gun proved invaluable supporting long-range Op Clarets. *(Author's Collection)*

29. Photo recovered from a dead IBT showing CCO activists with the guerrilla in the centre seemingly making a political point. They wear a mix of Dutch and US uniforms.

(Will Fowler)

30. Royal Marines dash for cover from a Wessex in a jungle clearing. *(Author's Collection)*

31. 1965. Major General Walker talks to Lieutenant Colonel Carroll, CO 1/7th Gurkha Rifles. In the centre is Major Denis O'Leary.

32. Lieutenant Colonel Chris Pike, 1/10th Gurkha Rifles. An outstanding company commander who successfully used the same ambush position twice during Operation Claret on 4 March 1966. *(Brigadier Chris Pike)*

33. A captured Indonesian is escorted from a Wessex by a Gurkha with a dressing on his chin. *(FAA Museum)*

34. May 1966. Gurkhas embark in a Royal Navy Wessex from a prepared LP near Bario. *(Will Fowler)*

35. Early 1966. Serudong Forward Locality Base, Sabah, occupied by D Company, 2nd Royal Green Jackets. *(Brigadier Henry Wilson)*

36. 1966. 2nd Royal Green Jackets 81mm mortar detachment in the familiar 'mortar men crouch'. The No. 1, without shirt, is Lieutenant Henry Wilson (now Commissioning Editor Pen & Sword Publishing). *(Brigadier Henry Wilson)*

37. 1965. Hearts and Minds. Queens Dragoon Guards medics treat an Iban woman. *(Will Fowler)*

38. 3 September 1966. The blurred photo of Lt Sumbi taken by Major Alan Jenkins 1\7th Gurkha Rifles. In the background is CSgt Phattabahadur Sunwar. *(Major Alan Jenkins)*

his men to surrender. On 2 November, 48 Squadron Hastings and Argosys dropped pamphlets over Sumatra and Riau Island urging Indonesians not to be misled about their perceptions of the Malaysian people's attitude to the war. The Indonesian reaction to this psychological tactic was unexpected. Contrary to declaring Sutikno to be a traitor, he was held up to be an example of heroic courage and revolutionary spirit since it had taken 5,000 Commonwealth troops to capture him.

The fighting in Borneo was affecting regional stability and the landings brought Malaysia and Indonesia very close to open hostilities. When revelations emerged in October that the British had plans to destroy the Indonesian Air Force and Navy in order to prevent further attacks on the Malaysian mainland, as far as Malaysia was concerned, a strike would have undermined her relationship with the Security Council that she was the victim of aggression. Had an attack been launched, while it would have undoubtedly undermined Sukarno's hold, it probably would have assisted the political aspirations of the PKI, who could then accuse Great Britain of colonialism. Indonesia was being marginalized in the United Nations, anyway, and was moving toward alignment with China. Nevertheless, several British warships were brought out of retirement and a second carrier task force built around HMS *Eagle* was despatched to the Far East, as was the guided-missile destroyer HMS *Kent*. In total, the Royal Navy fleet in the region numbered eighty ships, which included the aircraft carrier HMS *Centaur* and the commando carrier HMS *Bulwark*. It was the largest naval assembly since the Korean War and consisted of a third of the Fleet. Commonwealth warships operated openly in Indonesian waters off Sumatra. It is interesting that one commentator wrote: 'In the early stages of the campaign, it was apparent that some ships had not digested that this was not a peacetime Casualty Exercise or Gun Exercise but a genuine war, albeit on a small scale.'

By the New Year of 1965, a strategy had emerged to detect, capture or deflect Indonesian incursions by dominating the Straits of Malacca, Straits of Singapore and territorial waters outside the internationally recognized 3-mile limit. Intelligence was vital in identifying likely landing points, with signals intercepts a crucial element to pinpointing Indonesian naval and merchant ship intentions. Nevertheless, even though there was a fair amount of action with fragile sampans fighting back with vigour against heavily armed patrol boats and minesweepers, many incursions were poorly planned, badly co-ordinated and inadequately resourced. Interrogations by naval officers usually proved more successful than by Special Branch because the latter had little knowledge of naval matters.

The first line was horizon defence carried out by British and

Australian warships. The second line was Ton class minesweepers of the Inshore Flotilla and patrol boats of the Seaward Defence Boats of the Far East Fleet. As the Royal Navy had dispensed with its Coastal Forces fast patrol boats, Singapore and Malaysian Maritime Police units were particularly useful in checking islands and keeping in touch with isolated communities. Over 80 per cent of incursions were intercepted at the second defence. The third line was coastal defence of small police craft and inshore naval patrols with the final line being land-based coast watchers, patrols and home guards. Patrolling was often uneventful and repetitious, separated by visits to such ports as Bangkok, and refits, dry dock maintenance and exercises. Operations against the blight of pirates continued. Daily operational control was exercised by Local Operations Officers, whose nomenclature of LOO drew the inevitable cloakroom jokes. In addition to defensive operations, the SBS disrupted Indonesian activity on Sumatra. Typically patrols in Klepper canoes were dropped by submarines, such as HMS *Amphion*, close inshore. On completion of the tasks, the SBS would paddle to a pre-arranged rendezvous, form up line abreast and pass a line from one canoe to the next. The submarine would then raise its periscope and coming from astern of the canoes, it would snag the rope, tow them out of range and recover them.

Meanwhile niggling incursions continued. On 29 October, when a fourth raid of fifty-two infiltrators were seen by fisherman landing north of the mouth of the Sungei Kesang, south of Malacca, Brigadier P.A.L. Vaux, who was Commander, Malaysia, with a force from 28 Commonwealth Brigade, including the 1st RNZIR and 3rd Royal Australian Regiment (RAR), flung a cordon around the mangrove swamps and fruit plantations of the area, and then 102 (Australian) Field Battery, which had relieved 103 Field Battery in 28 Commonwealth Brigade, pounded the Indonesians. Within thirty-six hours, most of the trapped infiltrators were captured and the remainder surrendered three weeks later, exhausted and starving. Two groups, which landed in south-east Johore on 7 November were quickly rounded up. The consequence of this landing was to condemn the Australian gunners into six months of coast watching and observation posts. Involved on the periphery of this operation was 4th Royal Tank Regiment (RTR), which was in the process of taking over from the QRIH as the Armoured Reconnaissance Regiment, and was already patrolling the coast. Having just arrived from operations in the Radfan, the mismanagement of travel arrangements meant that some soldiers had not seen their families for eighteen months. The Saladins, under the rules of engagement, were forbidden to fire the 76mm main armament and were limited to single shots with their 0.30-inch Brownings coaxial machine guns.

140

On 6 December, HMAS *Teal* exchanged shots with an Indonesian vessel in Singapore waters and captured three Indonesian soldiers, including an officer. A week later, it intercepted two unlit Indonesian vessels looking for each other in the dark, and in a brief clash killed three Indonesians and captured four, one of whom turned out to be an Indonesian Marine officer. Also seized was a large quantity of explosives. On 23 December, twenty-eight Indonesians who had landed in south-west Johore, were destroyed in a swamp when they were split into small groups by Operation Birdsong in which 20 Squadron Hunters and 45 Squadron Canberras carried out real and simulated attacks. Operation Birdsong was repeated on Christmas Eve and Boxing Day when 103 Squadron Whirlwind and Belvederes supporting ground forces systematically split the survivors into smaller groups. On Christmas Eve, near One Fathom Bank, the frigate HMS *Ajax*, intercepted sixty-one infiltrators in an armed Indonesian Customs cutter and ten hijacked Malaysian fishing boats en route to a beach north of Kuala Lumpur; seven boats and a large quantity of supplies and material were captured. The niggling sabotage and raids continued in the first months of 1965. A Liberian freighter anchored in Singapore harbour was attacked in January and on 25 and 26 February, forty-four Indonesian police and volunteers landed east of Kota Tinggi. Eighty infiltrators in two groups landed in late March but were seen by locals and finished off by Security Forces. On 13 March, HMAS *Hawk* had the unusual experience of being bracketed by an Indonesian coastal battery while patrolling not far from Raffles Light, at the southern point of the Singapore fishing area. Two nights later, she intercepted a sampan with five Indonesians. Saboteurs in a sampan then attacked a French ship as she was piloted into the Western anchorage but in doing so blew themselves to pieces when a grenade bounced of its hull and landed in the sampan. In April, a bomb planted in the military ranges at Blakang exploded with a spectacular noise but little damage. Close to the Shell refinery on Pukum Bukom and in full view of several 2/10th Gurkha Rifles married quarters at the former Blakang Mati coastal battery, now their barracks, the Malaysian patrol boat *Sri Pahang* and some police launches intercepted a flotilla of sampans en route from Riau Archipelago to Singapore, destroying one and capturing another. The following day, the captured sampan was found to have a bomb on board and was blown up.

In April 1965, the Malaysians carried out another leaflet drop on Indonesian bases in Sumatra highlighting the futility of further raids, nevertheless during the night of 31 May, a platoon of twenty-five regulars landed on the south-east coast of Johore near Tanjong Pengelih, about 7 miles east of RAF Changi, and concealed themselves in abandoned Japanese coastal defences. Their aim was to seize a firm base for reinforcements and then move inland to Kelantan to train dissident Chinese communist and pro-Indonesian groups. During the night, they ambushed a platoon of the Singapore Infantry Regiment, killing eight and wounding five soldiers, the only successful engagement by any of the raiding parties. Next morning, 4 RMR and a police company watched as four Hunters rocketed the emplacements and then strafed them with 20mm cannon fire. When the Indonesians abandoned the position during the night, they were relentlessly pursued by the Malaysians and Singapore police, losing thirteen in a series of engagements as they headed inland. Over the next fortnight, without accurate maps and constantly on the move, leading to hunger, they were harried until 12 June when the survivors of the group were decimated with one more killed, eighteen wounded and six surrendering.

By the end of Confrontation, there had been forty-one Indonesian incursions by about 740 soldiers and police officers, of whom 451 actually landed. Of these, 142 were killed and 309 captured, some of whom were wounded. The raids were an irritant and tied down police and troops, some of which were resting after a tour in Sarawak, and kept the civil population on edge, a factor that was magnified by the need to create plans against air raids and impose an internal security regime with curfews. To that extent the Indonesian operations against Malaysia diverted some attention from operations in Borneo, however, there is no doubt that since the people of Malaysia and Singapore were kept informed about Indonesian incursions, they made a willing contribution to the defence of Malaysia – not that they needed much encouragement.

CHAPTER TWELVE

Operation Claret

The escalation by Indonesia of attacking Sarawak and raiding Malaysia with regular forces heralded a significant evolution in Confrontation. Although Prime Minister Douglas-Home's government was under considerable pressure as it neared the General Election, in August, the Cabinet agreed that Sukarno could no longer be permitted to retain the initiative and Admiral Begg was given permission for selective retaliation, as he had recommended in March, of allowing small forces to operate up to a limit of exploitation of 5,000 yards inside Indonesia. One of the last defence decisions of the government, it was never formally announced because general knowledge of this politically sensitive issue could cause very serious harm to the Nation. Known as Operation Claret, it was authorized in the knowledge that the border was so badly defined that incursions were deniable. Recce patrols and 'hot pursuit' did not represent the offensive action envisaged by Operation Claret. Every Indonesian incursion now risked retaliation.

Field Marshal Hull, the Chiefs of Staff, and the Foreign and Commonwealth Office were anxious about the strategy because they believed that Sukarno would use it to maintain Indonesian morale. Begg and his commanders were more concerned with deterring the establishment of 'liberated areas', not by invasion, but by inflicting minimal damage without Sukarno losing face, and keeping Indonesian commanders off balance by forcing them onto the defensive. Killing a few men in an ambush was preferred to wiping out an infantry company because body bags could not always be concealed from the inquisitorial media. Determined to keep cross-border operations under strict control, Major General Walker drew up 'The Golden Rules', which were applied on such a strict need-to-know basis that troops often had, and still have, no idea that they had crossed the border:

1. The Director of Borneo Operations authorised every operation.

2. Only experienced troops were to take part. No soldiers were to cross the border during their first tour of duty in Borneo.

3. Every operation must be planned and executed with maximum security. Every man must be sworn to secrecy, full cover plans must be made and the operation given code names and never discussed in detail on telephone or radio.

4. Depth of penetration was limited to 3,000 yards and attacks must only be made to thwart offensive action by the enemy and must never be in retribution or solely to inflict casualties.

5. Every operation must be planned with the aid of a sand-table and thoroughly rehearsed for at least two weeks.

6. No soldier taking part must be captured by the enemy – alive or dead.

In analysing the Rules, while local commanders frequently suggested targets, the strategy meant discreet penetration, shock impact and quick withdrawal. Three thousand yards was selected because it was well within the artillery umbrella of guns in forward FDLs. Plans were meticulously scrutinized, checked and rechecked at all command levels to resolve weaknesses, and reduce the risk of failure and the consequent political implications of the British as aggressors. They were then ratified by 10 Downing Street. Accurate intelligence was vital with patrols, interrogation and air photo recce being vital in planning and electronic warfare key to keeping columns advised of enemy intentions. Early operations relied on a high degree of junior leadership and an ability to assess situations accurately and, since Operation Claret exacted a great mental and physical toll on the troops, discipline, courage and skill were an absolute necessity to overcome the tensions of operating inside enemy territory in the knowledge that if captured, life would be distinctly uncomfortable. No evidence of a British presence was to be left – identity discs were not carried, and spent cartridge cases and discarded ration packs collected. The dead and wounded were to be brought back, a physically demanding task for tired soldiers, working in relays, carrying heavy loads, some of them in considerable pain, along narrow jungle paths, negotiating slopes and across rivers as quietly as possible, with the ever-present threat of being ambushed. No close air or helicopter support could be undertaken, except in exceptional circumstances, which greatly reduced the chances of survival. In short, once south of the border, the troops were deniable. Fortunately, patrols were too rigorous for most journalistic interference, a far cry from their meddling in Aden, Northern Ireland and the Middle East where naivety of military matters still threatens lives. Considering the numbers of troops involved, Operation Claret was one of the best-kept military secrets of modern warfare, and great credit must be given to those who planned and took part in it. It was only during the early 1990s that information about it began to seep out.

Every soldier needs reassurance that if he is wounded, injured or is ill, there is an efficient medical system. As the size of British Forces, Borneo increased in 1963, Medical Services, Brunei was established by Colonel E. Guish to support 99 Gurkha Infantry Brigade, with medics supplied by 16 Commonwealth Field Ambulance. 3 Commando Brigade was supported by naval facilities on board HMS *Albion*. Later that year, Medical Reception Station (MRS) facilities were extended throughout Borneo with a ward at Labuan Hospital, and two wards each at Brunei Town Hospital and the Shell Hospital in Seria, also supported by 16 Commonwealth Field Ambulance. In 1965, medical services grew with the arrival of the airportable 19 Field Ambulance, which set up in Sibu to support First, Second and Third Divisions and consisted of seven officers, including two Queen Alexandra Nursing Corps (QARANC) sisters, and 120 men. 53 Field Surgical Team (Major Ian Lister) operated on military and civilian casualties. When, in July 1966, 15 Field Ambulance took over from 19 Field Ambulance, who departed under glowing terms, it brought a Field Surgical Team, a mobile dental surgery and three QARANC Sisters.

Every FLB had RAMC representation. Thirty of the toughest accompanied patrols, carrying not only their personal equipment but also the paraphernalia of a patrol medic. With regimental medical orderlies, they were responsible for immediate treatment. All soldiers were taught advanced first aid and some SAS were trained in basic surgery. If a helicopter was available, casualties were evacuated from a prepared LP or were winched through the trees, sometimes using a stretcher.

Perhaps the most extraordinary surgery involved Captain Pat Crawford RAMC, the 1/7th Gurkha Rifles RMO, in April 1964. Flying in a Scout with Major 'Birdie' Smith to visit B Company (Major Douglas Moore), which was then the 99 Gurkha Infantry Brigade reserve company, the helicopter crashed short of the LP and plunged down a steep slope before coming to rest against a tree stump. The seat belts of both officers had snapped and Smith found himself suspended in mid-air with his right arm trapped in the wreckage. Judging that Smith's life could only be saved if his arm was amputated, Moore supported Smith while Crawford stood in the smashed cabin and, surrounded by intense jungle heat and aviation fuel fumes, for an hour in the gathering gloom, amputated Smith's arm with his clasp knife. After this ordeal, there was no place for Smith to lie down and, in intense pain, he remained on his feet while Moore organized an improvised hoist. Crawford then accompanied Smith to Simanggang hospital in another helicopter. Smith, who had served for twenty-two years with the Gurkhas, returned to command 1/2nd Gurkha Rifles before the end of Confrontation and later became an author on Gurkha military history. Captain Crawford was awarded the George Medal.

The hot and sweaty climate induced all sorts of skin diseases and the self-help personal hygiene regime taught to the troops became critical, with the prevention of sepsis a major problem. Apart from sprains and fractures, other common afflictions included scrub typhus in which tiny mites penetrate clothing and folds in the skin, and induce fever. An antidote was liberally applied insect repellent. Since jungle warfare is fought on foot, stringent care of feet is critical and all soldiers were reminded that clean, dry socks were important and the liberal powdering of feet important – a tall order in the jungle! Knowing that feet would get wet, many did not bother with socks. Leeches were usually removed with a lighted cigarette or a blob of insect repellent. Pulling them out often leaves the head and teeth firmly attached to the skin and risks infection. Mosquitoes, particularly those with an evening lullaby, are an infernal nuisance. The breakthrough against malaria occurred in 1961 with the development of the Paludrine tablet, which, taken daily, deflects cerebral malaria. A liberal coating of insect repellent, whenever possible, and the rolling down of sleeves reduced mosquito bites.

Leptospirosis is caught from rodent urine washed into rivers and, drifting downstream amongst the effluence, is usually contracted when infected water splashes either into the delicate membranes of the outer lining of the eye, through the lining of the nose and mouth or contacts cuts and abrasions. As a precaution, recreational swimming was forbidden in some rivers but it was not infrequent that on patrol rivers had to be crossed, which increased the risk. When wading, great was the temptation to swill cool water across the head and face. Not much was known about treatment of leptospirosis until the RAMC and the US Army Medical Research Station at Kuching gained a better understanding of its origins. In 1963, there were fifty-five cases, two of which were fatalities. Marine Tony Daker, who took part in the Limbang operation as a Vickers machine-gunner, was invalided out of the Royal Marines after contracting leptospirosis and was left to his own devices to deal with his ill-health.

In mid-July, 1/2nd Gurkha Rifles returned for their third tour and, under command of HQ East Brigade, took over from 2/7th Gurkha Rifles in Fifth Division. For two years, the two battalions would rotate with each other. Lieutenant Colonel Clements was still in command and when local Muruts reported that the abandoned village of Nankator had been re-occupied by the Indonesian Army, this was confirmed by a Canberra air photo recce. Clements considered its occupation was of sufficient threat to Fifth Division and Sabah for it to be attacked in the Battalion's first Operation Claret. The village also happened to be on the Sungei Sembakang main supply route. Clements selected A Company (Major Digby Willoughby). Willoughby was the former Adjutant who had pursued Major Muljono after Long Jawi.

A week after losing Trooper White, Sergeant 'Gypsy' Smith's SAS patrol and their Border Scouts, on the SAS's first formal Operation Claret, crossed the border on 15 August to gather intelligence on Nankator. Accompanied by Lieutenant (QGO) Manbahadur Ale, the 2 Platoon Commander, the patrol took three days to cover the 3,000 yards to the Sembakang and for the next week watched activity in the area. From their information, Intelligence assessed that Nankator was held by a 518 Para-Raider Battalion platoon, which was part of the Brawijaya Division. Sitting astride a steam junction and a track leading north to Sarawak, the village had been converted into a formidable camp with several sentry posts facing north, mined approaches and two machine-gun posts on high ground. The approach was rugged with rivers carving through steep-sided, jungle-covered cliffs. It was the monsoon and rain was inevitable. In spite of no reliable maps of the area, Willoughby built a sand model of Nankator from air photographs and the information gained by the SAS. Deciding to attack from the south-west during the weekend of 5/6 September, 3 Platoon was to occupy a stop position to the south and east, and ambush the Indonesians as they were driven out of Nankator by 2 Platoon, covered by the firepower of Company HQ. 1 Platoon was in reserve. Each platoon was fifteen strong and Company HQ was reinforced by two 3.5-inch Rocket Launchers and two GPMGs. When Major General Walker approved of the plan, the Gurkhas rehearsed over ground similar to that around the village.

On 4 September, A Company was helicoptered to a border LP and, next day, was guided by Muruts across the frontier; by 8.00 am the following day they were south-west and above Nankator in thick jungle. As the recce group was moving out, there was a scuffle and when two Muruts were captured, it turned out they were related to Willoughby's guides and reported that Indonesian soldiers were picking fruit along the track no more than four minutes away. Since the raid depended on surprise, Willoughby cancelled the recce and led Company HQ and 2 Platoon along the narrow track towards Nankator, but was impeded by

147

large logs. After the scouts reported they could see a basha, Company HQ covered 2 Platoon as it slowly advanced and then everyone froze when an Indonesian soldier ambled up the track. Everyone hoped that he would pass, however, he saw Lance Corporal Sherbikram Ale and fired, the bullet skimming through the Gurkha's hat. Sherbikram, who had recently passed bottom of a JNCO cadre, killed the Indonesian with a single snap shot. Surprise lost, Company HQ immediately blasted the basha with the Rocket Launchers and GPMGs. The Indonesians responded quickly and a .30-inch Browning machine gun, which had not been picked up by the SAS, opened fire, however its aim was high and the bullets tore through the foliage and branches above the Gurkhas. When Willoughby instructed 2 Platoon to knock it out in tactical bounds, they slashed their way through the vegetation and overran it in a flanking attack. One GPMG gunner calmly replaced a broken trigger under fire.

Still under fire from another machine gun, Company HQ, with the judicious use of grenades, advanced across the thick scrub and fallen logs. For Sherbikram, it was not learning that counts; it was the application. Leading his section with considerable élan, he burst into the camp. Three enemy positions were identified at the bottom of a steep slope with one covering a track to the north-west and two to the north-east near a longhouse beside a stream. Covered by machine guns, a small group of TNI counter-attacked up the hill but were stopped by Lance Corporal Hastabahadur Pun, a big man carrying 500 rounds of link ammunition. Placing his GPMG on a tree stump in open ground and oblivious to their fire, he broke up the attack, using nearly all his ammunition. 3 Platoon realized that the Indonesians had more than the two reported positions and attacked the longhouse. Lance Corporal Manbahadur Thapa was badly wounded by a mortar bomb exploding in trees above him while he was silencing a Czech 52/57 LMG with his GPMG.

After about an hour, A Company had captured Nantakor. During the search, the Indonesian commander, who was wearing campaigns medals for fighting against the Japanese and Dutch, was found among the dead. It is thought that at least twelve Indonesians were killed and, judging by blood found in the longhouse, several others had been wounded. The village was then set alight. The Gurkhas, faced with the awesome prospect of carrying four wounded men back to Sarawak, were relieved when Major General Walker permitted a helicopter to evacuate them to Brunei Hospital. When it turned up, Willoughby was delighted to welcome Lieutenant Colonel Clements, who had hitched a lift as a door gunner. Willoughby was awarded the MC and Hastabahadur and Sherbikram each received MMs.

Meanwhile incursions persisted. In early September, two B Company, 2/2nd Gurkha Rifles platoons clashed with an Indonesian patrol on a Second Division border ridge they were about to ambush as a known incursion route and lost a Rifleman killed. As they pursued the Indonesians withdrawing across the border they came under accurate mortar fire. When an Energa grenadier fired at an Indonesian lying behind a tree, his projectile hit the Indonesian's grenades and shrapnel seared through the trees, wounding six Gurkhas, one of whom had his foot blown off, and killing four Indonesians. As a result of this, Major Mike Joy, the Company Commander, could not follow up because he needed to evacuate the casualties.

2/10th Gurkha Rifles experienced several contacts in the border area of Lundu District. On 15 September, two patrols clashed near Pueh and then all was quiet for a fortnight until the infamous DShK machine gun at Aruk fired at an Auster, but stopped when the Battalion retaliated with a 3-inch mortar. Aruk was occupied by two companies totalling 400 men from the 438 and 445 Para-Raider Battalions, both of which were part of the Diponegoro Division. They were supported by about 400 IBTs. Elements of a RPKAD company were then reported to have penetrated First Division. On 2 October, Captain St Martin, who commanded D Company, left Biawak with several men to recce an ambush site near a hill that was being used by the Indonesians to machine-gun local Dayaks. As they neared the area, an Indonesian Army cap and boot prints were found, apparently carelessly left on the track, and then as the lead scout crested a small rise, he shouted 'Dushman!' ('Enemy!') and, stepping back, he pushed St Martin as a bullet fired from the jungle five yards away thudded into a tree. St Martin shot one of four charging Indonesians whereupon, with Captain Manbahadur Rai giving covering fire, the patrol broke contact, and under fire from a .30-inch Browning machine gun, grenades and 50mm mortar bombs, raced back down the track to another position. Manbahadur then scampered back and rejoined the patrol withdrawing in bounds, cautiously followed by the Indonesians, who soon broke contact apart from firing speculative, long-range machine-gun bursts down the track. A Company moved into cut-off positions, but for Battalion HQ it was a day of confused reports of enemy activity. When, next day, a big camp was found not far from the border, Lieutenant Colonel Fillingham realized that a major incursion had taken place and organized retaliation.

In August, 1st RUR, which had taken over from the Leicesters, changed over with 4 RMR and moved from Third Division to First Division to take over Serian District. Their area was split in half by the Kuching-

Simanggang road and a maze of paths connecting the kampongs. B Company was reinforced first by 4 Platoon, and then 2 Platoon, A Company, 1st Durham Light Infantry (DLI) from Hong Kong. The DLI were earmarked to deploy to Borneo in the autumn. An ambush of the junction of four streams was carried out in such relentless rain that even the tracker contracted pneumonia, nevertheless on the last night, soon after the area was mortared, they killed three IBTs. Otherwise it was a question of patrolling, although an old Indonesian camp was avoided after Lance Corporal Pugh of 2 Platoon stumbled on a resident family of unfriendly cobras. One soldier who made a name for himself was Private Edmund Christopher. A former medic in a colliery, he found himself running the medical centre at Long Jawi, not only dispensing medicine for the locals but also as a veterinary surgeon when an injured pet monkey was brought in for treatment.

Within days of the Ulstermen's arrival, two Dayak women from Tepoi were working in a paddy field about 70 yards from the border when they were asked by some Indonesians if there were any troops in the area. Replying that there were none, the women reported the incident to D Company, 1/6th Gurkha Rifles (Major Harkasing Rai MC*), which was under command of 1st RUR. With 10 Platoon, D Company, 1st RUR (Lieutenant Paddy Doyle) covering the track from the kampong to the border, Harkasing arranged for tin cans to be strung across the path and placed his Gurkhas and Doyle's platoon in ambush positions. After dark, some IBTs entered Tepoi and, after the usual shouting at everyone, they walked straight into the tin cans. Harkasing immediately fired a flare. Caught in its glare, the IBTs ran along the track leading to the river and straight into a trap laid by Corporal Deignan's section. One Indonesian was killed and the remainder were pinned down by Deignan's machine gunner for the night. Next morning, when three dead IBTs were found, the Ulstermen were taken aback when Dayak women danced on the bodies. 1st RUR claimed several more dead and wounded when a 176 (Abu Klea) Battery Pack Howitzer fired on likely withdrawal routes and the Medium Machine Gun Platoon engaged enemy setting up an OP about 600 yards from Kujang Sain, which sits on a spur jutting into Indonesia. It happened that Lieutenant Colonel Purdon was in the area in the Battalion Air Platoon Scout and, after being briefed by Lieutenant Nigel Taggart about the OP, he took off again. While the pilot, Staff Sergeant Hall hovered above the OP, Captain Brian Gallagher, from Battalion HQ, opened fire with a GPMG, while Purdon dropped grenades from a box he always took with him. A follow-up found no dead but plenty of blood trails leading to the border. The Indonesians never returned to Kujang Sain.

The RPKAD were then reported to be considering Mongkus as a

Wingate-style stronghold. The longhouse lay across Track 15 about 1,000 yards north of the border. When an elderly man and a sixteen-year-old girl were murdered while working in fields on 5 October, twenty-three men from 2 Platoon, A Company, 2/10th Gurkha Rifles (Sergeant Barmalal Limbu), which was under command of D Company, 1st RUR, deployed to Mongkus to ambush likely approaches. The Gurkha had a Bren and 2-inch mortar in a position on a knoll about 100 yards south-west of the longhouse. To the south was the river and to the east, a small overgrown rubber plantation; otherwise the remaining two sides were open cultivation. In support was a 176 Battery Pack Howitzer commanded by Bombardier Ward.

MAP 11 - BATTLE OF MONGKUS, 5 October 1964

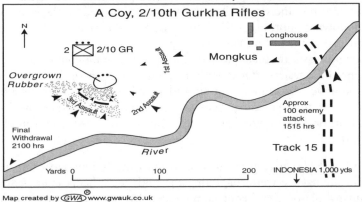

Map created by GWA® www.gwauk.co.uk

At about 1.50 pm Barmalal sent fourteen men to ambush a track about 2,000 yards to the north, leaving him with nine Gurkhas, four armed with Sterlings. It was raining. At about 3.30 pm there was a commotion at the longhouse and Corporal Damberbahadur Gurung, of Track 6 fame, fired at a group of enemy seen in its vicinity with the Bren. An estimated 100 uniformed Indonesians, covered by a light machine gun about 100 yards to the east of the longhouse, assaulted the knoll but were defeated by well-controlled shooting. Soon after he had informed Company HQ of his situation as an attack developed across the river from the south-east and advanced to within 50 yards of the Gurkhas, Barmalal called for artillery fire. Even though the rounds fell about 200 yards away, it was enough to convince the Indonesians to withdraw into cover from where they sniped at the Gurkhas, who replied with their mortar. Except for the fourteen-man ambush party, the prospects of reinforcements were slim, as was an air drop to replenish their seriously depleted ammunition stocks, but within the hour it would be dark. A third attack, supported by a heavy machine gun and mortar fire, developed from the south through an overgrown plantation. When some

151

mortar bombs fell among the crawling Indonesians, Barmalal, deciding that attack was the best form of defence, instructed Damberbahadur to give covering fire with his Bren, whereupon he and several men clashed with the Indonesians in the undergrowth, quickly despatching two. With Ward dropping 105mm rounds with monotonous but welcome regularity, and the judicial use of the Bren and grenades, Barmalal gradually drove the Indonesians to the river bank, by which time ammunition was down to one magazine per weapon. Although most of the Gurkhas had bullet holes in their hats and webbing order, none were casualties, which proves just how poor Indonesian marksmanship was. At last light, the ambush party rejoined Barmalal and, with spasmodic firing from the Indonesians, it looked as though it was going to be a long night, but by about 9.00 pm, there was silence. Barmalal remained on the knoll until the following morning and then sent out a clearing patrol, which reported that the Indonesians had departed.

Mongkus was another epic action in which a junior commander again had met Indonesian attacks with aggression and, in so doing, retained the initiative. Accurate shooting and grenade conservation had been critical. For their gallantry, Sergeant Barmalal was awarded the DCM and Corporal Damberbahadur the MM. Ward fired 155 rounds in support.

When 1st RUR were warned to deal with the Indonesian camp from which Intelligence were suggesting the raids were being launched, a C Company platoon at Tepoi commanded by the Irishman Lieutenant Niall Ryan was tasked to recce it. Accompanied by Lieutenant Colonel Purdon, he led the platoon across the border and, surrounding the camp, found it empty. However, carved on several trees were Indonesian slogans, including 'RPKAD'. As the platoon filed onto the track to Sarawak, Purdon noticed several newly carved slogans – 'Up the Irish' and 'RUR'. Mindful of the delight the international press would have if this was exploited by the Indonesians, he and his HQ hacked the comments from the trees and that night arranged for the 5.5-inch howitzers to shell the camp. Next morning, a helicopter recce reported the area was a tangle of uprooted trees and widely dispersed undergrowth and vegetation. Interestingly, 170 (Imjin) Medium Battery had supported the Ulstermen eleven times since 1944, the last in action being Korea.

Tebedu again became a focus of Indonesian attention when a mortar was fired at the town on 10 October. In the village was Bombardier Richardson's 5.5-inch howitzer from E Troop. Due to the number of houses and shops in the area, and because short- to medium-range counter-mortar fire was difficult, Richardson and the Section

Commander, Captain C.P. Masters, measured probable mortar base plate positions by direction and distance, and then Richardson opened fire. Next day, a patrol found that shells had impacted within 100 yards of the position and it had been hurriedly abandoned.

2/6th Gurkha Rifles (Lieutenant Colonel Tony Harvey), had arrived in Brunei as the resident battalion from Hong Kong and took over from 1st Argyll and Sutherland Highlanders in Fourth Division under command of Central Brigade. Tactical HQ was first at Miri and then Bario, the companies rotating about every six weeks at Pa Main and Long Banga with the reserve company at Seria. The Battalion and their families were based in Medicina Camp in Seria, which was a comfortable barracks rented from the Shell Oil Company, and was named after an action in Italy in 1945 in which the Battalion and the 14/20th Hussars had stormed German positions. When the Sultan of Brunei learnt from Major General Walker that some married quarters were poor, he financed a new barracks near Brunei town. Admiral Begg was delighted, but the Whitehall mandarins were not because the Works Department had not been consulted and there was suspicion that the Sultan might try to avoid paying Brunei's share of the costs. The Sultan, unconcerned by the hiatus, remarked to Walker that, 'On the one hand I am dealing with a sahib [Walker] – on the other with a lot of Whitehall babus [clerks].'

Intending to dominate the border ridges, the Battalion was soon in action when on 19 October, 5 Platoon, B Company, bumped an IBT patrol and sustained its first casualty. When information was then received that Pa Main and the Pa Lungan FDLs were under threat, B Company Commander, Major Vyvyan Robinson, sent two platoons to ambush two likely crossing points, and attacked a camp on Operation Claret. Two days later, when 1 Platoon was ambushed, it counter-attacked and killed two Indonesians. By now it was clear that the battalion was faced with a combative enemy and Robinson led a patrol armed with shotguns across the border and ambushed a track where they shot up two Indonesians. Meanwhile, soon after D Company had taken over from C Company at Long Banga, Lieutenant (QGO) Ranbahadur Pun's 11 Platoon laid a long ambush not far from the border. However, the route used to resupply the administrative base from Long Banga was attacked by Indonesian Marines and in a fierce battle, three Gurkhas, including Platoon Sergeant Kamabahadur Gurung, were killed and several others wounded. The Indonesians lost five killed and had several wounded, but then made the mistake of mutilating the bodies of the dead Gurkhas.

During October, Prime Minister Harold Wilson's Labour Party won a narrow election and almost within days, the new Deputy Secretary of State for Defence, Fred Mulley, a former Worcestershire Regiment sergeant who had spent several years as a prisoner of war after being captured at Dunkirk, visited Borneo. Major General Walker knew that Great Britain could not risk further alienation from the Communist and Afro-Asian blocs in the UN by declaring war on Indonesia, but was adamant the Indonesians could not be allowed to violate the border. He emphasized to Mulley that attack was the best form of defence and that the geographical limits marking the border were so confused that only by precise map reading could pursuing forces stop themselves encroaching into Indonesia. Operation Claret was not intended to hold ground but was aimed at creating a sanitized area in which Indonesian forces risked being attacked. Mulley was non-committal but promised to raise the issue with Secretary of State for Defence, Denis Healey. The Cabinet quickly agreed that Operation Claret should continue.

2/2nd Gurkha Rifles, still commanded by Lieutenant Colonel Neill, continued to harass the Indonesians on both sides of the Second Division border. 700/701 Para-Raider Battalion had been identified as having recently moved into the area and it was therefore important to put them on the defensive. From his C Company base at Batu Lintang, Major Geoff Aslett crossed the border with two platoons and ambushed a column of seventy Indonesians, however when a counter-attack, supported by mortar and machine-gun fire, swung in from the right, Rifleman Rudrabahadur slowed it down with his Bren. The Indonesians withdrew taking six killed with them.

In the second week of October, Major Mike Joy drew up plans for Operation Nelson's Eye to deal with an Indonesian unit opposite the B Company FDL at Jambu that was proving particularly troublesome with hit-and-run raids, however it took weeks of persistence by Neill to gain permission to attack the enemy. Joy had a score to settle, anyway. Assembling as many machine guns as he could, he placed them under command of Lieutenant (QGO) Samuel Tamang. The operation was significant because it was the last time that the Vickers went into action with the British. The plan was for B Company to take the Vickers and GPMGs 5,000 yards into Kalimantan and shoot up the Indonesian camp from distances of 1,200 yards for the Vickers, and 800 yards for the GPMGs. During the early morning of 14 October, Recce Platoon, E Company, which had been the former Medium Machine Gun Platoon, waited for enemy patrols to return to their camp and then opened fire with their Vickers, its comforting, heavy thumping echoing along the sides of the valley. There was very little retaliation and Joy ordered a ceasefire. When he later recced the camp, it was deserted and was never reoccupied. Intelligence reports indicated that the venerable Vickers and modern GPMGs had accounted for thirty-seven dead. Neill continued aggressive patrolling; on 1 November 1964 and 1 January 1965, Major Johnny Lawes led two E Company patrols across the border, which resulted in two Indonesians being killed. On 22 November, A Company (Major Len Lauderdale) attacked an Indonesian post killing four enemy. On 22 December, a joint C and D Company ambush in Kalimantan killed seven Indonesians.

Meanwhile, A Squadron SAS had carried out several Operation Claret interdiction patrols, laying ambushes and leaving booby traps, grenade necklaces and Claymore mines on tracks used only by Indonesian forces. In October, it was relieved by B Squadron on their first tour after being reformed. When the Squadron arrived, thirty Cross-Border Scouts were led by their commander, Major John Edwardes, across the border to set up a base from which to search for a CCO camp, thought to be somewhere near Batu Hitam.

By November, the number of incursions across the border had decreased to five. The last major action of the year in First Division occurred near Tebedu on 10 November when farmers reported to 10 Platoon, D Company, and a patrol of 1st RUR that they had seen ten Indonesians to the south. Captain Boucher was commanding the patrol and, after rendezvousing with a Border Scout corporal in Tebedu, and while going to where the Indonesians had last been seen, they met a Dayak, who said that he had directed them by a circuitous route to the village, in order to buy time for the Security Forces to arrive. Agreeing to show Boucher where the enemy could be intercepted, he then led the patrol at a fast pace 3,500-yards down a hill and up another until they came to a small ford. While the Border Scout was looking for enemy spoor, Corporal Labalaba, the section commander, signalled that Indonesians were approaching and a hasty ambush was laid in the very thick jungle around the stream. When the first five of the column entered the killing zone, the ambush was sprung and all five were shot by Labalaba. The remainder withdrew into thick cover and returned fire until the first artillery round called down by Boucher ended the firefight. The rest of 10 Platoon and a small tracker dog team, dropped by helicopter, set off in pursuit, but by nightfall it was evident they had withdrawn across the border. The Ulsters claimed three killed and three wounded.

December was a quiet month with just four incursions reported to Walker's headquarters, nevertheless 40 Commando, which arrived at Tawau in mid-July to defend an area of jungle and 150 square miles of near impenetrable mangrove swamp and countless rivers, streams and rivulets, obtained permission to raid a small OP on Sebatik Island about 500 yards south of the border near a river. Part of the island was in Indonesia, the other in Sabah. The OP was manned by about five Indonesian Marine Corps, who openly lived in an attap hut on the beach. Although the OP posed no direct threat to 40 Commando, its destruction would probably sap Indonesian morale. It had been examined earlier in the year by two 1 SBS swimmers who had crawled up to it. They had not found any defences or obstacles in the palms and scrub. The jungle reached to the water's edge, while nearby was a small, narrow beach suitable for a small landing.

B Company (Captain Bacon) provided the assault force of fifteen Royal Marines from 6 Troop. Lieutenant R. Seeger, who had recently completed a tour with the SBS, commanded the raid and planned for the patrol boat *Bob Sawyer*, which was manned by the Tawau Assault Group, to simulate a routine patrol north of Sebatik Island. Two Geminis would land the assault force of Seeger, his Troop Sergeant Costley, Corporal Tomlin's section, all armed with Sterlings, and Marine Allen with a GPMG. The Commando had just been equipped with GPMGs. Two Troop scouts, both good shots, had torches fixed to their SLR barrels. Bacon was the operational commander in a third Gemini, with a signaller and a reserve rifle section. The cover story was a broken-down outboard engine and an accidental drifting to the island.

Late in the afternoon on 8 December, the Royal Marines boarded the *Bob Sawyer* at Kalabakan and motored the 6 miles to the objective. After darkness, the three Geminis were launched and the force split into two groups, as planned. Shortly after Seeger's group landed on the small beach, an automatic weapon opened inaccurate fire from the tower. Surprise was lost and soon after Seeger had instructed everyone to spread out, he was wounded in the elbow. Sergeant Costley and Allen waded thigh deep into the sea to give covering fire. Seeger pressed on until looming out of the shadows was the hut. Shouting 'Grenades!' he threw two. Costley and Allen had nowhere to take cover except under-water, but were still spattered by fragmentation. As the grenades exploded, Allen opened fire on the burning hut and then, using the camp fire as a marker, specifically shot up any enemy who moved. Soon after, Tomlin's section then arrived after being briefly held up by the jungle. With the hut destroyed and three Indonesians sprawled on the ground, and with no time to search the bodies for documents and other intelligence, Seeger ordered the Royal Marines to withdraw. Scrambling into the Geminis, the outboards had just been started when mortar bombs, fired by Indonesian marines on Nunukan Island, bracketed the burning hut. The two Geminis rendezvoused with Bacon and then met up with the *Bob Sawyer*. Seeger was awarded the MC, Costley and Tomlin were both Mentioned in Despatches.

As 1964 drew to a close, President Sukarno's promise to crush Malaysia by the time the cock crowed on 1 January 1965 looked decidedly precarious, his forces having failed to achieve any significant success. It is not known if his commanders were acknowledging increasing evidence of Indonesian bases in North Kalimantan being attacked from Sarawak and Sabah. In any event, he could hardly admit this without being accused that Indonesian forces had been operating north of the border for nearly twenty months. His claim that they were 'volunteers' had been discredited and the attempt to stir up trouble in Malaysia had been a disaster. The reaction by the Commonwealth security forces showed just how restricted Indonesian capabilities were. If he was to crush the 'puppet state', Sukarno had no alternative but to raise the stakes. But he had an immediate problem. Even though he saw the CCO as allies, the failure of the IBT guerrilla bands to establish Wingate-style strongholds had decimated his support from Indonesia. In reality, by the end of 1964, Sukarno had no real choice except either to sue for a face-saving settlement or commit more troops to battle. But the Indonesian Army had not been in favour of the Malaysian landings because it believed that escalating the conflict would stretch naval and military sources to the limit. Senior Army officers were keen to rein in Sukarno because of his close links with the PKI, however, by mid-1964, some had become so disillusioned with the direction that *Konfrontasi* was taking Indonesia that peace feelers were extended to Malaysia in September through Des Alwi. Alwi was the adopted son of the imprisoned Sarakit Party leader, Sula Sjahir, and was employed in the Malaysian Foreign Ministry. Seemingly, he had made contact with General Yani during an overseas trip, an event sanctioned by Major General Suharto through Lieutenant Colonel Ali Murtojo and his contacts in Special Operations Intelligence. Murtojo is thought to have been smuggled in and out of Malaysia by Chinese fishermen during September and October. Early in 1965, Lieutenant Colonel 'Benny' Moerdani, of the Army Airborne Infantry, was smuggled to Malaysia disguised as a steward on an Indonesian national airline (Garuda) aircraft to continue the negotiations.

CHAPTER THIRTEEN

The Thin Red Line

During the autumn of 1964, British Military Intelligence had detected changes in Indonesian command and increases in their troop levels with the doubling and, in some cases trebling, of forces along the border. By the late autumn, the 12,000 troops that had faced Major General Walker in mid-year had grown to 16,000 by the New Year and would reach 22,000 in May 1965. Patrols, agents and informers were reporting better-equipped and better-trained troops backed up by light artillery. Increased troop levels on Sumatra threatened mainland Malaysia and Singapore. While Singapore and Borneo suggested that this was a prelude to an offensive, London suggested that Major General Walker was misreading the situation, although he did agree that the main threat was internal subversion.

The failure of the Malaysian landings had seriously undermined Air Marshal Dhani; in October 1964, Sukarno reorganized Vigilance Command and created an Inter-regional Command to cover Kalimantan and Sumatra, and placed it under the command of Major General Maraden Panggabean. Entrusted by Sukarno to quell mutinies, revolts and uprisings, he had done so with vigour. Panggabean was Yani loyalist, aged forty-two, who had been trained by the Japanese and then in the US; as Chief of Staff, East Indonesia Interregional Command, he had played a major role in the West Irian *konfrontasi*. General Yani retained Army control of operations by appointing reliable officers to key positions, in particular, on 1 January 1965, the politically astute Major General Suharto as Army Strategic Reserve commander. This undermined Dhani's military aspirations because he insisted that troops deployed to Vigilance Command must first be transferred to the Army Reserve.

Threatening Brunei and Sabah was an Indonesian Marine Corps brigade, which had been active. On the flanks of No. 4 Kalimantan Combat Command (still Brigadier General Supardjo) was East

Kalimantan Combat Command (Brigadier General Sumitro) and West Kalimantan Combat Command (Brigadier General Ryacudu) with its HQ at Pontianak, which the British believed was threatening Kuching with about eight TNI companies and eleven Brunei Regiment irregular companies. Although Brigadier General Kemal Idris had issued Sumatra Combat Command instructions to prepare to attack Malaysia, he had little enthusiasm for Confrontation, even less for an invasion of any sort in Malaysia, and seems likely to have been selected by General Yani because of his ambivalence to Sukarno's enthusiasm. He had been involved in coups in 1952 and 1956 against Sukarno and had then been prevented from filling any military appointments until 1963 when he joined Indonesia's UN commitment to the Congo. Major operations across the Straits of Malacca were unlikely.

In November 1964, the Chiefs of Staff had refused Admiral Begg's request to extend the limit of exploitation to 5,000 yards on the premises that, since Indonesian activity had decreased, raids would only escalate the crisis and that patrols operating deep inside Kalimantan could not be regarded as 'hot pursuit', were politically difficult to deny and might encourage Indonesia to escalate hostilities. However, on 12 January 1965, the build-up throughout Kalimantan and Sumatra led Begg to ask the Chiefs to extend Operation Claret up to 10,000 yards against staging areas, logistic routes, camps and garrisons as 'the Indonesian High Command might well remain in ignorance of them.' He justified his request by highlighting decrypted Indonesian intercepts indicating that it was not necessary to deny Claret because Indonesian commanders rarely reported clashes and if they did, it was to claim real and imaginary success, presumably to assure Sukarno that *Konfrontasi* was achieving its aims. While Walker could fly to his forward positions in First Division within fifteen minutes from Kuching, Indonesian Operations and Intelligence staffs were compelled either to fly long distances over inhospitable terrain, or use rivers, which could take days.

The following day, the request was authorized. The use of strategic intelligence to determine troop levels required to tackle *Konfrontasi* without provoking a full-scale war remained a vital factor in the context of Britain's over-stretched military resources, in particular the Army. Walker was content to dominate the border with the limit of exploitation to 5,000 yards and saw cross-border operations as a sharp stab to keep Indonesian commanders off balance, think defensively and not even consider offensive operations. He still insisted that only battalions on their second tour or more were permitted to execute Operation Claret, which rather confined operations to the Royal Marines and Gurkhas, and ignored the adaptability of the British infantry.

159

Defending East Malaysia were the 14,000-strong British Forces, Borneo, about 1,200 Sarawak, Sabah and Brunei police and 1,500 Border Scouts covering an area the size of England and Scotland. Singaporeans defended Kuching. About 22,000 Malaysian Army and 4,000 men of 28 Commonwealth Brigade defended Malaysia. During the New Year, Brigadier Patterson handed over West Brigade to Brigadier Bill Cheyne, a Seaforth Highlander. In Sabah, Brigadier Tunku Burhanuddin assumed command of East Brigade. By the end of January, Walker had strengthened the defence with an additional brigade, Mid-West Brigade:

- *West Brigade* – HQ 99 Gurkha Infantry Brigade defended First Division and 181 miles of border with five battalions.

- *Mid-West Brigade* – HQ 3 Commando Brigade covered Second and Third Divisions from Sibu with two battalions and 442 miles of border.

- *Central Brigade* – HQ 51 Gurkha Infantry Brigade defended Sarawak, Brunei and the Interior Residency of Sabah with two battalions and 267 border miles.

- *East Brigade* – HQ 5 Malaysian Infantry Brigade defended the rest of Sabah, 81 miles of the land border and 500 miles of coast.

Although RAF Transport Command flights were replacing the troop-ships, several ships ferried men to and from Singapore with the river motor vessel HMS *Auby*, which could ferry half a battalion at a time, doing a lion's share. Ferrying military equipment on usually fortnightly runs were three Malaysian-manned Mark VIII Landing Craft Tanks (LCTs) of 46 Squadron RASC (Water Transport), namely HMAV *Ardennes, Arromanches* and *Agedabia*, and two British-manned vessels, HMAV *Antwerp* and *Arakan*. These could carry 300 tons over 4,000 miles at 8 knots and were manned by two RASC officers and twenty-six soldiers, including two Royal Signals radio operators, who all conformed to Royal Navy and Merchant Navy proficiencies. Delivering stores to Sibu on the Sungei Rajang, and to Tawau and some destinations sufficiently close to the border, the LCTs were fitted with an Oerlikon, although none is thought to have fired in anger. For inshore operations and the provision of stevedores, 10 Port Squadron RE had detachments at Brunei, Kuching, Tawau and Sibu, and used Ramp Powered Lighters (RPL), a Ramped Cargo Lighter (RCL), the Z-craft *Nakhoda Manis*, which had been used in the Limbang operation, and a few Second World War landing craft. Tasks included the daily supply passage from Labuan to supply Central Brigade and weekly voyages from Kuching to Lundu, a distance of about 60 miles, and up the Rajang to Simanggang, a distance of about 100 miles. Both estuaries had treacherous sandbars, which skippers aimed to cross within two hours of high tides. 37 Maritime Squadron RE was equipped with general service launches and a RCL. One of its launches and a 10 Port Squadron Uniflote motorized raft supplied bases in Kalabakan and Wallace Bay, and delivered, in 1965/66, 9,000 passengers and 1,600 tons of stores while logging 32,000 miles.

The Brigade of Gurkhas 30 Company Platoon, Gurkha Army Service Corps of two Ferret Scout Cars, several Land Rovers and Bedford three-ton trucks rotated with 31 Company in Brunei on general transport duties, troop lifts and resupply tasks. By June 1964, Company HQ was in Brunei town with Composite Platoon in Tawau, a platoon at Seria and two platoons in Kuching. As the threat increased in First and Second Divisions in late 1964, the Composite Platoon moved to Kuching and, in January 1965, was joined by a Royal Marines transport platoon until it was replaced by 1 Company RASC when 19 Infantry Brigade arrived.

The Royal Army Ordnance Corps (RAOC) was responsible for storage of stores and equipment and during the Brunei Revolt, 99 Ordnance Field Park (OFP) was despatched to Labuan as part of 99 Gurkha Infantry Brigade. In January 1963, it was joined by 10 Field Workshops and 21 Air Maintenance Platoon of the Royal Electrical and Mechanical Engineers (REME), and moved to a depot in Parit Street with better access to a jetty and beaches. Interestingly, the Park had a 'shadow' role for deployment to Laos. 98 OFP organized logistic operations in Sarawak and was soon faced with establishing an ammunition point after the Kuching Port Authorities had refused ordnance to be discharged on to the Tanah Puteh Wharf, which was where civilian explosive was landed. Ammunition was therefore unloaded from ships to a lighter, manhandled up a slippery jetty to 3-ton trucks and then driven to the ammunition depot at a disused Public Works Department quarry. On one occasion, five soldiers unloaded 300 tons of ammunition in eight hours of darkness. Eventually the port authorities relented. When HQ 17th Gurkha Division arrived with Lieutenant Colonel Dally appointed as Commander RAOC, he found that the roles of the two OFPs were not fully understood by West and East Brigades, and the lack of handling equipment to move palleted and containerized supplies was complicating distribution. Renaming the two OFPs as 98 and 99 Ordnance Maintenance Parks and introducing measures to improve the systematic delivery of supplies, he instructed that both were to hold twenty weeks' worth of all stocks, which then reduced reliance on resupply from Singapore.

The Royal Pioneer Corps (RPC) organized local labour through detachments from 1202 Pioneer Corps Labour Unit (PCLU). Divisional and Brigade HQs usually had a RPC Defence and Employment Section of a sergeant and three sections of about eight men. 206 Company supported operations from Singapore. The increase in troop levels led to the expansion of logistic support and the establishment of two Brigade Maintenance Areas (BMA) at Labuan and Kuching. These consisted of a Transport Squadron, Port and Air Despatch unit, an Ordnance Maintenance Park, a Supply depot, barrack accommodation store, workshops and a PCLU.

In 1964, Lieutenant General Sir Archibald Nye chaired an Army Council committee examining the organization and function of the War Office and made several recommendations, including unifying the three Service ministries into the Ministry of Defence. In 1965, a committee headed by General Sir Roderick McLeod reviewing Quartermaster Services resulted in the disbandment of the RASC and the transfer of all transport services, including Port and Maritime Squadrons, to the new Royal Corps of Transport (RCT). The LCT Squadrons were grouped into 20 Maritime Regiment, while 10 Port and 37 Maritime Squadrons merged into 33 Maritime Regiment. The organization of non-transport logistics, such as the distribution of rations, petrol, oil and lubricants, married quarter and barrack services, fire services and the provision of staff clerks were transferred to the RAOC. The Sultan of Brunei still provided fuel for British use in Brunei free of charge. HQ Far East dissolved the RASC expensive 'dollar messing' system, which permitted those units not conveniently supported by a supply depot to purchase rations locally. Although an unpopular decision, the RAOC soon developed contracts for fresh food.

With the increase in strength of British Forces, Borneo, the helicopter force was strengthened in mid 1964 by the arrival of Spineforce, twelve 225 Squadron Whirlwind 10s and four 26 Squadron Belvederes from Exercise Triplex West in Libya. They joined 66, 103 and 110 Squadrons, and 845 and 846 NAS until October 1964 when 225 Squadron was disbanded and its aircraft dispersed between 103 and 110 Squadrons. In March 1965, even though twelve Whirlwind 10s from 230 Squadron arrived in theatre, there were still thirty-six helicopters too few to enable each battalion to deploy six aircraft.

Walker needed troops to caretake quiet sectors while those with jungle experience patrolled areas under greatest threats. When 1st Gordon Highlanders (Lieutenant Colonel J. Neish) arrived in late February from

162

the Strategic Reserve, the thirteenth British battalion to be deployed to Borneo, it moved into a camp about 50 miles north of Jesselton at Kota Belul, known as Paradise Camp, with instructions to develop jungle warfare training. On a coastal plain, amid beautiful low hills bordering sandy beaches and forest-clad hills, while the camp was idyllic, decent jungle was in short supply, nevertheless practically every unit that passed through climbed the nearby Mount Kinabalu, which dominated the area. Deployed from chasing communists on the Thai border, and arriving with the aptly named Major Gregor MacGregor of MacGregor as Second-in-Command, 1st Scots Guards took over from 1st KOYLI in 28 Commonwealth Brigade, and became responsible for the Kuching-Padawan sector, leaving 1/7th Gurkha Rifles to look after the remainder of First Division. Major General Walker told Lieutenant Colonel Charles Carroll, 'You hold the key to Kuching.'

Noting the defeats inflicted on the South Vietnamese by Viet Cong, Walker envisaged a similar situation developing in Borneo – if Indonesian insurgency was permitted to develop, and later claimed, 'The jungle belonged to us. We owned it, we dominated it, and we conquered it.' And his men had done well so far. Determined that incursions should never rest and must be destroyed, he fought hard to ensure his men were properly equipped, but was up against a complacent attitude in the Service ministries toward the campaign. When, in January, Lord Mountbatten, in his capacity as Chief of the Defence Staff, and Sir Solly Zuckerman, the Ministry of Defence's Chief Scientific Officer, visited Borneo, Walker gave them a prioritized list of his requirements in the knowledge that doing so at such a high level his chances of success were high. He emphasized the need for lightweight automatic Colt 5.56mm AR-16 Armalite rifles, a number of which were on trial with some units. Within weeks of Mountbatten's visit, an order was placed with Colt to supply several thousand, even before it was on general issue to the US Armed Forces. Nevertheless, some soldiers preferred the SLR because it was more powerful. The chubby 84mm Carl Gustav anti-tank gun replaced the cumbersome 3.5-inch Bazooka, and the 81mm mortar replaced the 3-inch mortar, although ammunition was in short supply. The 7.62mm GPMG had replaced the venerable Vickers and the Bren was finally retired in favour of the 7.62mm LMG. Seismic intruder detection systems, such as Tobias, were already deployed, while hover-craft trials were found to be too noisy. The Australian leather and canvas jungle boot with a metal plate to minimize punji stick injuries replaced the British canvas jungle plimsoll boot. Prince Philip, the Duke of Edinburgh, visited the same month and was annoyed to be restricted to flying in Twin Pioneers, which meant that he could not visit forward positions by helicopter.

Mountbatten's visit reflected a significant change in attitude in Whitehall and the outcome of Confrontation became important to regional security, particularly in the light of the instability in South Vietnam. As early as December 1962, Great Britain had urged Australia and New Zealand to commit to Borneo but Australia had good relations with Indonesia, indeed some Indonesian officers attended Queenscliffe Staff College during the war. In January 1963, during the Brunei Revolt, Canberra had permitted Royal Australian Navy (RAN) warships in Singapore to support the two Royal Navy Ton-class coastal minesweepers and a Royal Malaysian Navy patrol boat patrolling the British North Borneo coast, where Australian officers had noted that 'Royal Naval forces in the area are considered adequate to deal with naval problems arising from the Borneo situation.' Prime Minister Sir Alec Douglas Hume had reminded Australia and New Zealand that they should not interfere militarily except in response to a request from Malaysia and emphasized that Great Britain was firmly committed to the concept of defending Sarawak against incursions. Retaliation was out of the question except:

- In an attack either on a major facility, such as an airport, port or an essential defence establishment.

- Against a major city, in which case the decision to change the rules of engagement, such as with an air strike, lay with those on the spot.

By 1964, Canberra believed that if Sukarno was permitted to continue with his expansionist policy, then, in spite of the preferred option of not engaging, Australia would commit troops. The New Zealand Prime Minister K.J. Holyoake did not disagree that Malaysia should be supported but was keen to avoid hostilities with Indonesia because he believed it could have long-lasting, damaging political consequences with his Asian neighbours. Both countries had the same strategic aspirations:

- Establish the security of Australasia.

- Pursue a close relationship with non-Communist countries. This included Indonesia.

- Support SEATO.

- Counter Communist aggression.

- Support the UN.

164

When Malaysia eventually requested Commonwealth naval support, by May 1964 Australia had despatched two Ton-class coastal minesweepers to join the 16th Minesweeping Squadron patrolling East Malaysia, and two former Royal Navy Ton-class coastal minesweepers, HMNZS *Hickleton* and *Santon*, joined the frigate HMNZS *Taranaki* patrolling the Malacca Straits. The escalation in Borneo after Federation led the British to note that although there was a shortage of warships off Borneo, of greater value was the release of the Australian and New Zealand infantry battalions in 28 Commonwealth Brigade to serve in Borneo. The increased threat from Sumatra then led to the primary role of 28 Commonwealth Brigade being changed from defending Malaysia from external aggression to the 'maintenance of the security of Malaysia by support of the Malaysian Armed Forces in accordance with the agreement agreed' between the Commonwealth governments concerned.

On 10 November, after the Indonesian landings in Malaysia, Sir Robert Menzies announced to the House of Representatives that, since Indonesia was now the main threat to Australian security and to Papua New Guinea from West Irian, selective conscription would take effect from mid 1965. In January 1965, Canberra authorized for its resident 28 Commonwealth Brigade battalion, 3 RAR, the Australian SAS and combat and service support to deploy to Borneo. The Australian SAS Regiment had broken their links with the airborne element of the RAR in September 1964 but was still wearing red berets. When they arrived in Singapore en route for Borneo, within the day, Radio Jakarta reported that the British Parachute Regiment had been deployed to the Far East. 1 Squadron co-located its headquarters in the Haunted House and supported Central and East Brigades. The Australian Army Training Team was already in South Vietnam and Borneo would be a useful proving ground to evaluate tactics, equipment performance, loads and casualty evacuation. Australians later reported operations in Borneo far more strenuous than in Vietnam. Australian warships joined the Royal Navy patrolling the South China Sea.

New Zealand also realized the appeal for assistance could no longer be rejected and on 1 February 1965, Prime Minister Holyoake announced that 1 RNZIR would be deployed from 28 Commonwealth Brigade. It had also hunted the Indonesian infiltrators in Malaysia. 14 (RNZAF) Squadron deployed to Singapore with six Canberra bombers as part of the Commonwealth's air deterrent. Forty men of the 1st Ranger Squadron, New Zealand SAS (Major W.J.D. Meldrum) arrived in February. The term 'Ranger' is derived from Major Gustavus von Tempsky's Forest Rangers and Major Harry Atkinson's Tarankai Bush Rangers, both of which harried the Maoris during the nineteenth century Maori Wars. With some experience gained during the Malayan

Emergency, the Squadron joined D Squadron supporting West Brigade.

1/10th Gurkha Rifles arrived in Second Division on its fourth tour in January and were welcomed by 720/721 Infantry Battalion on their first night when Recce Platoon at Batu Lintang was mortared. Next day, work began to transfer the base to the reverse slope by burrowing through the hillside, leaving the bunkers facing south. C Company at Jambu undertook a similar operation with the aid of 200 Ibans. When an Intelligence Corps FIO and his Border Scout interpreter learnt that up to fifty soldiers of the 428 Para-Raider Battalion were using two huts in the village of Sadjingen, which was about 4,000 yards south of Biawak, on 2 February, D Company, 2/10th Gurkha Rifles (Major St Martin) attacked the village just after first light, however the Gurkhas were ambushed during the withdrawal and fought a confused battle as the four platoons dealt with hit-and-run tactics. During the month before it returned to Singapore, the Battalion fought several more engagements with more determined enemy troops than had previously been experienced.

After a nine-month casualty-free tour, on 10 February, 1st RUR handed over to the 1st Argyll and Sutherland Highlanders, which arrived from Singapore for its second tour. D Company was based at Plaman Mapu, a small hilltop village about 1,000 yards from Indonesian border, overlooked by the jungle-covered mountain Gunong Rawang, translated as Melancholy Mountain. Although its peak was frequently covered in mist, the Indonesian OP on the summit gave the units in Plaman Mapu the uneasy feeling of being under permanent observation. The base was strengthened with a network of trenches and bunkers connected to the Command Post in the centre and surrounded by dannert wire, punji sticks and other obstacles.

In January 1964, evidence of increased Indonesian activity south-west of Pensiangan, in Fifth Division, emerged when Murut villagers in the long, lush Ba Kelalan Valley reported that their cross-border trade with their cousins in the Long Bawan valley had been stopped by Indonesian troops building a military base at Long Medan. This was causing hardship. The Indonesians did not appreciate that a key to any campaign is winning the hearts and minds of the local people. In July, C Company, 1/2nd Gurkhas (Captain Bruce Jackman) deployed to Ba Kelalan, which at its nearest point is about 800 yards from the border, and built a formidable company base, with bunkers and tunnels, on a nearby hill. The nearest airstrip was at Long Semado, about 15 miles to the north and had been built by the Borneo Evangelical Mission. Capable of taking Twin Pioneer aircraft and parachute airdrops, it was defended by the RAF Regiment. Airdropped and helicopter supplies frequently included provisions for the local Muruts who had been deprived of trade. This was an important 'hearts and minds' operation, as were the weekly medical patrols to kampongs where Private Leeming RAMC performed a multitude of 'miracles', including the successful delivery of a breech birth despite never having been trained in midwifery.

C Company had 25 miles of border to cover and an area of responsibility about three quarters the size of Wales. The border ridges rose to 4,500 feet and were covered in inhospitable primary jungle where water was scarce. No incursions occurred until late October 1964 when the Indonesians ransacked a longhouse used by Indonesian refugees at Pa Tawing, about 12 miles from Ba Kelalan, an incident that induced a delegation of Murut headmen to demand action. Emphasizing that he was not allowed to cross the border, Jackman tried to reassure the headmen that he was providing protection by conducting an aggressive patrol and ambush programme along the border. Indeed, shortly afterwards, 11 Platoon (Lieutenant Sukdeo Pun) ambushed a nine-man patrol killing two and wounding three. The Indonesians retaliated by carrying out a stand-off attack against the C Company FDL with Czech RPG-7 rocket launchers. The Gurkhas counter-bombarded with 3-inch mortars and scored a direct hit on ammunition piled between the launchers. From the amount of blood found the following day, Jackman's estimate of three Indonesians killed was confirmed several days later.

As a consequence of this incident Jackman approached his commanding officer, Lieutenant Colonel Clements, seeking permission to destroy the Indonesian base at Long Medan. Recce patrols found the Indonesian camp to be on a spur running down from a jungle-clad ridge and surrounded on three sides by paddy fields. The camp, comprised of a headquarters hut and eight bunkers with attap overhead cover, was occupied by about sixty soldiers supported by two 60mm mortars, two medium machine guns and an assortment of light machine guns; 400 yards to the south was a river that was wide enough to be a serious obstacle. Brigadier Tuzo, who commanded Central Brigade, checked the plans, as did Major General Walker, the Director of Operations, and then Admiral Begg, all being briefed at Ba Kelalan over several weeks. After each visit, Jackman invariably had to take a recce patrol over the border to confirm some aspect of the plan. On one occasion, he took cine film and still photos to record details of the camp layout.

Finally, the plan was accepted for a night approach through the jungle prior to a dawn attack. Two platoons would attack from dead ground on a flank, with close fire support from the third platoon armed with four 3.5-inch rocket launchers, four M26 grenade launchers, four LMGs, in addition to their personal weapons. A Fire Support Base with

167

two 3-inch mortars and two GPMG (SF) would be on a nearby hill on the right flank. It would be guarded by 13 Platoon, D Company, who also provided the reserve. On 20 January 1965, six months after Jackman was first approached, Operation Moonbeam was authorized with the provisos that the river was the limit of exploitation and that no more than an hour was to be spent in the location because of the risk of being cut off from neighbouring military bases.

Jackman chose 29 January, the night of a full moon, for the approach and the attack at first light on 30 January. During the afternoon of 27 January, while final rehearsals were under way, Ba Kelalan was again pounded by a barrage of RPG-7 rockets from the same firing point as in November. Corporal Dhane Ghale, who happened to be cleaning his mortar, single-handedly brought it into action and fired ten rounds in one minute straight onto the Indonesian position. A follow-up patrol found two bodies and blood trails for two wounded enemy. For his skills, Corporal Dhane Ghale was Mentioned in Despatches.

On 28 January, 9 and 10 Platoons secured the border while Captain Tofield, the FOO, established his OP with 10 Platoon, where he had good observation of Long Bawan Valley and could bring down artillery fire with the Pack Howitzer flown to Ba Kelalan for the operation. Next afternoon, 11 and 13 Platoons and the Fire Support Base filed along Ba Kelalan valley, each man carrying two mortar bombs and machine-gun ammunition in addition to his own weapon, ammunition and equipment. Whilst having their last meal in the assembly area on the edge of the jungle below the border ridge, there was a shot followed by a short fusillade from 10 Platoon. Jackman learnt that a three-man Indonesian patrol, equipped with a RPG-7, had approached from the south. Rifleman Dilbahadur Thapa, who had very recently left recruit training, spotted the Indonesians but since he was unable to attract anyone's attention without giving away his position, he held his fire, hoping that someone would assist him. No one did and so he shot the leading Indonesian at such close range that he fell on top of Dilbahadur. The Gurkha was unable to shoot the other two, who ran back across the border. The Indonesians reacted by mortaring 10 Platoon from the hill Jackman had selected for his Fire Support Base. Jackman had a dilemma – attack or withdraw. The Battalion was already preparing to return to Hong Kong but, more important was the fact that the Muruts had been requesting action since October 1964. Opting to attack, Jackman instructed Tofield to neutralize the Indonesian mortar, which he did by forcing them to abandon the hill.

At 5.30 pm, the 148 men of the C Company group moved across the border and padded through the dark and silent jungle on a 4-mile approach march against an enemy assumed to be alert. By 5.45 am next morning, C Company was in position and the Fire Support Base established. As 11 Platoon were taking up their close fire support position on the fringes of the jungle, an Indonesian soldier carrying a LMG emerged from a hut and walked toward their position. Lieutenant Sukdeo immediately ordered the Rocket Launchers to open fire at the bunkers, as had been agreed if they were compromised, and as the first four projectiles smashed into the enemy bunkers, quickly followed by a second salvo, 9 and 10 Platoons ripped aside the bamboo fence, charged up the slope and stormed the eight bunkers with rifle, kukri and grenades. 9 Platoon lost Rifleman Shyambabahadur Thapa killed by machine-gun fire, Rifleman Amarbahadur Thapa wounded with a shattered leg and Rifleman Jagatbahadur Pun creased in the head.

As the platoons reorganized, an Indonesian heavy machine gun and two medium machine guns plus light machine guns and rifles opened up from a hidden position 400 yards in depth across the river. The situation for 10 Platoon looked grim as they faced the brunt of this stand-off counter-attack. It was then that Jackman realized that the Indonesians had thinned the defence of the base camp, after being alerted by the soldier, and had taken up a secondary position. Running with his signaller across open ground to assess the situation, they were floored by four mortar blasts. Corporal Birbahadur, the Mortar Fire Controller, used his knuckles to calculate adjustments and, hitting the Indonesian mortar pit with his second bomb, then plastered the area where the machine guns were located. Unfortunately, early morning mist surrounding the OP was preventing Tofield from directing artillery fire. Meanwhile, Jackman moved 11 Platoon's machine guns to join 10 Platoon and, working with the Fire Support Base, they silenced the Indonesian position except for the heavy machine gun. Someone would have to hunt for it. Jackman instructed a 13 Platoon Rocket Launcher team commanded by Corporal Lokbahadur, who was nearest to the enemy, to destroy it. Stalking through a chest-high sodden paddy field, they knocked out the machine gun with their first round, effectively signalling the end of the fighting at about 7.00 am. Eight dead Indonesians were found. After the Gurkhas had torched the camp, at 7.30 am, forty-five minutes after his time limit and with the risk of being cut off uppermost in his mind, Jackman ordered the withdrawal. With Shyambahadur's body and Armabahadur on improvised stretchers cut from the jungle, it took eight hours to climb the steep 4,000-foot ridge to the border under intermittent 120mm mortar fire from Pa Bawan, until the morning mist rose and Tofield could direct counter-bombardment.

Next day, the inhabitants of the Long Bawan valley streamed into Ba Kelalan delighted to be reunited with their cousins. Several days later, villagers from Pa Bawan said that they had buried thirty-two TNI who had been killed at Long Medan. The Indonesian forces vacated their camps in the Long Bawan valley for the duration of Confrontation. Private Leeming was Mentioned in Despatches for collecting the wounded during the battle and then treating Amarbahadur during the long carry back to Sarawak, in addition to the work he had done through his 'hearts and minds' patrols. Jackman was awarded the MC and Corporal Birbahadur Gurung the MM.

On 28 February, a SAS patrol was involved in an incident which is sometimes used to epitomize Confrontation; in fact, it was a near disaster had it not been for the resilience of those involved. Sergeant Eddie Lillico, of D Squadron, was instructed by Major Woodiwiss to establish an OP south-west of Plaman Mapu on the Sungei Sekayan, which had been identified as a main communication and supply route. The patrol totalled eight men and included four new arrivals on familiarization training. About 2 miles south of the border, the patrol stumbled upon an old Indonesian camp. Lillico left four men at their previous night's camp near Gunong Rawan, which had been designated as the emergency rendezvous, and then led the remaining three down a spur toward the camp. Trooper Ian Thompson was leading when, after crossing 1,500 yards of primary jungle, he saw the 'bashas' underneath high trees and beside a stream, and signalled 'Take cover'. After ten minutes, Lillico signalled Thompson to break cover, however as he stood up, Thompson was shot in the left femur at a range of about 12 yards, but still shot the Indonesian. Lillico, a veteran of the Malayan Emergency, fell wounded through the pelvis and in his buttock. Both men linked up and returned fire, felling two more Indonesians. Believing that Thompson could walk, Lillico sent him back to Gunong Rawan to bring the patrol forward. As night fell, Lillico was in deep trouble – on the wrong side of the border and partially paralysed – however, he dragged himself 400 yards into the shelter of a muddy pig hole lapping around the roots of a felled tree in secondary jungle. Dressing his wounds and injecting himself with morphine, he drifted in and out of consciousness.

When the firing began, the other two SAS returned to the emergency rendezvous and reported the contact to be a few soldiers, suggesting that Major Woodiwiss ask for support from a platoon of 1/6th Gurkha Rifles at Sain. Woodiwiss was in a dilemma because he was not sure of the status of the missing SAS, nevertheless next morning, when Brigadier Cheyne and SAS Commanding Officer, Lieutenant Colonel Mike Wingate-Gray, authorized a helicopter search, Flight Lieutenant David Collinson was given the task.

After spending the night not far from the rendezvous, Thompson found it had been abandoned and the Bergens ransacked by animals. Jabbing himself with morphine, he crawled towards Sain but, after 500 yards, collapsed from sheer exhaustion and the effects of his wounds. Resting underneath some bushes near a stream, he heard Collinson's Whirlwind and opened fire at it in the belief that it was enemy. During the afternoon, the Gurkha platoon, with six SAS scouting ahead to avoid friendly fire, found Thompson after he had fired three spaced signalling shots. Trooper Kevin Walsh reassured him he was safe. Rain prevented Collinson from evacuating Thompson and so the Gurkhas built a shelter and, next morning, carried him to a LP hacked from the jungle with their kukris.

Meanwhile, Lillico awoke to brewing coffee about 30 yards away. The Indonesians carried out a lacklustre search and when one climbed a nearby jackfruit tree, Lillico, his body covered in mud and bluebottles laying eggs in his wounds, lay very still. Although he heard the Whirlwind, he did not activate his search-and-rescue beacon. During the afternoon, when he reached the border, he activated his beacon and Collinson, in a demonstration of precision flying, descended between tall trees. Although weak, Lillico struggled into the strop, however, to his intense annoyance, he dropped his rifle as he was lifted out. Thompson, with his wounded leg shorter, served for several more years, as did Lillico. Collinson was awarded the DFC.

On 12 March, Major General Walker handed over British Forces, Borneo, and Director of Borneo Operations to Major General Lea. Although he had laid the foundations for the defeat of Sukarno, he was denied a knighthood, a fact accidentally or, more likely, deliberately let slip by Lord Mountbatten, when he had visited Borneo, mentioning that Field Marshal Hull had rejected the recommendation. Instead, Walker was awarded a third bar to his two DSOs, his citation written in terms of often being under fire, which was simply not true. But such are the inconsistencies of the military awards system.

Major General George Lea was aged fifty-three. Commissioned into the Lancashire Fusiliers in 1933, he had fought with his Regiment and the Parachute Regiment in Africa, Italy and North-West Europe, followed by regimental and staff duties with the Parachute Regiment and 3 Commando Brigade. Awarded the DSO in Malaya while commanding 22 SAS, in between staff officer appointments with the War Office, he commanded 2 Infantry Brigade from 1957 to 1960 and 42nd (Lancashire) Division from 1962 to 1963 before being posted as Commander, Northern Rhodesia and Nyasaland until 1964. Lea had steely charm entirely suited to the next phase of the campaign. His relations with Lieutenant General Hunt were good as they were with Admiral Begg.

While Lea reviewed Operation Claret, he kept the enemy off balance by ordering the SAS to attack opportunity targets south of the border during the last two days of their recce patrols. HQ 19 Infantry Brigade then arrived from the UK and took over Mid-West Brigade from HQ 3 Commando Brigade, which returned to Singapore as Theatre Reserve. Its 2 Intelligence Platoon identified the Police Mobile Brigade as a major threat. Seventy-two police were captured during Confrontation. The combination of increased troop levels and the absence of co-ordinated preparations for a major offensive – assembly of new troops, new camps and stockpiling of stores – was leading to uncertainty about Indonesian intentions. Nevertheless, opposite First Division, patrols were still finding evidence of unco-ordinated strong incursions.

B Company, 1/7th Gurkha Rifles (Major Alan Jenkins) was based at Serekin near a trading route running along the jungle-covered razor-backed Gunong Jagoi from Babang in Indonesia to Bau in Sarawak. The Battalion searched the valleys and low ground for signs of the infiltration. In support was the West Brigade Artillery Reserve which was 'galloped' from its base in the idyllic Simpangkuma Valley. The FOO was Captain Sandy Attoe from 70 Light Battery, who styled himself 'Forward Adviser to the Serikin Area Commander'. Below the northern slopes of the mountain was another gun at Stass, although this had a higher priority elsewhere. The Troop Commander was Lieutenant Pinnion.

Mid-morning on 11 March, a B Company patrol ambushed a long Indonesian column high on the route and then found themselves under severe pressure. Within a minute of Captain Attoe calling for an emergency fire mission from Stass on a likely forming-up place in a clearing south of the border, shelling covered the withdrawal of the patrol. However, by the afternoon the pressure was such that the Serekin gun was switched to support Attoe while Pinnion used the Stass gun to harass the Indonesians with salvoes of two white phosphorous to three high explosive for two hours. In between breathless radio messages, Attoe confirmed the fire was 'Fine, absolutely fine.' During the early afternoon, Attoe asked Pinnion to shell a clearing at the eastern end of Gunong Jagoi to encourage the Indonesians to withdraw. When the patrol and Stass were subjected to mortar fire, Pinnion used the Serekin gun to shell nine registered targets in the Kuloh area. The patrol remained on the ridge overnight under the artillery umbrella and when B Company arrived with Pinnion the following morning and found several large camps on the ridge, it was clear that they were being used as a springboard for a major attack into First Division. Radio Pontianak admitted twenty-eight soldiers killed during the fighting, although reports from a trader suggested that this figure was low. The radio claimed eighty-six Gurkhas killed when, in fact, not one casualty had been suffered.

1/10th Gurkha Rifles began its third tour in Borneo by taking over from 2/2nd Gurkha Rifles in Second Division on 19 January 1965. 700/701 Para-Raider Battalion had not been active for some time, however, when a defector suggested that the Indonesian battalion was planning a major attack in retaliation for raids conducted by 2/2nd Gurkha Rifles the previous year, several Operation Clarets destabilized their plans. B Company, after a two- day approach march, ambushed a boat 1,000 yards south of the border, killing three Indonesian soldiers. In this operation, artillery support was provided by 4th RTR Saladin armoured cars on a border ridge.

Meanwhile the financial requirements of *Konfrontasi* were beginning to affect the economic health and political stability of Indonesia and Sukarno badly needed a military victory.

CHAPTER FOURTEEN

The Battle of Plaman Mapu

On New Year's Day 1966, 2nd Parachute Battalion (Lieutenant Colonel Ted Eberhardie) (2 Para) flew out to the Far East from Aldershot to carry out four weeks jungle warfare training at Kota Tinggi prior to a six-week exercise in Malaysia. In a strategy not dissimilar to that employed by Lieutenant Colonel 'H' Jones in 1982, it seems that Eberhardie persuaded HQ Far East that with his battalion in the Far East, it made sense that it should reinforce British Forces, Borneo. In March, 2 Para took over from 1st Argyll and Sutherland Highlanders in First Division under command of West Brigade. At the same time the Rifle Brigade, which was scheduled to take over from a Gurkha battalion in Hong Kong, was flown out for a short tour in Borneo.

C (Independent) Company was attached to the SAS as part of the agreement that the three para battalions would provide a patrol company. Deployed to Fifth Division for familiarization, it took over from the Gurkha Independent Parachute Company at Sibu and supported Mid-West Brigade from Nangga Gaat with six weeks of intelligence gathering, mapping and watching for infiltration. On 12 April, two 845 NAS Wessexes carrying the four-man patrols of Lieutenant Johnson and Sergeant McNally collided in the gathering evening near the base, killing them, two JNCOs from the RAMC, three naval officers and three other ranks. A small cenotaph raised to them was renovated in 1990. This was the worst aircraft crash during Confrontation so far, closely followed by the crash of a 66 Squadron Belvedere on 4 May 1963 when several SAS and the aircrew lost their lives. Other fatal aircraft incidents included the loss of a Twin Pioneer on 14 February 1963, a Hiller on 9 April 1964, an Army 656 Squadron Scout on 15 July 1964 and a Royal Navy Wessex going down on 4 March 1965. Considering the conditions and the amount of flying hours, the fact that so few aircraft were lost speaks volumes for the training and skill of the Royal Navy, Army and RAF aircrews, and ground maintenance staff. A task inherited from the Guards and the Gurkha paras to link up with the nomadic Punan fell to Lieutenant John Winter's patrol. On the rare occasions that his patrol emerged from the jungle, they could be seen in the corner of some bar in Sibu, quietly muttering to each other, apparently in Punan. The Company's credentials established, four patrols under Lieutenant Simon Hill were transferred to First Division to work with A Squadron, which was still commanded by Major de la Billiere, on Operation Claret raids. By this time, Hill had developed a tactic in which he and his radio operator, Lance Corporal Burston, would leave the other two members of the patrol near the border crossing point while they disappeared into Indonesia to reappear about ten days later.

Lieutenant Colonel Eberhardie had seen active service in the Far East during the Second World War as the 12 Para Intelligence Officer, and with 5 Parachute Brigade in Java between 1945 and 1946. He had also fought in Korea and consequently had some novel ideas. Training 2 Para to use small patrols, as opposed to the platoon-strength patrols, a view not rejected by the Jungle Warfare School, his Education Officer, the Maori Captain Huia Wood, taught three men in every section the art of tracking. In line with most other units, he banned alcohol in the bases, however the grey-suited Fleet Street warriors of Fleet Street, as usual, printed half the story. The 'scandal' ventured into a public relations disaster and HQ Far East suggested that he either rescind the order or he would be relieved. When he chose the latter, the editors settled back into their comfortable offices and took credit for something about which they had no understanding; not for the first time had the Staff undermined a commander for political expediency. The fact is that most of the paras agreed with Eberhardie's philosophy.

Lieutenant Colonel Sarwo Edhie Wibowo, who commanded the Javanese-based 3rd RPKAD, was an experienced soldier who, bizarrely, had recently attended the Queenscliff Staff College in Australia where a fellow student was Major Jeremy Moore, the Royal Marine who had commanded the Limbang operation in 1962 and was then on the Operations Staff, HQ 17th Gurkha Division. Although Moore had discussed with him that dealing with regular forces was significantly different to dealing with irregulars, Wibowo was convinced that, since small Dutch units had defeated large guerrilla forces during the Dutch police actions, his para-commandos could do the same. Wibowo selected the company FDL at Plaman Mapu to test his theory. As an Indonesian officer was later to claim, the idea was to give 2 Para a bloody nose – after all they were inexperienced in the jungle.

Formed in April 1952, the elite Army Commando Corps (Korps Kommando Angatan Darat (KKAD)) was incorporated into the

Siliwongi Infantry Division until, in 1955, it was renamed the Army Commando Regiment (Regimen Pasukan Komando Angatan Darat (RPKAD)). A year later, it was embroiled in political affairs when its commander moved the regiment to the outskirts of Jakarta in anticipation of the coup planned by Colonel Lubis, however when this did not materialize, a mutiny among non-commissioned officers (NCOs) gave Army commanders the opportunity to regain control. The RPKAD first saw active service when, in 1958, 600 men parachuted into Sumatra, captured the city of Pakanbaru and helped suppress the PRRI rebellion. In October, the Regiment was renamed the Army Para-Commando Regiment (RPKAD) and in 1962, it landed with Air Force parachute units in the West Irian operation. The Regiment was then three 600-strong battalions of 1st Para-Commando Battalion in Jakarta, 2nd in Ambon on the Maluku Islands and 3rd in Solo in central Java. By October 1963, elements were training 'volunteers' of the Brunei Regiment infiltrating into Sabah and provided cadres for cross-border operations into Sarawak. The Regiment was distinctive in that the men wore red berets.

The FDL was perched on a conical hill surrounded by jungle and, in common with every other base, was supported by a network of LPs, winch sites and artillery and mortar direct-fire registered targets. In support at Gunan Gavak was artillery from 102 (Australian) Battery.

When Intelligence identified Wibowo to be facing First Division in February, Moore reported his conversations to General Hunt and warnings of a likely attack were sent to 2 Para. In mid February, refugees escaping looting by Indonesian patrols, and forced conscription as porters or 'volunteers', suggested increased enemy activity. Patrols found OPs and positions hacked out of the jungle for rocket launchers, mortars and RPGs, and newly cut routes and clearings. D Company found a camp capable of housing at least thirty men. The new headman in Kampong Daha Tama was also suspected by the FIO of passing information to the Indonesians.

During the night of 25/26 April, leaving a company to provide a firm rear security base on the border, three companies of 3rd RPKAD, numbering about 200 men, entered Plaman Mapu at 9.00 pm, cut the early warning telephone line to the base and intimidated the inhabitants into silence. Next night, one company set up a fire support base with RPGs and ten DShK machine guns south-west of the base.

In the base were thirty-four men commanded by Acting Major Jon Fleming, the B Company Commander. His other platoons were on operations and training. The FOO was Captain John Webb who was linked to a Pack Howitzer at Gunang Gajak. The garrison consisted of CSM

John Williams, CQMS Goodall, seven men from the Mortar Platoon commanded by Sergeant John McDonald, manning two 3-inch mortars, two Army Catering Corps cooks and fifteen 18- and 19-year olds who had just completed their recruit training and jungle warfare course. Eberhardie had kept them together as a platoon and placed them under command of Captain Nick Thompson of Support Company, in the absence of their platoon commander on a jungle warfare course. Also in the base was Craftsman Restorick, who had arrived the previous day to maintain weapons. When the company arrived, they had improved the defences creating fields of fire outside the perimeter. The soldiers slept in dugouts, wearing boots and trousers. Shirts were an option in the heat.

At 5.05 am, still dark and with heavy rain pounding the jungle, the RPKAD fire support base opened fire. Major Fleming thought the noise was rain until a signaller said, 'I think we are under attack.' Clipping his webbing over the sarong he wore at night, he went outside to a rain-sodden night illuminated by explosions, tracer and flares. The two water tanks were hit, as was the area around the sentry tower. Although the paras stood to very quickly, a mortar bomb killed Private Smith and wounded two others as they rushed to their mortar near the stores. A GPMG bunker was also rocketed. From the gully below the mortar pit, the Indonesians directed their attack at the mortar position and used Bangalore torpedoes to create paths through the double-coil barbed wire and 'punji' sticks, detonating Claymore mines. They then poured into the mortar position and milled around, seemingly undecided what to do next. CSM Williams, dressed in trousers and boots, had grabbed his webbing and rifle and ran to the sector where the fighting was taking place, where he encountered Private Kelly, a machine-gunner from the bunker that had been attacked, dazed from being shot in the head twice and waving a 9mm Browning pistol at virtually anything that moved. Disconcertingly alert, he pointed the pistol at Williams, shouting, 'They're in the position! You're one of them!' Williams coolly disarmed him and instructed a para to take Kelly to the Command Post where casualties were being assembled.

Meanwhile, Fleming had reported the attack to Eberhardie, however every time that he, still dressed in his sarong, went out to what was happening, he would be called back to the radio. He was therefore reliant upon Williams for updates.

With a crisis around the captured mortar pit, Williams left the paras on other parts of the perimeter to watch for attacks and with Lance Corporal Collyer, a cook, firing illuminating rounds from a 2-inch mortar, he ran to Captain Thompson and told him to follow with a section to counter-attack. Slipping and slithering as they ran across the muddy ground, several more mortar bombs fell into the base, wounding

177

Thompson and about half the section. Left with two men, one of them a cook, Williams told the Acting Platoon Sergeant, Corporal Malcolm Baughan, to give covering fire, agreeing that anyone in front was enemy and, in vicious hand-to-hand fighting with fist, boot, rifle butt and bullets, the three paras slowly drove the Indonesians from the mortar pit and down the steep flank of the base. Baughan's section lobbed grenades into the gully while the GPMG bunker raked them. With Captain Webb shelling the area, Sergeant McDonald had the surviving 3-inch mortar on near maximum vertical elevation to add to the discomfort of the enemy. Unfortunately the bombs were for 81mm mortars and they sometimes 'overcooked'.

MAP 12 - BATTLE OF PLAMAN MAPU, 27 April 1965

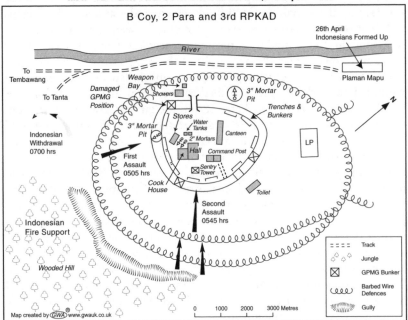

During a lull in the fighting, Fleming, Williams and CQMS Goodall organized the redistribution of ammunition and repaired smashed defences. When it became evident that Lance Corporal McKellar had a horrendous head wound, Williams asked Collyer, who had also been wounded, to remain with him. With the defenders down to twenty men, Fleming knew from Eberhardie that if he held out until dawn, which was not far off, reinforcements would be flown in and D Company was ready to cut the RPKAD off from the border.

Williams was helping a wounded man to the Command Post, which was now filling up with wounded, when, at 5.45 am, a second attack developed from the south, with about twenty-five enemy breaching the outer wire defences. Although heavily engaged with GPMGs and small-arms fire, they also crossed the inner wire. Instructing Baughan to counter-attack, shirtless, wet and muddy, Williams discovered that the GPMG in the smashed bunker was undamaged and, clipping two ammunition link belts together, he removed it from its tripod and then, firing from his hip, he raked the Indonesians hauling themselves up the slope through the barbed wire. Meanwhile, Baughan and about eight men were working their way through the trenches. Nevertheless, the Indonesians pressed home their attack and reached the British trenches before being thrown back, the closest man being killed 3 yards from Williams. It later turned out that this brave man had been wounded in the thighs during the first attack and had applied tourniquets. During the fighting, William was wounded in the head and partially blinded when his GPMG was hit and the foresight struck him on the head. The Indonesians left another killed near the outer defences.

As the first light of dawn filtered through the soaking trees, when the Indonesians withdrew toward Tanta, they were harassed by the guns and mortars. While the paras were searching the base, a number of unexploded British 36 grenades were found around the stores attap hut, leading to speculation that some locally employed labour had been feeding information to the Indonesians. Between 6.30 and 7.30 am, two small groups of Indonesians thought to be collecting dead and wounded were engaged. An hour later, a two-hour search found a trail of discarded first field dressings and abandoned equipment. The only unit identification was a name in a dropped wallet, although Eberhardie later thought the Indonesians were from 608 Infantry Battalion, or possibly a newly arrived one.

Soon afterwards, intense helicopters activity began with the arrival of the 1/6th Gurkha RMO who noted that Williams was blinded in one eye, deaf in his left ear and had head wounds from shrapnel and he had him casevacced to Singapore. John Williams was thereafter known as 'Patch'. For his exceptional leadership and gallantry, he was awarded the Distinguished Conduct Medal for 'One of the most outstanding acts of bravery and leadership witnessed during the Borneo Confrontation.' Retiring from the Army in 1989 after forty years of service, he died in 2002. Lance Corporal McKeller died in the British Military Hospital, Singapore. Corporal Baughan was awarded the Military Medal and Private Murtagh, who had been wounded in the first counter-attack, received a Mention in Despatches.

The Brigade Reserve, A Company, 1/6th Gurkha Rifles, went under command of 2 Para to defend the base. 6 Platoon, B Company was inserted into an ambush position while 5 Platoon was recalled from a jungle camp to reinforce D Company's base at Gunong Gajak. Directed by a helicopter OP, 102 (Australian) Battery carried out a programme of harassing fire on routes to and across the border. Apart from a short clash near a LP, in which A Company, 1/6th Gurkha Rifles was prevented from landing when a helicopter was hit by ground fire, there were no contacts. When a Royal Artillery Field Platoon roped down and found tracks of fifty Indonesian soldiers moving south, it was concluded the RPKAD had escaped the cordon.

For the next fortnight, 3rd RPKAD made several attempts to cross the border in the Mongkus/Mujat sector suggesting that, in spite of their reverse, more powerful attacks were being planned. After reports of recce patrols around Mongkus, as it was getting dark on 15 May, 12 Platoon (Sergeant Barker) ambushed a patrol near Mongkus and next day found tracks of five soldiers. When villagers in Mujat telephoned to a Border Scout screen that seventy para-commandos had entered the kampong the previous night, Major Barnes, who commanded D Company, despatched 10 Platoon (Lieutenant Gavin Coxen) to investigate. Suspecting a 'come on' ambush along the main path and stream bed, Coxen moved carefully but nevertheless clashed with a small enemy party and wounded one. In a planned battalion operation, Recce Platoon (Captain John Collinson-Jones) and a Combat Tracker Team commanded by Sergeant Murray then joined 10 Platoon. As the Australian gunners shelled suspected withdrawal routes, the dog, which was handled by Corporal Jocelyn, led both platoons along the track until it split into three at a junction. When the dog indicated spoor along a track and up a stream, Murray was suspicious of an ambush and led the two para platoons around a hill and then charged into it from a flank, during which Private McLeod was killed. The ambush collapsed and the RPKAD withdrew, taking with them five casualties. Outnumbered, D Company called up artillery fire. During the follow-up, Jocelyn and his dog became exhausted and the Iban tracker, Rayong, took over and, feeling for Indonesian boot marks in the darkness, very slowly followed the spoor. Shortly before midnight, Sergeant Murray reported a very recently abandoned ambush position. When the advance continued, Rayong became apprehensive and then the paras smelt the distinctive smell of coffee and tobacco. Murray pressed on until the smell was nearly overpowering and then halted until first light. Early next morning, the two platoons were on a border ridge when they found a large camp for about 150 men, which had been abandoned about half an hour before. From the layout, the camp was believed to be a base camp for ambush parties and patrols which had withdrawn the previous day. Possible withdrawal routes were shelled.

By 22 May, when information was circulating that about 100 Indonesians regulars were in the border area of Gunan Niyat south of Mongkus and Mujat, Lieutenant Colonel Eberhardie planned to surround them. With artillery suppressive fire controlled from an Auster, B Company, 1/6th Gurkha Rifles patrolled several routes to flush out the enemy while D Company, 2 Para roped down from helicopters along the border. Two KRRC platoons were brought in as the immediate reserve. Corporal Tindale, who was a 10 Platoon section commander, was scouting the ridge when about forty Indonesians were spotted advancing across the *lalang* toward them, laughing and joking, and waving in the apparent belief they were approaching their firm base. Organizing a quick ambush, Tindale waited until they were within about 10 yards and then ordered open fire, his two LMG gunners cutting down about fourteen Indonesians. They proved to be the advance party of a larger force and when Tindale found that he was in danger of being surrounded, and mortars bombs were dropping close to his position, he withdrew without any casualties. Tindale was awarded the MM.

The following month on 24 June, 10 Platoon was about to ambush a column of about fifty-five TNI, when a long Morse-coded message being unwittingly sent by the platoon signaller, Private Eltringham, was heard by the enemy lead scout, who opened fire. Although the ambush had been compromised, 10 Platoon opened a blistering volley, which felled about ten Indonesians, however the counter-attack forced the paras to withdraw. When Eltringham called for artillery fire to shell the ambush site, his radio was out of range. By chance, a helicopter was in the area and its pilot relayed the messages to D Company and soon 105mm shells were smashing into the jungle.

This was the last action of 2 Para and in late July, it returned to 16 Parachute Brigade in the UK, having lost eleven killed and thirty-eight wounded.

CHAPTER FIFTEEN

The Battle of the Rivers
June to October 1965

Plaman Mapu was a major assault on a British base and had been undertaken by experienced troops as part of an experimental Indonesian strategy that small forces could defeat larger guerrilla forces. It had failed largely because the opponents were a disciplined and motivated battalion, part of whose history focused on being cut off at Arnhem in 1944. To a great extent, it was a focal point in Confrontation and gave the British forces the opportunity to extend Operation Claret. Nevertheless, Indonesian intentions were still unclear and because it did seem that Plaman Mapu had not been co-ordinated with other incursions, Major General Lea instructed the SAS to undertake offensive operations, as opposed to just recces, providing guides for Operation Claret and acting as a rearguard to infantry columns.

One patrol encountered two Dayaks armed with muzzle loaders dated 1863. On 28 April 1965, two days after Plaman Mapu, Captain Robin Letts, who had been on Lillico's near disastrous patrol, attacked the rivers linking the Indonesian garrisons at Berjongkong and Achan, and ambushed two longboats heading in the direction of Sarawak near the Ayer Hitam boat station. Ten days later, a patrol led by Sergeant 'Lofty' Large waded through a swamp for several days, evaded a large Indonesian patrol and then watched the Sungei Koemba near Poeri from a rubber plantation. Large had been captured with 1st Glosters at the Battle of the Imjin River in Korea, and after physiotherapy to a wounded arm that had not been treated in captivity, had joined the SAS in Malaya. On 11 May, the patrol was about to fire on a launch flying an unidentified Indonesian Army ensign when a pretty woman was seen and chivalry overtook operational necessity. The ensign belonged to Lieutenant Colonel Moerdani, the same officer involved in extending peace feelers to Kuala Lumpur in November 1964 and the woman was his wife. Next day, in driving rain, the patrol ambushed a longboat manned by two soldiers. As the four men withdrew, a large king cobra confronted Large by spreading its hood and then slithered into the jungle.

After the 1st Argyll and Sutherland Highlanders, who were based at Lundu, had lost Private William Hill killed in a firefight north of the border in May, on 5 June, Lieutenant David Thomson and his platoon crossed the border and, supported by a Pack Howitzer, 'galloped' forward, fought a series of engagements over two days near Kandai and accounted for eleven Indonesians at the cost of one Argyll slightly wounded. In late June, the Battalion returned to Singapore and was posted to Aden where Thomson, who had been awarded the MC, was the Battalion Intelligence Officer when the Battalion controversially entered Crater District. After the KRRC (Lieutenant Colonel Edwin Bramall) took over from 1st Scots Guards in May in First Division, A and C Companies forced the Indonesians to abandon a large camp at Kepala Pasang, however, when one of the companies swam a river swollen by rain, six soldiers contracted leptospirosis. C Company isolated the camp at Mankau by attacking its lines of communications. After a two-day approach in difficult jungle, Lieutenant Mike Robertson was awarded the MC when he led a 14 Platoon patrol and killed seven TNI near Sungar Salaya in an ambush and then killed seven more in subsequent fighting. The action is immortalized in the Terence Cuneo painting showing Sergeant Hunt supporting the wounded Rifleman Martin en route to the rendezvous. By the end of their tour, the KRRC claimed at least forty-three kills for one man killed and two wounded.

Even though issues over rations, clothing and pay had not been solved, 3rd RAR took over from 1/7th Gurkha Rifles in First Division in Bau District on 14 June. Although Major General Walker had frequently asked that British troops be issued with rations conducive to jungle warfare and not the general service 'compo' used in Europe, the Australians were still supplied with British rations and a cash allowance to compensate for the deficiency of meat in the rations – some antipodean wag commented that British rations had to be pretty awful if Australians were paid to eat them. At the end of May, after the Indonesians had mortared several kampongs, Lieutenant Patrick Beale ambushed four boats smuggling supplies and men into Sarawak in a poorly mapped area. Several days later, when Second Lieutenant Byers's patrol had ambushed twenty-five Indonesians and killed seventeen, it was counter-attacked until Byers called down artillery fire, forcing the enemy to withdraw without their wounded. At the end of July, the

Australians completed their operations in Malaysia, having dealt with thirty incursions and having killed or captured an estimated fifty Indonesians. They later went to Vietnam.

On 22 June, eight days after 1st RNZIR (Lieutenant Colonel R.M. Gurr) took over from 1/10th Gurkha Rifles in First Division, Lieutenant Marshall, tasked to ambush two well-known tracks near Lubok Antu, was scouting a position previously used by the Gurkhas when his men captured two Indonesians; a third man escaped. Marshall's FOO, Captain Harbans Singh, of the 1st Malaysian Artillery Regiment, immediately shelled nearby border crossing points to catch any Indonesian patrols lurking in the area. Soon after Marshall's patrol had attacked a mortar crew setting up on a track junction, he learnt from his platoon that one of the wounded Indonesians had said, before he died, that he was part of an advance party of two companies tasked to attack Lubok Antu. Leaving Singh to harass several tracks leading from the border to prevent the Indonesians from withdrawing, Marshall took two sections to the track junction and killed two enemy lurking in the jungle. Checking a track leading south to the border, he swung east through the jungle, picked up a track heading north and returned back to the platoon without finding any Indonesians. Ordered to ambush the track junction the next night, Marshall's platoon settled down with two Claymores covering the approach from the border. At about 1.00 am, a sentry heard noises to the south-east and then, ten minutes later, the Indonesians opened speculative fire with a machine gun and a light mortar. Hoping to deceive the Indonesians into believing that they had left, the New Zealanders held their fire and then as they quietly withdrew 500 yards, the Claymores were detonated. Covered by Singh's shelling, in pitch blackness with each man holding on to a toggle rope, Marshall occupied a secondary prepared ambush site by 2.30 am. Five minutes later the Indonesians mortared the abandoned base and when they were shelled with Recce Platoon directing the guns to their muzzle flashes from an OP to the west, they retired across the border.

To the east, on 6 May, 42 Commando handed over its sector in Sabah to 1st Gordon Highlanders. D Company moved into Serudong and found that living conditions required a considerable amount of repair and the only water was from the sky. Over the next few weeks, the Battalion had several contacts near the border and pursued an IBT who had raided Tawau in January 1964.

At the junction of the Sabah and Sarawak border, on 25 June, after a month's planning, Corporal Robinson, of D Squadron SAS, led C Company, 2/7th Gurkha Rifles (Major Lloyd) to a military longhouse for sixty men at Labang, 5 miles south of the border on the junction of the Sembakung and Pensiangan rivers. Located in a clearing on the southern bank of the Temburong, the longhouse was supported by mortars, light machine guns and a DShK machine gun. When Major General Lea stipulated that the wide and deep Sembakung was not to be crossed, Lloyd planned to shoot up the longhouse, however the jungle was so thick that, under cover of torrential rain, trees were felled so that 81mm mortars could be positioned without being detected. Early next morning, as mist swirled around the river, the mortars opened fire and then 8 Platoon machine-gunned the longhouse. The Indonesians, who had just sat down for breakfast, reacted quickly but were unable to pinpoint the Gurkha position. When the Gurkha mortar bombs fell randomly all over the place, it emerged that the base plates were being driven into the wet ground by the recoil. C Company withdrew to Sarawak accompanied by the population of Labang, who were afraid of retaliation. The kampong was never used again.

The brigades each had Royal Military Police (RMP) Provost Units charged to help civil police with law and curfew enforcement, checking out-of-bounds bars for military personnel. An anti-vice squad combated the spread of sexually transmitted diseases. At first, the detectives in the Special Investigation Branch (SIB) were flown from Singapore, however when British Forces, Borneo increased, detachments were sent to Brunei and Labuan to investigate crime, breaches of discipline and weapon negligent discharges. Perhaps the most public case was the attempted murder of a village chief by several soldiers who mistakenly believed that he was a collaborator. Provost Units were heavily involved in convoy escorts, in particular on the road from Kuching to Serian, Balai Ringin and the route to Bau. At sea level, the road was narrow and, when not passing through paddy fields and rubber plantations, was often hemmed in by jungle. Bridges were liable to be washed away. When the road climbed, it passed through cultivated properties in a series of steep gradients and hairpin bends. Since ambushes were a threat, convoys were escorted by Saladins and Ferret scout cars.

Although the Indonesians threatened Kuching in early 1965, the CCO remained inactive and, as a consequence, the Serian district authority refused to allow 'hearts and minds' operations, even though there was a clear military threat to the District from them. The CCO saw this as a weakness and supported a small group of TNKU exiled by the Brunei Revolt who had returned into Sarawak. On 26 June, a 5-mile-long convoy was being escorted by a troop from C Squadron, 4th RTR, en route from Semengo to Kuching via Serian, when there was an explosion ahead. A recce found that the Milestone 24 bridge had been damaged but was crossable. Two dead Chinese lay in the rubble. The convoy motored on until, in the vicinity of the Milestone 18 Police Station, Sergeant K.B. Brown, leading the convoy in his Saladin, saw two suspicious objects on the road about a mile from the station. While he was reporting the situation to his HQ, there was an explosion near a bridge and then terrified Chinese civilians appeared and said that a group of Chinese guerrillas were killing police officers and civilians. Brown collected two RMP, Corporals Collins and Bain, only for the two armoured cars to skid on oil spread on the road for that very purpose. When they reached the Police Station, it was deserted except for dead and wounded police officers, several inquisitive children and a family hanged by the guerrillas.

With the local authorities clearly miscalculating the mood of the CCO, Major General Lea ordered Operation Hammer to screen about 8,000 Chinese forcibly evacuated between Milestones 13 and 25 on suspicion of CCO membership. With C Squadron providing communications and armoured escorts, early on 6 June, the RMP manned three vehicle check points along the road and then, in an operation that took six days, A Company, KRRC, 2/2nd Gurkha Rifles and B Company, 1/6th Gurkha Rifles helped the authorities move the Chinese, complete with pigs, chickens, dogs and ducks to screening centres, and then to resettlement areas near Kuching, a tactic used with success in the Malayan Emergency. 2/2nd Gurkha Rifles instituted Operation Tiger Balm in which the Pipes and Drums played nightly in kampongs while the Battalion HQ basketball team challenged villagers to matches. Gradually, the rear areas reverted back to a semblance of tranquillity although roadblocks, military and police patrols and the arrests kept the CCO guessing.

After a Special Branch report suggested twenty CCO had been seen on the road near Serayan, 2/2nd, 1/7th and 1/10th Gurkhas Rifles supplied companies to search the 3,000-foot-high Gunong Gadang, a steep-sided feature covered in jungle. Support Company, 2/2nd Gurkha Rifles captured a female supplier and her baby and, for four days, ambushed a CCO hide full of equipment and supplies in a well-concealed cave. 1/7th Gurkha Rifles captured a Chinese courier in a cave on 20 September and placed him and his Gurkha escort in a Scout flown by Sergeant Douglas Waghorn RAMC to be taken for interrogation at Lundu. Last seen flying at about 3,000 feet en route for Lundu, the Scout disappeared. Several reasons were suggested, including catastrophic mechanical failure, the prisoner attempting to escape and smoke from farmers burning dry undergrowth and 'slashing and burning' affecting navigation. In any event, its wreckage lies somewhere in the jungle.

The Rifle Brigade arrived in the Balai Ringu sector on its last tour on 6 July and settled into the routine of patrolling and 'hearts and minds'. Corporal Millard RAMC treated 4,147 patients, mostly Iban who did not understand the concept of the early morning sick parade. Corporal Jones extracted sixty teeth. The Battalion had the usual crop of short sharp contacts but lost five men killed in action or in accidents. A patrol from 7 Platoon, C Company (Lieutenant Alistair Stewart) and Recce Platoon (Sergeant Cameron) killed eight TNI and wounded five when they caught an Indonesian patrol in its bivouac. On another patrol, Rifleman Evans, of 11 Platoon, D Company, had climbed a tree with a radio antenna to improve communications with a helicopter due to recover his patrol, when it arrived earlier than expected. As the pilot was descending through the trees, he was astonished to see an anxious Evans at the same height grimly hanging on to the tree thrashing in the turbulence and not far from the whirring blades. The pilot gingerly rose into the air and saved Evans from being catapulted into the jungle. He climbed down, shaken and stirred.

Since the CCO remained a considerable threat to First Division, the SAS and 2 Detachment/1st Ranger Squadron NZSAS were instructed by Brigadier Cheyne to concentrate on finding the elusive Batu Hitam (Black Rock) CCO training camp. B Squadron and the Cross-Border Scouts had already spent weeks searching without success and suspicions that it was at Bemban dissolved when an infantry patrol killed thirty-two IBTs from Bemban. With Intelligence convinced that it was somewhere in the 6 miles of jungle between the Bemban and Sempayang rivers, when A Squadron crossed the border on 10 September, Trooper Blackburn, of 3 Troop, became separated during a clash with TNI near Batang Ayer and evaded capture for eight days until he reached First Division, largely guided by the Gunners firing signal shots. 1 Troop, on the right, found a large, empty but recently used fort. The camp was never found.

In Central Brigade, the Australian SAS's (Major Alf Garland) inexperience emerged when a 1 Squadron patrol led by Garland recceing several Indonesian bases was not without incident. Twice patrols were compromised near kampongs by dogs. It was, in his words, 'Not an outstanding success'. Later, when Sergeant Roy Weir's signaller, Trooper Paul Denehy, was gored by an elephant, Weir returned across the border to seek help from 2/7th Gurkha Rifles, however Denehy had died by the time they reached him. On 3 July, Sergeant John Perrit ambushed a longboat containing ten soldiers and killed eight; three weeks later, when Lance Corporal Chris Jenison, the LMG gunner in Second Lieutenant

Roderick's patrol attacking the Sungei Salilir, noticed military equipment lying in the bottom of a boat, he shot all but six men on board, all wearing identical T-shirts. In early August, 1 Squadron handed over to No. 1 Guards Independent Parachute Company and later deployed to Vietnam where the lessons learnt in Borneo proved invaluable. The Guards were soon involved in Operation Claret with the patrols of Sergeant McGill and Mitchell ambushing forty Indonesians. In 1966, the Company was transferred to the SAS as G Squadron.

By mid 1965, the Commonwealth forces were still faced by determined Indonesian forces. The Plaman Mapu and Milestone 18 Police Station attacks prompted Major General Lea to intensify Operation Claret on 1 August by extending the limit of exploitation to 10,000 yards, although for some operations, the distance was extended to 20,000 yards. When 2/10th Gurkha Rifles took over from 3rd RAR at Bau in July on their third tour, West Brigade issued orders that it was to:

Step up the offensive action and seek entirely to eliminate the current threat to Sarawak by dominating the area up to 5,000 yards over the border, to the extent that the enemy's forward bases become untenable, and to follow this up by further forcing the Indonesians to retreat to the 10,000 yard line from where meaningful incursions simply could not be mounted.

By attacking garrisons and logistic and communications routes, enemy commanders were to be persuaded either to devote time and effort to defending their rear or abandon their bases. Essentially, the Indonesians were to be besieged and reminded that North Kalimantan was not safe. The long-range strategy was risky because columns need to carry, for longer periods, everything required to attack enemy bases – machine guns, mortars, anti-tank weapons to bust bunkers, ammunition, rations. The risk of being cut off from the border increased. The golden rules still applied and units on their first tours were permitted to plan raids. CSM Lawrence Smith of A Squadron SAS was noted for several extremely successful recces opposite Fourth and Fifth Divisions, as were the four Guards patrols of Captain Charles Fuglesang's Troop. Intelligence Sections analysed information up to 20,000 yards south of the border, FIOs debriefed traders, 81 Squadron Canberras flew air photo recce and electronic warfare listened. Rebroadcast stations placed on high ground gave the column signallers an improved chance of successful communications, and logistic areas were established north of the border to receive casualties and provide rest areas. False stories were fed to journalists about the wounded. Politically, the Indonesians were still in a cleft stick. With troops in North Borneo, the Indonesians could not admit that

British forces were in Kalimantan and thus, to the world, the Indonesians were the instigators of Confrontation. Since most engagements centred on rivers, the period is sometimes known as the Battle of the Rivers.

The lack of artillery in early Confrontation meant that the presence of guns in FLBs had sometimes become status symbols, however, with the infantry regularly crossing the border, the Gunners became a vital asset, particularly as taking 81mm mortars was usually impractical. When 4th Light Regiment (Lieutenant Colonel R. Lyon), which was part of the Strategic Reserve, arrived from Bulford and replaced 45th Light Regiment, 170 (Imjin) Medium Battery, as the independent battery, remained in Borneo. Lyon was also appointed Senior Artillery Officer, Borneo and, against some opposition in HQ 17th Gurkha Infantry Division, moved his HQ from Labuan to St Barbara's Camp, near Kuching Airport. Communicating on the artillery command nets at 9.00 am and 3.00 pm daily for an hour and visiting all detachments at least once a month, Lyon quickly integrated the artillery with infantry HQs at every level, in particular FOOs. The regiment covered First and Second Divisions with one section of three guns per battery, complete with a command post and first-line ammunition in reserve, either to be 'galloped' forward by Belvedere or Wessex helicopters, 'cantered' in bits by Whirlwinds or 'trotted' in smaller components by light helicopters.

By the beginning of August, the ideological differences between Tunku Abdul Rahman and Lee Kuan Yew had developed into a serious rift when the ruling Chinese-dominated Peoples Action Party in Singapore had exploited the Chinese work ethic to develop an economically powerful state. The Party also attacked demands that Malay should be the national language and that the historical rights of the Malaysians, as the majority racial group, should dominate a Malaysian Malaysia. In a speech to the Federal Parliament on 27 May, Lee had said, 'If we find Malaysia cannot work now, then we can make other arrangements.' This added fuel to the fire and while the Tunku was recovering from an operation in London, he decided to expel Singapore from the Federation. One underlying reason why Singapore had been invited to join the Federation was to ensure that Lee Kuan Yew's left-wing leanings were monitored inside the Federation, as opposed to him undermining from outside. Returning to Kuala Lumpur, the Tunku kept his decision secret, even from the British government, until 9 August when he suggested to the House of Representatives that Singapore should be allowed to cede from the Federation. The cessation led to Malaysia becoming concerned about the viability of Federation and when David Stephens in Sabah championed the cause of numerically dominant

Kadazan-Dusums, this was seen by the Tunku as separatism and Stephens was sidelined. Resistance to the Japanese Occupation, the Emergency, Federation, Confrontation, the refusal to allow the Philippines to claim Sabah and the cessation of Singapore combined to develop a keen sense of Malaysian nationalism, but this did not resolve ethnic problems plaguing the Federation. Sukarno attempted to make capital out of the rift by claiming that the Commonwealth alliance was falling apart, however his statements were far too uncompromising for Singapore to accept. And so Singapore left the Federation but retained her defence links with the Commonwealth.

In their third major move of the year, 1st Gordon Highlanders handed Sabah over to 1st Scots Guards, who arrived, for their second tour, in September 1965 with a 1st Irish Guards company and a 1st South Wales Borderers platoon. The Guards then replaced 2/6th Gurkhas Rifles, which was the Brunei resident battalion, in Fourth Division under command of Central Brigade. The South Wales Borderers were based in Hong Kong and frequently reinforced British battalions with a platoon. However, any notion that the Battalion would have more exciting time than experienced so far was dispelled when the Indonesians concentrated on attacking First and Fifth Divisions and the Interior Residency of Sabah. Nevertheless, it carried out several Operation Claret raids against Dargai.

While the fighting along the border was relentless, there was still a need to maintain an effective internal security regime, as we have seen. In early December 1964, Corporal David Kitching, Intelligence Corps, joined HQ Mid-West Brigade as a FIO and, after a short familiarization course, was sent to Sarikei, which was the administrative centre for the Lower Rajang District. The town was the fourth largest in East Malaysia and consisted of ramshackle Chinese bazaars and a Malay river kampong. Kitching was lucky enough to be accommodated in the government rest house and although there were about twenty Europeans in the town, he spent most of his time with the locals. With Inspector Huang of Special Branch, he was soon involved in investigating CCO suspects. On one occasion, documents discreetly removed from the local offices of the Sarawak Advanced Youth Organisation were photographed and returned before the custodian realized they were missing. He also had two vital skills taught to every member of the Intelligence Corps – typing and an ability to organize an Intelligence office.

In April 1965, Kitching was moved to Lundu. About 70 miles of the district bordered Indonesia and compared to Sarikei, this was a dangerous place with about 50 per cent of the Chinese population reckoned to be in cahoots with the CCO. The 1st Scots Guards

Intelligence Officer and his sergeant, who had recently arrived, were sceptical about the needs of a FIO. Having learnt Iban, Kitching made contact with Ibans living across the border and unearthed information about the little-known People's National Commando of Sarawak (Kommando Nasional Rajkat Sarawak – KONAS). Most informants and sources are persuaded to collect information either by a reward or are blackmailed, or volunteer. In Kitching's case, he helped deliver a baby to the wife of a trader, who frequently crossed the border and talent-spotted potential for informants. Although not terribly successful, he reported that the principal function of KONAS was to support Indonesia by subverting Dayaks in Sarawak, and then persuaded four members to cross the border. After being met by Kitching, they spent the next month being debriefed. Kitching then received a letter from Alexander Nyaring, the KONAS leader, who confirmed his philosophy was to subvert the Dayaks and, interestingly, most members were Catholic and unarmed. Kitching finally met Nyaring. It was a major coup in the fight against subversion, particularly as he also acquired current information on CCO activities which led to successful Operation Claret patrols against the Sarawak People's Guerrilla Movement and other subversive CCO organisations.

In June, 1/2nd Gurkhas Rifles arrived from Hong Kong and again took over Fifth Division and the Interior Residency of Sabah from 2/7th Gurkha Rifles. When the Cross-Border Scouts reported contact with villagers conscripted to build an Indonesian camp in the upper reaches of the Sungei Agisan, about 1,000 south of the border, A Company (Captain Peter Duffell) was tasked to destroy it. An air photograph showed two attap huts separated by the Agisan, otherwise little was known of the camp layout although it was thought to be occupied by about sixty Indonesian Marine Corps and some TNKU.

On 4 August, Recce Platoon (Lieutenant J.B. Smart) descended from a ridge to the overgrown banks of the Agisan to about 2,000 yards south of the camp as a cut-off. Next day, A Company crossed and after four days of arduous tactical marching, was 1,000 yards west of the camp. Hot meals and drinks, and smoking, were prohibited, just in case a noise or smell in the pristine jungle alerted the Indonesians or an inquisitive animal. As the Gurkhas cautiously approached the Agisan, Duffell realized that he was between two huts. As evening approached, Duffell sent his second-in-command, Captain (QGO) Bhojbahadur Gurung, to check the hut on the east bank while he checked the one on the west bank, which was found to be empty. For three hours, Bhojbahadur's fire support group slowly crept through glutinous swamp and thick under-growth and then halted as darkness was falling when Bhojbahadur thought he was opposite the hut. He ordered an evening meal of dry rations and water – no cooking. Next morning, as the scent of roasted pork wafted across the 15-yards-wide river, he peered through the undergrowth and saw, gathered in front of the hut, several bearded Indonesians sitting around a pig roasting on a spit. The river was fordable and a shingle beach led to a medium-sized longhouse on the edge of the jungle. To its left and behind were two more huts. The entire camp was surrounded by stone sangars and weapon pits but there was no barbed wire or punji sticks. Bhojbahadur's fire support group quietly wriggled into position while Duffell and the two assault platoons spread out in the thick undergrowth lining the river bank.

Bhojbahadur opened the attack when a rocket launcher projectile broke the idyllic silence of the jungle by exploding against the longhouse, and then the 2-inch mortarmen opened fire. The Indonesian Marines reacted quickly and a .30-inch Browning in one of the huts opened fire on the mortar. Lance Corporal Manbahadur Thapa, who had been wounded at Nantakor, moved onto the shingle and silenced it. Meanwhile, Duffel's group splashed across the river and broke into the camp, despatching several naked Indonesians defending the hut. Resistance soon ceased, however after about half an hour, as the Gurkhas were searching for items of intelligence value, they broke up a counter-attack by twenty Indonesians led by one wearing PT shorts and a bandage covering a head wound. At 10.00 am, A Company began the long march back to the border.

At about mid morning, Recce Platoon killed four Indonesians travelling from the camp in a small boat. During the mid-afternoon, a small boat containing four men, covered by two men patrolling the banks, appeared, probably in the belief that the ambush had been lifted. Five of the six were killed. Smart changed his position but after a day of no results, he reached the border on 15 August. There was a confirmed body count of sixteen but the success of the operation was reflected in intelligence reports that thirty-nine of the sixty in the camp failed to return to their Marine Corps base.

By the beginning of 1965, the Indonesian base at Pa Bawan about 4 miles south of the border and had been so effectively isolated that supply was by parachute and it had become a DZ for parachute units before they crossed into Sarawak. When C Company, 1/2nd Gurkha Rifles, fired at a C-130 with paratroopers standing at open doors when it veered off course over Ba Kalalan in low cloud, its Dutch mercenary pilot banked toward Pa Bawan only for it to crash after being shot down by air defence gunners. The wreckage was still evident in 2004. After two 45th Light Regiment Pack Howitzers from Long Pa Sia and Bario were cantered to the ridge overlooking the airstrip, on 17 August, C Company, 2/6th Gurkha Rifles and a Guards Parachute Company patrol approached Long Bawan and saw an Indonesian marking out a DZ. As the parachutes spilled from the C-130, the two howitzers opened fire. Believing the aircraft to be dropping bombs, the gunners opened fire and damaged its starboard engines to such an extent that it made an emergency landing. The airstrip was not used again during Confrontation.

In June, 2/2nd Gurkha Rifles, still commanded by Lieutenant Colonel Neill, took over from 1st Argyll and Sutherland Highlanders in Lundu. Their area of responsibility was flat and criss-crossed with rivers that regularly overflowed when it rained, the border a line on a soggy map. For the first few weeks, the Battalion was confined to internal security and then on 1 August, the day that Lea intensified Operation Claret, a patrol led by Captain (QGO) Suredraman Gurung killed eight Indonesians by ambushing the Sungei Sentimo and a track below Babang Baba in Operation Guitar Boogie, signalling Neill's intention to dominate the Indonesians. The SAS worked very closely with the Battalion.

On 7 August, using an air photographic mosaic, in the first Battalion-sized operation 5 miles south of the border, Neill issued orders for A, C and Support Companies to disrupt the Indonesian logistic network over a 10-mile frontage in the general area of the Babang Baba garrison by attacking the River Sentimo, in Operation Kingdom Come. With six ambushes planned, 1 and 3 Troops, A Squadron SAS, who had recced the area, supported the Gurkhas; in support was a Pack Howitzer troop and the Mortar Platoon. But it rained continuously for five days flooding the jungle and all but two ambushes were withdrawn. A Company (Major Lauderdale) crossed a swamp with some difficulty and ambushed a longboat, killing all ten Indonesians, who had put up vigorous resistance.

Support Company (Captain Bullock), who was on a three-year secondment from the KRRC, attacked a main supply route identified by CSM Smith along the Sungei Puteh between Babang Baba and Berjongkong. Crossing the border on 14 August, his eighty men marched through rain-soaked primary jungle and shortly before dark reached the edge of a swamp. Next day, the Gurkhas waded through the morass and lay up on a huge mass of fallen trees. The third day was slightly easier and by midday, when they found land above the water north-east of Babang Baba, Bullock realized that he had been diverted by the fallen trees too far to the north. Next day, he headed south-west to hit the Sentimo downstream of Babang Baba, but encountered another swamp, which proved trying for the smaller Gurkhas. While searching for the river, Bullock and a small recce patrol was nearly compromised by several Ibans and their dog walking along a track. When a Gurkha then climbed a tree and reported that they were about 500 yards west of Babang Baba, for the first time in four days, Bullock knew exactly where he was. Next morning, after resting his men, several of whom had dengue fever (picked up from brushing ticks off trees) and who should have been in hospital, he led them through the swamp to a low dry hill about 700 yards north of the Sentimo, which he had selected for his administration base. With chest-deep water everywhere, Bullock almost despaired of finding a suitable ambush site until Lance Corporal Birbahadur Pun, of Recce Platoon, literally stumbled on a logging track alongside the river bank. When Bullock found a small mangrove thicket, he placed the Recce Platoon and his 170 (Imjin) Medium Battery FOO, the Royal New Zealand Artillery Captain John Masters, and a platoon at the ambush base on a hill overlooking the ambush site.

Next morning, the sixth since crossing the border, Bullock and ten tall men, first from the Anti-Tank Platoon, occupied the thicket, the men being rotated every ninety minutes throughout the day. The only interruption was a canoe. Next day was also fruitless, the only event being a huge python swimming with ease against the current. The third day dawned bright. At about midday, Bullock's patience was rewarded when the Assault Pioneers killed all four Indonesians in a longboat from a range of about 15 yards. When a counter-attack developed from the east, it was time to leave. After assembling his platoons at the ambush base, Bullock first headed south-east, in order to frustrate Indonesian attempts to cut him off from the border, and after two days of anxious marching, crossed the border on 23 August. Neill was delighted with Operation Kingdom Come.

Meanwhile, C Company (Major Geoff Ashley) accompanied by 1 Troop, A Squadron SAS, in Operation Blood Alley, accounted for six Indonesians in a longboat in two ambushes on the Sentimo. A platoon-sized counter-attack was stopped in its tracks by Sergeant Lasing Thapa's supporting ambush accounting for fifteen confirmed kills. An attempt to roll up the ambush from the flank cost the TNI six more casualties.

When good intelligence emerged that the Indonesians were sending a convoy to supply the garrison at Berdjonkong using the Sentimo, Lieutenant Colonel Neill briefed Bullock that he was to ambush the convoy in Operation Hellfire . The village of Achan was known to contain an Indonesian company. CSM Smith was to be his guide; on call was a Pack Howitzer at the D Company base at Kandai and a section of

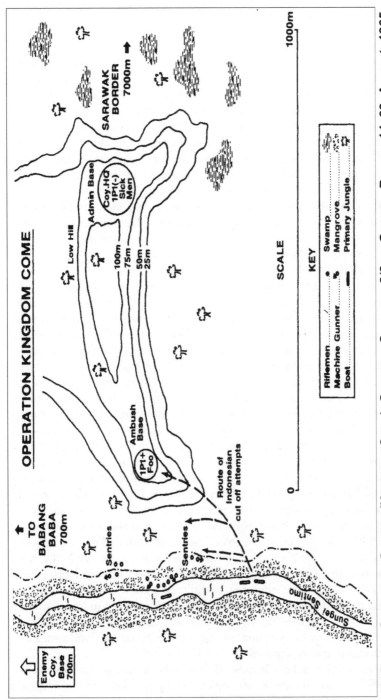

MAP 13. OPERATION CLARET (KINGDOM COME) SUPPORT COMPANY 2/2ND GURKHA RIFLES. 14–23 August 1965.
With thanks to Brigadier Bullock.

195

two 81mm mortars. With sick men recovering from Operation Kingdom Come, others on leave, and not allowed to take new recruits, Support Company was down to fifty men.

With a platoon of recruits securing the border, on 28 August, several men of Support Company, including Captain Masters, quickly succumbed to scrub typhus, nevertheless it made good timing to the Sungei Achan, which the Assault Pioneers bridged with a log. It rained very heavily during the night and next day, and when they encountered a swamp they were unable to find the Sentimo. The third day dawned bright and during the morning they reached the objective, about 5 miles south of the border. Bullock selected an ambush site and placed the Anti-Tanks to overlook the killing zone of a newly cut path and the river. The Assault Pioneers and Recce provided flank protection. Behind the ambush was the checkpoint manned by CSM Harpisarsad and a small team of men who converted a low hill into a defended strongpoint centred on several fallen trees. Weapon pits were dug and the ambush was positioned about 350 yards from the strongpoint.

The next day, 2 September, was one of downpours and sunny periods. The assumption was that military river traffic would be powered by outboard motors. When at about midday, twenty-four Indonesians in two longboats, each poled by an Iban, silently glided through the killing zone from the west, Bullock, warned by tugging vines from the Recce Platoon, frantically ordered the Anti-Tanks to crawl over the path to catch any more boats, but none appeared. Shortly before last light, he withdrew the three platoons to the administration base and reviewed the plan. The next day again dawned bright and when Support Company reoccupied the ambush site, it was adjusted to cover the river and path as well. Bullock was unaware that SAS patrols in the area for three days had ambushed two boats shortly before Support Company arrived. This had alerted the Indonesians and a strong patrol checking the supply route to Berdjonkong clashed with the Recce Platoon. Amid rifle fire and exploding grenades and Claymore mines, Bullock ran to find enemy on the southern bank being engaged. When the Anti-Tanks then opened fire at a RPG set up across the river, Bullock abandoned the ambush and ordered the Assault Pioneers to occupy the strongpoint, while the Anti-Tanks and the Recce Platoon returned to the ambush base. When Corporal Bhagtasing mentioned to Bullock that the checkpoint party had not reached the strongpoint, Bullock went forward to look for them but ran into a party of Indonesians and was fortunate to be rescued by Rifleman Harisprasad Gurung, of the Assault Pioneers. Two attacks on the strongpoint were repulsed.

Lieutenant Colonel Neill radioed that Bullock was to assemble in the ambush base and return to Sarawak. A third attack on the strongpoint was stopped when a LMG gunner, Lance Corporal Resembahadur Thapa, loosed a complete magazine into the jungle, and convinced the Indonesians to reconsider their options. On reaching the ambush base, Bullock was briefed by his second-in-command, Captain Surendraman, that CSM Smith, with Captain Masters missing, had worked out a defensive fire plan. Ordering a fire mission on the ambush site, it was with a heavy heart, because men were missing, that an hour later Bullock and Support Company withdrew. Meanwhile, the checkpoint party signaller, Lance Corporal Tekbahadur, had reached Kandai, covered in blood, and reported that he had become separated in the fighting. Shortly before dark, Support Company reached Kandai after six hours of marching. It had taken five days to cover the same distance going south. An exhausted Captain Masters then appeared and reported that CSM Harpisarsad was wounded and concealed south of the border.

During the withdrawal from the ambush the checkpoint had become involved in a very short-range melee and Tekbahadur had shot an Indonesian, who fell on him, covering him in blood. Harpisarsad was shot five times in the thigh. A Gurkha medical orderly disappeared but was subsequently recovered. Tekbahadur then became separated and made his way to Kandai. In spite of dengue fever, Masters hoisted Harpisarsad on his back and, avoiding Indonesian patrols, carried him 4 miles through unforgiving jungle until he reached the Achan. Too deep for him to cross with Harpisarsad, Masters dragged him into cover, re-dressed his wounds and after leaving his water bottles with him, swam the river and headed for the Pack Howitzer acting as a beacon for Support Company.

Meanwhile, Neill heard, from intercepts of Indonesian radio traffic, that a captured British officer and a Gurkha NCO were being sent downriver to Siluas. This information could only have been elicited from intercepting a British radio conversation about the missing men, and so it was with some relief that he heard that Masters was safe. Bullock planned that D Company (Major Piers Erskine-Tulloch) should join elements from Support Company to look for the CSM. Overnight it rained, which should have reduced the ability of the Gurkha trackers to retrace Master's route, however they picked up his boot prints and in the late afternoon, Harpisarsad was found by Support Company. When Captain Howard Manuel, the RMO, diagnosed gangrene, he assessed that unless he was immediately treated in hospital, he would lose his leg. Under the golden rules, helicopters were not permitted to cross the border, however Neill authorized one to evacuate Harpisarsad and, in so doing, was reprimanded by Brigadier Cheyne. D Company cleared an area and, in the midst of another downpour, Flight Lieutenant Brian Sillikon manoeuvred his Whirlwind over the narrow hole in the canopy and winched up the stretcher.

In the debrief, Captain Bullock was critical of the lack of operational co-ordination with the SAS. Support Company could have been wiped out, however inadequate Indonesian tactics and inaccurate shooting versus the superior training and fitness of the Gurkhas meant that Bullock regained the initiative. An interesting result of this action was that the ambush with flank protection layout became the accepted tactic, as opposed to linear, which had been used hitherto. By the end of August, 2/2nd Gurkha Rifles were claiming forty-nine TNI and IBTs killed in one month. Masters received the MC for his gallantry, the first of two to be awarded to 170 (Imjin) Battery. CSM Smith's professionalism throughout Confrontation earned him the MC, a decoration then awarded to officers and only to other ranks in exceptional circumstances.

On its return to Borneo in September, the Gurkha Independent Parachute Company was deployed to Fifth Division with Central Brigade. Commanded by the experienced jungle fighter, Major John Cross, it recced enemy bases and ambushed tracks south of the border, reporting that a force of about 500 men had moved into the Risau area. On one patrol, Cross and three Gurkhas became separated from three other patrols and, while trying to find them, found the initials 'RPKAD' and the previous day's date carved on a tree. This was serious news because it meant that the Army Para-Commando Regiment was still opposite the Division. Using a method of communication developed during the Malayan Emergency and in the full knowledge that cuckoos did not exist in Malaysia, he 'cuckooed' and, within fifteen minutes, the force had re-assembled in a clump of trees in the middle of open terrain. Next day, while marching north to Sabah, Cross was resting near a well-defined LP when an Indonesian helicopter, escorted by fighters, suddenly landed troops. The Gurkhas deployed but no enemy appeared, leaving Cross to cross the border without interference.

In July 1965, General Yani cheekily suggested that Air Marshal Dhani's Vigilance Command should select the right moment to attack and destroy Singapore – no mention of Borneo, however when Army commanders failed to organize assault transports and landing craft, Brigadier General Idris, who commanded Combat Command Sumatra, was accused by Dhani of delaying the transfer of troops to Sumatra on the basis that there was no accommodation. In fact, vacant barracks in North Sumatra were falling into disrepair. In the same month, Brigadier General Supardjo's authority as the commander of the No. 4 Kalimantan Combat Command was eroded when his units were transferred to Brigadier General Sumitro's East Kalimantan Combat Command. In September, the Army strengthened its influence when Vigilance Land Strategic Command (Komando Strategis Darat Siaga – KOMSTRADAGA) was formed within Dhani's Vigilance Command and placed under command of Idris. All units in Kalimantan and Sumatra were included in its order of battle, including two units of Sarawak Chinese, who were inducted in a ceremony officiated by Major General Suharto in North Kalimantan. With no command, Supardjo returned to Jakarta, a city that was tense as the ideological struggle between the PKI and the Army, that had been evident throughout 1964 and 1965, was about to explode.

CHAPTER SIXTEEN

Turmoil in Indonesia

Economic decline in Indonesia had accelerated since September 1963 after President Sukarno had increased military expenditure for Confrontation. An attempt, in May 1964, to stabilize the economy had failed and by mid 1965, inflation was out of control, budget deficits out-weighed revenue, exports decreased and foreign governments were unwilling to prop up an ailing economy. Infrastructure fell into disrepair.

With the apparent approval of Sukarno, anti-PKI protest was gradually silenced and when, on 4 August 1965, he fell seriously ill while receiving a delegation, his Chinese doctors warned that recovery was unlikely. Into the vacuum stepped the PKI, whose leaders realized that if Sukarno died, the Party would be at risk from the Army. They launched a propaganda campaign against business and suggested arming workers as a 'Fifth Force', and sending advisory teams into the Armed Forces to further 'Guided Democracy'. The Party had already achieved influence over the media and had even persuaded Sukarno to use communist slogans in his speeches. Sukarno briefly recovered and in the 17 August Independence Day speech, he referred to the 'Fifth Force' in terms of 'we cannot defend our nation's sovereignty without the people, who should be armed, if necessary.' Significantly, he failed to give a firm commitment about its development, because he was under intense pressure from Army commanders to drop the idea. When pensioned Army Warrant Officer Sudjono was killed in a clash with communist peasants in Sumatra in May, General Yani took a tough line and told Sukarno that he rejected the involvement of the advisory teams in Army units. Air Marshal Dhani supported the 'Fifth Force' and nego-tiated an agreement with China to arm the workers and agreed that it could protect air force bases and thereby make up for the shortfall of airmen. At Halim Air Base, outside Jakarta, the defence commander, Major Sujono, discreetly formed a company of 120 volunteers and ran two courses per month for selected trainees, as opposed to volunteers, at a small village outside the base known as Lubang Buaya (Crocodile Hole). By September, his defence force had grown to 1,200, which was considerably in excess of the requirement. When Commodore Ignatius Dewanto, the base commander, found out, he instructed that all recruits must be from nationalist and religious organizations.

Army commanders were suspicious of the motives of the PKI and Air Force but were careful not to be seen on the political defensive. They could count on the Navy and the police, although the latter was the most faction ridden and at risk from subversion, however the three forces had been sufficiently infiltrated for the PKI to form a Special Bureau through which subversive and clandestine activities were managed. One problem was that sympathizers, particularly in the Air Force, often agreed with the PKI ambitions but rejected Party membership. It was inevitable that the combination of the differences between the PKI and the Army, the tense political situation and the dire economic atmosphere would generate a crisis. In September, Sukarno relapsed and when it seemed that recovery seemed slim, at least according to his doctors, left-wing officers formed the 'Thirtieth of September Movement' and plotted a coup d'etat against the 'Council of Generals', who, it claimed, not without good cause, was CIA sponsored and had been very active since Sukarno had collapsed on 4 August. The 'Council of Generals' was a shadowy organization probably formed to assess Sukarno's policies, although General Yani had assured the President that it reviewed only promotions and postings, and avoided politics. However, with the Army's close involvement in political affairs, it is inconceivable that it did not have a cabal of senior officers planning political activity.

Lieutenant Colonel Untung was the Army Airborne Infantry battalion commander of the Cakrabirawa Palace Guard. Recruited by the PKI to forestall any actions by the Army to take over should Sukarno die, with the President apparently so unwell, Untung believed the time was ripe for insurrection and, during the early hours of 1 October 1965, the 'Thirtieth of September Movement' sprang a coup d'etat. Six battalions of troops, including the pro-communist Central Java-based 454th Para-Raider Battalion from the Brawijaya Division, the East Java-based 539th Para-Raider Battalion from the Diponegoro Division and the Palace Guard deployed in Merdeka Square to dominate the Presidential Palace and key buildings. When small groups were sent out to arrest prominent individuals, Lieutenant Dul Arief led the pre-dawn raids on the homes of six senior generals and Defence Minister Nasution on the pretext that they had been summoned by Sukarno, dead or alive. Three generals, including Yani, challenged the summons and were murdered. The remaining three were taken by jeep to Halim. At Nasution's house, the Defence Minister escaped by scaling a wall into the Iraqi Embassy, but his five-year-old daughter was killed. A lieutenant aide-de-camp was captured and also taken to Halim where he joined the three generals. Later in the day, they were executed at Lubang Buaja and their bodies thrown into a well, along with the three who had resisted.

At 7.00 am, the rebels broadcast that 'a military movement has taken place within the army assisted by troops from the other branches of the Armed Forces' and that 'The Thirtieth of September Movement' had arrested the 'Council of Generals' because of its connections with the CIA, and for using troops assembled from throughout Java for the 5 October Armed Forces Day parade to stage a coup against the President. There is no evidence to suggest that the Council was planning a coup, however the 20,000 troops assembled for the parade were in retaliation for the large PKI march held the previous year.

When the broadcast claimed that President Sukarno was being protected by the Movement, in fact, Brigadier General Supardjo, one of the Movement's leaders and formerly the No. 4 Kalimantan Combat Command commander, had left Halim to persuade Sukarno to return with him to the base where, it was hoped, he would support the coup. However, no one seemed to know where Sukarno was. In fact, he was with his third wife when he heard the firing at Nasution's house and decided to return to the Presidential Palace. On being told of troops in Merdeka Square, he then joined his fourth wife on the outskirts of Jakarta and made his way to Halim, arriving at about the same time as Air Marshal Dhani was announcing that the 'Thirtieth of September Movement' had 'protected and safeguarded the Revolution and the Great Leader of the Revolution against subversion' and that the Army was being purged. He also emphasized that the Air Force would support 'all progressive movements'. Supardjo finally met up with Sukarno at about 10.00 am, however when the President heard about the murder of the six generals but that Nasution had escaped, he suggested that the coup should be stopped. For the conspirators, this was disappointing because by 11.00 am, Central Revolutionary Councils were being formed throughout Indonesia and, although power was to be passed to them, Cabinet ministers were to remain in post. Decrees were issued under the names of Untung, Supardjo, Air Force Lieutenant Colonel Heru Atmodjo, Navy Colonel Ranu Sunardi and Police Senior Adjutant Anwas Tanuamidjaja. By 4.00 pm, Sukarno had appointed Major General Reksosamudro Pranoto as Army Commander.

However, the Movement had failed to neutralize Lieutenant General Suharto, the Army Strategic Reserve commander, one of whose roles was to deal with internal unrest and attempted coup d'etats. Woken by a neighbour with the news of the shooting at the houses of the abducted generals, he made his way to his HQ where, with Yani missing, he immediately assumed command of the Army and instructed that all troops be confined to barracks, and that the Air Force, Navy and police commanders report to him. When the Air Force refused to accept his authority, suspicions that the Air Force was involved in the coup were confirmed. Suharto and Major General Wirahadikusuma, the Jakarta garrison commander, assembled loyal forces, which included 328th Para-Raider Battalion, from the Siliwongi Division, which had seen action in Borneo, and 1st and 2nd RPKAD. The 1st was normally based in Jakarta and had resisted attempts by the conspirators to be posted to Kalimantan, while the 2nd was in the capital to attend the annual 5 October parade. The 3rd RPKAD was still on the border. The presence of these battalions in October led one suspicious Diponegoro officer to ask Air Marshal Dhani why an unprepared brigade, namely 5 Infantry Brigade, had been sent to North Kalimantan when others ready for action were not. Was something going to happen in Java?

Determined to avoid fighting, officers sent by Suharto to negotiate with the two battalions in Merdeka Square persuaded 454th Para-Raider Battalion, with the help of the Brawijaya Division commander and promises of food, to switch sides and purge its communist elements. Major Sutikno, who commanded the 530th Para-Raider Battalion and was a friend of Untung, refused to budge and, although his tired and hungry men watched 454th Para-Raider Battalion leave the square, he led them back to Halim. Suharto had regained control of the strategically important Merdeka Square and the Palace. When 1st RPKAD recaptured Jakarta radio station, Suharto broadcast that he was taking command of the Army and that the 'Thirtieth of September Movement' at Halim Air Base would be crushed. Attempts by the conspirators to persuade Sukarno to leave Jakarta failed and when he realized the coup had run its course, he returned to the Presidential Palace, which signalled its collapse and sent the plotters into panic.

In spite of threats to Suharto that Halim Air Base would be defended, Lieutenant Colonel Sarwo Edhie, the officer who had led the attack on Plaman Mapu, recaptured it against feeble resistance by remnants of the 454th Para-Raider Battalion and a few Air Force 'volunteers', and received its surrender from Commodore Dewanto. The bodies of the murdered generals were recovered from the well. By daybreak on the 2nd, Suharto was demanding that Sukarno deny that the Air Force had not been involved in the uprising. Sukarno could not and refused to implicate the PKI; nevertheless Suharto was not ready to challenge his authority and permitted the politically critically wounded Sukarno to remain as President. However, he forced Air Marshal Dhani to resign and the Diponegoro Division was purged of 1,500 officers and men honourably discharged, and about 1,100 suspended, punished under military law or pensioned into retirement. Some deserters made their way to North Kalimantan. Twenty-five years after the coup, General Nasution told an Australian historian that although he initially thought that Sukarno had supported the 'Thirtieth of September Movement' because of the involvement of the Palace Guard, he changed his mind when he learnt that Sukarno had, on 30 September, summoned General Yani to see him next day, 1 October, in order to sack him. Nasution died in 2001, aged eighty-one, a firm critic of Suharto's regime.

In addition to British psychological operations in Sarawak, the shadowy Information Research Department (IRD) of the Foreign and Commonwealth Office had been co-ordinating black propaganda to discredit Sukarno, the Chinese in Indonesia and the PKI. Described by the journalist John Pilger as 'one of Her Majesty's most experienced liars', Norman Reddaway arrived from Beirut as the Political Warfare Co-ordinator; he was an expert at manipulating the British press and the BBC to ensure that comments were unattributable and official links concealed. British Intelligence links to the IRD are always denied. Reddaway's contribution to Confrontation was described as 'considerable' by the political advisor to the Commander-in-Chief, Far East. The coup presented a massive opportunity to smash the PKI.

On 8 October, the IRD fed a false story to several outlets, including the BBC, that the communists were planning to slaughter the citizens of Jakarta and discredited the coup leaders by highlighting alleged acts of brutality, in particular that the six generals had been tortured and their sexual organs mutilated by female members of the Party. The BBC was selected because it was banned from Indonesia and therefore its reporters were unable to verify the allegations. The Army were portrayed as patriots defending Indonesia against communism and Red Chinese interference in Indonesian internal affairs. Suharto knew the mutilations were untrue because he had attended their autopsies, however, as with other Army officers, he was in the pay of the CIA.

The PKI had three million members and eleven million sympathizers so could not be ignored, a fact accepted by the Army. The US Embassy helped by furnishing the Army with the names of 5,000 suspected active communists and supplied modern communications equipment so that moves against the PKI could be co-ordinated. The allegations had the desired results and on 8 October, the Army and police stood by as rioters sacked the PKI headquarters in Jakarta and also found arms and a transmitter. The coup leaders fled to central Java in the hope of gaining popular support for an armed struggle but were hunted down by an Army Airborne Infantry brigade. As law and order collapsed and interfactional fighting broke out, the PKI reverted to crime, terrorism, murder and kidnapping, but retribution was swift when anti-communist elements retaliated. 3rd RPKAD was recalled from North Kalimantan and joined its Regiment to crush rebels in Semarang and Solo before deploying to Bali where it played a major role in destroying the PKI. The PKI leader, D.N. Aidit, was murdered. Estimates of those killed by the Army and Muslim groups range between 80,000 and 1 million, an event that remains largely unreported. Thousands of people were accused of involvement in the killings but only about 800 were brought to trial.

On 2 and 3 November in Bangkok, the Army's highly secret Special Operations Group, with the agreement of Sukarno, arranged for Brigadier General Achmad Sukendro to meet the Permanent Secretary at the Malaysian Ministry of External Affairs, Dato Ghazali Shafie, where he confirmed that British operations in North Kalimantan were hurting. A US Intelligence assessment dated 18 November is interesting:

> Although there was a massive Indonesian build-up along the Borneo border and in Sumatra beginning last December and largely completed by May military activity against Malaysia has declined in the last six months. The last attempt to infiltrate as armed guerrilla units into the Malaysian peninsula occurred last March ... In Borneo, effective British cross-border operations have disrupted Indonesian planning and placed the approximately 17,000 Indonesians in the area on the defensive. Since August, British and Malaysian security forces have captured or killed over 500 of the nearly 700 Indonesian guerrillas involved in these unsuccessful efforts.

Sukendro explained that the Army needed six months to consolidate its political position of destroying the PKI, in the meantime it would broaden its power among the population. It will be recalled that the Army never totally supported *Konfrontasi* and when Sukendro showed Shafie a document suggesting that the PKI had pressured Sukarno to fight Malaysia, he asked that propaganda be used to undermine Foreign Minister Subandrio, even suggesting he be assassinated because he was a hindrance to negotiations. The latter suggestion was not taken up. Meanwhile, the IRD's strategy of undermining support for *Konfrontasi* by highlighting the patriotism of the Army and discrediting Sukarno and his senior loyalists, led to General Nasution's deputy, Admiral Sjaaf, agreeing that Commonwealth warships could pass through Indonesian waters on rights of passage, provided that notice was given. The survey ship HMAS *Moresby* was the first to test the commitment.

Amid the chaos that had engulfed Indonesia, on 13 February, at a

205

National Front rally, Sukarno expressed his willingness to challenge the Army. When, three days later, Defence Minister Nasution appealed for law and order in the face of PKI terrorism, Sukarno sacked him because his appeal was contrary to a broadcast that he had made two days earlier praising the efforts of the communists in the struggle for independence. In an attempt to re-establish his authority, in a Cabinet reshuffle, Sukarno replaced the Navy Chief of Staff and several other pro-Suharto officers with loyalists. Foreign Minister Subandrio was reinstated but since he was being implicated in the October coup d'etat and was being accused by British propaganda of moving money to Hong Kong, his credibility amongst the Army power-brokers was low. Sukarno's risky challenge to the Army can be traced to his assertion that he was head of state and by dismissing Nasution, he believed that most Army officers would not oppose him; he had miscalculated. The reshuffle indicated to the Army leadership that Sukarno was failing to recognize the new 'reality' and senior officers, including several in North Kalimantan, plotted to remove Sukarno. Brigadier General Idris was now Chief of Staff to the Army Strategic Reserve Command, with direct responsibility for the defence and internal security of Jakarta. Knowing that he could count on the Siliwangi Division, he subverted several anti-Sukarno officers with the tacit agreement of Suharto. Colonel Edhie thought more pressure should be brought on the President.

Encouraged by the Army, students marched against the reshuffle and when two were shot by the Cakrabirawa Palace Guard, internal security deteriorated and civil unrest flared. On the day of their funerals, Suharto chaired the first meeting of the newly constituted Crush Malaysia Command to review Confrontation but spent the session discussing the domestic situation. Suharto hoped that Sukarno would recognize the dominant role of the Army in national politics, however, the President saw this acceptance as a weakness and rejected suggestions that the situation would quieten if named Army officers were removed from the Cabinet. Revelations of a plot by several radical officers to force Sukarno to acknowledge the 'new reality' by kidnapping Dr Subandrio were seen by the President as a rehearsal for his kidnapping. The longer that he resisted, the worse the internal security situation in Jakarta became. For the next few months, Sukarno procrastinated about finding a solution to the crisis but insisted that Guided Democracy must remain. Although the PKI had been crushed by the Army, its surviving leadership were reluctant to force a final showdown with Sukarno, primarily to avoid clashes between rival military units, in which the communists would undoubtedly lose.

When reports emerged at a Cabinet meeting, on 11 March 1966, that the RPKAD was about to attack the Presidential Palace, Sukarno was assured that the Marine Corps would defend it until he was handed a note that an unidentified Army unit had appeared in front of the Palace. The troops were the pro-Suharto 1st RPKAD and, minus their red berets, they had been deployed by Idris and Edhie to intimidate the President, threaten the Cakrabirawa, protect the students and arrest Subandrio and Sukarno loyalists. It was a high-risk strategy, nevertheless Sukarno recognized the weakness of his position and, quietly leaving Jakarta, handed power to Suharto. Within twenty-four hours, Suharto effectively undermined a fundamental principle of Guided Democracy by accusing the PKI of irresponsibility and demanded that it be purged. Sukarno's government machinery was subjected to arrests and dismissals and the Air Force was compelled to launch a major purge which, by April, had resulted in the dismissal of 306 officers, including Air Marshal Dhani. He and several other left-wingers were later tried. Sukarno supporters were also purged from the police and Cakrabirawa Palace Guard.

The strength of the Armed Forces inherited by Suharto stood at 505,000, with 300,000 Army, 125,000 Police, 44,000 Navy, including 20,000 Marine Corps, and 36,000 Air Force. The Army believed that the combined strength of likely opponents, which would include pro-Sukarnoists in the Army, would not guarantee security and therefore there was always the risk of coups. Suharto was determined that the Armed Forces must be capable of defending Indonesia against the threat of communism seeping throughout South-East Asia and although there was speculation that it might end Confrontation, its political liabilities and anti-Malaysian orientation led to continued hostilities. Army Headquarters expressed some concern about the loyalties of the CCO but since very few of them had links with the PKI, they were not seen as a destabilizing force.

CHAPTER SEVENTEEN

The British Offensive
October 1965 to February 1966

Operation Claret had become a useful stick and carrot in the negotiations between Kuala Lumpur and Djakarta, and as the turmoil in Indonesia unfolded, Major General Lea suspended operations in periods that were known as 'be kind to the Indos'. He re-organized British Forces, Borneo when, in October, HQ 19 Infantry Brigade Group handed Mid-West Brigade to HQ 5 Infantry Brigade (Brigadier Rollo Pain). The Brigade had moved from West Germany to the UK eighteen months earlier in an attempt to relieve cost pressures. Brigadier House, who had formerly commanded 1st Green Jackets, took over from Brigadier Tuzo in HQ Central Brigade.

Between November 1965 and March 1966, 4th Light Regiment deployed guns ninety times to support Operation Claret, with most guns moving every two days. When a gun was moved, another one usually fired on the first gun's targets to screen its deployment. From August 1965, there was an average of four FOOs on patrol at the same time in West Brigade. Since periods of rest and refitting between patrols were short, FOOs were among the fittest, and slimmest, of the Royal Marines and Army. As one 129 (Dragon) Light Battery FOO later commented: 'The jungle is hard, wet and uncomfortable always – and our many different infantry companies were efficient, helpful, cheerful and friendly and we couldn't have wished for more. The FOO parties had an interesting life, sometimes exciting and satisfying and this went a long way to compensating for the physical hardships encountered.'

The extent of Operation Claret is reflected in the inability of the Gunners to supply sufficient FOOs, however a proposal that warrant officers and sergeants should command was rejected on the grounds that the responsibility was unjustified, although few doubted their capability. The problem was resolved by reducing the FOO to an officer and a

208

signaller, leaving the remaining two signallers manning a gunner rebroadcast station on the border. Although the A42 and C42 were not compatible, by flicking switches, voice messages could be automatically transferred from one set to another. If communications were poor, signallers manually switched the automatic relay system on the words 'Over' or 'Out'. Lyon commented that VHF worked well in the jungle, provided that the signallers were determined to 'get through'.

40th Light Regiment from the Strategic Reserve took over from 4th Light Regiment in November 1965, and between 10 November and 29

Table 2. Artillery Deployment in Borneo			
WEST BRIGADE		CENTRAL BRIGADE	EAST BRIGADE
December 1964			
1 x Light Battery (6 x 105mm Pack)			1 x Commando Battery (4 x 105mm Pack How)
1 x Low-Level Air Defence Battery (8 x 40mm Bofors and 2 x 4.2-inch mortars)			1 x Medium Troop (2 x 155mm How)
	MID-WEST BRIGADE		
November 1965 – August 1966			
2 x Light Batteries (12 x 105mm Pack How)	1 x Malaysian Light Battery (4 x 105mm)	1 x Malaysian Light Battery (4 x 105mm)	1 x Malaysian Light Battery (4 x 105mm)
1 x Commando Battery (6 x 105mm)			1 x Light Section (2 x 105mm)
1 x Medium Troop (3 x 155mm Howitzer)			Naval Gunfire Support Battery
1 x Low-Level Air Defence Battery (8 x 40mm Bofors and 2 x 4.2-inch mortars)			
1 x Locating section (2 x Green Archer) (2 x Sound-Ranging Bases)			

March 1966, fired 1,100 rounds of 105mm and 313 of 5.5 inch at identified targets, and 5,317 rounds of harassing and registration targets. Between 6 November 1965 and 18 June 1966, they imposed a curfew on the 10-mile strip of jungle south of the border between 7.00 pm and 6.00 am with harassing fire on track junctions and border crossing points, usually in support of Operation Claret columns. With the guns so widely dispersed, when there were insufficient officers to man Command Posts, or provide Gun Position Officers (GPOs) and FOOs, warrant officers and sergeants found themselves commanding gun positions.

The Sarawak-recruited 1st Malaysian Rangers, which had been formed after the Sarawak Rangers was disbanded as part of the Malaysian

Army reorganisation on Federation, moved into Second Division. Of the four battalions raised, two saw active service in Borneo. On its left flank in Third Division was 1st KOSB, which had arrived from Hong Kong in October and was the only battalion to have served in Korea, Malaya and Confrontation. When the A and C Company patrol bases at Katibas and Long Jawi were attacked respectively, Major General Lea was uncertain whether this was authorized or an independent action, nevertheless it was sufficient for him to lift the suspension on Operation Claret.

Lieutenant Colonel Neill, as usual, allowed the Indonesians opposite the Lundu sector no time to relax. When, on 20 October, A and Support Companies, 2/2nd Gurkha Rifles again attacked the Sungei Sentimo in Operation Monsoon Drain, Captain Bullock was concerned because he felt that the Indonesians would be alert. Although the swamps were deeper from the 'wet' monsoon, when A Company found an ambush position, Bullock asked Major Lauderdale to wait until Support Company was in position. Next day, 24 October, the column bumped into a large Indonesian patrol and when A Company were also seen moving into the ambush, Lauderdale and Bullock left the area to attack the Sungei Berbjonkong, using a site not far from Bullock's Operation Hell Fire ambush site. Although there were difficulties finding a site long enough for a two- company ambush, several boats crewed by boatmen dressed in the same singlets and slacks were allowed to pass through the killing zone because it was not certain that they were military. As there was always the overriding concern of being cut off from the border, on 30 October, when it appeared the ambush base was under threat, the companies returned to defend it. The threat turned out to be a false alarm, nevertheless Neill terminated Operation Monsoon Drain. B Company (Major Erskine-Tulloch) blew up a launch after a three-day ambush and claimed nineteen Indonesians killed. D Company (Major Mike Joy) sank another launch containing senior Indonesian officers.

From 15 to 19 November, in an operation devised by Major Ashley, C and Support Companies, on Operation Pallo Patti, attacked a main supply route linking two Indonesian camps and a route to the border on the River Separan, 10,000 yards south of the border. With the two ambushes set 5 miles apart, Neill hoped that the actions of one ambush would feed the enemy into the second ambush. Support Company bridged two rivers and then on 17 November, while searching for the Separan, at about 11.10 am, Captain Bullock radioed Battalion HQ reporting a RAF Whirlwind hovering overhead. A DShK then opened fire and he watched the helicopter disappear trailing smoke. Brigadier Cheyne, who happened to be visiting the Battalion, suggested to Major General Lea that Bullock and 2/10th Gurkha Rifles, which had patrols not far away, should rescue the crew, however Lea vetoed the proposal. Bullock assumed the machine gun was located in a base across the Separan.

The pilot, Flight Lieutenant Albert Fraser, was killed but his passenger, Gunner A. Martin of the Royal Horse Artillery (RHA), attached to Radar Troop, 40th Light Regiment, had suffered a broken leg, although it seems he despatched a couple of Indonesians before he was killed. Fraser had been posted to 103 Squadron two days previously. Earlier in the day, he had flown to Stass from RAF Kuching with a pilot who knew the area, however, when he returned to Kuching, he was sent on another sortie to Stass and was joined by Martin, but was not given a co-pilot familiar with the ground. It seems he mistook high ground west of Stass for Gunong Jagoi and inadvertently crossed the border. Coming under fire from the machine gun about 150 yards in front of Bullock's column, he banked left to return to Sarawak but came under fire from another machine gun, suffered catastrophic damage and crashed into a swamp. His body was never found; he left a wife and two children. Martin's body was returned to the British authorities and was buried in Folkestone, Kent.

Believing that the Indonesian base was still unaware of him, Bullock pushed on, however when he reached the river, it was about 80 feet wide, in full spate and not navigable. He decided to attack the track south of the river between the two Indonesian camps and instructed the Assault Pioneers to build a bridge, using a tree that had fallen across the river. Bullock placed the Anti-Tanks in an ambush a short distance south of the bridge. Recce Platoon and his FOO, Lieutenant Chris Mutton, who was attached to 40th Light Regiment from 49th Light Regiment, and Gunner 'Chalky' White, were on a small hill covering the approaches from the south. In support was Sergeant Bill Walton's Pack Howitzer at Stass. The Assault Pioneers improved the stability of the bridge and guarded its approaches.

The ambush was in position by 9.45 am on 18 November, the sun was up and the insects annoying. At about 11.00 am, a small party of Indonesians walked through the killing zone and then when a longer column followed the Anti-Tanks sprung the ambush with a volley of fire, Claymores and grenades. When the Indonesians launched a quick counter-attack supported by mortars and heavy machine-gun fire from Kindau, slightly wounding Bullock and a lance corporal, Sergeant Walton, directed by Mutton, shelled the Indonesian positions. Realizing that a second weak counter-attack was a probe for an organized attack, Bullock instructed the Anti-Tanks to abandon the ambush and cross the bridge, which by now was under mortar attack, and then he systematically assembled Support Company, struck east and crossed the border next day. Even though he later learnt the ambush site was only 50 yards from an Indonesian camp, it was a model ambush and, as a result, the Indonesians took no more offensive action in the Kindau area during Confrontation, although the garrison remained a threat. Bullock received a well-deserved MC.

Meanwhile, 2/10th Gurkha Rifles (Lieutenant Colonel Peter Myers) were tackling camps occupied by 5 Infantry Brigade along the Sungei Koemba, which is about 5 miles south of Bau. Myers had been Chief of Staff to Major General Walker and was another veteran of Burma and

MAP 14. OPERATION CLARET (PALLO PATTI) Support Company, 2/2nd Gurkha Rifles, 15–19 November 1965.

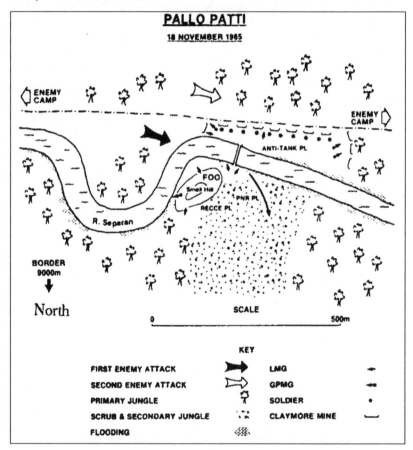

Malaya. C Company (Captain Chris Maunsell) was tasked to map the layout of 'J' Parachute Infantry Battalion, which was believed to be

deployed between Risau and Babang. The terrain was littered with razor-sharp ridges and hills covered in primary and secondary jungle. Maunsell withdrew after an ambush occupied for five days was compromised by civilians on 30 September and a prisoner-of-war snatch party was spotted next day. Myers then instructed C Company to destroy a large force reported to be about 5 miles south of the border opposite Bau. In Operation Time Keeper, 7 Platoon was to dominate the Koruh to Risau track; 8 Platoon was in reserve; 9 Platoon was to cover the approaches from Babang; and Recce Platoon was to snatch a prisoner from 'J' Battalion at Koruh. The Pioneers were to provide a firm base on the border and protect the radio-relay station. On call were two Pack Howitzers from 129 Battery (Major G.N.W. Locke) and a 5.5-inch Troop through the FOO, Lieutenant Douglas Fox, of 170 (Imjin) Medium Battery, with Gunner Cuthbertson as his signaller.

On 16 November, C Company crossed the border. It was next evening that Maunsell initially received instructions to rescue the Whirlwind aircrew. On the 18th, after the Recce Platoon had found Koruh to be alert, Maunsell suggested to Myers an alternative prisoner snatch from the Indonesian platoon on Gunong Tepoi, also known as Hill Top Post. The feature was about 500 feet high, covered in *baluka* (fern, scrub) and surrounded by secondary jungle. Three ridges led west to Babang, south to Koruh and east to the border. From an excellent OP 1,000 yards to the east, Maunsell could see the Indonesian position was occupied by a platoon manning several trenches on the summit of a steep-sided hill. HQ was in an attap hut at the head of the track from Koruh.

When Myers agreed, with H-Hour timed for 2.00 pm, the Recce Platoon cut a 400-yard tunnel with secateurs through the *baluka* from the platoon base toward the track that led north up the hill; by about 1.00 pm, the Gurkhas were 100 yards below the summit after negotiating a recently felled tree. Recce and 9 Platoons provided fire support and received extra ammunition as 7 and 8 Platoons advanced up the hill. About 100 yards short of the enemy position, for about twenty minutes, they were delayed by an Indonesian moving around in the jungle. The Gurkhas were negotiating the next barrier, a line of trees, when a soldier came out of the platoon HQ attap hut and wandered down the track – toward the prone Gurkhas. Stopping about 10 yards from the scouts, something alarmed him and so he was shot as he unslung his rifle. Surprise lost and with his men on a four-man frontage on the narrow path, Maunsell widened the axis of attack by instructing 7 Platoon (Lieutenant (QGO) Ranjit Rai) to seize the attap hut, which Rai did with four men. He and his signaller then found a position from which to control the battle and ordered the platoons to spread out. As 8 Platoon (Lieutenant (QGO) Bhagat Bahadur) fanned out to the right, a

MAP 15 - OPERATION CLARET (TIME KEEPER), 21 November 1965

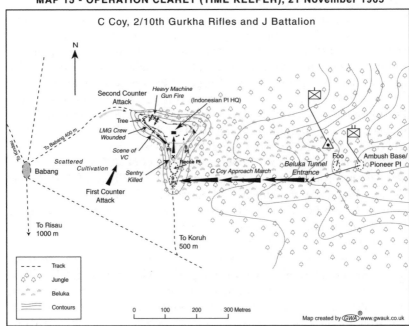

Gurkha was killed and when another was badly wounded, Maunsell dragged him into cover; for this act of inspirational gallantry, he was awarded the MC.

The leading section of 7 Platoon wheeled left and, advancing below the summit covered by its LMG group commanded by Lance Corporal Rambahadur Limbu, came under heavy fire from its right flank. Forced to take cover in an enemy trench, Rambahadur appreciated that until the machine guns were dominated, his section was pinned down. Leading his two colleagues toward a tree to improve their fields of fire, they dropped a grenade into a trench, but before it exploded, its Indonesian occupant placed his AK-47 on the lip of the trench and opened fire, wounding both of Rambahadur's colleagues. Because of the noise of the battle, Rambahadur was unable to tell Lieutenant Ranjit what had happened and he started back to the hut. Infuriated that his two colleagues were wounded, he crawled back to them but was repeatedly forced to take cover. Deciding the only alternative was to run, he dashed forward and carried one wounded Gurkha back about 50 yards across bullet-swept ground to the hut. He then returned and fetched the second man. To everyone's dismay, both Gurkhas were dead. When Rai

214

instructed the machine guns be knocked out by the section, Rambahadur charged the Indonesian positions, firing his LMG from his hip, and personally accounted for at least four of the enemy. He attributed his survival to his small height and the tendency for bullets fired downhill to go high unless carefully aimed.

With the left flank secure, Maunsell transferred 7 Platoon to the right and over the next hour, C Company systematically overran the Indonesian defences. After re-organizing on the crest of the hill, they beat off two counter-attacks from Babang. With 8 Platoon sent ahead to carry the three dead and two wounded, after ninety minutes, C Company withdrew from Gunong Tepoi with Lieutenant Fox shelling mortars firing from Risau and Koruh. Captain Wynters, the RMO, met the column, treated the wounded and, holding the intravenous drip of one, accompanied them on the 1,500-yard march in pitch blackness to Serikin. C Company killed an estimated twenty-four TNI. The Pack Howitzers of Bombardier Holness and Sergeant Walton fired 106 rounds while the 5.5-inch howitzers of Sergeant Richardson and Bombardier Saunders fired eighty-five rounds. It was during this engagement that communications were made difficult by interference from American B-52 bombers over Vietnam. One memorable exchange was reputed to have gone something like this:

US aircraft, 'Unknown station. Get off the air. We're fighting a war. Over.'

British signaller, 'So are we but at least we're winning. Over.'

Nothing more was heard from the Americans.

Lance Corporal Rambahadur Limbu was awarded the only Victoria Cross of Confrontation but such was political sensitivity of Operation Claret that his citation and the press releases were carefully written to screen the fact that the action had taken place about 4,000 yards inside North Kalimantan. His was the thirteenth VC awarded to the Gurkhas and the first to a Limbu. The previous Gurkha to win a VC had been Rifleman Lachhiman Gurung of 4/8th Gurkha Rifles in Burma in 1945; his Company Commander then was Major Peter Myers, who was now commanding 2/10th Gurkha Rifles. Rambahadur received his medal on 22 April 1966 from Lieutenant General Sir Alan Jolly, the Army Commander in the Far East. On 2 February, his wife had died following complications to the birth of his second son. Maunsell, Fox and Ranjit were awarded Military Crosses.

2/2nd Gurkha Rifles ended their last tour in Confrontation in a typical flourish when, on 30 November, Lieutenant Colonel Neill planned Operation James Bond, a battalion ambush south of the border of approaches to First Division. When Major Lauderdale, who was leading

A and C Companies, clashed with a TNI column on a track, Rifleman Balhbahadur was severely wounded in the lungs and kidneys but kept firing his LMG until he collapsed. Evacuated to Kuching Hospital, he died eighteen days later. The occupation by Major Erskine-Tulloch with B and D Companies of a small hill, sparsely covered in thin trees, preparatory to sending out patrols to locate an ambush site, was seen by a TNI company. Had it not been for the inspirational leadership of Corporal Siriparsad Gurung and his section defeating two attacks from the south, Erskine-Tulloch may well have been in serious trouble. Short of ammunition, Siriparsad's section, all yelling the battle cry 'Ayo Gurkhali! Right flank attack!' broke up a third attack. The Indonesians faltered and withdrew. Siriparsad was awarded the MM and Erskine-Tulloch the MC. On 13 December, the Battalion exchanged Lundu District with 42 Commando arriving on HMS Albion but lost twelve Gurkhas when two Wessexes collided. Its return to Singapore was then delayed when Prime Minister Wilson, in attempting to resolve the Unilateral Declaration of Independence by Rhodesia's Prime Minister Ian Smith, offered Zambia military aid. A fully-equipped and battle-hardened, if weary, Gurkha battalion was an obvious choice and Albion headed into the Indian Ocean until the politicians took wiser counsel.

Since the Royal Marines' order of battle was still three rifle companies, as opposed to four, Brigadier Cheyne moved the inter-battalion boundaries so that Bokah was included in the neighbouring 1/10th Gurkha Rifles sector. This meant that the company FLB at Serekin became superfluous and it was destroyed. The base at Bukit Knuckle had become uninhabitable and was transferred to another hill 1,500 yards away known as Gumbang. The Gurkhas were commanded by Lieutenant Colonel Ronnie McAlister, who later wrote the comprehensive account of the 10th Gurkha Rifles since 1945 entitled *Bugle and Kukri*. The Royal Marines relied, and still do, upon the commando-trained Royal Navy and Army for most combat and service support so when Commander Royal Artillery, West Brigade instructed that 129 (Dragon) Battery, who knew the area well, would support the Commando, and not 79 (Kirkee) Commando Battery, this was not well received by the Royal Marines, who questioned whether the FOO had the ability to keep up with them. The Gunners, who knew the area, proved more than once that the Green Beret is a symbol of a physical course.

Having handed over to the 1st Queens Own Buffs in Hong Kong and seen their families depart by aircraft to Colchester, 1st DLI (Lieutenant Colonel G.J. Maughan) took over Paradise Camp at Kota Belud from 1st Gordon Highlanders, who then relieved 2/6th Gurkha Rifles in

Brunei and were based at Seria for the next four months. Maughan had known for a year that his Battalion would be deployed to Borneo and had arranged for several platoons to be attached to 1st RUR in 1964. He strengthened the rifle companies by reinforcing A Company with the Anti-Tank Platoon, from D Company. The Bugles joined B Company, Recce Platoon went to C Company and the Mortar Platoon was split among the companies, so that the twelve rifle platoons were over thirty strong. The Assault Pioneers trained with 32 Field Squadron RE and were distributed among the rifle companies; with the nearest bright lights at least 50 miles away, the Regimental Police was reduced to four men, the remaining four being posted to rifle companies. In the idyllic surroundings, the Intelligence Section was accused of 'dividing their time between talking Malay, being Intelligence and collecting butterflies'. On 18 December, Maughan took over the Balai Ringen sector from 3rd Royal Green Jackets in the eastern sector of West Brigade. Battalion HQ was at Balai Ringen where badminton was the favoured sport. Included in their order of battle was 13 Platoon, 1st South Wales Borderers, Air Flight, 8 (Alma) Commando Battery and 514 Signal Troop providing the rear link to West Brigade. On their right was 1st Argyll and Sutherland Highlanders, who had begun their third tour in November with companies located at Serian, Pang Amo and Plaman Mapu. The only other British infantry battalion to complete three tours was 1st Green Jackets. Both battalions had been neighbours during the EOKA crisis in Cyprus.

In a series of small actions, 1/2nd Gurkha Rifles from Fifth Division so totally dominated the valley between Long Bawan and Long Medan that the Indonesians withdrew from seventeen outposts and bases to a depth of 10,000 yards, which was exactly what Operation Claret envisaged. There was, therefore, not much activity except to patrol, dominate the jungle, carry out 'hearts and minds' activities and wait for events in Indonesia to develop. Mines on tracks caused several casualties. 1/7th Gurkha Rifles had its first battle casualty since early 1964 when, in November 1965, Lance Corporal Bajurman Rai stepped on a Yugoslavian mine and, although quickly lifted out by a 103 Squadron Whirlwind, lost his leg below his knee. The following month, Rifleman Masterman was the eighth man in a B Company, Rifle Brigade column when he stepped on an anti-personnel mine on a track running along the top of steep-sided primary jungle slopes. Major David Ramsbottom, the Company Commander, had the area searched for other mines while arrangements were made to evacuate Masterman to a LP. Ramsbottom later rose to General and, in the 1990s, was the controversial Inspector-General of HM Prisons. An Iban tracker with the Battalion named Jalim also stepped on a mine, but since it happened south of the border and he could not be evacuated, it took two days to stretcher him to Sarawak.

As 1965 drew to its end, the level of incursions decreased as the crisis in Indonesia deepened. Since 1963, British Forces, Borneo had killed an estimated 300 Indonesians with about 120 being accounted for by West Brigade. On 31 December, Indonesia withdrew from the UN on the pretext that it objected to Malaysia taking a non-permanent seat on the Security Council and Sukarno then attempted to set up the Conference of New Emerging Forces, however with few friends, he felt he had no alternative but to seek support from China. China was more than happy to ally herself with an anti-colonialist but gave little practical help. This only inflamed the shaky scene in Indonesia where the Army, indirectly supported by British propaganda, was savaging the PKI. The IRD was undermining the reputations of advocates of *Konfrontasi*, such as Foreign Minister Subandrio, by linking him with the communists and accusing him and Sukarno of salting away money to Hong Kong. The dropping of China's first nuclear bomb undermined the *rapprochement* since Indonesia was a signatory to the 1963 Test Ban Treaty.

The garrison at Siding was harassed by 2/10th Gurkhas Rifles in an Operation Claret that began on 23 December and involved 8 and 9 Platoons, both led by Lieutenant (QGO) Puransing Limbu, attacking the track from Babang to Serikin. 9 Platoon allowed a ten-strong TNI patrol through the killing zone, because the Indonesians were alert and springing it would have been counter-productive. At midday on 28 December, a group of nine Indonesians assembled in the killing zone and, hoping for more to enter, Puransing waited an hour before ordering open fire, accounting for all nine. When the search teams were counter-attacked, Captain John Peel, the FOO, arranged for harassing fire from E Troop, 129 (Dragon) Battery to cover the withdrawal, but when the Indonesians diverted the Gurkhas by mortaring their intended route, the Green Archer locating radars were unable to pinpoint the mortars. During the action, Sergeant Walton's Pack Howitzer overheated and would not run out so Walton reverted to the emergency drill of firing it with a lanyard. When this snapped, rather than report his gun out of action, he stood near the muzzle and forced the breech mechanism open by ramming a cleaning pole down the barrel after each round. In doing so, both his eardrums were perforated, he was medically evacuated and his health assessment downgraded.

Departing on 3 January 1966 to ambush the Siluas to Risau main supply route on which 'J' Battalion entirely relied, B Company (Major J.A.F. Bailey) carried out a deep raid accompanied by Captain Peel, who had returned from supporting Lieutenant Puransing only five days earlier and had been on near continuous operations since 12 December.

The Gurkhas had penetrated nearly 15,000 yards when they ran into a gauntlet of enemy patrols and hostile civilians, and it soon became apparent that the Indonesians had good intelligence of their presence. When Bailey reached the ambush site, he was compromised by the dogs of five civilians, however such was the domination of the jungle by 2/10th Gurkha Rifles, that B Company evaded further contact until it crossed the border on 14 January. Relieved in the Bau sector on 25 January by its sister 1st Battalion, 2/10th Gurkha Rifles returned to Singapore having carried out seventeen Operation Clarets at the cost of five killed and two wounded, but an estimated eighty-four enemy killed. It had been awarded one VC, five MCs, two MMs and two Mentions in Despatches; it would not return to Borneo.

First introduced into theatre in October 1965 by 2nd Locating Troop, from 45th Light Regiment, the three Green Archers performed well by locating forty-three mortars. However, by the time 3rd Locating Troop, from 3rd Royal Horse Artillery, arrived from Detmold in West Germany in the New Year, the climate and lack of spares in the Far East had taken their toll and two Green Archers were frequently out of action, while the third radar was in the workshops under continual repair. On 1 January 1966, 42 Commando at Biawak experienced the first of eight mortar attacks. Although Operation Claret had been suspended pending events in Indonesia, the Royal Marines were forced to mount shallow incursions to find 'the enemy had flown'. The problem persisted after March when 2nd Locating Troop, 6th Light Regiment arrived.

Following the visit in September 1965 by Major Dick Graf, from the School of Artillery, to advise on the feasibility of using counter-battery Sound Ranging, C Troop (Captain R.B. Myburgh), 22nd Locating Battery, 94 Locating Regiment, arrived on 31 January, direct from winter in Larkhill, and deployed in First Division. Such was the importance of the Troop that it did not attend the jungle warfare course and was not given an acclimatization period. Deploying Sound Ranging was not as difficult as first thought, although an attempt to emulate a successful experiment in England using helicopters to lay D10 cable to L Company, 42 Commando on 2 March at Biawak nearly had a disaster when the combination of humidity creating lack of lift and an inability to fly slowly almost led to the Sioux crashing. After a request to use a Whirlwind was rejected, a section commanded by Second Lieutenant D.J. Miles laid microphones by hand from Biawak to positions close to the border in climatic conditions in which the equipment had never been tested. Under normal circumstances, microphones were laid in the ground, but since holes rapidly filled with rainwater, they were attached to trees or placed on locally made stands, complete with a tampering detection device. One listening post was established on a high hill, which meant an exhausting eight-hour climb. One technical problem followed another, nevertheless the Troop persevered through experimentation and a second base with three microphones was established at Stass. They were manned by about fourteen gunners with a Pack Howitzer, a 4.2-inch or 81mm mortar on call for counter-battery fire. The Gunners laid all 120 miles by hand – no mean feat, considering that each man carried at least 80lb of equipment, the heaviest item being the mile of twisted cable in a metal cable dispenser. One listening post was joined by an Army Catering Corps private who gave up his rest and recreation for a spell of front-line duty. Maintaining the cable always meant that patrols had to be sufficiently large to withstand an ambush. 2nd Locating and C Troops were amalgamated into the Locating Battery, Borneo on 28 March and were commanded by Major C. Beeton, who had Artillery Intelligence experience and recognized the value of a combination of intelligence and locating devices as the best counter-battery asset in Borneo. The examination of mortar craters also indicated the calibre of a weapon and the direction of fire. The Locating Battery remained in Borneo until early July when A Troop, 94th Locating Regiment, took over from its sister C Troop and 2nd Locating Troop exchanged with G Locating Troop from Terendak Camp. By August, 65 light and 39 medium mortars, 13 howitzers and 33 anti-aircraft guns had been plotted.

When, on 13 January, intelligence reports suggested that small groups of Chinese-trained Indonesians troops were deploying along the Sungei Sekayan intending to infiltrate into Sarawak, SAS B Squadron (Major Terry Hardy) was tasked to destabilize a suspected incursion being planned from Kampong Sentas, a village some 3,000 yards south of Tebedu in First Division. With 9 Troop on other tasks, the Squadron was reinforced by the New Zealand SAS and four from 2 (Australian) SAS Squadron, who had arrived a fortnight earlier. The force was reinforced by a 1st Argyll and Sutherland Highlanders platoon, plus Captain Peel and Gunner Jimmy Grant from 40th Light Regiment. Crossing the border on 30 January, by the third day, the 53-strong column had reached the Sekayan about 1,200 yards upstream from Sentas. Leaving the Argylls to secure the crossing point and the emergency RV, after dark, B Squadron crossed the river and followed a track east toward Sentas, intending to surround the kampong and attack at first light. A telephone line alongside the track was cut. Of two huts on two hills, one was thought to be occupied by a pepper farmer and the other was known to be a machine-gun post. Hardy approached the farmer's hut to persuade him and his family to remain inside, however the occupants turned out to be TNI. As Hardy beat a hasty retreat, Trooper Ken Elgenia, of the Australian SAS, threw a phosphorous grenade at the hut, but in the darkness, his aim was erratic and the grenade hit an upright, bounced on to the ground and exploded, showering Sergeant Dick Cooper, of B Squadron, and Sergeant John Coleman, of the Australian SAS, with phosphorous. Phosphorous burns are only extinguished by dousing in water. With a firefight developing and the operation compromised, Hardy ordered withdrawal to the Argylls where a headcount revealed that four men were missing. By 10.00 am, Hardy decided that he could wait no longer and set off for the border.

After the instruction to withdraw, Coleman, Sergeant Lou Lumby and Trooper 'Ginger' Ferguson ran along a ditch until undergrowth forced them to skirt the second hill, however Coleman's glowing uniform and equipment was an easy target for enemy machine-gunners. Returning fire, the group reached the river and bumped into Indonesians pursuing B Squadron. After a brief exchange of fire, the trio broke contact and headed east, crossed the river and were heading for the rendezvous when Captain Peel shelled the enemy camps, so they headed for the border and met up with B Squadron. The fourth missing man, Trooper Elgenia, did not hear the order to withdraw until he realized that he was on his own and was followed by some TNI as he left the area, assuming he was one of theirs. Crossing the river and heading towards the emergency RV, B Squadron saw Indonesians running along the riverbank and detonated a Claymore hurling Elgenia into the river. When he dragged himself to the northern bank, he was minus his weapon and his clothing and webbing were in tatters, nevertheless he crossed the border three days later. Kampong Sentas remained of concern. Another attack by the SAS in mid-February failed when the thirty-strong patrol was unable to cross the Sekayan because it was flooded after heavy rain.

Meanwhile, Prime Minister Wilson's Government had concluded in its Defence White Paper that the Conservative Government had deployed overstretched and under-equipped forces in which political necessity had not necessarily matched military capability. Aden was a classic example. The previous government had allowed for an annual increase of 3 per cent per year for the defence budget, but in 1964/65, spending had risen by 8.7 per cent and was projected to rise to 8.9 per cent for 1965/66. The White Paper recognized that although instability in Africa and the influence of China in the Far East were of concern, the principal threat to the UK was nuclear, from the Group of Soviet Forces Germany, and the government must revert to its historical strategy of defending the nation by fighting in Western Europe. The government undertook to get defence projects back under financial and contractual control, and, accepting that research and development in UK must be protected, collaborative projects with international partners would be sought. In terms of force levels, when the White Paper stated that commitment must match capability, with three Service ministries already combined into the Ministry of Defence with a single Service chief, the Armed Forces knew famous names would disappear. Of the units in the Far East, 1st Green Jackets, the KRRC and Rifle Brigade had pre-empted disbandment by brigading into the Royal Green Jackets on 1 January 1966. In other brigades, junior battalions, such as the DLI, were at risk.

In Indonesia, President Sukarno, weakened by the increasingly influential Major General Suharto, who was endeavouring to convince him of the new 'reality' that the Army's influence was supreme, tried to influence military strategy by realigning the Supreme Operations Command with Crush Malaysia Command on the pretext that the former was moving toward militarism. This was not rejected by Suharto, who welcomed the opportunity to dispel accusations of a military dictatorship, because he knew that very discreet peace talks were underway. On 29 January, Major General Lea suspended Operation Claret.

CHAPTER EIGHTEEN

The End of Confrontation
February to September 1966

After a year in Borneo, 1st Gordon Highlanders handed Fourth Division over to 1st Scots Guards and returned to Scotland. The Guards were reinforced by a 1st Irish Guards company and a 1st South Wales Borderers platoon to complete a Celtic line-up. On 8 February 1966, 132 (The Bengal Rocket Troop) Medium Battery replaced 170 (Imjin) Medium Battery. Although the turmoil in Indonesia marked a distinct slackening of activity in Kalimantan, when Crush Malaysia Command was realigned, this indicated no firm move toward concluding *Konfrontasi*. On 8 February, Major General Lea renewed Operation Claret.

Border Scouts and other intelligence agencies reported a marked increase in Indonesian military activity and, on 15 February, a Border Scout found tracks north of Tebedu suggesting another major Wingate-style incursion threatening First Division, possibly accompanied by several women. Lieutenant Colonel 'Runce' Rooney, commanding 2/7th Gurkha Rifles, directed the ten-day Operation Mixed Bag from a helicopter. Reinforced by C Company, 1/10th Gurkha Rifles, which was the West Brigade Reserve company, a platoon from D Company, 1st Argylls and elements of B Squadron SAS, Rooney deployed his 600-strong force to throw a cordon of ambushes around likely enemy routes, with the Chinese enclave around Milestone 24 being the probable Indonesian objective. The Argylls killed six Indonesians as they struggled to avoid contact, although on 16 February, C Company, 1/10th Gurkha Rifles lost one killed and five wounded near Tebedu. The incursion split into two groups, one group converging on several Chinese villages on the Kuching to Serian road. During the first week of March, several Indonesians rounded up inside a Chinese resettlement compound at Milestone 24 by the Sarawak Police Field Force signalled the defeat of

223

the incursion, at the cost to the Indonesians of six dead, several wounded and most captured. A few struggled across the border.

1st DLI was involved in several Operation Clarets. On one occasion, when 13 Platoon, South Wales Borderers, was sheltering under fire in a harbour area and Battalion HQ was trying to establish whether it was artillery or mortars, Lieutenant Colonel Maughan 'gave an inspired imitation of the whistle of a shell over the radio'. A patrol led by the second in command, Major J.H. Jacobs, was lifted out of the jungle when a boat capsized in floods. To add insult to injury, he was the most experienced jungle fighter in the Battalion. On 26 February, Private Tom Griffiths was killed and five wounded when 2 Platoon, A Company were ambushed. Apart from Griffiths, Private Miller died in a road accident and Private Roy Newton died at Catterick Military Hospital in September 1967 after being casevacced from Borneo due to ill health.

In early March, D (Patrol) Company, 3 Para replaced the Gurkha Independent Parachute Company in Central Brigade and undertook several intelligence-gathering Operation Claret patrols. A radio set used by the signallers was the lightweight 125 HF set, which had been used by the Special Operations Executive during the Second World War. Robust and light, it was nevertheless difficult to keep dry. One of the platoon commanders was Lieutenant David Chaundler who, in 1982, took over command of 2 Para after 'H' Jones was killed at the Battle of Goose Green.

The success of Operation Claret opposite First Division by 2/2nd Gurkha Rifles had forced the Indonesians from Siding and isolated Kindau. The Sungei Koemba remained a main logistic artery and 1/10th Gurkha Rifles, which was based in Bau, scored an outstanding success when D Company (Major Chris Pike) crossed the border on 27 February to attack Indonesians building a base 1,500 yards west of the junction of the Koemba and Separan rivers. On 4 March, after a five-day approach march through primary jungle, the company waded into a swamp, to avoid leaving tracks, and then tunnelled through secondary jungle to dry ground about 300 yards from the junction, where Pike established an ambush base before placing his three platoons in ambush positions. Two days later, a landing craft containing thirty-five TNI motoring downstream was struck by devastating fire from 11 Platoon at a range of 15 yards and beached on the riverbank about 30 yards downstream. When the Indonesians opened small-arms and mortar fire, Pike withdrew 11 Platoon and left 10 and 12 Platoons in the ambush. The Indonesians failed to send a clearing patrol and, at about 5.00 pm, two small boats containing nine TNI chugged into the 12 Platoon killing zone and were sunk. Under mortar fire and expecting a counter-attack, Pike withdraw the platoons, however when there was no follow-up, he sent 12 Platoon back to the ambush in the hope of more kills, but none materialized. By 8 March, D Company was back in Sarawak, claiming an estimated forty-four TNI killed, which was the highest number of casualties inflicted on the Indonesians and their surrogates in a single patrol. Daring, impudence and cunning planning were key factors.

Meanwhile, 42 Commando (Lieutenant Colonel Peter Whitely) had turned its attention to Sedjingan in Operation Lively Cricket, largely because L Company at Biawak had been mortared eight times since it arrived in November and the village was thought to be a staging post for CCO infiltrating into Sarawak from Batu Hitam. The camp was defended by the 304 Infantry Battalion from the Siliwangi Division and had taken a largely defensive profile after being attacked by D Company, 2/10th Gurkha Rifles in February 1965. The Gurkhas had been forced to fight through several ambushes as they withdrew to the border. The plan was for L Company (Captain Jack Smith) to assault Positions 'C' and 'D' while M Company (Captain Tom Secombe) was to protect the right flank of L Company by ambushing Indonesians deploying from Position 'B'. Mortar Troop was to neutralize 'A'. The frequency of Operation Claret by British units is illustrated in that this was Secombe's seventh incursion in his six-month tour. 129 (Dragon) Battery supported the attack with Captain George Correa, the F Troop Commander, and Bombardier Milson attached to M Company, and the FOO, Lieutenant Christopher Hill and Lance Bombardier Collett with L Company. In Biawak, the F Subsection Officer, Lieutenant L.R. Simpson controlled fire direction with the Pack Howitzers of E Subsection (Sergeant R.A. Ross) and F Subsection (Sergeant H.M.R. Largo), which had been helicoptered from Lundu. He also had under command the Commando Mortar Troop of four 81mm mortars.

When, on 3 March, HQ West Brigade gave authorization for Sedjingan to be attacked within fourteen days, twelve volunteers commanded by Lieutenant Iain Clark, of L Company, recced Sedjingan, his limit of exploitation being north of the river to the south of the village. He, Sergeant Peter Pearce, Clark's Troop Sergeant, and Lance Corporal Price did the bulk of the close recces. On one occasion, Pearce crept to within 5 yards of the Indonesians without being detected and on another recce was behind a bush onto which an Indonesian urinated. No dogs or civilians were noted. On the final patrol, Clark was accompanied by Second Lieutenant Miles, of the Biawak Sound-Ranging Detachment. A papier-mâché model was built under an attap hut at Biawak, as specified in the 'Golden Rules', which was uncovered after local labourers left during the late afternoon.

There was a very brief delay when Major General Lea again briefly suspended Operation Claret in response to events in Indonesia when Major General Suharto overthrew Sukarno in a bloodless coup on 12 March. The man who had said to *Daily Telegraph* journalist John Ridley that 'I am Indonesia. I created Indonesia. As long as the world lasts, my name will be remembered' had led his country from substantial wealth to economic poverty and had, since 1 October, been quietly stripped of his power and reputation by relentless political pressure. Nevertheless the Mobile Police Force, the Marines and Air Force remained loyal to Sukarno and showed no inclination to quit fighting. In addition, at the beginning of the year, D Company, 1st RPKAD had sent a platoon each to East and West Kalimantan Combat Commands to co-ordinate deep-penetration operations with the TNKU and CCO, and set up Wingate-style strongholds from which to subvert the population and mount raids.

When Brigadier Cheyne returned to the UK on medical leave, on 13 March, Whitely, who had assumed command of West Brigade, authorized 42 Commando to raid Sedjingan. L and M Companies left their bases at Biawak and Samatan respectively early next day and rendezvoused 2,000 yards north of the objective that evening. After a recce patrol found that Position 'B' was unoccupied, at about 5.00 pm on 15 March, when it was assumed all Indonesian patrols would have returned to camp, both companies moved to a forming-up place 200 yards north of Sedjingan. 5 Troop protected the position. At about 2.00 am next morning, after M Company had placed ambushes west of 'B', L Company attacked 'C' and then advanced to 'D' where a telephone line between two attap huts was cut. 4 Troop wheeled left to attack another hut, while 6 Troop assaulted two huts on a bank.

The blowing up of the lower hut with Claymore mines attached to 10 feet bamboo poles by Sergeant Pearce was the signal for the attack, however, at about 3.45 am, they were seen by a sentry and a furious battle developed around the two huts, during which Lieutenant Clark was very badly wounded and two others were also wounded. Covered by Lieutenant Hill shelling both objectives, L Company withdrew to the forming-up place where Medical Assistant Scott RN and Private Towers RAMC said that the wounded could be carried to LP 1. It was then discovered that Lance Corporal Tom Collins, who had last been seen by his Number Two, Marine Thom, firing from behind a tree, was missing. A patrol sent to find him returned empty handed.

L Company withdrew up the track to the assembly area, hindered by carrying the dead and wounded, and under fire from two Indonesian mortars. These were silenced in between the demands for defensive

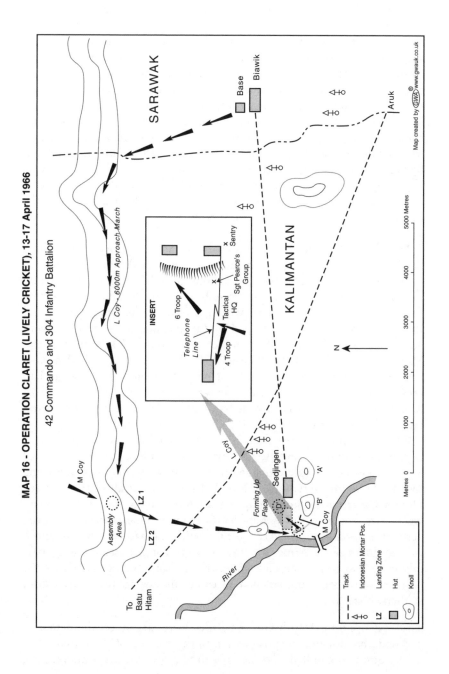

MAP 16 - OPERATION CLARET (LIVELY CRICKET), 13-17 April 1966

42 Commando and 304 Infantry Battalion

SARAWAK

Base

Biawik

Aruk

KALIMANTAN

M Coy

Assembly Area

LZ 1

LZ 2

To Batu Hitam

L Coy - 6000m Approach March

River

Forming Up Place

Sedjingen

L Coy

'A'

'B'

'D'

M Coy

N

INSERT

Sentry

6 Troop

Telephone Line

Sgt Pearce's Group

Tactical HQ

4 Troop

Metres 0   1000   2000   3000   4000   5000 Metres

Track
Indonesian Mortar Pos.
LZ   Landing Zone
Hut
Knoll

Map created by GWA® www.gwauk.co.uk

227

sweeping fire missions to prevent 304 Infantry Battalion from pursuing the Royal Marines. When the Indonesians then bombarded Biawak with a 60mm mortar, Sound Ranging plotted its position, but it was close to a Sarawak Police Field Force ambush. After the thirty minutes it took to withdraw the police, Captain Cameron in the 40th Light Regiment Auster Air Observation Post organized a quick shoot on the mortar. At about 9.00 am, radio communications were almost lost and the barrage slowly crept toward L Company until Lieutenant Colonel Whitely and Major Locke, the battery commander, then arrived in a Scout and rotated with another Commando Flight helicopter to relay messages. Meanwhile, Whitely had authorized a 103 Squadron Whirlwind, piloted by Flight Lieutenant A.R. Miller, escorted by Lieutenant Lyons in a 40th Light Regiment Sioux, to collect the casualties from LP 1. Soon after a mortar firing on M Company was silenced by Sergeant Largo, the Indonesians broke contact and both companies returned to Biawak on 17 March.

Arguably, had it not been for Lieutenant Simpson coolly controlling the fire support with guns and mortars firing on different targets, 42 Commando would have been in serious trouble. Sergeants Ross and Largo had fired 149 and 135 rounds respectively and two mortars finished the day bedded in to within a foot of their muzzles. Sound Ranging was frequently swamped by the shelling. Interestingly, for an action deemed to be successful, very few gallantry medals were awarded. More seriously, with Lance Corporal Collins missing, a Golden Rule had been broken. Since it could not publicly be admitted that he had gone missing south of the border, he was posted 'believed killed' on 18 March and his family told that he had fallen over a cliff while on patrol. His mother, in particular, refused to believe the account.

When Corporal Kitching, the FIO, was tasked to discover the extent of the Indonesian casualties, he learnt from traders that Positions 'C' and 'D' had been badly damaged and the Indonesians were admitting five dead and fifteen wounded. Five 304 Infantry Battalion graves in the Heroes Cemetery in Sinkawang are attributable to the battle. Several weeks later in Biawak, Kitching learnt from an elderly man who lived across the border that the day after the battle, he had been press-ganged by the Indonesian Army to crew several commandeered longboats taking twelve heavy bundles downstream from Sedingjen. When the bundles were being unloaded, one came undone to reveal two dead soldiers, head to toe.

The TNI opposite 1/10th Gurkha Rifles were largely on the defensive and had abandoned their positions until the evening of 11 March when a field gun manhandled into the area fired a few rounds. Captain Peel, the FOO, alerted the Stass Sound-Ranging Base and an E Troop, 129 (Dragon) Light Battery fired five speculative rounds. Nothing more was heard of the gun. Lieutenant Colonel McAlister was then surprised to be informed that in mid-April his Battalion was to deploy from Bau to Serian in order to make way for 4th RAR (Lieutenant Colonel D.S. Thomson MC) from 28 Commonwealth Brigade, which had replaced 3rd RAR. When 3rd RAR occupied the base, the Australian Government had paid for improvements and now insisted that it must be occupied by Australians. The valuable intelligence and local knowledge gathered by the Gurkha battalions over the past three years was now at risk for the sake of political expediency. McAlister, facing a dilemma of either action before redeployment, or inaction, applied to HQ West Brigade to eject the Indonesian garrison out of their nearest border village, Kindau, in a full battalion attack.

197 Light Battery was in direct support and with every officer committed to the operation or involved in supporting other units, command of the gun positions was devolved to warrant officers and sergeants. Drivers filled gaps on the guns and gunners reinforced the rebroadcast signallers. A Sioux helicopter piloted by Captain D. May from the Regimental Flight was allocated to the Battery with Captain Alcock, the Battery Captain, acting as observer. After the field gun incident on 11 March, a 5.5-inch howitzer was moved from Pejiru along a new road and joined by a second howitzer allocated to support A Company. A Troop, 5th RTR defended the gun positions. The date for the attack was set for 25 March.

The Recce and Pioneers Platoons, led by Major Thompson, of HQ Company, left Stass on 12 March and after struggling through feature-less jungle, arrived outside Kindau and radioed, 'I don't know where I am nor where the enemy is, but I can assure you we are both in the same place.' Leaving Thompson 800 yards east of Kindau, McAlister instructed:

- A Company to divert attention from the assault by keeping the hill-top OP on Gunong Tepoi and Babang Garrison occupied.

- B Company to 1) dominate the Upper Macham area where Captain Peel was to establish an artillery OP; 2) harass Kindau from the north-west and its lines of communications to Siluas.

- HQ and C Companies, under command of Thompson, to assault the southern perimeter of Kindau.

- D Company – 1) in a separate operation to recce the Sungei

Separan; 2) move south-east to search for the Siluas to Kindau lines of communications in an area of jungle not yet mapped and penetrated. Its task had been planned from a roughly gridded air photograph.

By 23 March, in teeming rain, after a five-day approach march, mostly through flooded swamp, D Company had crossed the swollen 30-yard wide Sungei Separan with great difficulty and found Separan empty of TNI. When it then seemed that his column had been seen by a farmer, Major Pike moved into a 'hide' and sent out recce patrols, who reported two Indonesian camps to the south-west and south-east, and that the occupants were taller, strongly built and paler than had been seen before. During a 24-hour delay imposed by HQ West Brigade demanding more information, a TNI platoon arrived very near the 'hide'. Although both accepted that D Company had probably been compromised, McAlister agreed that Pike should ambush a junction of main tracks before withdrawing. By first light on 25 March, D Company was in position, however its bad luck continued when two civilians rested in the 12 Platoon killing zone and were captured. During the mid-morning, when nine TNI cooking a meal at a track junction covered by 10 Platoon were joined by a second group, the platoon opened fire but then lost two GPMG gunners killed by several Indonesians trapped in the killing zone. Captain Templer, the FOO, lost communications with the Pack Howitzers, however he arranged for Lieutenant Hogarth's 5.5-inch howitzer to fire thirty shells, which scattered the Indonesians. While 10 Platoon was withdrawing, Lance Corporal Hindupal Rai's section lost two Gurkhas killed and two wounded. Although the Indonesians were alert to a British unit south of the border, helicopter casualty evacuation was considered too dangerous and D Company carried its four dead and two wounded, and crossed the border at about 9.45 pm on 26 March. In spite of the fact that Confrontation had developed into a company commander's war, Pike was the only one to be awarded the DSO. Hindupal was awarded the DCM.

With the Indonesians alerted to the incursion, Brigadier Cheyne ordered that the attack on Kindau be confined to shelling by E Troop and harassing fire from rifles, machine guns and mortars. At about 3.00 pm, the FOO, Lieutenant Welby-Everard, climbed a tree about 150 yards from Kindau and, with Gunner Evans halfway down and Captain Hughes at the bottom, relayed corrections to two Pack Howitzers ranging with smoke and then firing 120 HE rounds. Meanwhile, Second Lieutenant Bloxam in an OP 800 metres from Kindau, and Captain Alcock in the Sioux, engaged opportunity targets with the two 5.5-inch guns, including a field gun at Risau. A 5.5-inch dealt with several TNI on Gunong Jagoi who had, rather unwisely, fired on A Company. While this action was going on, there was intense diplomatic activity between Kuala Lumpur, Jakarta and London and at 4.15 pm, 1/10th Gurkha Rifles received orders originating from London, several thousand miles away, to withdraw across the border.

In the early days of his office, General Suharto had retained the command structure developed by Sukarno, including Crush Malaysia Command, but it was an inactive headquarters for public consumption. Supported by Adam Malik, the leader of the small nationalist-communist Murba Party, who had replaced Dr Subandrio as Foreign Minister and was leading negotiations with Malaysia, Suharto suggested that *Konfrontasi* had run its fatal course. The Murba Party had been formed in 1948 with an ethos of state communism, as opposed to alliances with Moscow or Peking, and was despised by the PKI. Not surprisingly, Malaysia was suspicious, however when, in April, Indonesia established diplomatic and commercial relations with Singapore, the thaw set in and then on 12 April, Suharto indicated that Indonesia would recognize Malaysia. Major General Lea again suspended Operation Claret but insisted that recce patrols should continue.

Since the SAS had left the Far East, most of these patrols – which were mounted by 2 (Australian) SAS Squadron and 2 (New Zealand) SAS Detachment, and were sometimes accompanied by officers from battalions planning raids – found the TNI alert and were often forced to abandon close recces. Still reeling after losing the four men killed, on 26 April, 1/10th Gurkha Rifles handed over the Bau sector to 4th RAR and, shuffling to the left, took over Serian from 1st Argyll and Sutherland Highlanders. Since arriving in December 1965, the Argylls had carried out several Operation Claret patrols against an enemy focused more on training CCO than with inviting trouble, although a patrol shot up several Indonesians swimming in a stream. 1/10th Gurkha Rifles continued with several Operation Claret recce patrols and 40th Light Regiment handed over to 6th Light Regiment. 42 Commando at Biawak continued to be spasmodically mortared until it handed over to 1st Malaysian Rangers (Lieutenant Colonel Yusif Bin Abu Bakar) on 6 May. Two days earlier, the 1/6th Gurkha Rifles tempted Assistant Lieutenant Sumbi, from 600 Raider Battalion, into attacking a vacated platoon post near Bario and although themselves ambushed, drove Sumbi's force of 100 men back across the border. In late May, 1st DLI, after three years in the Far East and en route to Colchester to join the Strategic Reserve, handed over to 1st RNZIR (Lieutenant Colonel Bryan Poenanga) on its second tour. Their departure was typical:

Our move to UK was complicated as it involved four separate media, helicopters, road transport, boat and fixed wing aircraft. The companies moved tactically out of their bases by helicopter and moved from the helicopter head some 60 miles by road to ships awaiting them in Kuching. We sailed in three ships for Singapore while Battalion Headquarters and a small rear party moved by air. It was fortunate that the MV Auby on which the bulk of the Battalion moved did not sail for 36 hours. This enabled us, with the courtesy of the skipper, who was himself a Geordie, to hold a cocktail party on board at which we entertained Brigadier Cheyne and 99 Gurkha Infantry Brigade Staff and various Kuching friends. It was an evening not to be forgotten whilst the troops' consumption of 'Tiger Beer' after enforced abstinence in the jungle was quite staggering.

After a 32-hour air trooping flight, the Battalion arrived home to be welcomed by military bands and Her Majesty's Customs and Excise before they joined their families.

Table 3. L Company, 42 Commando at Biawak – Statistics 26 November 1965 to 6 June 1966	
Duration	144 days.
No of patrols	69. Men on patrol one day in every four.
No of contacts	4
Killed	2 – Lt Clark and LCpl Collins (actually missing) at Sedjingen.
Wounded	2 - Lt Wantage (groin) and Mne Healey (chest) at Sedjingen.
Enemy killed	15
Enemy wounded	18
7.62mm rounds fired	1,427 equating to 21 tons costing £29,755.
81mm rounds fired	689 equating to $1^7/_4$ cwt
Accidental discharges	4 – All Armalites resulting in four injuries. This led to an inquiry.
Athlete's Foot	10
Dengue Fever	6 – All casevacced to hospital.
Dysentery	1
Diarrhoea	49
Impetigo	5
Rashes	49
Ringworm	38
Worms	12
	Source *Biawak Diary, FAA Museum*

Throughout April and May, Suharto told Indonesians that it was time to resolve *Konfrontasi* diplomatically. In mid-May, eight senior Crush Malaysia Command officers took a message to Kuala Lumpur that although Confrontation would continue, the door was open for negotiations. On 25 May 1966, a close colleague of Suharto, Lieutenant Colonel Moerdani, who had led discreet negotiations in 1964 and had nearly been shot up by Sergeant Large's patrol in 1965, led a diplomatic mission to Kuala Lumpur. Three days later, Major General Lea terminated Operation Claret and ordered British Forces, Borneo to revert to internal security and guarding the border. Malik and Malaysian Deputy Prime Minister Razak then met in Bangkok and, on 4 June, agreed to end Confrontation. British withdrawal from Singapore was no longer a pre-condition, simply because the Defence White Paper had indicated withdrawal from the Far East, except Hong Kong. Although this was quickly ratified by Malaysia, Indonesia procrastinated because of strong criticism from Sukarno who, sensing that since Indonesia had made the first moves, saw an opportunity to regain power, and was publicly suggesting that agreement equated to capitulation. When former Defence Minister General Nasution acknowledged that the concept of 'Maphilindo' was unlikely and that national principles important to Indonesia should not be discarded in favour of peace, his views won considerable support among officers who feared international humiliation. Fighting hard to keep the peace talks on track, Suharto shifted supporters into positions vacated by Sukarno's military loyalists, some of whom were coincidentally sent on upgrading courses at the Army Staff College. Although nothing specific was agreed in Bangkok, because of tensions in Indonesia, at a Crush Malaysia Command meeting on 10 June, a minute was endorsed as 'having established mutual trust and goodwill between the two countries'.

In spite of the moves to ending hostilities, the Indonesians continued military operations. On 13 June, after Stass Sound Ranging detected an Indonesian field gun shelling Bau District, V Battery returned fire, reports later indicating that the shells had landed within 100 yards and the Indonesians had hurriedly abandoned the gun. They later retrieved it. Intelligence then reported that two small groups of RPKAD and TNKU, 'Manjaps 1 and 2' were planning to enter First Division in order to gather intelligence on Commonwealth military activities and stir up subversion among the Chinese during the Bangkok Talks. Directed by 2 (Australian) Squadron SAS, on 15 June, a C Company, 4th RAR patrol commanded by Lieutenant Curtis intercepted five Indonesians on Raya Ridge, at the cost of one killed and another wounded, and recovered documents casting doubt on the commitment of the TNI and IBT to end Confrontation and implied continued active support of the CCO. C and D Companies, 2/7th Gurkha Rifles, in Operation Last Chance, working on Special Branch information, killed four and captured two of a six-strong TNI patrol, dressed in civilian clothes, and captured a large cache of weapons and equipment near Kampong Tundang. This was last major operation for 2/7th Gurkha Rifles, on its fourth and last tour in Borneo.

The British continued to rotate units through Borneo. On 5 May, 40 Commando, on its fifth tour, took over Second Division from the 1st Malaysian Rangers and had a quiet time with a few internal security incidents. After training at Paradise Camp having arrived from Netheravon, on 1 June, 1st Royal Hampshires (Lieutenant Colonel M.F.A. Wilson) took over from 2nd RGJ in Sabah just as the Bangkok talks were beginning and were then relieved in mid July by the 1st Queen's Own Buffs (Lieutenant Colonel E.W. MacDonald), which was the fifteenth and last British battalion to be deployed to Borneo. When the CCO began to agitate, A Company at Pango Amo mounted Operation Side Hat, killed one Chinese and made several arrests. 1st Royal Warwickshire Fusiliers took over Paradise Camp but arrived too late to be deployed operationally. 4th RTR handed over to a composite regiment with squadrons from the Life Guards, Queen's Dragoon Guards and 5th RTR. Within forty-five minutes of Second Lieutenant Crawshaw arriving from Tidworth, he was on escort duties commanding 4 Troop, H Squadron, 5 RTR, and days later, lay beside a rain-soaked track for forty hours. On 30 July, Lieutenant Mike Halliwell was the FOO to a 4th RAR Operation Claret when shortly after arranging 5.5-inch fire, one of his signallers exclaimed, 'We've beaten the Germans!' The Australians were wondering if the British knew exactly who they were fighting, little realizing England had just defeated West Germany 4 to 2 in the Football World Cup.

1/7th Gurkha Rifles (Lieutenant Colonel Carroll OBE), on its fifth tour, took over from 1/6th Gurkha Rifles the 160 miles of border in Fourth and Fifth Divisions. His combat team consisted of a 38 Light Battery Pack Howitzer, a Gurkha Engineers troop, the Gurkha Air Flight of three Sioux, Patrol Company, 3 Para, 2 (New Zealand) SAS Detachment, eight platoons of the Sarawak Police Field Force, 230 Border Scouts in villages and three Intelligence Corps FINCOs. The terrain was rugged with rivers threading through jungle-covered ridges, some rising to 2,500 feet. Rivers in flood were usually full of logs and trees hurtling downstream and so patrols were confined to tracks winding their way through the dripping canopies of the primary jungle.

Although the level of activity had decreased, intelligence assessments were suggesting co-ordinated incursions by two groups into Fifth Division and the Interior Residency of Sabah, with the aim of carrying out acts of sabotage intent on destabilizing Sarawak and Brunei in order to undermine the peace negotiations. It was not known if these incursions were supported by Jakarta.

In June, specific information, including from a prisoner captured by 2/6th Gurkha Rifles, began flowing into HQ Central Brigade that

Assistant Lieutenant Sumbi was training a mixed force from 600 Raider Battalion and TNKU at Long Bawang with the intention of blowing up the oil refineries at Seria, Brunei. Thought to be a formidable guerrilla, who may have trained at the Jungle Warfare School, Brigade HQ assessed that he would either move fast using well-defined routes and risk interception, or take the slower option of following features, such as a mountain ranges or rivers. The Sabah incursion was a mixed force from the RPKAD and TNKU. The FINCO border tripwire of sources and the Border Scouts network were alerted to gather information.

In his sector, Carroll believed that Sumbi could only cross somewhere within the 16 miles of border between Ba Kelalan and Long Semado, and the belief that he would fight governed Carroll's doctrine over the next two months. For maximum flexibility and balance, he placed all platoons under his direct command and had them issued with HF radios to improve communications. Company HQs would be inserted either as tactical HQs to operate with platoons in difficult conditions, assist with tactical decision making or improve communications. He planned to exercise command and control from a helicopter while operational matters were to be resolved at Battalion HQ. New LPs were hacked out of the jungle and the guns and mortars carried out target registration and prepared for rapid moves.

Major Alan Jenkins was the B Company Commander at Ba Kelalan and as information built up around Sumbi, he began a diary entitled 'The Sumbi Saga'. During the Bangkok talks, he had received a letter from Sergeant Major Sjakur, the Indonesian 509 Infantry Battalion post commander at Lian Tuar, advising that a TNI unit wished to fire its mortars across the border and pleaded with Jenkins not to retaliate, because both sides were looking for communists. It seems that his battalion had been pushed deep into North Kalimantan by Operation Claret and had been replaced by a mixed bag of the RPKAD, Sukarno 'fighters' known as 'Sukarnolewan', Diponegoro Division deserters and hardcore TNKU. By 7 July, Sumbi had briefed the fifty men he had selected that the mission was to train dissidents in Temburong District and then attack the oil refinery complex at Miri. Temburong had been the most resistant area during the Brunei Revolt. On 13 July, when Sumbi received his last supply drop by air, this was reported by the FINCO to HQ Central Brigade and the alert state was raised.

It was not until 25 July that Major Jenkins learnt from a reliable source that Sumbi had crossed the border two days earlier. Carroll sent seven Gurkha platoons and four 2 (New Zealand) SAS patrols to scour the area. Also in the area was a five-man Gurkha Independent Parachute Company patrol on exercise about 4 miles north of Ba Kelalan, and on 31 July, it found the tracks of thirty men, about five days old, heading

235

north. For the next forty-eight hours, without cooking or making camp, the Gurkhas tracked the Indonesians until they found in a bivouac, about 11 miles north of the border, three pairs of discarded British Army canvas jungle boots and sacking, probably used to wrap around boots. When Gurkha patrols found more camps in the area, Carroll instructed 6 Platoon, B Company, to take over the pursuit. Recce Platoon (Lieutenant (QGO) Kulbahadur Rai) moved into the field and during the evening of 3 August, while a suspected bivouac was being checked, a sentry guarding the patrol base saw several people, including Sumbi, it was later learnt, crossing the track about 300 yards down a hill and opened fire. After lying in ambush all night, Kulbahadur led a charge into their camp, however the Indonesians fled, taking with them one man who later died of his wounds.

Carroll laid a communist-style annihilation ambush along the Sungei Kelalan by having the Recce Platoon beat the east bank while the Anti-Tanks took the west bank, the plan being to drive the Indonesians toward two rifle platoons in blocking positions to the north, who had been landed by helicopters on a sandbank in the middle of the river. No one walked into the trap. Next day, the Anti-Tanks found more tracks and these were doggedly followed by Acting Sergeant Kaluman Rai, a section commander. It had been raining heavily for days. A company HQ was inserted to stabilize command and control, but supposed sightings were followed by the frustrations of false leads. Nevertheless, 1/7th Gurkha Rifles, now reinforced with B Company, 2/6th Gurkha Rifles, relentlessly followed the tracks until they were lost in the mud and rain, only to find them again. For a week Carroll rotated patrols between operations and rest. Brigade and Battalion intelligence assessments frequently confused the picture and it seemed that Sumbi had disappeared into the vast wet mist of thick jungle.

And then on 12 August, the day that Confrontation ended, when a bedraggled Indonesian staggered into Long Lopeng and was handed over by the villagers to the Gurkhas, he revealed, under interrogation, that Sumbi was camped about 2 miles to the west and that he had split his forces into two, handing over about half to Sergeant Rampingen, which had unsettled his anxious men. Of interest was that Sumbi had been shaken by the 3 August encounter because he believed that he had not been detected. He had not reckoned on operational security indiscretions at Long Bawan and that Intelligence Sections were analysing his every move.

Meanwhile, the thaw between Indonesia and Malaysia blossomed into another meeting in Bangkok and British Forces, Borneo was ordered to cease offensive operations, which included the pursuit of Sumbi. Indonesia began withdrawing troops from the border and the Riau

236

Archipelago, while Great Britain formally announced her intention to reduce her military presence in Malaysia and held out a promise of rescheduling Indonesia's £10 million debts. Sukarno and Nasution insisted that although the military confrontation might be over, political confrontation would continue until Great Britain adhered to the Manila Agreement and that, in any event, the war with colonialism would continue. General Suharto's ambition to replace Sukarno formally was strengthened when the People's Consultative Committee asked him to form a cabinet. At its first meeting on 4 August, he announced that hostilities would end before 17 August – Independence Day. In fact, Confrontation had effectively ended on 12 August and the British were already withdrawing. Four days earlier, Mid-West Brigade had disbanded and HQ 5 Infantry Brigade was returning to the UK. In 1982, it would fight in the Falklands Campaign and was commanded by Confrontation veteran, Brigadier Tony Wilson.

On 16 August, Deputy Prime Minister Razak visited Jakarta to sign the peace agreement, 'in order to resolve the problems between the two countries arising out of the formation of Malaysia'. It was agreed that Malaysia 'would give the people of Sarawak and Sabah the opportunity to reaffirm, in a free and democratic manner through general elections, their previous decision about their status in the Federation of Malaysia'. The final statement was a masterpiece of Far East face-saving. Malaysia emphasized that the wishes of the two Borneo states had been upheld in 1963, while Indonesia could claim that the 1963 act of self-determination should be repeated. Today, both states remain within the Federation and judging by Indonesia's misbehaviour in East Timor, their selection was wise. Although full diplomatic relations were not immediately established, TNI and CCO factions were reluctant to quit infiltrating into Sarawak. 1st Queens Own Buffs suffered its only fatality when Private Mark Barton, of C Company, was killed on 14 August in a brisk battle with an Indonesian patrol intercepted near Tebedu. Sumbi took the time to rest and split his forces further in the hope that some would reach Temburong.

Lieutenant Colonel Carroll, still convinced that Sumbi's men would fight, moved the centre of operations to Long Semado where Captain David Morgan organized the logistics of 1/7th Gurkha Rifles and two reinforcement companies from 1/6th Gurkha Rifles, a total of fourteen platoons. Among recent prisoners were two TNI lieutenants refusing to talk under interrogation. A Gurkha major then arrived on a fishing trip and when he suggested that a mock execution might convince them to co-operate, the ploy worked and, both believing that the other had been shot, the two men divulged that Sumbi was heading for the 6,070-feet-high Bukit Pagon and that his men were determined. The mountain straddles the southern tip of Brunei's Temburong District with Fifth Division, and was the same feature that had given Lieutenant van der Horst's 42 Commando patrol such a torrid time in January 1963. Below is the Sungei Pasia, which flows north to the Temburong and into Brunei Bay. If Sumbi managed to reach the Pasia, he could use boats to take him north to relative safety among sympathisers. This information was relayed to London for further instructions; however it was not until 20 August that Carroll received authority from HQ Central Brigade to continue the pursuit.

With the sharp decrease in incursions, British Forces, Borneo focused on the pursuit of Sumbi. Next day, Major Jenkins, Second Lieutenant Nigel Warren and 4 and 5 Platoons were inserted into the jungle to the east of Bukit Pagon to continue the pursuit. Jenkins:

> found the going was horrendous – steep, mountainous jungle slopes, rivers in full flow and persistent rain. On one occasion, Company Headquarters and the two platoons were confronted by a near vertical cliff, up which the Gurkhas hauled themselves. On reaching the top, I was dismayed to find that we were on a sheer-sided, round, jungle plateau with the patrols unable to find a reasonably safe way down. A helicopter from Battalion Headquarters identified the best route for us to follow.

Meanwhile, 12 Platoon, D Company, accompanied by the two TNI officers, was patrolling west from Long Merarap. On the 25th, Carroll had concluded that Sumbi had not occupied Bukit Pagon so he ordered Jenkins to search the Parsai valley for tracks and then link up with 12 Platoon, which had found some Indonesian bivouacs and had captured a number of Indonesians, including Sergeant Rampingen and several men. From his Air Flight Sioux, Carroll, concerned about the fatigue, health and fitness of the Gurkhas, nevertheless encouraged them to be alert to ambushes. By the 31st, 4 and 12 Platoons met but the ten days of patrolling in appalling conditions had taken a severe toll on the Gurkhas, and Jenkins reduced the force to a composite section of the ten fittest men. Meanwhile 5 Platoon, patrolling north along the Pasai, had captured three Indonesians on 31 August and a further five the following day. All were physically exhausted. 12 Platoon had been in the field since 1 August bar three days.

The composite section found two more camps and then, during the evening of 2 September, the lead scout reported a small bivouac about 200 yards across a shallow river. Since it was nearly dark, Jenkins ordered a 'quiet' camp. Next day at 9.03 am, the section passed through the camp and was following the track through the jungle when they saw four Indonesians. Jenkins challenged them to surrender and three did so immediately, but the fourth shouldered his weapon and turned to walk away, only to be stopped by a shout from his colleagues. It was Lieutenant Sumbi. He offered no resistance and was disarmed of his pistol and dagger, which are now on display in the Gurkha Museum at Winchester. At 9.10 am, Jenkins reported to Carroll that he had captured Sumbi and needed a helicopter. Within a few minutes, a Scout piloted by Major Maurice Taylor, of the Army Air Corps, perched on a wet rocky outcrop beside the swollen Trusan. With his back propped against the pilot's door, Jenkins took a photograph of Sumbi, but sadly he had not accounted for the helicopter vibration and it is a little blurred. Sumbi was then flown to Long Semado for interrogation.

Forty-two of Sumbi's men had now been accounted for but three Indonesians and four TNKU led by Corporal Ibrahim were still missing. In spite of his tribulations, Sumbi was in good condition and resisted interrogation until he was invited by the 1/7th Gurkha Rifles Anti-Tank Platoon commander, Lieutenant (QGO) Kharkabahadur Rai, to join him in a glass or two of rum. In the third week of September, A Company captured the Indonesians of Ibrahim's group in the lower reaches of the Trusan, which left four TNKU missing. By the end of October, border incursions had ceased, nevertheless, the Brunei Government needed confirmation that the oilfields were not at risk. When Lieutenant Colonel Cross, the officer who had formed the Border Scouts and now commanded the Gurkha Independent Parachute Company, joined a patrol that found very recent evidence of a small IBT unit, he contacted the newly-formed 1st Royal Brunei Malay Regiment and several days later a patrol captured the four TNKU after they had wandered into an Iban longhouse, emaciated and starving.

The pursuit of Sumbi had been meticulously planned and directed by Lieutenant Colonel Carroll. Apart from the engagement on 3 August, no shots had been fired by either side during the six week, fox-and-goose pursuit in the soaking jungle. The helicopters of 230 and 845 Squadrons had played a crucial role moving troops and flying out prisoners. By any stretch of the imagination, it was a remarkable operation and worthy of the many accolades that 1/7th Gurkha Rifles received. Major Jenkins was awarded a MC, not for gallantry, but for leading a relentless and potentially hazardous pursuit resulting in the capture of twenty-four Indonesians.

In East Brigade, on 28 August, 1st Royal Hampshires laid several ambushes in west Sabah in response to the incursion directed at the Interior Residency and co-ordinated to take place at the same time as Sumbi's. A week later, when intelligence emerged of subversive interest in several security bases, on 2 September, 3, 7 and 8 Platoons searched the village at Milestone 12 and arrested a Chinese who could not satisfactorily account for 100lb of rice. When these operations sparked off reports of more sightings, including barefoot, armed men in the jungle, the Intelligence Section made five crucial conclusions: 1) that an incursion was directed at Kalabakan; 2) the enemy strength could be estimated; 3) equipment had been identified; 4) the enemy were short of food; 5) the enemy were lost. In an operation not dissimilar to that mounted by 1/10th Gurkha Rifles in January 1964, in the Brantian area, Lieutenant Colonel Wilson denied the incursion food, shelter and tranquillity by ambushes, harassment, responding quickly to sightings, and guarding villages and towns, which netted several tired and starving TNI and IBTs. On 14 September, the Battalion handed the pursuit to a Malaysian battalion and left for UK.

On 10 September, 4th RAR handed over to 3rd Malaysian Rangers and within a few months was in South Vietnam. In First Division, HQ West Brigade was replaced by 3 Malaysian Infantry Brigade and 248 Signal Squadron handed over to a Malaysian squadron equipped with modern communications equipment. During the thirty-two months since it had arrived in April 1964, 248 Squadron had converted from an airportable unit to a static one and VHF radios had replaced the HF sets in all command posts, with communications distances of over 120 miles being achieved by the exploiting antennae. The rebroadcast station on top of the 3,000-feet Gunong Serapi had become a sophisticated facility and at one stage handled five rebroadcast stations, which allowed the Squadron not only to meet its normal commitments but also supported naval, military and police communications, particularly when Operation Claret raids were under way. On the lighter side, the Nuffield Trust had financed a longboat, which was named *Bahadur*, for rest and recreation. By the time that the unit left Sarawak in September, the boatman, Corporal Dalbahadur Thapa, had just about mastered parking the boat at Kuching against a 5-knot current and in limited space.

By the end of the year, all British, Australian and New Zealand forces had left Borneo. Within months, some Australians and New Zealanders fighting a hopeless war in Vietnam successfully applied lessons from Confrontation. Meanwhile, many of the British found themselves fighting an altogether different type of jungle war in the concrete housing estates and green fields of Northern Ireland.

CHAPTER NINETEEN

Conclusions

Confrontation was the first war to be fought by British Regular Armed Forces since the Second World War. During a visit to the Far East, on 11 July 1966, Secretary of State for Defence Denis Healey visited Borneo and at Labuan made a speech in which he paid the following tribute:

> The records and achievements of the British Forces in East Malaysia are quite literally incomparable. I do not think the troops of any other country could have handled this type of problem more successfully and maintained stability for so long with so little loss of life.
>
> The other thing that stands out in peculiar types of campaign which have been all too common since the Second World War is that political control of operations should be exercised uniformly with every level from cabinet down to platoon. The Services have dealt with this problem with our Malaysian allies without putting one foot wrong.
>
> It has been a model of inter-Service co-operation between the Forces of the old and new Commonwealth.

Healey, who was probably one of the best post-war defence ministers, declared the campaign to be 'one of the most efficient uses of military forces in the history of the world'. From December 1962 until August 1966, the British lost 19 killed and 44 wounded and the Gurkhas, who with the Royal Marines had necessarily taken the brunt of the fighting, lost 43 killed and 83 wounded. The Australians lost 22 killed with 7 killed in action and the New Zealanders had 7 killed and 7 wounded and injured. Of the three known to have been captured by the Indonesians, Trooper Condon of the SAS, Gunner Martin and Lance Corporal Collins, none returned alive.

Twenty-five years after the engagement at Sedjingen, following repeated requests by his mother, Mrs Margaret Collins, for an explana-

241

tion of the death of her son, Colonel Ian Ker, the Defence Attaché at the British Embassy in Jakarta, undertook to see what he could find out. During Confrontation, Ker had served in the Malaysian Army as a company commander in Sarawak and Malaysia and was familiar with the area around Biawak and Sedjingan. During one of several visits to North Kalimantan between 1990 and 1991, he met a Dutch pastor who remembered seeing a dead British soldier being brought into Kampong Sebedang, which is some 70 miles from Sedjingan. The pastor put Ker in touch with a Chinese called Ah Choi, who along with three other young locals, had been ordered by the Indonesians to bury the body., They had had marked the spot with a simple wooden cross and agreed to look after the grave. Very soon after Collins had been buried, President Sukarno paid a rare visit to North Kalimantan and when he was told about Collins, he joked that the death of 'Collinsism' was as dead as colonialism. No doubt everybody dutifully laughed at this observation. In 1991, Ker, several senior Indonesian officers, a patholo- gist and a dentist were present and when the body was exhumed, the combination of British military relics and Ah Choi's evidence proved beyond doubt that the body was Lance Corporal Collins. With due ceremony, the Indonesians flew the Union Flag-draped mahogany coffin to Jakarta, where it was formally handed by Air Marshal Suakadirul, the Head of Armed Forces Personnel, to the British Ambassador, Mr Roger Carrick. The coffin was then flown to the United Kingdom a few days later for a private family service and reburial in the same plot as his father in the cemetery next to the cathedral in St Helens. A bearer party and buglers from the Royal Marines Training Unit at Lympstone provided the escort. How Collins met his death will probably remain a mystery. Research suggests that he was killed after running out of ammunition, having evaded capture for some time, after which his death was apparently swift and summary. The Indonesians admitted that the majority of their casualties in this particular action were caused by Collins's determination to prevent 304 Infantry Battalion from closing in on L Company during their withdrawal from Sedjingan. If this is the case, then the bravery of Lance Corporal Collins should be recognized.

Indonesian losses are estimated to be 590 killed, 222 wounded and 771 captured. Of the 546 prisoners of war repatriated from Malaysia in October, 4 were Customs officials, 21 Army, 34 Navy, 72 Mobile Police Brigade, 109 Indonesian 'volunteers', such as fisherman, 117 Quick Mobile Force, most captured on the Malaysian mainland, and 189 TNKU, CCO and other 'volunteers' from Brunei, Sarawak and Sabah. There is no doubt that most Indonesians fought hard and they had their successes, however their forces evolved from guerrilla-style campaigns and were dependent on the support of the local population. Indonesian strategists appear not to have appreciated that Great Britain would provide the bulk of the defenders and that its Armed Forces were highly experienced in a jungle setting, having just defeated communist guerrillas in the Malayan Emergency.

In the nearly four years of conflict, thirty-six civilians were killed and fifty-five wounded, most during operations conducted by the CCO. Four are reported to have been taken prisoner. The very few civilian casualties can be directly attributed to the fact that most of the fighting took places on isolated tracks and rivers. Unlike the US strategy in South-East Asia, carpet bombing and the destruction of villages were not part of either side's strategy, largely because wrecked trees become major obstacles and refugees and homeless people are a logistic nightmare and a media scoop. The 'hearts and minds' of the local population was of value to both sides in different ways. For the Commonwealth forces, it was a tripwire and proven intelligence resource and, provided that internal security was maintained, there was less of a threat to the units in depth. The Indonesians were reliant upon sympathizers, principally Chinese, to provide support and succour as they moved deeper into Malaysia to set up 'liberated areas' from which to mount attacks on the defences and economic infrastructure.

Comparisons between Confrontation and Vietnam are frequent; however, there are fundamental differences. The US was a relative newcomer to South-East Asia and did not have a cultural, political and military history as the British had developed in Borneo and at home. British North Borneo had stable administrations whereas the South Vietnamese government was corrupt. The North Vietnamese were totally committed to their ideology and were actively supported by Viet Cong embedded in South Vietnam. The same could not be said of support to the CCO. The Commonwealth and the US approach to war differed. The counter-revolutionary strategy adopted in Borneo was similar to that used in Malaya and relied on retaining 'hearts and minds', dominating the jungle with imaginative tactics and good quality intelligence to ensure that almost every Indonesian move was detected. Jubilant and full of confidence as the Indonesians set off, once in Malaysia, they soon risked death, injuries and wounds, capture or being forced to survive on the run in inhospitable jungle, on the wrong side of the border and without support. Morale collapsed. The length of the demilitarized zone and the border with Cambodia was about the same length as the one that Commonwealth forces defended in Borneo.

Confrontation is often described as a secret war – it was not, although few in Great Britain realized, and still do not, the extent of the fighting. This was largely because very few journalists applied, or indeed were invited, to report on the fighting and very few incidents provoked the interests of the media, in the context of events in Aden and later in Northern Ireland, largely because of their unwillingness to join troops on patrol. While television was deployed in the front line in Vietnam, it played no role in Confrontation. The absence of journalists permitted the military to apply the full weight of military functions, such as interrogation. The journalists who swarmed the streets of Northern Ireland and deserts of the Gulf from hotel bars and airport lounges would have found few journalistic hotels and watering holes in Borneo. The few articles written about Borneo are generally supportive of British troops. Journalists today are apparently experts on military strategy, tactics and culture and, while claiming to be guardians of democracy, most are self-centred and do not realize that their disclosure, innuendo, gossip and rumour can affect military operations. In Northern Ireland, their disclosures affected the pursuit of an enemy regarded by politicians to be criminal and yet who styled themselves in such terms as 'army', 'brigades', 'battalions' and 'companies', just as the Indonesians' surrogates had done when they also crossed a border on military operations from a country that allowed them sanctuary. Interrogation was widely used by the military and Special Branch and undoubtedly contributed to the low number of military and civilian casualties. In comparison, interrogation of the 'soldiers' of the IRA was fatally emasculated by media disinformation to be near meaningless. A vital cog in the military intelligence cycle that had proved so successful during Confrontation was replaced by sophisticated source-handling techniques, which has since led to demoralizing investigations.

The absence of journalists allowed the British to conduct one of the largest clandestine operations in military history – Operation Claret. Commonwealth forces were initially at a disadvantage behind their defences in North Borneo but by destabilizing Indonesian initiatives with attacks on their military infrastructure, the offensive initiative was wrested from the Indonesians and they were pushed onto the defensive, except when the political situation meant that Operation Claret was suspended and the Indonesians mounted attacks. The operation also isolated the CCO from succour.

Did the Indonesian High Command know about Operation Claret? Certainly the Army was not keen to be accused of not supporting a war of national pride, and from signals intercepts, it seems that Indonesian military commanders were claiming successes. Captain Christopher Bullock was on holiday in Bali a year after Confrontation and met an Indonesian officer opponent who said that the British had 'raided into North Kalimantan regularly and just as regularly had been driven off so they had won'. It seemed to Bullock to be 'a soldierly explanation'. It is interesting that British units were able to range almost at will in North Kalimantan against an army that had evolved on guerrilla wafare and rear area operations. Whereas the British tactic was to cut Indonesiasn incursions from the border, few attempts were made to cut British units off from their withdrawal routes to Sarawak. To that extent, it must be concluded that Operation Claret achieved its strategy of sanitizing a substantial area south of the border.

To what extent Claret contributed to the political process that ended Confrontation is debatable. The strategy did not involve positional warfare of capturing ground as a bargaining counter and therefore did not hurt Indonesia markedly. If Indonesian commanders in Jakarta were receiving information that British raids were being driven off, which falls into the strategy of quick impact and withdrawal, then it is difficult to agree to the argument that Operation Claret was a major contributor to bringing Indonesia to the negotiations. In fact, peace feelers had been extended before the strategy was developed.

Confrontation was fought in a period of the social upheaval of the Swinging Sixties, with the arrival of the Beatles, Carnaby Street and Mary Quant. Those in the Armed Forces who know veterans of Confrontation regard them with the same respect as those who defeated Argentina in the 1982 Falklands campaign. To a great extent it was the culmination of the campaigns fought by the Army since 1945. To the north, armed forces from across the Far East were involved in a war in which lessons learnt by the British since 1941 in conventional, revolutionary and guerrilla jungle warfare were largely discarded as, home and abroad, discipline collapsed in the face of highly motivated Vietnamese Communists. A country was swallowed up and 55,000 dead US servicemen, several hundred thousand wounded and a national guilt adopted over its international humiliation still pervades today. Australasian military discipline prevented the drug abuse that was to blight US Forces.

During Confrontation technology was tested to the limit. The British developed the use of helicopters to move men, guns and supplies over huge distances, albeit generally without interference. Ground sensors and mortar-locating radar played an important role in an environment in which observation was often very difficult. Lighter VHF radio sets replaced HF sets and improved the quality of communications. The Armalite replaced the heavy SLR and was ideal for short-range jungle warfare in which quantity of firepower is important in the first few seconds of an engagement. That the versatile Italian 105mm Pack Howitzer could be dismantled for transportation was important. The hovercraft was too noisy.

A key principle learnt from the Malaysia Emergency was that counter-insurgency relies upon a joint political and military response. In spite of some opposition, Major General Walker, supremely supported by Admiral Begg, insisted on Joint Service and civil command and control, and an intelligence-sharing approach. Imagination, mature battle craft and good leadership at all levels defeated insurgency. There are lessons to be learnt from Confrontation even today.

Within four years, many of the British Regulars who had defeated the Indonesians found themselves experiencing savage defence cuts that ensured that Confrontation was the last war for several famous regiments – the Durhams and King's Own Yorkshire Light Infantry were absorbed into the Light Infantry, the Warwickshire Fusiliers were merged into the Royal Regiment of Fusiliers, the Queen's Own Buffs joined other South-East and Home Counties regiments to form the Queen's Regiment, while the Royal Ulster Rifles joined the Royal Irish Rangers. The SAS profited from Confrontation in that the officers who fought in Borneo created a belief that it should operate entirely independently of conventional units. While there is no doubt that Special Forces must have an independent role, they also have an information-gathering one to provide intelligence for the anvil of conventional units. Many of those who took part in Confrontation found themselves fighting an altogether different type of war in Northern Ireland, where political expediency and survival, media interference in military operations and the force of law were placed above the lives of soldiers. Too close to home for many who served there, politicians exerted control of operations, laid down policies which directly affected military strategy and then, in the pursuit of peace with an organization that admits to negotiating down the barrel of a gun, actually apologized for the actions of the British Army.

In the end, it was the Commonwealth soldier containing and driving his Indonesian opponent from the border, backed up by the political instability in Jakarta which brought down Sukarno. Efficient and effective acquisition of intelligence enabled the British Army to deploy its own and allied Commonwealth forces, and their resources, with the greatest effort. And then when political cracks appeared in late 1964, Britain exploited propaganda and psychological warfare to conclude Confrontation to her satisfaction and Indonesia's embarrassment. It was an outstanding victory, and it was a victory.

APPENDIX 1

FUNDAMENTALS OF GUERRILLA WAR

A summary of the theories of Colonel Nasution are:

1. War in this century has become total people's war.
2. Guerrilla warfare is a war of the weak against the strong.
3. Guerrilla warfare cannot, by itself, bring final victory: guerrilla warfare can only weaken the strength of the enemy.
4. A guerrilla war is usually an ideological war. Warfare is a total people's war.
5. Guerrilla warfare does not mean that all the people are fighting.
6. A guerrilla war must not consist of unorganised destruction; it must be of systematic character.
7. A guerrilla movement has its base within the people. The people support, care for and conceal the guerrillas.
8. The enemy's arsenals are the guerrilla's sources of weapons.
9. The principal requirements for guerrilla warfare are: a people who will give assistance, sufficient geographical room, and a war of long duration.
10. A total people's war needs a unified leadership, not only at national level but also down to the local level.
11. The anti-guerrilla war must aim at severing the guerrilla fighters from their base, 'the people', and must therefore emphasize political, psychological and economic movements. The guerrilla must be opposed with his own tactics.

In a chapter entitled 'The Guerrilla and our Future War', Nasution predicted that guerrilla warfare would govern the strategic defence of Indonesia after 1953, and was therefore relevant to Indonesian strategy during Confrontation.

1. Have your umbrella ready before it rains (Keep your powder dry). Citing that the Cold Car turned into real wars, Nasution says the Indonesia must be able to defend itself if dragged into war. Armed forces must be organized, technical troops trained and weapons systems kept up to date.

2. For the next ten years or so guerrilla warfare will be the main item on our program of defence. Guerrilla warfare will be the national strategy only when Indonesia is unable to defend itself by conventional means. Most of the action will take place on land. As the armed forces develop, the effectiveness of guerrilla warfare will decrease.

3. At present, and in the years to come, we will continue to be engaged in anti-guerrilla activities. Nasution examined the guerrilla warfare being conducted by rebel factions in Java and the Celebes, and accepts that civil war cannot be concluded quickly. He accepted that official corruption, political cronyism, economic instability and ineffective security forces were major factors in inducing unrest.

4. The guerrilla war we waged was militarily speaking of an immature nature. Nasution examines the fighting against the Dutch and concludes that static and defensive tactics were no match for the flexibility of the Dutch. Although there was sufficient manpower, military organization was weak because too many battalions and brigades were formed to permit offensive action.

5. We must as soon as possible develop a truly regular army. The formation and development of regular forces were essential for the defence of Indonesia. Guerrilla warfare is, by nature, long and exhausting while conventional forces can absorb the pressures of guerrilla activity. Regular forces must be territorial and regional in nature with its own depots and training units to support home guards, people's defence forces and guerrilla units. Nasution had recommended these principles in 1948 after the Dutch First Police Action.

6. Organization and training for a future guerrilla war. To defend Indonesia, Nasution suggests three lines of defence - resistance by the army, resistance by the people's guerrilla army and the defence of the people. The Infantry must be lightly equipped, flexible and capable of being deployed quickly as organized units. Veterans are an important element of developing militias. Home guard units, partisans and student corps must be encouraged to become involved in defence. Volunteers are worth ten pressed men. Formed Home Guards are the most effective against guerrillas.

7. Guerrilla leadership and growth must be indigenous. The geography of Indonesia means that the Army must be simple in structure and regionally based in order to maintain national defence. The development of roads would be important as would the migration of people from

Java to the sparsely populated Kalimantan. The army should encourage this movement, particularly by veterans. While guerrilla warfare is necessarily localized by nature, attacks on Indonesia are also likely to be localized so that the regular army would fight in urban areas while the guerrillas dominated the rural areas and interior.

8. Guerrilla troops are the vanguard of an ideological war, usually a political-ideological war. The Indonesian National Army had been subjected to controversy about its involvement in politics, however, as an instrument of government, the Army is an ideological tool in the development of Indonesia and therefore guerrilla and soldier must fight shoulder to shoulder as standard bearers of the revolution.

9. The people's army and the guerrilla forces. Those who question the need for guerrilla forces and a people's army must realize that in the event of a modern war, the permanent army will require the support of a large number of militarily trained people. Everyone is expected to contribute to national defence and therefore the people's army must develop through organized militias properly trained by a core of instructors. Guerrillas can come and go, depending on the strategic situation.

10. The primary task of the army for the coming years is to restore domestic security. All preparations for guerrilla warfare are pointless unless the domestic security situation is under control.

APPENDIX 2

OFFICIAL CITATION

21148786 Lance Corporal Rambahadur Limbu
10th Princess Mary's Own Gurkha Rifles

On 21 November 1965 in the Bau District of Sarawak, Lance Corporal Rambahadur Limbu was with his Company when they discovered and attacked a strong enemy force located in the Border area. The enemy were strongly entrenched in Platoon strength, on top of a sheer hill, the only approach to which was along a knife-edge ridge allowing only three men to move abreast. Leading his support group in the van of the attack he could see the nearest trench and in it a sentry manning a machine gun. Determined to gain first blood, he inched himself forward until, still ten yards from his enemy, he was seen and the sentry opened fire, immediately wounding a man to his right. Rushing forward he reached the enemy trench in seconds and killed the sentry, thereby gaining for the attacking force a first but firm foothold on the objective. The enemy were now fully alerted and, from their positions in depth, brought down heavy automatic fire on the attacking force, concentrating this onto the area of the trench held alone by Lance Corporal Rambahadur Limbu.

Appreciating that he could not carry out his task of supporting his platoon from this position he courageously left the comparative safety of his trench and, with a complete disregard for the hail of fire being directed at him, he got together and led his fire group to a better fire position some yards ahead. He now attempted to indicate his intentions to his Platoon Commander by shouting and hand signals but failing to do so in the deafening noise of exploding grenades and continuous automatic fire he again moved out into the open and reported personally, despite the extreme dangers of being hit by the fire, not only from the enemy but by his own comrades.

It was at the moment of reporting that he saw both men of his own group seriously wounded. Knowing that their only hope of survival was immediate first aid, that evacuation from their very exposed position so close to the enemy was vital, he immediately commenced the first of his three supremely gallant attempts to rescue his comrades. Using what little ground cover he could find he crawled forward, in full view of at least two enemy machine gun posts who concentrated their fire on him and which, at this stage of the battle, could not be effectively subdued by the rest of his platoon. For three full minutes he continued to move forward but when almost able to touch the nearest casualty, he was driven back by the accurate and intense weight of fire covering his line of approach. After a pause he again started to crawl forward but he soon realised that only speed would give him the cover which the ground could not. Rushing forward he hurled himself on the ground beside one of the wounded and calling for support from two LMGs which had now come up to his right in support, he picked up the man and carried him to safety out of the line of fire. Without hesitation he immediately returned to the top of the hill determined to complete his self-imposed task of saving those for whom he felt personally responsible. It was now clear from the increased weight of fire being concentrated on the approaches to and in the immediate vicinity of the remaining casualty, the enemy were doing all they could to prevent any further attempts at rescue. However, despite this, Lance Corporal Rambahadur again moved out into the open for his final effort. In a series of short forward rushes, and once being pinned down for some minutes by the intense and accurate automatic fire which could be seen striking the ground all round him, he eventually reached the wounded man. Picking him up and unable now to seek cover he carried him back as fast as he could, through the hail of enemy bullets. It had taken twenty minutes to complete this gallant action and the events leading up to it. For all but a few seconds, this young NCO had been moving alone in full view of the enemy and under the continuous aimed fire of their automatic weapons. That he was able to achieve what he did against such overwhelming odds without being hit, was miraculous. His outstanding personal bravery, selfless conduct, complete contempt of the enemy and determination to save the lives of the men of his fire group set an incomparable example and inspired all who saw him.

Finally rejoining his section on the left flank of the attack, Lance Corporal Rambahadur was able to recover the LMG abandoned by the wounded and with it won his revenge, initially giving support during the later stage of the prolonged assault and finally being responsible for killing four more enemy as they attempted to escape across the border. This hour-long battle which had throughout been fought at point-blank range and with the utmost ferocity by both sides was finally won. At least twenty-four enemy are known to have died at a cost to the attacking force of three killed and two wounded. In scale and in achievement this engagement stands out as one of the first importance and there is no doubt that, but for the inspired conduct and example set by Lance Corporal Rambahadur Limbu at the most vital stage of the battle, much less would have been achieved and greater casualties caused.

He displayed heroism, self-sacrifice and devotion to duty and to his men of the very highest order. His actions on the day reached a zenith of determined, pre-meditated valour which must count amongst the most notable on record and is deserving of the greatest admiration and the highest praise.

• **AWARD – VICTORIA CROSS**

Date of Action   London Gazette
21 November 1965   22 April 1966

BIBLIOGRAPHY

Allen, Charles, *The Savage Wars of Peace: Soldiers' Voices 1945-1989*, Michael Joseph, London, 1990.

Andaya, Barbara Watson and Leonard, Y., *A History of Malaysia*, Palgrave, Basingstoke, 2001.

Blaxland, Gregory, *The Regiments Depart: A History of the British Army 1945-1970*, William Kimber, London, 1971.

Bowyer, Chaz, *The Encyclopaedia of British Military Aircraft*, Bison Books, London, 1982.

Bullock, Christopher, *Hazardous Journeys: Gurkha Clandestine Operations in Borneo*, Square One Publications, 2000.

Clayton, Dr Anthony, *Forearmed: A History of the Intelligence Corps*, Brassey's(UK), London, 1993.

Conboy, Ken, *South-East Asian Special Forces*, Osprey, London, 1991.

Cross, J.P., *Jungle Warfare: Experiences and Encounters*, Guild Publishing, London, 1989.

Crouch, Harold, *The Army and Politics in Indonesia*, Cornell University Press, 1978.

Easter, David, 'British Intelligence and Propaganda during the Confrontation, 1963-1966', *Intelligence and National Security*, vol. 16, No. 2 (Summer 2001), pp.83-102.

—, *Britain and Confrontation with Indonesia*, IB Taurus, 2004.

Everett-Heath, John, *British Military Helicopters*, Arms and Armour Press, London, New York, Sydney, 1968.

Flack, Mike, www.ton (Ton Class Association)

Fowler, William, *SAS: Behind Enemy Lines*, HarperCollins, London, 1997.

Grey, Jeffrey, *The RAN, Confrontation and the Defence of Malaysia*, Allen and Unwin, London, 1998.

Habesch, David, *The Army's Navy. British Military Vessels and their History since Henry VIII*, Chatham Publishing, London, 2001.

Harclerode, Peter, *Para! Fifty Years of the Parachute Regiment*, Brockhampton Press, London, 1992.

—, *Fighting Dirty. The Inside Story of Covert Operations from Ho Chi Minh to Osama Bin Laden*, Cassell, London, 2001.

Healey, Rt Hon Lord Denis, *Time of My Life*, Penguin Puttnam, London, 1993.

Jackson, General Sir William, *Withdrawal from Empire*, Batsford, London, 1986.

James, Harold and Sheil-Small, Denis, *The Undeclared War*, Leo Cooper, London, 1971.

—, *A Pride of Gurkhas, 2nd King Edward VII Own Goorkhas (The Sirmoor Rifles) 1948-1971*, Leo Cooper, London, 1975.

Jones, Matthew; *Conflict and Confrontation in South-East Asia 1961-1965: Britain, US, Indonesia and the Creation of Malaysia*, Cardiff University Press, Cardiff, 2001.

Keegan, John, *World Armies*, Gale Research Company, Detroit, 1983.

Ladd, David, *SAS Operations*, Robert Hale Ltd, London, 1986.

Lee, Air Chief Marshal David, *Eastward: A History of the Royal Air Force in the Far East 1945-1972*, HMSO, 1984.

Lee, David, *A Year in 42 Commando, November 1963-1964, Singapore and Borneo*, www.britains-smallwars.com

Lord, Cliff and Watson, Graham, *The Royal Corps of Signals, Unit Histories of the Corps (1920-2001) and its Antecedents*, Helion & Co Ltd, Solihull, 2003.

Lovell-Knight, Major A.K., *The Story of the Royal Military Police*, Leo Cooper, London, 1977.

Mackie, J.A.C., *Konfrontasi: The Indonesia-Malaysia Dispute 1963-1966*, Oxford University Press, London, New York, Melbourne, 1974.

McAllister, Major General R.W.L., *Bugle & Kukri: The Story of the 10th Princess Mary's Own Gurkha Rifles*, The 10th GR Regimental Trust, 1985.

McCouaig, Simon, *South-East Asian Special Forces*, Osprey, London, 1991.

McNab, Chris, *Twentieth-Century Small Arms*, Grange Books, Rochester, 2001.

Mockaitis, Thomas R, *British Counterinsurgency in the post-Imperial Era*, Manchester University Press, Manchester and New York, 1995.

Pilger, John, 'Iraq. Indonesia. We Need To Be Told', *New Statesman*, 18 October 2005.

Pimlott, Dr John and Gilbert, Adrian, *Modern Fighting Men*, Guild Publishing, London, 1986.

Phelps, Major General L.T.H., *History of the Royal Army Ordnance Corps 1945 -1982*, Trustees of the Royal Army Ordnance Corps.

Pocock, Tom, *Fighting General: The Public & Private Campaigns of General Sir Walter Walker*, Collins, London, 1973.

Porrit, Vernon L., *British Colonial Rule in Sarawak 1946-1963*, Oxford University Press, New York, 1997.

Poulgrain, Greg and Pramoedya Ananta Toer, *The Genesis of Konfrontasi: Malaysia, Brunei, Indonesia, 1945-1965*, C. Hurst & Co (Publishers) Ltd, London, 1998.

Purcell, Victor, *Malaysia*, Thames and Hudson, London, 1965.

Sarawak Government, *Sarawak Annual Report 1962*, Sarawak Government Publishing Office, Kuching, 1962.

Smith, E.D., *Counter-Insurgency Operations 1: Malaya and Borneo*, Ian Allen, Shepperton, 1985.

—, *East of Katmandu. The Story of The 7th Duke of Edinburgh's Own Gurkha Rifles, vol. II, 1948-1973*, Leo Cooper, London, 1976.

—, *Britain's Brigade of Gurkhas*, Leo Cooper, London, 1973.

Spirit, Martin, www.britains-smallwars.com

Strawson, Major General J.M., Pierson, Brigadier H.T. and Rhoderick-Jones,Brigadier R.J., *Irish Hussars. A Short History of the Queen's Royal Irish Hussars*, The Queen's Royal Irish Hussars, London, 1986.

Thompson, Major General Julian, *The Royal Marines: From Sea Soldiers to a Special Force*, Sidgwick and Jackson, London, 2000.

—, *Ready for Anything: The Parachute Regiment at War*, Fontana, London, 1989.

Wah, Chin Kim, *The Defence of Malaysia and Singapore. The Transformation of a Security System 1957-1971*, Cambridge University Press, 1983.

Warner, Philip, *The Story of Royal Signals 1945-1985*, Leo Cooper, London, 1989.

White, Dr Terry, *The Making of the World's Elite Forces*, Sidgwick and Jackson, London, 1992.

Regimental Periodicals

Queen's Royal Irish Hussars, *The Crossbelts*, 1963.

Queen's Own West Kents, *Invicta*, 1966.

The Hampshires, *Tiger*, 1966.

1st Green Jackets, *Chronicles 1963 to 1965*.

Kings Royal Rifle Corps; *Chronicles 1965*.

Kings Own Yorkshire Light Infantry, *The Bugle*, 1963 and 1964.

Gordon Highlanders, *Tiger and Phoenix*, 1965 and 1966.

Leicesters, *The Green Tiger*, 1964.

Royal Ulster Rifles, *Quis Separabit*, 1964-65.

Royal Signals, *The Wire*, 1966.

Royal Marines, *Globe and Laurel*, 1963-1966.

The Brigade of Gurkhas, *Kukri*, 1967.

Durham Light Infantry, Regimental Journal 1965-1967.

Kings Own Scottish Borderers, *Borderers Chronicle*, 1966.

Royal Engineers, *History of the Royal Engineers*.

Royal Navy, *Naval Review*.

Army Catering Corps, *Sustainer*.

Royal Pioneer Corps, *The Royal Pioneer Corps*.

Royal Army Medical Corps, *Journal of the Royal Army Medical Corps*.

129 (Dragon) Light Battery Operational Tour in Borneo 1965-1966.

Further Reading

'A sort of Advanced Boy-Scouting: The Borneo Campaign August 1963 – January 1966', *The History of 45 Regiment, Royal Artillery*, Chapter 6.

Assessment of Present Operational Situation in the Borneo Territories, PRO DCF 11/487.

Assessment of the Situation in the West Brigade Area 25 March 1964, PRO DCF 11/487.

Beeston, Major C., 'Locating in Borneo', *Royal Artillery Journal*, 1966.

Indonesia, Memo 4 October 1963, PRO WO 32/20364.

C-in-C Land Forces, Far East, *Anti Guerilla Operations in the South East Asia*, Crown Copyright.

Director of Operations, Malaya, *The Conduct of Anti-Terrorist Operations in Malaya1958*, Crown Copyright.

Fillingham, Lieutenant Colonel J.A.I., 'Operations in Sarawak', Royal Artillery Museum.

Gregorian, Raffi, 'The Black Cat Strikes Back. Claret Operations during Confrontation 1964-1966', Department of War Studies, King's College, London.

Heelis, Lieutenant Colonel B.D, 'REME in Borneo 1956-66', Museum of Technology (REME).

Jenkins, Colonel Alan, 'The Sumbi Saga'.

Lyons, Lieutenant Colonel R., 'Borneo Reflections', *British Army Review*, 1967.

Ministry of Defence, Land Operations, vol. V, Operational Techniques under Special Conditions, Part 2 – Jungle, B – Jungle Skills and Drills, Crown Copyright, 1974.

Naval Review, 'Ratings Police the Coast of North Borneo, 1964'.

—'Naval Operations in the Malacca and Singapore Straits 1964-66'.

'Patrolling Borneo Waters with a Motley Fleet', The Times, 15 April 1964.

Personal Directive from Commander West Brigade to Lieutenant Colonel D.G. House, Comd 1 Green Jackets, PRO WO 305/2576.

Post-Borneo Report, 2 Para, 1965, Airborne Museum.

Ricketts, Major R.A.S., 'Borneo', The Royal Engineers Journal.

'The Malaysia Campaign 1 to III', The Times, August 1964.

'The War in Borneo', The Daily Sketch, 17, 18 June 1964.

Treen, Paul, '16 Light Air Defence Regiment RA', www.britains-smallwars.com

Walker, General Sir Walter, How Borneo Was Won. The untold story of an Asian victory (courtesy of Colonel Alan Jenkins, 1/7th Gurkha Rifles).

'Health in the Army', 1963-1966.

Index

Edwardes, Maj John, 36, 155
Egypt, support for NLF in Aden, 43
Elgenia, Tpr Ken ASAS, 221
Eltringham, Pte, 181
Engkilili, 4, 66
Erskine-Tulloch, Maj Piers, 197,
  210, 216
Esteridge, Maj Mike, 48
Evans, Gunner RA, 230
Evans, Rfm, 187
Exercise Sea Serpent (1963), 64
Exercise Trumpeter, 43

Falklands Campaign (1982), 237
Falle, Lt Frank, 96
Far East Air Force, 104-5
FARELF (HQ Far East Land Forces)
  *Anti-Guerrilla Operations in South
  East Asia*, 18
  FLASH signal about Tebedu attack,
  39
  response to Brunei insurrection,
  32
  suggestions to combat Indonesian
  incursions, 34
Fenner, Sir Claude, 31, 75
Ferguson, Sir Bernard, 3
Ferguson, Tpr 'Ginger', 221
Ferret Force, 55
Ferret scout cars, 57, 185
Ferry, Maj RA, 127-8
Fillingham, Lt Col Jack, 86, 114-
  18, 149
Fiskerton, HMS, 32
Fleet Air Arm (FAA) *see* Royal Navy
  (Fleet Air Arm)
Fleming, Maj Jon, 176-8
Flores Sea, security of
  Commonwealth shipping, 133
Flower, Capt Nigel, 79
Flowers, Capt RA, 119
Forsa, RASC Vessel, 113
Forward Locality Bases (FLBs), 44-
  8, 58
  artillery deployments, 107, 119,
  127-9, 189
  medical facilities, 145
  Plaman Mapu, 176-80

platoon routine, 47-8
supply drops, 106
Fox, Lt Douglas RA, 213, 215
France, 23, 63-4
Fraser, Flt Lt Albert RAF, 211
Fuglesang, Capt Charles, 188

Gallagher, Capt Brian, 150
Garland, Maj Alf ASAS, 187
Ghale, Cpl Dhane, 168
Gilchrist, Sir Andrew, 74
Glennie, Brig Jack, 32-3, 76, 86, 91,
  95-6
Goodall, CQMS, 177-8
Goode, Sir William, 8, 31
Gooding, Mne Jim RM, 110
Graf, Maj Dick RA, 219
Grant, Gunner Jimmy RA, 220
Graves, Wing Cdr RAF, 31
Great Britain *see* United Kingdom
The Green Tiger, comment on heli-
  copters, 92
Green, Tpr Jimmy, 128-9
Griffiths, Pte Tom, 224
guerrilla warfare
  Indonesian army and, 242-3
  Nasution on, 16-18, 247-9
  'Territorial Warfare', 19-20
'Guided Democracy', 14-15, 124,
  200, 206-7
Guish, Col E. RAMC, 145
Gumbang, 40, 66
Gunung Serapi, rebroadcast station,
  240
Gurr, Lt Col R.M. RNZIR, 184
Gurung, Cpl Bhojbahadur, 191-2
Gurung, Cpl Birbahadur, 169-70
Gurung, Capt (QGO) Birbahadur,
  136
Gurung, L/Cpl Damberbahadur,
  115, 151-2
Gurung, Rfm Harisprasad, 196
Gurung, Sgt Kamabahadur, 163
Gurung, Rfm Kharkabahadur, 82-3
Gurung, Lt (QGO) Matbarsing, 70-
  1
Gurung, Lt (QGO) Nandaraj, 126
Gurung, Lt (QGO) Pasbahadur, 84

at Tepoi/Kujamg Sain, 150
Idris, Brig Gen Kemal, 159, 198,
206-7
Indonesia, 1-2
anti-British riots (Sept 1963), 74-5
Bangkok ceasefire talks (1964),
98-100, 111
British overflying restricted, 75
China and, 14, 139, 204, 218
civil unrest (1966), 207
communist coup (1966), 135
continues military operations in
Borneo (1966), 233-6
'Council of Generals', 201-2
'Crush Malaysia' (*Ganjung
Malaysia*) campaign, 65, 86, 94-
8, 124, 131-42, 157, 206, 222,
231, 233
debt rescheduling, 237
declares 12-mile coastal limit, 133-
4
diplomatic relations with Malaysia,
26, 38, 67, 74-5, 231-3
economic decline, 15-16
economic effects of *Konfrontasi*,
173, 200
independence achieved, 10-14
knowledge of Operation Claret,
244-5
peace declared, 236-7
performance of armed forces, 242-
3
PKI's 'Fifth Force', 200
political infighting between
generals, 124, 133, 157, 198-9,
201-2
propaganda radio stations, 38,
132
protest, rebellion and coup, 200-7
regional ambitions, 10, 24, 26
response to ethnic and religious
uprisings, 13-14
seizure of international assets, 15
students supported by Army, 206-
7
support for Brunei rebellion, 32
suspicion of all colonial ties, 64-5

'Thirtieth of September
Movement', 201-3
UN Congo Commitment, 159
Wingate style strategy, 59, 69, 76,
80-1, 92, 94, 109, 119-20, 151,
157, 223, 226
withdraws from UN, 218
see also National Army of
Indonesia (TNI)
Indonesian Air Force (Angkatan
Udara Republik), 19-20, 226
Air Base Defence Force, 131
left wing (PKI) sympathies, 123-4,
200-1
parachute base incursion (Labis, W.
Malaysia), 135-8
purged by Suharto, 207
Quick Mobile Force, 20, 131,
135-8
raid on Kuching and First Division
positions, 86
West Malaysia attacks and, 131
Indonesian Central Intelligence
Bureau, 37, 76, 86
ciphers broken, 79
propaganda radio, 132, 173, 197
Indonesian Marines (KKO), 21-2,
153, 226
deployment (Oct. 1964), 158-9
'electronic ambush', 104-5
Kalabakan raids, 94-8
Sebatik Island, 112
Sungai Agisan, 191-2
Indonesian National Party, 74-5
Indonesian Navy (Angatan Laut
Republik), 20-1
clashes with Malaysian patrol
craft, 133
Crush Malaysia Border Area
Command, 131-42
Marines (KKO) *see* Indonesian
Marines (KKO)
Indonesian Police
Mobile Brigade, 12, 22
prelude to Suharto coup, 201
Information Research Department
(IRD), 204-5, 218

270

272

Treen, Gunner Paul RA, 107-8
Tringuss, IBT attacks, 110
Truell, Maj G.D.S. RA, 129
Trusan Valley, 5-6
Tucker, S/Sgt John, 79
Tudor, Sgt, 128-9
Tuzo, Brig Harry (51 Infantry Bde), 108-9, 167

U Thant (UN Secretary General), 31, 67, 73, 94
United Kingdom
  black propaganda to subvert Indonesia, 204-6, 218
  Brunei contingency plans (Plan Ale), 31-2
  complacency in Service ministries, 163
  defence cuts, 246
  Defence Ministry formed, 162, 222
  financial implications of Confrontation, 90-1
  government change to Labour, 153-4
  internal events August (1963), 68
  Jakarta riots and Embassy burnt, 74-5
  Malaysian Commission Enquiry, 27
  Manila Pact (1954), 63-4
  NATO and, 23-4, 90
  Operation Claret anxieties, 143-4
  peace arrangements with Indonesia, 237
  plan to knock out Indonesian Navy and Air Force, 139
  political concerns in SE Asia, 23, 25-6, 67-8, 90
  presence of in East Malaysia discussed, 99-100
  see also British Army
United Nations
  ceasefire talks (Jan/Feb 1964), 98-100
  Committee of Good Offices, 12
  Confrontation and, 94
  and Sarawak/North Borneo self-

  determination, 65, 67, 72-3
  West Irian and, 16
  withdrawal of Indonesia, 218
United Nations Security Council, considers Indonesian 'aggression', 137
United States
  attitude to the Confrontation, 93-4
  concerns about Chinese subversion in SE Asia, 26, 33
  disbandment of Gurkha regiments and, 33
  economic sanctions against Indonesia, 75
  Manila Pact (1954), 63-4
  reassurances to Indonesia, 67-8
  South-East Asia strategy, 49, 93-4
  US Army Medical Research Station (Kuching), 146
United States Central Intelligence Agency (CIA), 14-15, 18-19, 30, 79
  anti-PKI factional fighting and, 204-5
  assessment of Confrontation (Nov. 1965), 205
  clandestine operations, 86
Untung, Lt Col (Cakrabirawa Palace Guard), 201-2

van der Horst, Lt Rupert RM, 35, 238
Vaux, P.A.L., Commander Malaysia, 140
Vickers heavy machine gun, 154
Vickers, Maj Richard, 57-8
Victoria Cross, L/Cpl Rambahadur Limbu, 215, 250-2
Victorious, HMS, 134-6
Vietnam
  affect of the social context, 245
  Australian and New Zealand contingents, 43, 184, 188, 240
  compared with 'Confrontation', 243-4
  jungle warfare experience, 49
Voice of Freedom Fighters of North Kalimantan, 38